Social Psychology: A Practical Manual

Social Psychology:
A Practical Manual

Edited by Glynis M. Breakwell, Hugh Foot
and Robin Gilmour

The conclusions drawn and opinions
expressed are those of the authors. They
should not be taken to represent the views
of the publishers.

First published 1982 by THE BRITISH
PSYCHOLOGICAL SOCIETY and THE
MACMILLAN PRESS LTD.

Distributed by The Macmillan Press Ltd,
London and Basingstoke. Associated
companies and representatives throughout
the world.

ISBN 0 333 34009 4 (hard cover)
ISBN 0 333 34010 8 (paper cover)

Printed in Great Britain by The Lavenham
Press.

Contents

List of contributors

Peter Ball
Department of Psychology, University of Tasmania, Hobart, GPO Box 252C, Tasmania, Australia 7001

Glynis M. Breakwell
Nuffield College, Oxford, OX1 1NF

Ray Bull
Department of Psychology, North East London Polytechnic, Three Mills, Abbey Lane, London, E15 2RP

Antony J. Chapman
Department of Applied Psychology, UWIST, Llwyn-y-Grant, Penylan, Cardiff, CF3 7UX

Mark Cook
Department of Psychology, University College, Singleton Park, Swansea, SA2 8PP

Hugh Foot
Department of Applied Psychology, UWIST, Llwyn-y-Grant, Penylan, Cardiff, CF3 7UX

Howard Giles
Department of Psychology, University of Bristol, 8-10 Berkeley Square, Bristol, BS8 1HH

Robin Gilmour
Department of Psychology, Fylde College, University of Lancaster, Bailrigg, Lancaster, LA1 4YF

Rom Harré
Linacre College, University of Oxford, Oxford, OX1 4JJ

Mansur Lalljee
Department for External Studies, Rewley House, 3-7 Wellington Square, University of Oxford, Oxford, OX1 2JA

Bram Oppenheim
Department of Social Psychology, London School of Economics, Houghton Street, London, WC2A 2AE

Paul Robinson
Department of Psychology, Hollymoor Hospital, Northfield, Birmingham, B31 5EX

Robert Slater
Department of Applied Psychology, UWIST, Llwyn-y-Grant, Penylan, Cardiff, CF3 7UX

Mike Smith
Department of Management Sciences, UMIST, PO Box 88, Manchester, M60 1QD

Peter B. Smith
School of Social Sciences, Arts Building, University of Sussex, Falmer, Brighton, BN1 9QN

Geoffrey M. Stephenson
Social Psychology Research Unit, Beverley Farm, University of Kent, Canterbury, Kent, CT2 7NS

Peter Trower
The Central Hospital, Hatton, Warwick, CV35 7EE

Maryon Tysoe
Flat 2, 19 Glenmore Road, London NW3

Frances M. Wade
Department of Applied Psychology, UWIST, Llwyn-y-Grant, Penylan, Cardiff, CF3 7UX

Preface

This is a collection of research exercises in social psychology. The purpose of these exercises is to give students practice in using a range of research methods and techniques to investigate a number of problems central to modern social psychology. They are, therefore, the stuff of which 'practical' classes are made. In fact, the text is addressed to the organizers of such classes and explains carefully how a class might be organized in order to do each exercise. Nevertheless, the book can usefully be read by students themselves because the description of each exercise also includes its theoretical background, the processes of data collection, and the ways in which results might be discussed.

This is a 'practical' manual in the broad sense: a reasonable sample of field studies are also included, so not all of the exercises are to be done in the laboratory. Nor are all of the exercises experimental or even quasi-experimental; several involve basic techniques of ethnographic research. Such an eclectic choice of exercises is necessary if the object is to reflect something of what is happening in social psychology now. Increasingly, social psychologists are seeking to integrate different methods of research and to use them in concert to examine social phenomena. Each method has its weaknesses and where one is weak another is strong: experimentation offers control but is confounded by artificiality; ethogenic methods offer realism but no control. Used together sensibly, methods which are each individually flawed can generate a more satisfactory picture than any could alone; hence the need to teach a broad range of methods and hence the eclecticism in the selection of exercises.

The exercises can be ranged along a continuum from those primarily concerned with a method or technique to those essentially concerned with a problem or phenomenon that needs to be researched. In a way, the continuum reflects the needs of a research methods course: the course has to teach specific methods and techniques in all their abstract purity but it must also show how they relate to particular research problems. Of course, some research problems become almost totally identified with a particular method or technique; just as some techniques only ever seem to be used to explore one sort of problem. This book is divided into three parts which represent distinct points along the continuum between technique- and problem-orientation. The first part contains exercises which are designed to introduce the student to a series of specific techniques of research; the second contains exercises which might be said to exemplify how some techniques have a special affinity for certain problems; and the third and final part contains exercises whose emphasis lies upon exploring a particular problem area in social psychology.

Part I consists of five chapters, each of which describes a technique which is standard in social psychology. In chapter 1, Robert Slater describes an exercise which will introduce students to questionnaire design. This is followed by an exercise on how to conduct a selection interview by Mike Smith who describes: how to open the interview and how to end it; how to cover systematically the important issues; how to make the interviewee talk; and what must be considered when drawing conclusions from an interview. The exercise in chapter 3 by Bram Oppenheim is a classical description of attitude measurement, an activity so central to the research goals of innumerable social psychologists. Chapter 4 by Hugh Foot is based upon the use of a modified version of the Bales Interaction Process Analysis which gives students a route to interactional analysis in the context of group discussion. Rom Harré, in chapter 5, portrays something of the epistemology and applications of ethogenic approaches.

The five chapters in Part II contain exercises which each illustrate how a particular method or technique can be especially suited to the study of a particular social psychological problem. In chapter 6, Peter Ball and Howard Giles demonstrate the matched guise technique, a method which has come to be associated with the study of the social psychology of language. In the following chapter, Tony Chapman and Frances Wade employ non-participant observation to examine the recreational use of the street by children; it is difficult to imagine what other technique would be effective in studying this phenomenon. Paul Robinson and Peter Trower, in chapter 8, take us into the realms of applied social psychology, using role-play exercises to show the importance of social skill in interpersonal relations. Mark Cook presents in chapter 9 an exercise specifically designed to show how results can be influenced by the techniques employed in a study of person perception. Chapter 10 concludes Part II with a study on negotiation processes by Geoffrey Stephenson and Maryon Tysoe; this exercise illustrates the commonly used technique of role-play in studies of bargaining.

Part III represents the 'problem' end of the continuum. These five chapters present exercises designed to introduce the student to specific problem areas in social psychology. Chapter 11 by Ray Bull is concerned with the problem of gathering eyewitness testimony and examines some of the factors which influence the accuracy of an eye-witness's recollections in a field setting. Mansur Lalljee describes a study whose object is to test certain central tenets of attribution theory. In chapter 13, Glynis Breakwell delineates an exercise which tests how group membership influences the expression of intergroup prejudices. The theme of 'group psychology' is continued in chapter 14 by Robin Gilmour who outlines a study of co-operation and competition in groups. The concern with groups continues in the final chapter by Peter Smith in which the emergence of group roles and norms is explored.

The structure of each chapter is obviously dependent upon the peculiarities of the subject matter covered. As far as possible, authors have used the tried and tested format of:

* theoretical introduction;
* procedure of the exercise;
* forms of analysis and dimensions of discussion.

With such a large range of topics there has clearly been some divergence from this straight and narrow path. However, each chapter begins with a section headed 'Specification notes' and this is designed to outline briefly the object of the exercise and the sorts of resources needed to do it. The specification notes are provided so that readers can pick the exercise most suited to their own ends and resources. Some of the exercises need to be done at particular times during the academic session if they are to work (e.g. Peter Smith's and part of Rom Harré's) and the specification notes give these sorts of details too. In fact, it is probably valuable to read through the specification notes on each of the exercises before choosing any one. This should preclude inappropriate timetabling of exercises.

It should be borne in mind when choosing exercises that they can be regarded as prescriptive and comprehensive patterns for a 'practical' class or they can be treated as suggestive. The exercises have a certain amount of built-in flexibility. In most cases, they start with a simple design for a study which can be used as a foundation for more complex designs. The basic studies can be used for students in the first years of their social psychology training either at A level or at undergraduate level. Where extra variables are woven into the design and more complex forms of analysis are applied to data, these same studies can be used for students with considerable experience of the discipline. This flexibility also means that exercises can be modified to suit the specific needs and experience of each student group. A tutor could equally decide to cannibalize exercises and play the vivisectionist: several of the exercises fit together neatly. For instance, that on selection interviewing (chapter 2) goes with that on the effects of language on interpersonal evaluation (chapter 6) and with that on social skills (chapter 8). Similarly, chapter 13 on intergroup prejudice complements chapter 15 on group norms. Extensions and modifications of exercises are facilitated because each chapter contains suggestions on various types of analysis which might be used on the data generated, and includes a body of self-criticism on epistemological or methodological grounds.

The exercises can be seen as building blocks. Each stands alone and yet they can be cemented together. Together they become a representative part of the edifice of social psychology, reflecting its methods and its problems.

Glynis M. Breakwell
Hugh Foot
Robin Gilmour

Part one Technique demonstrations

1

Questionnaire design
Robert Slater

Specification notes

AIMS OF EXERCISE: to assist students in appreciating the procedures involved in question and questionnaire design; to produce a questionnaire; by collecting and analysing data (i.e. by piloting the questionnaire), to be able to redraft unsatisfactory questions (and answer formats); to examine simple hypotheses about relationships between variables.

PRIOR KNOWLEDGE ASSUMED: little prior knowledge of the survey topic (smoking) is needed, but a basic understanding of sampling statistics (confidence limits for population estimates) and of 2 x 2 Chi Square analyses would be useful.

DURATION: it is an integrated exercise extending over two laboratory sessions (six hours) undertaken some three or four weeks apart, with intervening data collection if the second session is being undertaken. The first exercise can be carried out by itself (three hours) and a suggestion is given for reducing the second session to one hour's duration.

LOCATION: both practical sessions to be held in normal teaching laboratory; data collection to take place 'in the field'.

RESOURCES/FACILITIES: pencils, rubbers, wide-ruled A4 sheets, scissors, staplers, staples, sellotape, blackboards, handouts on various topics, reprographic facilities (for duplicating questionnaires, etc.), pocket calculators, Chi Square value significance tables.

SPECIAL REQUIREMENTS: the second practical cannot be undertaken without prior collection of data. In order for such data collection to be undertaken between practicals, quite heavy demands are made on the course tutor.

Introduction

Surveys are now found everywhere. We are bombarded by information based on surveys, for example from opinion polls, almost every day of our lives. Research on purchasing behaviour occupies many individuals in commercial agencies engaged in consumer research. Much of the research undertaken in the social sciences in general, and in psychology in particular, utilizes survey methods; but the ubiquitous nature of surveys brings with it a problem. People tend to think anyone can 'cobble' together a few questions into a 'questionnaire', and they do. These then get sent to busy people who may have neither the time nor the inclination to respond, especially to questions which to them - the respondents - perhaps appear unclear, nosey, irrelevant, impertinent, uninteresting, or

1

which concern a topic of little apparent importance to them.

The primary aim of this practical exercise is to help students appreciate the procedures involved in producing a viable questionnaire to be used as a scientific research instrument for collecting psychological data. A secondary aim is to facilitate the students' experience of decision-making in groups and the use of their colleagues as a feedback mechanism (in lieu of pre-testing the material on strangers), although the exercise requires extensive supervision by the course tutor. A third (and minor) aim is to obtain 'results' from the survey (if undertaken). The central aim, then, is to make students more proficient in question and questionnaire design.

In arriving at a final questionnaire it is necessary to obtain the reactions of the target population to various drafts of questions and questionnaires. In this exercise the choice of survey subject area has been explicitly made so that the students themselves are part of the potential target population. This being the case, the practical is appropriate for participants as young as sixth-formers or first-year students. (When contact with the 'general public' is involved, it is often best to restrict survey work to more mature - perhaps final-year - students, who are more credible as serious interviewers in public.)

The survey topic has been chosen because it remains an area of general concern given current (late 1980) government intentions to investigate 'smoking' yet again and Eysenck's (1980) further contribution to the debate over cancer causation.

This practical exercise, then, aims to give students the experience of deciding upon the areas of importance when constructing a questionnaire on a topic of potential interest to themselves: and also to psychologists, health educationists, politicians (and cigarette manufacturers!). Why do adolescents start, continue or stop smoking? The 'problem' of people taking up smoking seems rather intractable, but in the context of <u>laboratory</u> studies in social psychology the survey research question of 'Why do they start?' is complemented by more experimentally-based work on what

sort of communications will influence them to stop. Research on the latter must of necessity be informed by research on the former. Thus the topic demonstrates the interdependence often found in social psychological research between fieldwork-based and laboratory-based studies.

Theoretical and methodological background of survey methods

The first systematic social survey undertaken in Britain was a study of living conditions and poverty among the working classes (Booth, 1904), which markedly influenced the economic and social policies of subsequent governments. Other 'poverty surveys' followed rapidly, but it is Bowley who is credited for first seriously taking into account such technical matters as how 'selection effects' influence the generalizability of the data: that is, the possibility that 'refusers', or those who are 'not at home', may in some important way be different from the people from whom data <u>are</u> obtained (Bowley and Burnett-Hurst, 1915). The need for sampling to be rigorous, if generalizations were to be at all accurate, was increasingly recognized from Bowley's time onwards, although there is continuing debate about the necessity for, and cost-effectiveness of, random sampling techniques. Various government surveys, on nutrition, family expenditure, and ill-health, were brought together under the umbrella of the Government Social Survey which was set up in 1941. In America, during and after the Second World War, survey research methods came into their own in the field of public opinion polling and in advertising. Since these fields were monopolized by commercial agencies, ever cost-conscious, the development of sophisticated sampling procedures was rapid; poorly selected samples can result in inaccurate results, high costs and slow turn-around of the data. Nowadays some market research agencies are geared up to conducting 3,000 short interviews in the morning and having simple frequency tabulations of the data ready the same afternoon.

Apart from market research surveys and opinion polls, most surveys carried out today are probably for research purposes: to establish the prevalence of, say, psychiatric ill-health in a community; to establish norms of human performance or characteristics, as in the development of intelligence and personality tests; and to examine social attitudes and relate them to biographical data. Many such surveys are intended to be descriptive rather than analytical; that is, to produce an accurate picture of the state of affairs in a population by surveying a sample rather than explicitly setting out to examine hypotheses. In such descriptive surveys, having the right size of simple random sample to obtain the requisite accuracy of description for the entire target population is essential. Otherwise, statements about what percentage of voters say they will vote Conservative in an election, for example, may have to be elaborated by perhaps 'plus or minus 15 per cent', which makes the information - that between 25 per cent and 55 per cent of voters say they will vote Conservative - hardly worth having.

Other research surveys are intended to provide the data with which hypotheses can be tested. Even here, though, one might wish to demonstrate that a relationship between two variables observed in a sample was likely to hold in the population from which the sample was drawn. Thus, if one wishes to test hypotheses that are framed in general (i.e. population) terms, such as, for example, 'there is a relationship between social classes and child-rearing patterns, in which the higher the social class the more instructions to children are accompanied with rational explanations', then sample size becomes as important as it was in the descriptive survey, since one is trying to describe a relationship in the population that is hypothesized to exist.

The more one is confident that the standard deviations of the variables under investigation are small (i.e. the more confident that 'man' can stand for 'men'), then the less need there is for large samples. Conversely, the more varied the behaviour of attitudes and opinions under investigation are thought to be, the more necessary are random sampling methods, with relatively large samples. Since survey sample sizes are frequently in the 500-4,000 range, it can be seen at once that surveys can make heavy demands on resources. As a consequence, most surveys with large samples, as with the census, confine

themselves to relatively few, simple questions. Of course, what appear at first to be simple questions may not be: for example, the difficulties with census questions concerning households with showers, which produced data not thought worthy of publication. An illuminating illustration of this and other census difficulties with 'simple' questions (when is a 'household' not a household?) is found in the 'quality check' on the 1966 sample Census (Gray and Gee, 1972).

Important survey data of interest to psychologists have been collected in the past to answer such questions as 'Is there a relationship between family size and intelligence of children?' and 'Is the average intelligence of the nation declining?' (Maxwell, 1969). And while it is probably a truism to say that a survey has no doubt been conducted (probably badly) somewhere on almost any topic you care to name, since the early 1950s little in survey research methods and techniques has changed, save for the advent of computer-readable questionnaires, and multivariate analysis of data by computer. The future may see us all pressing buttons on our televisions in response to some question given 'over the air', with more or less instantaneous 'playback' of results, but the central problem for most survey research will still remain: namely, asking questions which have reliability and validity.

Specific background to this exercise

As suggested earlier, studies of the effectiveness of persuasive communications in general, and of anti-smoking propaganda in particular, need to be informed by a knowledge of why some adolescents (and, of course, children) take up smoking whilst others do not. What differences are there between the reasons for starting smoking and the reasons for continuing and for wanting to stop? Are smoking patterns changing: for example, are women becoming more like men in their smoking patterns, and is this connected with aspects of women's liberation? A whole gamut of sensible questions, some largely sociological, some largely psychological, can be posed in order to explicate smoking attitudes and behaviour. Surveys by Bynner (1969) and by McKennell and Thomas (1967), on which this exercise will draw heavily, showed that by the age of 15 some 80 per cent of a sample of 5,601 schoolboys had smoked a cigarette. Smokers (boys who were smoking one or more cigarettes each week) were found to be always behind non-smokers in the extent of their acceptance of health education arguments, and the more heavily they smoked the less they appeared to be put off by 'Their' belief that they would get lung cancer from it. Bynner (1969) found that smokers and non-smokers could be discriminated best by four 'variables': number of friends who smoked; anticipation of adulthood; parents' permissiveness; and whether they, the boys, were put off smoking by the danger of lung cancer. He also found that smokers appear to go around in groups largely composed of other smokers, while non-smokers go around in groups largely composed of other non-smokers. Findings such as these are of relevance to social-psychological studies of persuasive communications, such as 'boomerang' effects (Jones and Gerard, 1967), latitudes of acceptance (McGuire, 1969), and presentation orders (Hollander, 1981), as well as to those of pressures to conform in small groups.

Merits of the exercise as a training device
This exercise has the merit of being relatively realistic, in so far as any survey into the smoking behaviour of adolescents would probably begin with qualitative group discussions and/or open-ended fully-probed interviews with adolescents. It should enable students to examine the pros and cons of various standard question and response formats (see also Payne, 1965). Furthermore, the exercise should allow the formulation of questions in order to gather a spectrum of information, ranging from relatively straightforward factual data on age and number of older brothers, for example, to more complex sociological data, such as ascertaining social class, to psychological data on self-image and ideal self-image, perhaps, or on discrepancies between thoughts and actions. Finally the exercise should have the merit of making students realize that while the 'cobbling' together of a questionnaire is relatively easily done, constructing one that is a precise scientific data collection instrument takes a lot of time and effort, testing and re-testing.

Derivation of aims and hypotheses
The aim of the exercise is to produce a questionnaire that could be used to collect data to test a variety of hypotheses concerning why, for example, adolescents start, continue or stop smoking. Many sensible hypotheses are likely to be generated in the class by the students themselves. Bynner (1969) suggests that smokers are seen as 'tough', 'educationally unsuccessful', and 'precocious'; that all boys tend to value toughness and educational success, but that only smokers tend to value precocity. Since Bynner's data were collected on a sample of boys, the image of female smokers is not elucidated. What is the female equivalent of 'tough' in this context? Since female smoking habits have been changing and coming more into line with male smoking patterns in terms of overall consumption (McKennell and Thomas, 1967), one might derive a variety of hypotheses concerning sex differences in reasons for, say, starting smoking, or wanting to give it up.

Method

Resources
The first practical requires a room large enough for students to move from individual work to group work without much disruption of the class (each student will need a table or desk to work at, preferably with a surface roughly 1½ x 3 ft). If it is possible for each student to have one table for individual work and one for group work, so much the better, otherwise it is probably best for tables to be maintained in a group-work position throughout the practical.

In advance of the session the course tutor should prepare handouts on example question formats (taken, perhaps, from the Appendix). Each student will need one set of such handouts. Students will need pencils and rubbers (using pens and biros and the crossing out of errors is to be avoided) and separate sheets of wide-ruled A4 paper. At least one stapler and pair of scissors per group will be needed, plus spare staples, and a couple of rolls of sellotape. A large blackboard/writing surface for the course tutor to use must be available. As the session lasts a continuous three hours, it would be helpful if access to tea/coffee can be laid on in the practicals room.

The above resources are those required for the first of what are two integrated practicals to be run three or four weeks apart. (The first practical can, however, stand on its own.)

For the second, associated practical the course tutor must be able to reproduce questionnaires, administration instructions, editing and coding instructions, and handouts suggesting further analyses of the data. Again a large blackboard/writing surface for the use of the course tutor is essential, and two or more such surfaces may be useful (for when the data are being collated). Several pocket electronic calculators should be available as well as sets of tables for determining the significance of Chi Square values.

Organization of the exercise

At the outset the class should be told that the aim of the practical is to produce a pilot questionnaire concerning aspects of adolescents' (young adults') smoking behaviour, that the three-hour session will be run to a tight timetable, and that much of the time students will be working in groups. (If a second practical exercise is to be undertaken by the course tutor - see below - this should be mentioned to students at this point.) The number of groups will vary according to the size of the class, but it is advised that each group should comprise no more than five students (otherwise groups tend to fragment into sub-sections, with one section getting on with the work and the other watching, or worse!). It is useful to prepare a listing of groups, selected on a proper random basis. Random selection makes the group-work process more realistic, ensuring more varied input of ideas concerning areas of the survey, and enhancing to a certain extent the 'testing' of items on people who are at least not likely to be best friends. It may be useful to point out to students that the grouping is based on random num-

bers selection, and that the allocation to groups in alphabetical order surname clusters is not random. The class should also be told that where necessary, to keep to the timetable (see below), the course tutor will have to take some decisions out of students' hands.

Timetable

A suggested timetable follows. Whilst there must be some flexibility in timing the various activities, the tendency will be for sessions to overrun: it is vitally important not to let this happen with early sessions. When sessions seem to be coming to an end before their 'allotted time', move straight away to the next activity.

STEP 1 (15 minutes). Arrange students physically into groups (course tutor to decide, and to delegate role of chairman, secretary, and/or spokesman if thought necessary); explain that most of the exercise will be group work; mention random sampling; state that the exercise is to construct a questionnaire concerning one of the following topics (it is impossible to cover all three in one three-hour practical):

* why adolescent girls (and/or boys) start smoking?
* why adolescent girls (and/or boys) continue smoking?
* why adolescent girls (and/or boys) stop smoking?

Explain the constraints on the practical: that is, they are going to have to use themselves as the target population. Request each group to decide on its survey topic preference, and to be prepared to 'justify' its decision.

STEP 2 (15 minutes). Students in groups decide on topic preference and feed this information back to the rest of the class via the course tutor. It is likely that in this and the subsequent step a group (or groups) will find it difficult to reach agreement on the topic for the survey. Although getting such agreement should enhance students' involvement in the exercise, it may be necessary for the course tutor to impose a decision.

STEP 3 (15 minutes). Course tutor leads the whole class in obtaining a consensus on survey topics. This consensus should be achieved on a rational basis. For example, in a group of older adolescents, many may have been smoking for some time, so data on why they continue smoking, or why they have stopped, might be more reliable. If very few in the class have ever smoked, for example, one might be flexible and have as the topic why some adolescents do not take up smoking. The decision as to whether to focus on males or females (or both) should largely rest on the composition of the class, but in evenly matched classes, focussing on males has the advantage that there are comparative data available, whereas focussing on females has the advantage of being more novel: that is, looking at an area of change. The general intention is that this discussion should help students to realize that choice of topic and of target population have wide practical ramifications and that some choices are quite impractical.

STEP 4 (15 minutes). Each group should produce a list of broad areas of information that they consider relevant to an explication of the chosen topic. By broad areas is meant such possible aspects as: smoking behaviour of possible models; biographical information; attitudes to school; attitudes to adolescence; perceptions of smokers and of non-smokers; ideal and real self-image; knowledge about smoking and health; evaluation of knowledge about smoking and health; needs satisfied by smoking; and advantages and disadvantages of smoking. In a later session each group will take responsibility for elaborating one or more of these major areas which the questionnaire is to cover.

STEP 5 (15 minutes). The course tutor (and class) should obtain feedback from group spokesmen about the areas considered to be of relevance, and an attempt made to integrate these into conceptually clear and distinct groupings. If this proves very difficult one could try and impose the areas mentioned in Step 4, since these have been used in previous surveys. Again not all of those areas are relevant to each of the three possible suggested survey topics.

(A study of why people start smoking is less likely to be well-informed by questions concerning the needs satisfied by the continuation of smoking.) Thus, in this session, the areas to be covered must be put into a rank order of salience for the topic and, since it is probably best that each group concentrates on one area, some areas of low salience may have to be omitted in classes with relatively few students.

STEP 6 (15 minutes). Each group should be allocated one of the salient areas decided upon from the previous session. Each group should then proceed to determine what are the 'facets' of the area it is considering. For example, 'smoking behaviour' of possible models may have facets related to close relatives, teachers, friends, pop stars, television personalities and sports people. 'Attitudes to school' may be subdivided into attitudes concerning teachers, the work undertaken, the subjects studied, the degree of discipline and the extent to which schoolwork is seen to interfere with other interests. 'Knowledge about smoking and health' may be subdivided into knowledge about cancer, about heart disease, about shortness of breath, about smoking affecting unborn babies, and so on.

STEP 7 (15 minutes). The course tutor and the class should obtain feedback about the facets each group has produced, and have the opportunity to add to them and comment upon them. Attention here should be paid to retaining those facets which can be covered by collecting data via a questionnaire, and to rejecting those that are likely to be troublesome in this respect. For example, little seems to have been written directly on smoking and overt sexual behaviour, primarily because people may object (on moral grounds) to data on sexual habits being collected and because it is difficult to relate what people do to what they say they do (a major problem in all verbal surveys about behaviour). It is important in this session that all the participants feel they have a conceptually clear idea of what the major areas and their facets are tapping, so that they have some sense of the coherence of the survey in toto, even though at present they are working on it in groups. For the latter reason, in the following session agreed groupings of facets should be worked on by student groups other than those who originated them.

STEP 8 (15 minutes). Having re-allocated to the groups the sets of the agreed facets, each group should attempt to produce written questions pertinent to the survey topic concerning those facets. Before doing this, however, each group should familiarize itself with the common format options by inspecting copies of the sample material which the course tutor will have provided, and may wish to introduce (Payne, 1965, should be found most useful in this respect). The 'final' questionnaire should contain as few open-ended questions as possible to facilitate data coding and analysis in a subsequent practical session should this take place. Groups who wish to produce two-way or multiple choice response formats to questions may require classmates to respond to open-ended questions, or to sentence completion material, in order to undertake a content-analysis of response upon which they can base the range of answers available for the multiple-choice questions. The subsequent session will enable this to be undertaken to a limited extent.

STEP 9 (15 minutes). Groups wishing to pose open-ended questions (e.g. 'What were the reasons that made you start smoking?') or sentence completion material ('In my opinion the typical smoker is the sort of person who ...') should state them to the course tutor and to the class, and the class should proceed to act as subjects. The answers should be passed back to the appropriate groups (written on separate sheets for each question, so that an individual group member can analyse the responses to one question at a time). Since this process could take a long time if several groups are involved, the course tutor should be wary of letting more than two groups use the rest of the class as subjects.

STEP 10 (15 minutes). In this period, different tasks may need to be delegated to different groups. Groups involved in content analysis of open-ended material should continue with this, aiming to produce the desired multiple choice format for each question. Groups that have already formulated questions and their response formats should be requested to consider, first, the sequencing of those questions in relation to each other and, second, where the chosen sequence should occur in the questionnaire in relation to other areas being covered.

STEP 11 (15 minutes). The course tutor should try to obtain rational consensus agreement, having heard the group's views, on the sequencing of question areas within the questionnaire. Having agreed upon this the groups should be instructed to undertake two tasks: (i) to write a 30-word introduction to 'their' series of questions; and (ii) to ensure that each question or series of questions has clear instructions on how it is to be answered, where this is necessary.

FINAL 15 MINUTES. The groups should be requested to produce (i) a neatly written copy of each question, (ii) the introductions to their series of questions, and (iii) instructions for particular questions, all in the appropriate positions. These should then be stapled together in the sequence agreed upon. Effectively this is the end of this practical exercise.

The course tutor is advised to collate the material in the overall sequence agreed upon, and arrange for the material to be typed up and reproduced so that each class participant can subsequently have a copy of the 'end product' of the practical session. In writing up this exercise, students should be encouraged to review critically and constructively the questionnaire and the process by which it was constructed. They should examine questions for their clarity, and response formats for their mutual exclusiveness. They should be encouraged, by way of formulating a general conclusion, to anticipate how respondents will react to the questionnaire in general and to each question or series of questions in particular.

Data collection

It is highly desirable that students administer the questionnaire (to some 10 subjects) in order to see if their expectations about it as a data collection instrument are realized. The data thus collected can then be used for question redrafting in a second associated practical exercise. However, it would be sensible not to time-table this second session until three or four weeks after the first, in order to carry out the necessary preparatory work and to give students time to collect the data.

Preparatory work

Inevitably, the material collated from the first practical will require the course tutor to spend some time 'knocking it into shape' so that it follows an internally consistent layout format. (If some of the material collated is considered not to be 'up to scratch' for data collection, the tutor may wish to make use of material from the Appendix to this chapter and from the sources suggested there.) Having arranged the questionnaire into a presentable form - that is, one which can be handed over to respondents for them to complete - it is suggested that the course tutor writes simple instructions to students on how to proceed with data collection.

Since students will be administering questionnaires between the two practicals, it is important that the written instructions accompanying the questionnaires are comprehensive. The instructions should direct the student to inspect a copy of the questionnaire and to make a note of any queries they themselves have about it, or anticipate that respondents might have. It should be emphasized that when students administer the questionnaire they should be quite familiar with its contents and have prepared answers to the sort of questions they anticipate respondents might raise. They should be instructed to make a note of actual 'problems' with the questionnaire that do arise when respondents are completing them. These instructions to the students, together with the questionnaires, should be reproduced and collated in sufficient numbers for each student to administer the questionnaire to some ten subjects with the designated sample characteristics. Since these may well be peers, it might on the one hand be simplest to allow students to find their own subjects. This, of course, would facilitate the faking of responses. On the other hand, it may well prove administratively very difficult (although more desirable) to arrange for students to collect the data via classroom administration sessions. The course tutor will have to decide which is the more appropriate method of collecting the data, given the particular circumstances that prevail, and the interval elapsing between the two practicals.

Administration

Students should be instructed to check that each questionnaire is complete (no missing or blank pages) and that pages are in the right sequence. Each questionnaire should be given a unique identification number which can be linked to the student who administered it. Each student should have two or three questionnaires for emergency use.

Students will need to be informed of the arrangements for administering the questionnaires. If they are being given the responsibility of finding appropriate subjects, the defining characteristics of the sample population must be made clear. If the course tutor has decided to collect data via classroom (that is, group) administration of the questionnaires, students must be told which classes they are to be using, where they are located, and at what time they are to administer the questionnaires. Obviously the course tutor will have to have made arrangements well in advance with other teachers for them to cooperate. These teachers should have been forewarned of the arrival of the students at such and such a time, that administering and collecting the questionnaires will take approximately 15-20 minutes, and that with large classes, two or more students may arrive to carry out the questionnaire administration. It is recommended that with 'classroom' administration at least two students are present for every 20 respondents in order to help issue the questionnaires, answer queries about questions and collect the questionnaires. Students should remember to thank the class and the teacher for their co-operation.

Questionnaire data analysis

Timetable considerations
Since it is not considered feasible for students to collect data during the time allocated to the second practical itself (it should be collected between first and second practicals), the course tutor may feel that the second practical should be shortened to give students time off in lieu. If classroom (group) administration has been followed, it is likely that all in all this will have taken up perhaps two hours of the students' time (reading the instructions, going through the questionnaires, getting to the venue, administering the questionnaires). Similarly, if students have been delegated the task of finding appropriate subjects themselves, and have been conscientious about this, it is unlikely that they will be able to collect the data from 10 respondents in less than two hours. Consequently, course tutors may wish to stop the second practical after the first hour in the following timetable. However, for those who feel that data collection is legitimate homework for students to undertake between practicals, a full three-hour suggested time-table is given.

STEP 1 (15 minutes). Each student should now have in the region of 10 questionnaires to edit. If there are no open-ended answers to be coded at this stage (and it is advised that there should be as few as possible), editing will be largely a matter of ensuring that there is a code number given for each answer (e.g. Yes - code 1; No - code 2; Don't know - code 3; as well as omitted answer codes, ambiguous answer codes, and refusal/can't do codes). If an attempt is being made to allocate a social grade to, say, father's occupation (a tricky task at the best of times), a copy of a coding scheme of the kind to be found in the Market Research Society's (undated) 'Handbook for Interviewers' (pp. 57-70) will have to be provided by the course tutor for each student. Similarly, if parental levels of education are being

classified, a scheme like the one on pp. 135-137 of Atkinson's (1971) 'Handbook for Interviewers' will have to be available. By the end of this quarter-hour, each of the students should have edited and coded their questionnaires.

STEP 2 (15 minutes). Students should collate the material from their 10 questionnaires on to one 'master' (spare and unused) questionnaire; that is, they should summarize the frequency with which each answer is occurring for each question. At this point it might be useful to elicit feedback about 'problem questions' that were noted when the data were collected, in order to be wary of them in any subsequent analysis.

STEP 3 (15 minutes). The summarized frequencies from each student should now be collated to give a total frequencies description of the data collected. For large classes of students, in order to save time, it may be sensible for the course tutor to do this in two stages by splitting the class into groups which collate their data independently but simultaneously and afterwards collate the groups' data into a total set.

STEP 4 (15 minutes). The collated data should be noted by students on their master questionnaire, and they should be asked to get into groups (as in the first session) and produce descriptive comments on the findings. The emphasis here should be placed on the implications the descriptive findings have for revising the questionnaire (i.e. improving both the questions and the response formats). Are there many 'don't knows', response instructions not followed, undiscriminating questions, unanswered questions, questions answered that should not have been? Each group's comments should be fed back to the rest of the class.

STEP 5 (15 minutes). Each group of students should discuss which relationships between which variables (taken two at a time) should be analysed, and have a spokesperson ready to explain their decisions to the rest of the class. Again the emphasis should be on analyses which will help in the revision and improvement of the questionnaire.

STEP 6 (15 minutes). Each group in turn should explain its 'priority for initial analyses' to the rest of the class, and the course tutor should attempt to obtain consensus agreement concerning which analyses to undertake first. It may be decided that more time should be spent examining the implications of the descriptive findings for the improvement of the questionnaire.

STEP 7 (15 minutes). Any analysis of data in this raw form is inevitably cumbersome, and will illustrate to students the need to transform data into another format (e.g. computer cards) to facilitate sorting, or for non-mechanical means of performing the analysis (i.e. computers). After a few attempts at analysing data by sorting questionnaires students may begin to wonder how data ever came to be analysed before the invention of computers and card sorters!

Having agreed on the method of first analysis, and for practical purposes a simple 2 x 2 Chi Square table might be most appropriate (see Gregory, Hartley and Lewis, 1969, pp. 97-109, for a simple introduction), the questionnaire should be sorted into the appropriate (four) piles and counted and the contingency table produced. For example, in a sample of 100 female respondents there may be 27 girl smokers (GS) whose mothers smoke (MS), 23 girl non-smokers (GNS) whose mothers smoke, 10 girl smokers whose mothers do not smoke (MNS) and 40 girl non-smokers whose mothers do not smoke. This would produce the following contingency table (table 1).

Table 1

	GS	GNS	
MS	27	23	50
MNS	10	40	50
	37	63	100

STEP 8 (15 minutes). The contingency table should be set up on the board, together with instructions on how to calculate Chi Square, and, as a check on computational accuracy, each group should perform the calculation using the pocket electronic calculators provided. Ideally each group will arrive at the same value which can be examined for statistical significance using tables provided. Each group should formulate a comment on the result and a hypothesis for 'explaining' it.

STEP 9 (15 minutes). A second similar analysis should be undertaken. Each student should retrieve any 10 questionnaires and then place them in piles according to the analysis being performed.

STEP 10 (15 minutes). This should follow the pattern established for Step 8.

STEP 11 (15 minutes). Again, re-sort questionnaires according to the next analysis being undertaken which might, more ambitiously, be an n x k Chi Square.

STEP 12 (15 minutes). Again, follow the pattern for Step 8. (An alternative strategy to undertaking three different analyses in the last six steps might be to collate material in Step 2 and Step 3 in a grouped form for both males and females, 'older' and 'younger' respondents, etc. This will facilitate more Chi Square analyses being undertaken in the last half of the practical by individual students who can then have the choice of variables to relate to the variable on which the grouping has been based. If the course tutor follows this strategy, a lot of pocket calculators will have to be made available. It will also, if desired, enable a closer examination to be made of the implications for questionnaire redesign of the descriptive results.) Students should be given a handout by the course tutor suggesting further analyses of the data (which will have been prepared prior to the practical). The course tutor should collect the edited questionnaires, and point out to the class the need for access to a computer for fast and effective analyses of data of this type.

Data collection, analysis and results

Data collection

As will already have become clear, if only the first practical session is undertaken, there will be no 'data' available for analysis save for students' opinions concerning how the questionnaire may yet need to be modified. If the second practical is undertaken, the data will take the form of coded numeric information for perhaps some 20-30 variables for some 150-350 respondents. It is intended that during the second practical each student will have a set of the pooled data for the survey from which a descriptive account of the responses to the survey can be given. Apart from the Chi Square analyses undertaken in the practical, students will not be able to pursue with their simple frequency count data any further analyses which relate one variable to another, although they might attempt to ascertain whether selected frequency distributions obtained differ significantly from distributions theoretically anticipated.

Data analysis

Depending on the central aim of the survey the frequencies analysis should itself provide some answers to such basic questions as 'Why do adolescents start smoking?', 'Why do they continue smoking?' and 'Why do they stop smoking?' If time has permitted, it may have been possible to organize the data collation stage of the second practical in relevant groupings (e.g. for males and for females). Organizing the collated data in this manner will enable students to carry out basic statistical analyses like Chi Square. However, more complex analyses of the data (see below) can be undertaken by the course tutor if so wished.

The collected data

As we have noted in the opening sections of this practical, there are a variety of hypotheses that can be stated with respect to the images adolescents have of smokers and of non-smokers, and how these images relate to their own smoking behaviour. However, more complex analyses of the data (e.g. discriminant functions analyses to ascertain how best to discriminate be-tween smokers and non-smokers) needs to be undertaken via a computer and software like SPSS (The Statistical Package for the Social Sciences; Nie, Hull, Jenkins, Steinbrenner and Bent, 1975). If course organizers have access to a data preparation service that will punch cards direct from well-edited and coded questionnaires, and if they are familiar with SPSS (or a similar package) and have access to it, setting up such multivariate analyses, and more simple ones like cross-tabulations, will be a relatively straightforward matter. Data of the kind likely to be collected lend themselves to a variety of forms of statistical analysis, and as such can be a fruitful basis from which to teach the use of many statistical procedures.

Data presentation

The data from the second practical that are of the frequency-count type are likely to be best presented in one of two forms. For relatively continuous variables (e.g. age at which the first cigarette was smoked), a frequency curve may be drawn. For classificatory or discontinuous variables (such as whether the respondent has ever smoked, or reasons for starting smoking), bar charts and/or pie diagrams are more appropriate for illustrative purposes.

Discussion

The limitations to any conclusions drawn from the analyses will reflect, largely, the limitations of the questionnaire designed in the first practical, the genuineness of the data and the nature of the sample from which the data were collected. There will not have been sufficient time to undertake a proper pilot study; indeed, the data collected for the second practical should be regarded more as that required to assist in reformulation of the questionnaire before it is used in a survey proper. The construction of the questionnaire in the first practical will have been somewhat hasty and, even though the course tutor may have utilized some of the material in the Appendix to collect the data for the second practical, it is likely that certain questions will prove unsatisfactory (vague, biassed, ambiguous, etc.), and some answer alternatives will prove un-satisfactory also (unclear, not mutually exclusive, etc.).

Such limitations should be pointed out by the course tutor (and ideally by the students themselves) as part of the peda-gogic exercise; otherwise the practicals might, unfortunately, reinforce the com-mon belief mentioned at the outset, that anyone can string a few questions together into a questionnaire. Students should throughout be encouraged to be critical of the material they are producing, and be helped to realize that in a full-blown survey, with a relatively large-scale pre-test (Bynner's questionnaire was piloted on 1,180 boys and girls in the first and fourth years of 20 secondary schools), much time and effort is put in by a great many individuals proficient in the stages of conducting a survey and analysing the results.

The general lesson students should have learnt from these practicals is that al-luded to above when considering the limi-tations of the design procedure, namely that the production of a questionnaire to act as a scientific data collection instru-ment is no easy matter, and requires pre-liminary data collection (through pre-tests and pilot studies) and analyses before final drafts may be considered viable. In undertaking the practicals, students should have learnt to appreciate that it is in-appropriate to collect certain sorts of data through questionnaires, and that obtaining a satisfactory response rate is vital and is affected by the nature of the survey and the ease (or difficulty) with

which respondents are able to follow (and answer) the questions asked. More pre-cisely, students should have learnt that questions are formulations of words, and words have different connotations for dif-ferent people. Thus not only should the formulation of unambiguous, specific and understandable questions be recognized as a major task in constructing a questionnaire, but also as much thought must be given to the consideration of clear, unambiguous and mutually exclusive coding categories for respondents' answers.

Conclusion

By undertaking the first practical exercise students should have developed some insight into the way in which group discussions may be used at an early qualitative stage in survey research. They should also be fami-liar with the range of ways in which data can be collected by using a questionnaire, and have some understanding of how num-erical coding systems are utilized prior to data analysis. By undertaking data collec-tion students will have experienced at first hand some of the inherent problems of this method of data elicitation and some of the problems in the questionnaire itself. By carrying out in the second practical exercise a simple analysis of the data, further understanding of the necessity for adequate coding schemes, and of the limi-tations of the questionnaire, should be fostered. At the same time an appreciation of the need for further, more sophisticated statistical analyses of this form of data may be generated, especially if the survey data have revealed interesting results.

Acknowledgement

The example questions in the Appendix are reproduced with the permission of Her Majesty's Stationery Office from the report 'The Young Smoker', by J. M. Bynner, based on a survey carried out by Social Survey Division of the Office of Population Censuses and Surveys.

REFERENCES

Atkinson, J. (1971) Handbook for Interviewers. London: HMSO.

Booth, C. (ed.) (1904) Life and Labour of the People in London. London: Macmillan.

Bowley, A.L. and Burnett-Hurst, A.R. (1915) Livelihood and Poverty: A study in the economic conditions of working class households in Northampton, Warrington, Stanley and Reading. London: Bell.

Bynner, J.N. (1969) The Young Smoker. London: HMSO.

Eysenck, H.J. (1980) Causes and Effects of Smoking. London: M.T. Smith.

Gray, P. and Gee, F.A. (1972) A Quality Check on the 1966 Ten Per Cent Sample Census of England and Wales. London: HMSO.

Gregory, A.H., Hartley, J.R. and Lewis, D.G. (1969) Basic Statistics. London: Methuen.

Hoineville, G., Jowell, R. and associates (1977) Survey Research Practice. London: Heinemann.

Hollander, E.P. (1981) Principles and Methods of Social Psychology. London: Oxford University Press.

Jones, E.E. and Gerard, H.B. (1967) Foundations of Social Psychology. London: Wiley.

Market Research Society (undated) A Handbook for Interviewers. London: The Market Research Society.

Maxwell, J. (1969) Intelligence, education and fertility: a comparison between the 1932 and 1947 Scottish surveys. Journal of Biological Science, 1, 247-271.

McGuire, N.J. (1969) The nature of attitudes and attitude change. In G. Lindzey and E. Aronson (eds), The Handbook of Social Psychology. Reading, Mass.: Addison-Wesley.

McKennell, A.C. and Thomas, R.K. (1967) Adults' and Adolescents' Smoking Habits and Attitudes. London: HMSO.

Nie, N.N., Hull, C.H., Jenkins, J.G., Steinbrenner, K. and Bent, D.H. (1975) Statistical Package for the Social Sciences. New York: McGraw-Hill.

Oppenheim, A.N. (1966) Questionnaire Design and Attitude Measurement. London: Heinemann.

Payne, S. (1965) The Art of Asking Questions. Princeton, NJ: Princeton University Press.

Warwick, D.P. and Lininger, C.A. (1975) The Sample Survey: Theory and practice. New York: McGraw-Hill.

APPENDIX: A SELECTION OF EXAMPLE QUESTIONS

For a fairly exhaustive set of pertinent questions see the relevant appendices to Bynner (1969) and McKennell and Thomas (1967). For more general material on question and questionnaire design see: Payne (1965); Oppenheim (1966); Warwick and Lininger (1975); and Hoineville, Jowell and associates (1977).

	LEAVE BLANK
	COL/CODE

1. How old are you? I am _____ years and _____ months.   **1/2/3**

2. How many brothers and sisters have you altogether? _____   **4/5**

   <u>If you have brothers and sisters</u>

       How many of them are older than you are? _____   **6/**

       How many of them are younger than you are? _____   **7/**

3. What is the name of your father's job?

   _____   **8/**

                                           TICK HERE

4. Have you ever tried smoking a cigarette?

              Yes ... ____ 1

              No ... ____ 2   **9/**

5. Have you smoked more than one cigarette?

              Yes ... ____ 1

              No ... ____ 2   **10/**

6. How many cigarettes do you smoke now?

       I do not smoke now ... ____ 1

       Less than 1 each week ... ____ 2

       Between 1 and 9 each week ... ____ 3

   (Tick one) Between 10 and 19 each week ... ____ 4

       Between 20 and 29 each week ... ____ 5

       Between 30 and 39 each week ... ____ 6   **11/**

	LEAVE BLANK
	COL/CODE

7. What social class do you think you and
    your family belong to?

Upper middle class	... ___	1
Middle class	... ___	2
(Tick one) Working class	... ___	3
No particular class	... ___	4
Don't know	... ___	5

12/

8. Do you ever feel nervous or tense?

Often	... ___	1
Sometimes	... ___	2
Hardly ever	... ___	3

13/

9. Now we would like to know what kind of person you are

Dare to take risks ☐ ☐ ☐ Want to be safe

If you are the kind of person who dares to take risks, put a
tick (✓) in the box on the LEFT.

If you are the kind of person who wants to be safe, put a tick
in the box on the RIGHT.

If you really can't decide what kind of person you are, put a
tick in the box in the MIDDLE.

Now put a tick by each of these questions in the box which is
right for the kind of person you are.

Good at school/   ☐ ☐ ☐   Not so good at
academic work   school/academic work

14/

Interested in   ☐ ☐ ☐   Not much interested in
girls/women   girls/women

15/

etc., etc.

	LEAVE BLANK
	COL/CODE

10. Now we want to know <u>what kind of person you would like to be.</u>

We want you to answer some of the same questions as before, but this time <u>with the person you would like to be in mind.</u>

Good at school/ academic work ☐ ☐ ☐ Not so good at school/academic work   25/

etc., etc.

11. Please answer the following questions by putting a <u>ring</u> round the words YES or NO, like this:

(YES)   NO   1   2

Do your nerves often feel on edge?   YES   NO   36/

Do you often have an upset stomach?   YES   NO   37/

Do you find it difficult to relax?   YES   NO   38/
etc., etc.

12. (FOR PEOPLE OPERATIONALLY DEFINED AS SMOKERS OR EX-SMOKERS)

How did you get your first cigarette?   TICK HERE

I bought it in a shop   ...   ___ 1

I was given it by my father or mother   ...   ___ 2

I was given it by my brother or sister   ...   ___ 3

(Tick one only) I was given it by an adult (not a relative)   ...   ___ 4

I was given it by a friend   ...   ___ 5

I got it from a slot machine   ...   ___ 6

I found it or took it   ...   ___ 7

I got it some other way   ...   ___ 8   48/

12a. <u>Why</u> did you smoke it?

I wanted to know what smoking was like   ...   ___ 1

I was dared to smoke   ...   ___ 2

I was showing off   ...   ___ 3

I wanted to be like my friends who smoked   ...   ___ 4   49/

	LEAVE BLANK
	COL/CODE

13. (FOR PEOPLE OPERATIONALLY DEFINED AS EX-SMOKERS)
Why did you stop smoking and for which of these reasons?

	1 TRUE	2 FALSE	

1. I didn't like smoking   ... ____   ____   50/

2. My parents didn't like me smoking   ... ____   ____   51/

3. I thought smoking cost too much   ... ____   ____   52/

(Tick each one either true or false)

4. I thought I might get lung cancer   ... ____   ____   53/

5. I thought smoking was bad for my health   ... ____   ____   54/

6. I thought smoking was a dirty habit ... ____   ____   55/

7. I thought it was making me unfit   ... ____   ____   56/

8. I wanted to prove I could stop   ... ____   ____   57/

Which of the above reasons was the most important for you? Write its number here ...   ____   58/

14. (FOR PEOPLE OPERATIONALLY DEFINED AS SMOKERS)
Why do you smoke now?

	1 TRUE	2 FALSE	

Because my friends smoke   ... ____   ____   59/

(Tick each one either true or false)

Because I enjoy smoking   ... ____   ____   60/

Because I can't give up smoking   ... ____   ____   61/

Because smoking calms me down   ... ____   ____   62/

Because smoking makes me feel adult ... ____   ____   63/

I smoke for some other reason   ... ____   ____   64/

15. We now want you to think about <u>the sort of male pupil/student who smokes cigarettes.</u> You have answered this sort of question before: just put a tick in the appropriate box, and only use the middle box if you really can't decide between the left side and the right side answer.

Good at school/ academic work [ ] [ ] [ ] Not so good at school/academic work   65/

etc., etc. (could be repeated for female smokers and for non-smokers)

16. People have different ideas about many things. Below is a list of ideas that some people believe in. You will <u>agree</u> with some of them and disagree with others. Sometimes you will <u>agree</u> strongly and at other times you will <u>disagree</u> strongly. Now and then you may be uncertain whether you agree or disagree. Read each statement below carefully, then put a tick by it in the column which is right for <u>you</u>.

	Strongly agree	Agree	Uncertain	Disagree	Strongly disagree	
Smoking is only dangerous to older people						76/
Smoking is a dirty habit						77/
Smoking makes you feel on top of the world						78/
Smoking gives your breath a bad smell						79/

etc., etc.

LEAVE BLANK

COL/CODE

2

Selection interviewing: a four-step approach
Mike Smith

Specification notes

AIM OF EXERCISE: to improve students' skills in the professionally important task of selection interviewing. Subsidiary aims are to provide insights into training techniques and person perception.

PRIOR KNOWLEDGE ASSUMED: no prior knowledge of interviewing is required. Prior knowledge of training techniques and theory of person perception is helpful but not essential.

DURATION: 2½-3 hours. Students need to complete an application form in advance. Time available can be divided into hourly segments.

LOCATION: for a group of 18 students, a large, flat (i.e. unraked) lecture room would be sufficient. If possible, small rooms for groups of three students to practise the exercise would be advantageous but not essential.

EQUIPMENT: closed-circuit television (CCTV) is highly desirable but not essential. A more sophisticated system involving three cameras, mixer and special effects generator can be used to advantage. Duplication of nine one-page handouts is desirable.

SPECIAL REQUIREMENTS: none.

Introduction

This chapter describes a sequence of four exercises designed to improve students' skills in selection interviewing. Each exercise has five parts: (i) a briefing by the tutor; (ii) a handout covering the material given in the briefing; (iii) a role-play which is recorded on CCTV; (iv) a replay with feedback and comments from the tutor; (v) completion of a check-list to summarize the major points.

Many practical classes in psychology give students practice in problem definition, investigation design or data analysis. In contrast, this practical focusses upon the acquisition of another important professional skill: the ability to conduct an effective selection interview. It is envisaged that the complete sequence of four exercises will take about three hours, whereas an industrial training course in interviewing skills would last a minimum of two days, so clearly the exercises can only start to develop interviewing skills. Considerable repetition of the final exercise plus variations in role-play (e.g. a very shy candidate, a very garrulous candidate) would be needed to produce a really proficient interviewer.

The selection interviewing exercises are based upon research on interviewing, which is briefly summarized in the next section, and theory. However, the exercises can also be related to industrial training.

(The exercises themselves are a condensed training course, where the task is first analysed and then imparted to the trainees using the Cumulative Part Method and the role-play learning method: see Toye, 1977.) The exercises can also be related to the social psychology of person perception, especially attribution theory. Furthermore, the skills of selection interviewing are partly transferable to other types of interviews such as appraisal interviews, counselling interviews and exit interviews.

Theoretical background

Systematic selection

Interviews must be seen within the context of systematic selection, which starts with the analysis of the job (see Landy and Trumbo, 1980). On the basis of the job analysis and exit interviews a draft job description is prepared. The job is then considered to see if it needs to be altered in some way; could it be abolished or merged with some other job? Could it be altered to make it more interesting and satisfying? When the modifications have been decided, a final job description is produced.

The final job description is used to prepare the second important document in the selection process - the personnel specification - which attempts to describe the ideal applicant. The format of the personnel specification can take many forms and perhaps the most widely used is Rodger's Seven-Point Plan (1968). It categorizes worker characteristics under seven headings:

1. physique: health, appearance, speech
2. attainments: education, work qualifications, experience
3. general intelligence: how much is there? How much is normally used?
4. special aptitudes: mechanical, spatial, verbal
5. interests: outdoor, scientific, computational, etc.
6. disposition and temperament: extravert, neurotic, independent?
7. circumstances: dependant relatives, family working in same job?

It is also common practice to sub-divide worker characteristics further into essential and desirable characteristics. These are indicated in the shortened personnel specification given in Appendix 1.

The personnel specification is used to draw up a job advert. The most promising applicants are interviewed and/or subjected to other tests, and the personnel specification is again used in the final stage of 'arriving at a decision'. From this very brief outline, it can be seen that the selection interview is only one stage of the selection process and the interview is easier to conduct if the preceding stages have been competently executed.

Research on interviews: the reliability problem

Probably the most serious criticism of selection interviews concerns their unreliability. As Hollingworth pointed out as long ago as 1929, a candidate interviewed by one 'experienced' manager can be a stunning success, while at an interview with another 'experienced' manager, the same candidate is an abysmal failure. Hakel and Dunnette (1970) point out that 'periodic reviews of research studies on the employment interview (Wagner, 1949; Mayfield, 1964; Ulrich and Trumbo, 1965) agree in concluding that most personnel interviews are conducted in such a way as to be quite unreliable and usually non-valid'. Such damning criticism may be a little unfair since many critics adopt simplistic and faulty methods themselves; nevertheless, the reliability of the typical selection interview remains very suspect.

Sources of unreliability can be collected together under five headings. First, different interviewers use the interview to look for different traits. For example, in selecting for the police force, one interviewer may look for a person who is affable and physically strong, while another interviewer may look for the intellect of Sherlock Holmes. Under these circumstances, it is only to be expected that the interviewers arrive at different evaluations of candidates' worth.

The second source of unreliability concerns the setting of the interview. The physical setting of the interview can influence the performance of the interviewee:

he or she must be able to hear the interviewer and feel that the surroundings are private, free from distraction and conducive to an exchange of information. The psychological setting is probably more important.

The interviewees must not be overawed by the interviewer's status symbols. The psychological climate of a business-like, sympathetic, problem-solving exchange must be established. Lewis (1980) draws attention to the need to establish an explicit contract whereby the interviewer agrees to treat the interviewee equitably if the latter agrees to provide valid data. Since much of an interviewee's behaviour is fakable, Lewis argues that to obtain reliable and valid data, the interviewer must adopt a reflective, trusting style, more typical of a counsellor, in the hope that the interviewee will adopt a complementary role. The opening phase of an interview is probably the most crucial time in establishing a rapport of this kind.

The third source of interview unreliability arises from the fact that most interviewers fail to structure the interview. Even when interviewers agree upon a common set of traits, or when a single interviewer is dealing with a succession of candidates, the questioning is often radically different. For example, during the first interview of the day, an applicant may be questioned about all aspects of his life. Towards the end of the day an applicant may be asked a few perfunctory questions about qualifications and work experience while home circumstances, interests and aspirations are given scant regard. The same applicant can give very different impressions under the two very different situations. Structuring an interview, therefore, almost certainly increases reliability. In 1969, Schwab and Henman found that unstructured interviews produced a reliability coefficient of 0.36, while a totally structured interview (i.e. a list of predetermined questions) produced a reliability coefficient of 0.79. Unfortunately, the totally structured interviews were inflexible, artificial and made it difficult to establish effective rapport. The semi-structured interview, which specifies the subject areas to be questioned, seems to offer an acceptable compromise.

Schwab and Henman found that interviews which were semi-structured produced a reliability coefficient of 0.43. Other research has shown that interviewers rarely cover all the relevant aspects of a candidate's background. In the light of these and other research findings, interviewers are advised to adopt an interview plan. The plan used in the following exercise is one example of the many plans available and it has a number of advantages: it is simple and easy to follow; it starts with the most relevant aspects; and the progression from factual to less structured information helps build rapport.

Even when interviewers have agreed upon the traits required, have produced the right climate, and have carefully followed a plan, the results of an interview can still be unreliable because of the fourth source of reliability: the interactive nature of interviews. Verplanck (1955) was one of the first investigators to research the interactive nature of interviews. He instructed interviewers to react in a specified way whenever candidates stated their opinions: agreement with the candidates increased the number of opinions they expressed, silence produced a small decrease, while disagreement produced a large decrease in the opinions given by the candidates. In a similar vein, Davis and Sloan (1974) manipulated the number of self-disclosures which interviewers made to candidates, and independent judges listened to audiotapes of the interviews.

Their results suggest that disclosing interviewers produced more disclosures from the interviewee, but the interviewer had to keep disclosing in order to keep the interviewee disclosing. Keenan (1976) conducted a similar experiment by manipulating the non-verbal approval or disapproval of interviewers and asking judges to rate videotapes which showed only the performance of the interviewees. Interviewers who emitted approving non-verbal cues tended to produce interviewees who are friendly, relaxed and successful in creating a good impression. The level of the verbal communication also influences a candidate's behaviour. Daniels and Otis (1950) reported that interviewers talked for 57 per cent of the time, candidates talked for 30 per cent of the time, while the remaining 13 per cent was spent in silence. With the interviewer claiming the lion's share of interview time, candidates have a poorer chance of revealing their abilities. In order to get the candidate to give extended answers, the interviewer needs to pose open-ended rather than closed questions.

If the interviewer has avoided the previous four sources of unreliability, there is a good chance that at the end of the interview accurate and relevant information about the candidate will have been obtained. However, the fifth possible source of unreliability remains. The interviewer must use the information to arrive at a judgement of the candidate's suitability. The first problem is one of human fallibility. Research suggests that by the time the interview is concluded, an interviewer has forgotten half of the information given by the candidate. Consequently, notes of key points are essential. Another common failure of interviewers is that they often make up their minds too early in the interview. Springbett (1958) suggests that interviewers make up their minds within the first four minutes of an interview and that the remainder of the time is spent looking for evidence which will support their early decision. Other interviewers arrive at a global evaluation of a candidate, and the halo surrounding the global judgement obliterates contrary evaluations on the individual traits contained in the personnel specification. Finally, there are the problems of how the interviewer interprets and weights the information obtained from the candidate. The phenomena of attribution theory and person perception are relevant here (see, for example, Gergen and Gergen, 1981, p. 57-70). When candidates relate incidents in their lives, the interviewer has to attribute the cause of the incident either to the candidate's 'personality' or to the situation in which the candidate was placed. A wrong attribution can lead to an erroneous conclusion and it has been suggested (Herriot and Rothwell, 1981) that interviewers may have a tendency wrongly to attribute causes to the person rather than the circumstances. To add to the difficulty the various attributions must be weighted before a final decision is reached. Bolsher and Springbett (1961) suggest that interviewers pay too much attention to negative

attributions but more recent work has suggested that any unexpected and unusual information about the candidate is given too much emphasis.

This catalogue of the five sources of interview unreliability highlights two points. First, the interviewer is faced with an inordinately complex task and, second, the reliability of the interview is intricately related to validity. Indeed, in many senses, the issues surrounding the interview decision could be regarded as issues of validity.

Method

The objectives of the sequence of exercises are to reinforce the research findings concerning interviews and to give students an opportunity to develop skills as interviewers and interviewees.

The exact organization of the practical session is easily adapted to different teaching situations and level of technical support. For clarity of exposition, the following organization envisages a practical group with about 18 students and a fairly simple CCTV system. Later, two variations in organization to meet different circumstances will be indicated.

Resources
For the fairly typical situation with a group of 18 students, the following materials are required and should be booked two or three weeks in advance.

1. Large screen television.
2. Recorder, tape and take-up spool.
3. Microphones, camera (with zoom facility) and tripod extension lead.
4. One set of documentation for each student, as follows:

   Person specification (Appendix 1)
   Application form (Appendix 2)
   Briefing notes for exercise 1
     (Appendix 3)
   Check-list for exercise 1 (Appendix 4)
   Briefing notes for exercise 2
     (Appendix 5)
   Check-list for exercise 2 (Appendix 6)
   Briefing notes for exercise 3
     (Appendix 7)

Check-list for exercise 3   (Appendix 8)
Briefing notes for exercise 4
   (Appendix 9)

5. Four or five file cards.
6. Two stop-watches.

It should be noted that since the factors involved in arriving at a decision are both varied and abstract, there is no check-list for the final exercise.

Copies of the documentation are given in the appendices. Universities, polytechnics and colleges of higher education may photocopy or otherwise reproduce them for teaching of full-time or part-time courses (but not short courses or other purposes) provided the source is acknowledged. It must be pointed out that, in the interests of clarity, the male referent has been used throughout the handouts, but of course they refer equally to both men and women.

Advance preparation

At least one day before the exercise, students are given a blank application form (Appendix 2) and asked to complete it as though they were each 20 year olds who had taken six 'O' levels at the age of 16, and had obtained passes in Mathematics, Engineering Drawing, Woodwork and Metal Work. After leaving school, an engineering technician course had been followed for two years before a friend's father made an offer of a lucrative job in a firm of bookmakers. The offer was accepted but as there were no promotion prospects, a career in the police force was sought after an interval of about two years. Students are told that they can invent any other details, provided they are sensible and realistic. However, one student's brief is slightly amended to include a period of six months in jail following a conviction for a betting shop fraud. This student is asked to omit this fact from his application form and he is asked not to volunteer this information at an interview but, if directly questioned, he is not expected to lie or prevaricate. This student is asked not to disclose these amendments until after the exercise.

The tutor should read through the earlier theoretical section of this chapter and appropriate texts on industrial training or person perception if these topics are to be included in the discussion periods. The tutor should also be familiar with the CCTV equipment. The tutor may also wish to prepare overhead projections for use in the briefing sessions.

EXERCISE 1: OPENINGS, JOB EXPLANATIONS, CLOSINGS (20 minutes). After a general introduction to selection interviewing (two minutes) the tutor briefs students on the points covered in Appendix 3 (seven minutes) and it is explained that two students will be asked to act the role of interviewers and one student asked to act the role of interviewee. The class is then divided into threes and appropriate roles allotted (democratically or otherwise!). Copies of Appendix 1 (Person specification) and Appendix 3 (Briefing notes for exercise 1) are distributed and the groups are given five minutes to prepare the openings, description of a job, and closing. At the end of this time one group of three is chosen (democratically or otherwise!) to role-play the exercise in front of the CCTV. These 'volunteers' are given the following instructions.

The objective of this exercise is to develop your skills in starting an interview, finishing an interview and in explaining the job. Please go through these stages of interview with this candidate. Do not bother about other stages of the interview. Aim to take under four minutes. If you go over your time I will give you this winding-up signal (demonstrate) and you are to finish quickly. You are not allowed to consult the briefing notes during the interview.

When the role-play is completed, the check-list (Appendix 4) is distributed to class members while the tape is rewound. The tape is then played, stopping for comment where appropriate (six minutes). The check-list is completed as the tape is played plus, perhaps, a little extra time at the end of the tape. Subsequent discussion (five minutes) should focus upon the check-list items which were ignored during the role-play. The times indicated for each stage are maximum times allowed.

In practice, the role-play of this stage is usually much shorter than the five minutes allowed and the whole of this exercise plus the introduction can be accomplished in 20 minutes.

EXERCISE 2: COVERING THE GROUND (30 minutes). The briefing session (five minutes) covers the material contained in Appendix 5. Again, the students are given time to prepare interviews (about six minutes). A volunteer trio (which happens to contain the student with the amended brief) is asked to role-play in front of the CCTV.

The interviewers are given the application form for inspection and the objectives of the exercise are explained. For example:

> The objectives of this exercise are to give practice at openings, job explanation and closings. However, the main purpose is to see how well you obtain the relevant information. You should open the interview, explain the job, question the candidate and then close the interview. In all it should take about 15 minutes. If you run out of time I will give you the wind-up signal. Pay particular attention to being systematic and comprehensive.

At the end of the mock interview, the tape is rewound, replayed and discussed. The check-list (Appendix 6) for exercise 2 is distributed as the tape is rewound. The discussion should emphasize the depth and range of questioning. Acceptance of superficial answers should be discussed in detail. If the interviewers have not detected the candidate's criminal history, it should be revealed and the omission discussed. During this exercise, the way that questions are phrased should not be criticized as they are the subject of the next role-play.

EXERCISE 3: WAYS OF MAKING THEM TALK (50 minutes). The briefing (five minutes) for the third session covers the material contained in Appendix 7 'Ways of making them talk'. Student pairs are given five minutes to prepare their interviews before a pair of volunteers and a volunteer interviewee are obtained. The other stu-

dents in the group are allotted specific tasks, such as:

* count the number of closed-ended questions;
* count the number of open-ended questions;
* time interviewer's speaking time;
* time interviewee's speaking time;
* count the number of gestures;
* count the number of 'guggles' (i.e. 'uh uh', 'ah', 'jolly good' and 'really').

After the interview (20 minutes) the videotape is replayed (25 minutes) and discussed (five minutes) before the check-list is completed. The maximum time for individual components is indicated in parentheses. Usually this exercise can be completed within 50 minutes and it is often followed by a coffee break.

EXERCISE 4: REVISION AND MAKING A DECISION (35 minutes). Exercise 4 commences with the traditional briefing (five minutes) but preparation time is not required since preparation for previous exercises can be utilized. Volunteers are obtained and without attracting attention the interviewee should be handed a card saying:

> For the first half of the interview answer with a single word whenever possible (e.g. yes, no, sometimes). In the second half, give long-winded answers. Mumble incoherently at least three times. Try to give answers which are consistent with the referees' comments which will be read out. Do not disclose these instructions until you are allowed to do so.

Immediately before the mock interview starts, the tutor announces to the whole group that a reference has been received from the candidate's ex-head teacher. It reads:

> The candidate is shy and very modest. The candidate has an IQ of 130 but this was not reflected in the 'O' level results. The candidate's 'O' levels had been interrupted by a two-week period in hospital. Although unable to swim, the

candidate had jumped into a lake to help someone who was in a dinghy and who was in difficulties. Unfortunately, the candidate had injured himself/herself and had nearly drowned. Subsequently, a local society had awarded him/her a medal for bravery.

The role-play (25 minutes) proceeds in the same way as previous role-plays, except that, at the end, the interviewers are asked to decide whether to engage the interviewee. When they have given their answer, the interviewers should be asked to give their evidence and the reasoning behind their decisions (two minutes).

A replay of the videotape is not necessary for the final exercise; the discussion (10 minutes) should focus upon the validity of the evidence and inferences used in arriving at a decision. At this point, the discussion can be widened to discuss problems of selection interviewing in industry (some students can be asked to relate their own experiences). A good way to end the session is to focus upon the training aspects and ask how interviewer training in industry would differ from the training just given (e.g. participants would have less theoretical background but more practical experience; more practice would be given to produce over-learning; and efforts would be made to assist transfer from the training situation to the 'factory floor').

Variations in the method
The practical can be amended to suit a wide variety of situations. In situations where fewer resources are available, the exercises can be run without a CCTV: the students simply make notes as they observe the role-plays. In this situation the time requirement is reduced by about 45 minutes. If copying or duplicating facilities are not available, the material contained in the handouts can be transferred to acetate sheets, displayed on the overhead projector

and copied by students. Check-lists can be read. While these alternative arrangements demand fewer resources, they are less effective. In situations where more resources are available, an improved CCTV system can be used. An ideal system requires two static cameras, plus one camera with automatic pan and tilt. The output of the cameras is relayed to a mixer, and an effects generator with split-screen facility. In this ideal setting (shown in figure 1), one of the static cameras is focussed upon the interviewee, while another static camera is focussed upon the interviewers. The tutor and the remaining students who are not involved in the role-play observe from an adjacent area where the tutor records events, switches from camera to camera and manipulates the remote control camera. Perhaps the observers could watch the role-play via a one-way mirror. The tutor's task is quite difficult and he or she should be familiar with the equipment before the exercise. The use of the remote control camera is particularly difficult. The tutor should switch to one of the static cameras while 'lining up' the particular 'shot' with the remote control camera.

If sufficient accommodation is available, the students can divide into groups of three and, while one group is being recorded on CCTV, the remaining groups can perform their own role-play and re-group to watch the video. Inevitably, the additional organization requires additional time.

Additional time could also be used to explore models of decision making. Worksheets could be prepared to ask for the traits which interviewers in the final exercise use to decide whether to employ the candidate. The worksheets could also ask for the importance of these traits. The information could then be used to demonstrate the additive model, the averaging model and the weighted averaging model of person evaluation (see Gergen and Gergen, 1981, p. 60).

Figure 1. Ideal arrangements for interviewing exercise

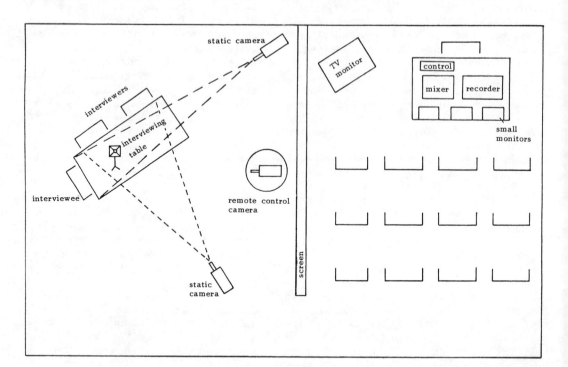

REFERENCES

Bolsher, B.T. and Springbett, B.M. (1961) The reaction of interviewers to favorable and unfavorable information. Journal of Applied Psychology, 45, 95-103.

Daniels, A.W. and Otis, J.L. (1950) A method for analysing employment interviews. Personnel Psychology, 3, 425-444.

Davis, J.D. and Sloan, M.L. (1974) The basis of interviewee matching of interviewer self-disclosure. British Journal of Social and Clinical Psychology, 13, 359-367.

Gergen, K.J. and Gergen, M.M. (1981) Social Psychology. New York: Harcourt-Brace.

Hakel, D.M. and Dunnette, M.D. (1970) Checklists for Describing Job Applicants. University of Minnesota, Minn.: Industrial Relations Centre.

Herriot, P. and Rothwell, C. (1981) The selection interview: a theoretical account and some data. Paper presented to Occupational Psychology Conference, York.

Hollingworth, H.L. (1929) Vocational Psychology and Character Analysis. New York: Appleton-Century-Crofts.

Keenan, A. (1976) Effects of non-verbal behaviour of interviewers on candidates' performances. Journal of Occupational Psychology, 49, 171-176.

Landy, F.J. and Trumbo, D.A. (1980) Psychology of Work Behavior. Homewood, Ill.: Dorsey Press.

Lewis, C. (1980) Investigating the employment interview: a consideration of counselling skills. Journal of Occupational Psychology, 53, 111-116.

Mayfield, E.L. (1964) The selection interview - a re-evaluation of published research. Personnel Psychology, 17, 239-260.

Rodger, A. (1968) The Seven-Point Plan. Windsor: National Foundation for Educational Research.

Schwab, D.P. and Henman, H.G. (1969) Relationship between interviewer structure and inter-interviewer reliability in an employment situation. Journal of Applied Psychology, 53, 214-217.

Springbett, B.M. (1958) Factors affecting the final decision in an employment interview. Canadian Journal of Psychology, 12, 13-22.

Toye, M. (1977) CRAMP: A user's guide to training decisions. Cambridge: Industrial Training Research Unit.

Ulrich, L. and Trumbo, D. (1965) The selection interview since 1949. Psychological Bulletin, 63, 100-116.

Verplanck, W.S. (1955) The control of the content of conversation: reinforcement of statements of opinion. Journal of Abnormal and Social Psychology, 51, 668-676.

Wagner, R. (1949) The employment interview - a critical summary. Personnel Psychology, 2, 17-46.

APPENDIX 1: POLICE PERSON SPECIFICATION

Note: this abbreviated specification is for demonstration purposes only.

1. PHYSIQUE	Essential:	Good eyesight, hearing, clear speech, adequate height (5' 4" women, 5' 8" men).
	Desirable:	Good standard of grooming.
2. ATTAINMENTS	Essential:	At least four 'O' levels or pass qualifying examination.
	Desirable:	Ability to drive.
3. INTELLIGENCE	Essential:	In top third of population.
4. SPECIAL APTITUDES	Essential:	Good written expression.
	Desirable:	Organized approach to words and dealing with problems. Ability to follow instructions.
5. INTERESTS	Desirable:	Persuasive, clerical, social service interests.
6. DISPOSITION AND TEMPERAMENT	Essential:	Self-confident, circumspect, even-tempered, able to use initiative, tough-minded.
7. HOME CIRCUMSTANCES	Essential:	Circumstances which do not prevent shift work and long hours of work.

CONTRA-INDICATIONS: criminal record, undue impulsiveness, age below 18½ years.

APPENDIX 2

**APPLICATION
FORM**

Please return this form to
Not later than:

---

1. POSITION APPLIED FOR

---

2. PERSONAL DETAILS

    Surname   Forenames _____

    Address   Telephone Number _____

                                 Date of Birth _____

                                 Marital Status _____

                                 Ages of children (if any)

                                 ____ yrs ____ yrs ____ yrs

                                 ____ yrs ____ yrs ____ yrs

Name and Address of Next of Kin

_____

_____Telephone:_____

Names of friends or relatives in this Company   Position

---

3. WORK HISTORY
Name and address of your present (or last) employer

_____

Date and job title on starting
Title of present job
Brief indication of type of work

_____

Reason for leaving

_____

Salary of present (or last) job
If you have already left your last job, give the date of leaving

              /continued ...

3. <u>WORK HISTORY</u> (continued ...)

Names and Addresses of other
previous employers   <u>Job Title</u>   <u>Date</u>   <u>Reason for leaving</u>

4. <u>EDUCATION AND TRAINING</u>

  <u>Names and Type of School or College</u>   <u>Dates</u>

Please list the examinations you have taken   <u>Results</u>

5. <u>MEDICAL HISTORY</u>

Have you ever suffered from

Back trouble   Yes/No   When?

Nervous trouble   Yes/No   When?

Alcoholism   Yes/No   When?

Would you be willing to have a medical examination?   Yes / No

6. <u>GENERAL</u>

What are your hobbies and pastimes?

7. <u>REFERENCES</u>

Please give the names and addresses of TWO people who know your work.

APPENDIX 3: BRIEFING NOTES FOR EXERCISE 1

OPENINGS, CLOSINGS AND JOB EXPLANATION

1.1 INTRODUCTION

A typical interview has four phases: the opening, questioning the candidate, explaining the job and the closing. Interviewers need to prepare the openings and closings very carefully since a good opening sets the right tone for the interview and a good closing sends the candidate away with a good impression. In these stages, events are very predictable and interviewers are able to build up a standard 'spiel'.

The physical setting for an interview is important. It should be private, free from interruptions and distractions, be suitably furnished and be supplied with a clock.

1.2 FOR OPENINGS

Greet candidate by name. It checks that you have the right candidate and establishes a friendly but formal tone.

Introduce yourself clearly. Give your name(s) and job title.

Indicate where candidate should sit.

Chat about something innocuous to put candidate at ease and used to the sound of his voice.

Thank him for his application and explain purpose of interview.

1.3 JOB EXPLANATION

Study the job description and work out a spiel. The job may not be to your taste but do not denigrate it. Beware of qualifiers such as 'just' or 'only'. Prepare answers for standard questions on pay, promotion, hours and reason why vacancy arose. Do not make rash promises. Do not tell lies. Mention the positive aspects of the job.

1.4 CLOSINGS

Say how helpful you have found the visit.

Except with a garrulous candidate, ask if there are any other questions.

Explain that you have had a wonderful response to the advertisement and that you must see several other candidates.

Ask him what other applications he has made.

Tell him when and how he will hear the result of the interview.

Thank him again for his application.

APPENDIX 4: CHECK-LIST FOR EXERCISE 1

OPENINGS AND CLOSINGS

Explanation

Watch the videotape carefully. To what extent did the <u>interviewer</u> cover all the main points? Tick them off the following list as they occur.

Opening

Is the candidate greeted by name? : _ :
Does the interviewer introduce himself clearly? : _ :
Does the interviewer give his own job title? : _ :
Does the interviewer indicate where the candidate should sit? : _ :
Does the interviewer put the candidate at ease? : _ :
Does the interviewer thank the candidate for his application? : _ :
Does the interviewer explain the purpose of the interview? : _ :
Is the opening stage kept under two minutes? : _ :

Closing

Does the interviewer say something positive but non-committal
  about the interview (e.g. it has been a useful talk)? : _ :
Does the interviewer say that there have been other candidates? : _ :
Does the interviewer tell the candidate when and how he will hear
  the result of the interview? _ :
Does the interviewer ask the candidate about his other
  applications? : _ :
Does the interviewer thank the candidate for his interest? : _ :

PHYSICAL SETTING

In this exercise, the physical setting was not under the control of the interviewer. But, nevertheless, how did the physical setting match up to requirements?

Was it free from interruptions? : _ :
Was it private? Could others see? Could others hear? : _ :
Could the interviewer see a clock without it being obvious? : _ :
Was the furniture suitably arranged? : _ :
Was the room located near a suitable waiting area? : _ :

GENERAL IMPRESSION

Did the interviewer give the impression that he was a fair and
  sympathetic person? : _ :
Did the interviewer give the impression that the job was important
  and worth while? : _ :
Did the interviewer give the impression that he was efficient and
  friendly? : _ :

APPENDIX 5: BRIEFING NOTES FOR EXERCISE 2

2. SYSTEMATICALLY COVERING THE GROUND

Research has repeatedly shown that interviews are much more reliable if they are properly structured. A number of plans exist but one of the least complicated is as outlined below.

2.1 JOB BACKGROUND

Ask candidate to describe his present job: establish exact nature of duties.
Ask why he has left, or wants to leave his job.

Repeat the above questions until a complete job history for the last five years is obtained.

Ask what he wants from his job.
Ask what he thinks he will be doing in a few years' time.
Ask why he wants this job.
Ask point blank questions about qualifications, licences and essential training.

2.2 INTERESTS

What are the candidate's interests and hobbies?
How deep is the interest, and what standard has been reached?

2.3 HOME BACKGROUND (Needs careful handling as many candidates are sensitive about their backgrounds. Be careful to ask both sexes similar questions.)

Ask whether the candidate has brothers and sisters, and then explore jobs held by family members.
Will home background help by providing support, knowledge or contacts?
Will home commitments (e.g. children, invalids, fiances) hinder discharge of duties?
How do family members feel about this job?
What will be the arrangements for travelling to work?

To test how well the candidate can reason, ask him for his views on some issue, then tell the candidate that, for the sake of argument, you will be taking the opposite view, but do not get carried away or bellicose.
    If the personnel specification calls for a special ability (e.g. ability to handle people) ask the candidate whether this ability has been needed in the past. Ask about a specific incident and ask him to elaborate on what happened and whether he would do things differently now.

APPENDIX 6: CHECK-LIST FOR EXERCISE 2

SYSTEMATICALLY COVERING THE GROUND

Explanation

This practice is concerned with the middle section of the interview where the interviewer is trying to get relevant information from the candidate. To what extent does the interviewer systematically cover all the ground? Tick off the points as they occur.

JOB BACKGROUND

Has the interviewer obtained a complete list of the candidate's
jobs over the last five years or the last four jobs?   : _ :

Is the employment history unbroken (i.e. no gaps)?   : _ :

Has the interviewer established exactly what the candidate's
duties were in each of his jobs?   : _ :

Has the interviewer established how well the candidate
performed his duties?   : _ :

Has the interviewer established why the candidate left each
of his jobs?   : _ :

Has the interviewer established why the candidate has applied
for this job?   : _ :

Has the interviewer established what the candidate wants from
the jobs he does?   : _ :

Has the interviewer established the candidate's qualifications,
the licences and training?   : _ :

INTERESTS AND HOBBIES

Has the interviewer established the candidate's spare time
activities?   : _ :

Has the interviewer established the depth of the candidate's
interest in his hobbies and his competence at them?   : _ :

HOME BACKGROUND

Has the interviewer established whether the family background
is favourable?   : _ :

Has the interviewer established how the candidate would travel
to work?   : _ :

APPENDIX 7: BRIEFING NOTES FOR EXERCISE 3

3.   WAYS OF MAKING THEM TALK

An interviewer aims to get information by getting candidates to talk freely and openly. Interviews are very interactive processes and the interviewer can exert a strong influence upon the willingness of the candidates to reveal information about themselves. The following 'eight commandments' should be obeyed.

3.1 Don't talk too much yourself. Generally, interviewers talk too much (about 57 per cent of the interview time). It is impossible for candidates to give information if the interviewer chatters incessantly.

3.2 Don't use stress tactics (except in exceptional circumstances, e.g. selecting foreign agents for MI6). Stress tactics force people into a defensive role where they refuse to reveal unfavourable information.

3.3 Do not emphasize status differentials. We normally confide in people of our own level. We are usually reminded of our status by our possessions and physical setting. Consequently, interviewers should not play status stunts. Do not interview across oceans of teak veneer and ranges of multicoloured telephones. Do not place candidate on a lower, obviously inferior chair.

3.4 Vary your voice and use gestures. Avoid giving candidates the impression that they are boring you. Vary the pitch of your voice and the speed of talking. Use facial expressions such as raised eyebrows or half smiles.

3.5 Use comments and 'guggles'. In most social situations comments are more adroit than questions and they are more effective in stimulating conversation. For example, 'That sounds interesting' is much more effective than the question 'What else did you find of interest?' To keep the candidate talking, make liberal use of approving 'guggles' such as 'jolly good' and 'really'.

3.6 Use open-ended questions: these are questions which cannot be answered by a one-word answer such as yes or no. The main purpose of open-ended questions is to get expressions of opinion, feelings, and attitudes. The majority of questions in an interview should be open ended.

3.7 Use summaries. At the end of each section of the interview, summarize the ground you have covered. It lets candidates know you have been attending, and it allows them to correct any misunderstandings.

3.8 Take notes but do not make an immediate note when the candidate says something against himself. Wait until the conversation has moved to a different topic.

APPENDIX 8: CHECK-LIST FOR EXERCISE 3

MAKING THEM TALK

Explanation

This exercise is also concerned with the middle section of the interview where the interviewer is trying to get relevant information from the candidate. For the purpose of this exercise, assume that the interviewer systematically covers all the ground. Instead, concentrate on how well the interviewer gets the candidate talking. Tick off the points as they occur.

KEY ASPECTS

Does the interviewer avoid undue stress?   : _ :
Does the interviewer avoid showing his own personal reactions
  to the candidate?   : _ :
Does the interviewer avoid status stunts?   : _ :
Does the interviewer avoid being openly critical of the
  candidate?   : _ :
Does the interviewer talk for less than 25 per cent of the time?   : _ :

OTHER ASPECTS

Does the interviewer vary the speed and pitch of his voice?   : _ :
Does the interviewer use any gestures?   : _ :
Does the interviewer use any guggles and comments?   : _ :
Does the interviewer use any open-ended questions?   : _ :
Does the interviewer summarize the candidate's answers?   : _ :
Does the interviewer seem to have kept an open mind until
  the end of the interview?   : _ :
Does the interviewer dogmatically state his own opinions?   : _ :
Does the interviewer avoid arguing directly with the
  candidate?   : _ :

APPENDIX 9: BRIEFING FOR EXERCISE 4

4. ARRIVING AT A DECISION

The final stage of interpretation is probably the most difficult stage. Skill in the interpretation of interviews takes years to acquire. Interpret the interview without delay because research has shown that interviewers quickly forget information about specific candidates.
Standard interviewer faults are outlined below.

4.1 Making a decision too early. Many interviewers come to a conclusion during the first four minutes of an interview, and are taken in by the 'smart Alec' who gives a good impression but who is useless except for talking. They also run the risk of overlooking an excellent candidate who takes a little time to settle down.

4.2 The halo effect. Do not allow your judgements to be swamped by one outstanding characteristic.

4.3 Weight information carefully. Be particularly careful not to give too much weight to negative information or unexpected information.

4.4 Make due allowance for the candidate's circumstances. Do not automatically attribute failures to the candidate's personality. Often, the circumstances surrounding a candidate are the most important factors in determining success.

3

An exercise in attitude measurement
Bram Oppenheim

Specification notes

AIMS OF EXERCISE: to introduce students to attitudes and their measurement by constructing a Thurstone attitude scale and to give them an understanding of practical and theoretical issues involved.

PRIOR KNOWLEDGE ASSUMED: little background theoretical knowledge is assumed but a basic knowledge of statistics would be useful (e.g. measurement scales, item statistics, coefficients of reliability and validity).

DURATION: two laboratory sessions of around $2\frac{1}{2}$ hours each, plus a prior introductory lecture.

LOCATION: the exercise can be conducted in a normal classroom or teaching laboratory.

RESOURCES: blackboard, paper, writing materials, rulers, a set of percentage tables or a pocket calculator, set of ogive graphs and envelopes are required. There is also a handout which will require duplication prior to the lecture, and for this, and for other preparation, some secretarial assistance would be extremely useful.

Introduction

Why do scaling?
It may be useful at the outset to distinguish between factual and attitudinal topics or questions in survey research. Such a distinction cannot be maintained precisely because the two areas overlap, and because in most cases even 'factual' questions contain many attitudinal and subjective components which will influence the answers, but - loosely speaking - a factual question is one for which there is or could be a 'true' or 'correct' answer, such as 'When did you last go to the dentist?' This is a much simpler problem than trying to find out someone's attitudes to civil liberties, to immigrants or to a political party; the exploration of these latter topics may require more and different questions, using a variety of methods or approaches.

Put in measurement terms, we generally find that it is possible to obtain reliable answers from single questions where the topics are 'factual', but not so when the topics are affective or attitudinal. A single attitude question such as 'How do you feel about people who drink and drive?' or 'What are your views about the teaching of Latin in schools?' can be asked, and can be quantified after a fashion by means of coding frames, but often such questions do not produce measurements which are sufficiently reliable or which do justice to the problem. This is because the issues are complex and often sensitive and emotional, and because the answers are likely to be influenced by various underlying components or dimensions such as the respondent's feelings about alcohol, about Latin, about schools, and so on. We find, therefore, that 'factual' topics are generally dealt with by means of single questions, whereas in the case of attitudinal topics this will not do.

This dilemma has, from the early 1920s onwards, produced a number of different solutions in the form of attitude <u>scaling</u> methods. (It has also led to the development or adaptation of a number of projective techniques for attitude measurement, and to still other methods such as the Semantic Differential.) It is the purpose of the present exercise to introduce the student both to some aspects of attitude <u>theory</u> and to some methods of attitude <u>measurement</u> by attempting to produce an attitude scale.

So let us first ask ourselves what an attitude is and how it works or what it does, and then go on to see what can be done to measure it reliably and - we hope - validly by means of a group of items that together form a scale.

What is an attitude?

There have been many attempts to define attitudes. One way is to think of them as 'states of readiness', as predispositions to notice, to perceive, to select, to feel, to remember and to react to a particular issue or topic (in reality, or in abstract verbal form) in a particular way whenever it arises. Thus attitudes affect most of our cognitive processes as well as our emotional ones; they dominate important aspects of our social life such as religion, marriage, politics, work and leisure, and they tend to be long-lasting and difficult to change.

An attitude is a construct, an abstraction which cannot be directly apprehended. It is an inner component of mental life which expresses itself, directly or indirectly, through such more obvious processes as stereotypes and beliefs, verbal statements or reactions, ideas and opinions, selective recall, anger or satisfaction or some other emotion; and in

various other aspects of behaviour. However, the links between underlying attitudes and, say, the expression of hostility towards an ethnic minority, are subtle and complex so we must never assume that attitudes can directly predict behaviour (nor, for that matter, can we reliably infer attitudes from observations of behaviour).

It may help us to conceptualize attitudes in terms of 'levels'. If attitudes may be said to 'underlie' more 'superficial' expressions, such as beliefs and opinions, then underlying these attitudes in their turn are still deeper and more abiding constructs such as 'values', 'philosophies-of-life' and, ultimately, some aspects of 'personality'. The deeper we go, the broader, more pervasive and influential will be the constructs we encounter, and the more long lasting and change-resistant they become. Thus a male chauvinist may, at a superficial level, seem to treat women as equals and may admire a 'clever' woman for her achievements, but deeper down his orientation will remain sexist, and this may be linked to a somewhat authoritarian and inflexible value system, and to a certain rigidity of personality throughout life.

This example, tracing some of the linkages of male chauvinism, also serves to illustrate another important aspect of attitudes, namely that they are not isolated 'boxes' but are linked and intertwined in many ways, upwards and downwards as well as across to other attitude domains. Attitudes form patterns, and in each of us such patterns create our own unique outlook on life. Yet in the formation of such patterns there are also common elements so that, in a given society or sub-culture, we frequently find certain patterns that repeat themselves in many people. For example, it would not surprise us if our male chauvinist also expressed himself in favour of strong political leadership, was against abortion on demand, against random breath testing of drivers for blood alcohol level, against legalized pot, in favour of wild-life hunting, and disinclined to believe that 'small is beautiful'. We come to recognize such patterns intuitively; we sometimes give them labels (such as 'left-wing' or 'bourgeois' or 'progressive'), and we are also aware that, over the years, issues that make up such a pattern may gradually change, and will differ from culture to culture.

We note also that these patterns are not logical, they are irrational or 'psychological'. There are no <u>logical</u> reasons why someone who favours abortion on demand should be unconcerned about homosexuality, or why someone who is hostile to immigrants should also want a return to capital punishment; such patterns come to exist because there is an underlying web of attitudinal strands which have more to do with emotions and with personality needs than with logical or scientific thinking. In any case, most of the attitudes we hold are not the results of our own analysis or experience; they are more likely to have been adopted or taken over from significant others as part of our culture and socialization.

If we try to think about our own attitude to almost any topic, we shall probably experience this as something subtle and complex, amorphously shaped and coloured by varied emotions; to try to approach it by means of some kind of linear scaling system would hardly seem likely to do it justice. This is probably because the art of attitude measurement is still in an early and relatively crude state. We can hope to deal with the more common attitude patterns that exist in large numbers of people, but not with the detailed subtlety of private attitudes; and the measures we can generate will, at best, be able to produce crude correlations or to divide large samples into five or six subgroups on some attitude continuum with a fair degree of reliability, but they should not be used for individual cases nor for the prediction of behaviour.

Let us now <u>sum up</u> what we have learnt from the above that may be relevant to our problem of attitude measurement.

First, an attitude is a construct, an organizing principle behind a pattern of feelings and expressions. We cannot hope to pinpoint it by means of a single item or question; it will need a multiple-item approach, using the attitudinal surface-expressions (beliefs and opinions) to map out the components beneath by means of a series of triangulations.

Second, we cannot be sure what we shall find. Neither logic nor dictionary definitions will be a good guide to the complex ways in which people think and apprehend their world. We must be ready for a mapping exercise, taking nothing for granted and following the paths through our data to see where they lead, and what pattern will eventually emerge. Thus we may think that 'cleanliness of mind and body' is a single attitude, but it may turn out to be two, or none, or to be but two small parts of a much wider attitude domain.

Third, we must not over-estimate what we can do. By applying a linear scaling model to such a complex, amorphous construct we can but hope to extract a relatively crude measure, effective only with large numbers. Attempts to go into finer detail tend to lose themselves in a morass of unreliabilities.

Problems of attitude measurement
Among the better known methods of attitude measurement is the Thurstone scaling procedure. This, like other scaling procedures, tries to fulfil the requirements of the linear scaling model as far as possible. The linear scaling model has been widely used in the fields of cognitive testing, personality testing, aptitude testing and so forth. Basically the model has the following requirements:

* unidimensionality (the measure should be 'about one thing at a time');
* reliability (consistency);
* validity (the scale must measure 'what it is supposed to measure');
* equal (or equal-appearing) intervals and scoring norms.

(Note that we are not dealing here with ordinal or nominal forms of measurement.)

The notion of <u>unidimensionality</u> is not difficult to comprehend when we deal with attributes such as length, weight or temperature; it becomes more difficult when we have to deal with space-form ability or neuroticism, and more difficult still when we try to measure attitudes. There is no evidence that an attitude such as vegetarianism, dislike of animals, or love of country can be conceptualized as a straight line, or as a single measure which is 'about one thing at a time'. Exploratory interviews with people about, say, their attitude to the police will probably show many components: links with own father, with teachers and school authority, with motoring offences, with childhood bogey-men, with uniforms and armed services, with traffic control, with burglary and crime generally, with helping the young or the infirm, with motorbikes, television fiction, and so on. If we were in the process of creating a scale of attitudes to the police we should have to take all these sub-domains into account and see if we could justifiably merge them into one conglomerate on which people can be given one score each, to represent their position on a single pro/con dimension.

The notion of a scale's reliability concerns its capacity to measure something consistently, so that we get approximately the same score if we repeat the measurement process over and over again. There will always be human and instrumental errors of measurement even under the most stable conditions, but we must try to minimize these. When we repeatedly administer verbal or pictorial scales to human beings we experience additional problems because the respondents may remember some of the items and will try either to be consistent with what they said before, or try to say something new; and if we wait for a time before repeating the scale, some genuine changes may meanwhile occur in the respondents, leading to inconsistencies. Several methods have been developed to overcome these problems, such as the 'split-half' measure of reliability, and the use of parallel scales. A scale's reliability is usually represented by a single correlation coefficient, such as Cronbach's alpha.

Reliability needs to be stressed as a most important requirement for, without it, there can be no validity: we shall never be able to measure length accurately if we use an elastic tape-measure!

A scale's validity is likewise expressed in the form of a correlation coefficient (note that a scale can have more than one validity coefficient, depending on its various applications). A scale has high validity if it measures what we want it to measure, and very little else. However,

this statement begs a further question, for how do we know what the scale really measures? It is not sufficient to go by the scale's label or by the word of its creator ('face validity'), nor can we rely on the scale's manifest contents when we read some of the items ('content validity'), for further research often shows that such assumptions are incorrect. Sometimes we can get a bit further in the process of validation by comparing our scale with some earlier scale, or some other measure which we believe to be valid ('criterion validity'), or by seeing if behaviour forecasts made with the aid of the scale actually come true ('predictive validity'). Another approach to validation is through 'construct validity', where we have strong theoretical reasons for expecting our scale to form a particular pattern with other neighbouring measures.

However, attempts at validation are often unsatisfactory in the field of attitude research, mainly because there are so few ways of obtaining an outside criterion measure of the attitude in question which is itself valid and reliable. Some researchers have tried to find behavioural criteria; but just what could be regarded as, say, a valid and reliable behavioural measure of people's attitude to the police? Membership of certain groups or associations might be indicators, for extreme cases, but clearly people join associations for many different reasons which may or may not reflect their attitudes directly. Other researchers have tried to use construct validity: presumably they would argue that respondents who score high on the F-scale should also score favourably on our attitude to the police scale, but this is hardly conclusive evidence of the scale's validity. Indeed, this whole problem highlights the fact that we do not yet have much well-established knowledge of the attitude systems in people's minds, nor do we know in detail how such attitudes contribute to the explanation of overt behaviour.

It is important to realize that validity and reliability interact: validity will inevitably be poor when reliability is too low, but if reliability is high (say, 0.80 or above), then there is at least the possibility of making the scale valid. We need therefore to make sure that, at the very least, our scale is sufficiently reliable.

Ideally, we should also like our scale to have equal (or equal-appearing) inter-vals so that we can give numerical scores to each respondent, and relate these to norms from which we can tell, by compar-ison with other groups, whether our res-pondents are particularly favourable or unfavourable in their attitude to the topic of the scale. When we review these scale requirements we may feel that this approach can never hope to do justice to the comp-lexity, subtlety and emotionality of indi-vidual attitudes, and hence many research-ers have preferred to use projective or other non-scaled methods of attitude study, and have sought to obtain evidence of reliability and validity in different ways. Yet it is not surprising, given the many advantages of the linear scaling approach, that other research workers have persisted in trying to apply it to attitude measure-ment, both for theoretical studies and for practical enquiries. The results of their efforts have produced several rather dif-ferent scaling methods based on the work of Guttman, Bogardus, Likert and Thur-stone, each of which fulfils some, but not all, of the scaling requirements we have listed.

In any piece of research, our choice of scaling method will be guided by its ap-propriateness: that is, we shall want to choose the method of scaling that is right for what we need in our particular study. For example, the Thurstone scaling method can often produce two parallel scales (two scales which use different items, yet pro-duce comparable scale scores); it follows that this would be the method of choice when we do a 'before-and-after' study of, say, the impact of a short film or a television presentation on our subjects. Each scaling method has its own strengths and weaknesses, and none of them fulfils all our scaling requirements.

The exercise

The purpose of this exercise is to give students some familiarity with attitudes and their measurement by getting them to try to construct a Thurstone attitude scale. Students will be given a preliminary lecture/discussion (reinforced with a hand-out: see the end of this chapter) dealing with basic attitude theory, and with the various methods that have been developed to measure attitudes by means of attitude scales. The class will then decide on the attitudinal topic which the scale will be designed to measure, and they will be asked to write attitude statements (see handout) which are to go into an item pool. In the first laboratory session they will collec-tively create a Thurstone attitude scale. The second laboratory session will be devoted to a detailed discussion of the results and a critical evaluation.

The theoretical background of the exer-cise stems from the field of social psycho-logy, in particular the field of attitude studies. This is an important and flourish-ing area which is highlighted in most social psychology textbooks (see also Further reading) and which throws up a number of important and controversial is-sues, some of which have been touched upon in the Introduction. The exercise aims to give the student a practical appreciation of the nature of attitudes, as well as some understanding of the theoretical issues involved.

The methodological background lies in the general field of mental measurement, interval scaling, problems of reliability and validity, etc. However, specialized scaling methods have have been developed within the field of attitude measurement, each of which has its own advantages and disadvantages. Through practical experience the students may come to appreciate some of these, and may be led to an awareness of other methods of attitude measurement such as the Semantic Differential, Guttman scaling, multi-dimensional scaling, and projective techniques, not dealt with in this exercise.

A general background in simple test-construction methods, including the notions of ordinal and interval measurement, item statistics, coefficients of reliability and validity, and the generation of scores and norms, would be helpful.

Many students probably have some vague ideas about attitudes, values and opinions and may assume that they can be measured by means of single questions in large-scale surveys, such as the public opinion polls. The present exercise should introduce them to some of the broader aspects of attitude theory in social psychology; to the difficulties and subtleties of conceptualization that arise when we try to measure attitudes about which relatively little is known; and to the unreliability of single-question measurement which has led to the evolution of classical scaling techniques.

The merits of the exercise are both practical and theoretical. At the practical level, students will begin to acquire scale-building skills: the care needed during interviewing and item writing when dealing with attitudes; the problems of conceptualizing the components of a given attitude; problems of language and the expression of feelings; and the risk of unintentional bias. The whole process of scaling will be brought down to a very simple level which the students can do for themselves, thus 'de-mystifying' the whole process. Having constructed one type of scale, students may now tackle other scaling methods with greater confidence.

By going through the exercise of building a simple attitude scale the students will also acquire a much more critical understanding of the theories involved. It is not important whether the building of the scale itself is successful; what is important is that the students begin to understand and to question some of the assumptions - both about attitudes and about the nature of scaling - upon which the procedure depends. Does it make sense to think of attitudes as straight lines? Are interval scales appropriate? How 'deep' can attitude statements go? Do attitudes overlap with each other? How can any item pool do justice to the variety of attitudes held by different people about a given topic? Can the meaning of items be accurately judged by item 'judges', and how can we choose the 'best' items? How can we evaluate any form of measurement, and more particularly an attitude scale? How should we choose between different methods available? What are some of the practical applications of attitude scales? These and many other issues can be raised, and partly answered, by the exercise that follows.

Method

RESOURCES AND SPECIFICATION. In terms of contact hours, the exercise will require one lecture and two laboratory periods of, say, 2½ hours each.

Some secretarial assistance will be needed. The text of the handout (see Appendix) will have to be duplicated in advance of the lecture. The items handed in by the students will need to be scrutinized and edited, typed and duplicated before the first laboratory session, and for each student one set of all the items will have to be cut up into item slips. A set of ogive graphs should also be duplicated (see table 1).

The students will need a classroom with desks or table-tops on which to work. They will also need writing materials, some scrap paper and rulers. The room should have a blackboard, whiteboard, or similar. The tutor will need a set of percentage tables or a pocket calculator. The set of ogive graphs should be available, with as many graphs as there are items in the item pool plus some spares. A set of envelopes in which to hold the item slips would be helpful.

The exercise is suitable for laboratory classes from ten students upwards. No additional subjects are needed, but before writing the attitude statements after the lecture, students will be encouraged to conduct a few interviews with each other or with others. During the first laboratory period each student will be asked to work out the item characteristics (median and semi-interquartile range) for a small number of items, say, three items per student. It would be helpful, therefore, if the size of the item pool were approximately three times as large as the number of students in the class, otherwise the exercise becomes too lengthy and cumbersome. When asking students to write attitude statements a somewhat larger number should be aimed at: say, five or six per student, and before these are typed they should be edited and scrutinized by the tutor. This process will eliminate duplications and near-duplications, colloquialisms and poor grammar, illegible items, etc., but the tutor should not leave out items which are ambiguous, double-barrelled, lengthy, too

Table 1. Cumulative frequency graph for item no. ...

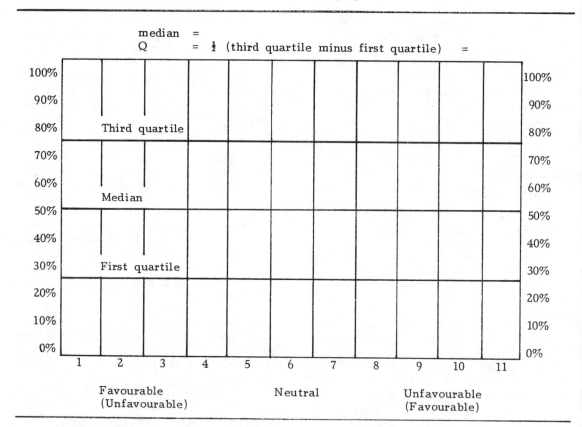

median =
Q   = ½ (third quartile minus first quartile)   =

cognitive, or which show some of the many other characteristics of 'bad' attitude items. The students will learn more if such items are included in the item pool and subsequently show up poorly in the scaling procedure.

If possible, the tutor might like to have available a number of other attitude scales or published collections, such as those by Shaw and Wright (1967). These can be passed round the class as additional background material.

The timing should not be too close. After the lecture the students will need a few days to assimilate and digest the handout, do some interviews and write the attitude statements. After these have been handed in, there must be adequate time for the item pool to be scrutinized by the tutor, for the items to be typed and duplicated, and for copies of the item pool to be cut up into item slips for each stu-

dent (either by secretaries or by a volunteer working party from among the students). After the first laboratory session, the second session can follow almost immediately.

Sequence of events, instructions and briefing

BEFORE THE LECTURE. The handout is duplicated (after adapting to student background where necessary). The tutor prepares a lecture based on the introduction and handout material, thinks up some suitable scale topics, and perhaps also gets copies of scaling books or other attitude scale material ready.

THE LECTURE. The tutor announces the practical exercise and leads the class discussion to propose and select a suitable topic for the attitude scale. Students should also be briefed on attitude statement writing, and urged to do some interviewing before writing statements. A firm date by which all statements must be handed in should be announced, and then the handout can be distributed. After the lecture, the tutor discusses the procedures with the secretary, indicating the date by which all statements will be handed in and arranging to have ample copies of ogive graphs duplicated. After collecting the statements, the tutor edits and assembles the item pool in random order, and numbers the items. The item pool is then typed, and duplicated twice. One set is assembled as a test booklet or questionnaire, the other set is cut up into item slips (one set of slips of the complete item pool for each student, in an envelope).

FIRST LABORATORY SESSION. The tutor hands out the envelopes with the item slips and draws the 11-interval attitude continuum on the board, indicating clearly which end is the positive end and which is the negative one, and then goes over the judging procedure, answering questions, emphasizing, too, that students must judge the contents of each item, not express their own agreement or disagreement.

Students go through the item-judging procedure after reading through the item pool. Each item must, as far as possible, be placed in one of the 11 categories according to its content. When this task has been completed, the student should enter, on each item slip (in the far right-hand margin) the category number in which it has been placed, from 1 to 11. After that, each student will reassemble the item pool slips in their numerical order, from 1 to 60 or 70 or however many items are in the pool.

Meanwhile the tutor will put two tables on the blackboard: (i) a percentage table for the number of judges in the class, rounded off to whole percentages; and (ii) an empty table showing the item numbers down the side (running from one to 60, 70 or whatever) and two headings across the top: 'median' and 'semi-interquartile range' (SIQ). The tutor will also divide the number of items by the number of students in order to decide how many items to allocate to each student for

the item analysis.

When all students have made their judgements, entered them on the item slips, and have reassembled their slips in numerical order (where necessary, quicker students may be asked to help the slower ones in the clerical work, but not in the making of judgements), the tutor will allocate items to each student. It is simplest to go round the desks, allocating sets of items in sequential order to each student. Thus, if each student will work on four items, then student D will be responsible for items 13, 14, 15 and 16.

At the blackboard, the tutor will now explain how to generate the two item statistics (median and SIQ) for each item (see under Data collection). The students will calculate and graph these item statistics for each of the items allocated to them. They will enter these in the relevant positions in the table on the blackboard. The tutor will, meanwhile, help students who have difficulties, deal with missing values, and so on.

The tutor will now hand out the item pool booklets and ask students to copy the item statistics from the blackboard. A copy of the table of item statistics should be retained by the tutor. Students should be urged to bring their item booklets and graphs along to the next laboratory session. The cut-up item slips can be discarded.

SECOND LABORATORY SESSION. It now becomes possible to construct a Thurstone scale, though perhaps not a complete one. Together with the tutor the class will peruse the item statistics, reading out the texts of items that did well or poorly, each noting the location (medians) of the items they had written themselves, and so on. The scaling process may then begin by setting some fairly arbitrary upper limit for SIQs depending on the item statistics available: for example, henceforth ignoring all items with SIQs above 1.7. After that the class must decide how many items there will be in the scale: 11, at unit intervals? Twenty-two at half-unit intervals? Or is perhaps some fine discrimination required on a particular sector of the scale, say in half units between six and eight, and in whole units above and below those values? And do they want to make up a parallel scale as well? Having made these decisions, the class and the tutor together can list, for each point on the intended scale, the medians of the items with values nearest to that point; say, for point 4, items with medians of 4.2, 3.9, 4.1, and so forth. From among these, they ought to choose each time the item with the lowest SIQ but, with a small item pool and an inexperienced group of item writers, this often becomes a trade-off problem: it may happen, say, that the item with the lowest SIQ is also the item with a median that is furthest away from the desired scale point, or else that an item with a median right on the scale point has an unacceptably high SIQ.

By proceeding in this way, and assuming fairly adequate item statistics, eventually a scale of, say, 11 items will emerge. These should be listed together with their medians or scale values, and critically examined. The tutor might also point out that in some research projects, if the results are not satisfactory, some items have to be revised and improved, new items have to be written, and the whole judgement procedure has to be repeated before the best possible set of scale items is obtained.

Finally, a discussion can be started on the Thurstone procedure, on attitude scaling generally, and on what such methods of measurement can tell us about the attitude domain under consideration (see below, under Discussion).

Data collection and analysis of results

CHOICE OF A SUITABLE SCALE TOPIC. As part of the initial lecture, the tutor will discuss and agree with the class what will be the topic of the proposed scale: to take some examples, attitude to statistics, to the Olympic Games, to the police, to margarine, to smoking, to alcohol drinking, to football, or to civil liberties. It is best to choose a relatively clear-cut and well-known topic for this first exercise, and to avoid novel or vague or hypothetical topics on which there may not be many clearly formed attitudes. By the end of the lecture, the class should have one definitely agreed topic, and members should be instructed to generate five or six attitude statements each, dealing with different aspects of the chosen topic, and to hand these statements in by an agreed date some days in advance of the first laboratory session.

Students' attention should be drawn not only to the problems of item writing (see handout), but also to the conceptualization of the item pool as a whole. Each attitude has numerous sub-areas, which partly overlap with each other, and the item pool should show a reasonable balance between areas. Positive and negative items should also roughly balance, and students might be encouraged to write a few extreme items for inclusion in the pool.

THE ITEM-JUDGING PROCEDURE. This will be the main activity of the first laboratory session. First, the tutor should briefly go over the steps in the Thurstone procedure (where necessary, taking examples from some other attitude topic). After that, the envelopes with the item slips should be handed out, and it may be as well to close windows and doors to prevent any breezes! On the blackboard should be a horizontal line representing the attitude continuum. It should have the number '1' at the left-hand extreme, and the number '11' at the right-hand extreme; it may be helpful also to write 'N' under the centre of the line, to suggest a 'Neutral' category. Explain to the class that an arbitrary decision now has to be made about the location of the favourable and the unfavourable ends of the continuum: either '1' will represent the most favourable category, and '11' the most unfavourable, or the other way around. Although this decision is arbitrary, once it has been agreed and recorded on the blackboard, it must be adhered to consistently.

Next, the students should be instructed to ignore their own attitudes and to act solely as item judges. They should take each item slip in turn, read the item, and then ask themselves: if someone agrees with this item, where does that person stand on the attitude continuum: in a favourable/very favourable/very unfavourable or neutral position, or where? Then they should place the item in the category that reflects this position. In this way they should go through all the statements; they must feel free to use all 11 categories as well as six, the neutral category, but there is no need to have the same number of statements in each category. Before the start, students should check that they have the correct number of statements in their envelopes. When they have finished, they should write on each statement the category number which they have given it (i.e. any number from 1 to 11) and put this number in the right-hand margin. After that, the statements should be re-shuffled in their item-number order, and returned to their envelope. (Alternatively or additionally, the tutor may like to hand out written instructions, such as those on p. 128 of Oppenheim, 1968.)

This judgement process can be quite time-consuming, and often produces wide individual differences in working speed. The tutor might encourage the early finishers to help slower students with the numbering and item sorting, but not with the actual judgement process. The tutor should move about the class ensuring that students have ample working space, helping with queries, and making certain that some students do not reverse the direction of the continuum: that is, write 8 or 9 when they should enter 4 or 3 and so on. Also, some students write the figure '1' the way others write a '7' so, to prevent misunderstandings, students might be encouraged to write a '7' in the Continental way: that is by placing a short stroke across its stem.

While the students are still entering their judgements, the tutor could write the relevant percentage table in a corner of a blackboard: that is, the percentage table for the number of students doing this exercise. The tutor might also wish to draw a sample of the ogive graph on the board, with a worked cumulative frequency example. However, most of the blackboard should be kept free for listing the medians and semi-interquartile ranges of the items as they become available in the next stage of the procedure.

THE GENERATION OF ITEM STATISTICS. Essentially, the Thurstone procedure collects all the judgements about each item and then engages in an item analysis or item selection procedure. First, items on

which there is much disagreement between judges must be eliminated; for this, we need a measure of spread, in this case the semiinterquartile range. Next, we seek items which are at equal-appearing intervals from each other; for this, we need a measure of central tendency for each item (in this case, the median).

A 'bad' item is one with a large spread: that is, one on which there is wide disagreement between judges about its degree of favourability or unfavourability. The medians will be used to produce, as far as possible, equal-appearing intervals between the items appearing in the final scale, chosen from the items with relatively narrow SIQs. If students are not familiar with the calculation of medians and SIQs the tutor will explain that, with the aid of a percentage table and an ogive graph (see table 1), these values can easily be read off, rather than calculated, as illustrated by going over the worked example on the board. First, for each item, produce a frequency distribution from 1 to 11 of all the judgements. (Total frequency must correspond to the number of student judges.) Then convert these frequencies into percentages by reading off from the percentage table on the blackboard, or by using a calculator. After that, convert the percentages into cumulative percentages. (Students often need help with this, and there will be totals of 99 or 102 due to rounding-off in the percentage table.)

EXAMPLE. For a hypothetical item no. 23, first create a frequency distribution based on a class of, say, 15 judges. By using the percentage table for N = 15 (previously put on the board) these frequencies will be converted to percentages. Next, these percentages will be converted into cumulative percentages (see table 2).

The cumulative percentage figures next have to be transferred to the ogive graph. It is sufficient to do this in a rough-and-ready way, by eye, and the entry marks can then be connected to produce the S-shaped ogive curve required. A long, low-angle ogive suggests a poor item with a big spread; we are looking for items with a steep curve, suggesting little disagreement among the judges.

Table 2. Item No. 23

Category	F	%f	Cumulative %
1	-	-	-
2	-	-	-
3	-	-	-
4	-	-	-
5	-	-	-
6	1	7	7
7	1	7	14
8	2	13	27
9	8	53	80
10	3	20	100
11	-	-	100
	15	100	

To find the median, students should drop a perpendicular to the baseline from the point at which the ogive crosses the 50 per cent line drawn across the graph. For the above example, the median will be approximately 8.4.

To find the quartile values, students should drop perpendiculars from the points at which the ogive crosses the 25 per cent and the 75 per cent lines on the graph. These baseline values should be read off by eye, and the difference between them calculated; half this difference is the SIQ value. Typically, for poor items, such values will exceed 1.5 and even 2.0. For the above example, the quartile values are approximately 8.9 and 7.8. The difference between them (the inter-quartile range) is 1.1, and the semi-interquartile range will be 0.55.

After explaining these procedures, the tutor should allocate items to students. If there are, say, three times as many items in the item pool as there are students in the class, then each student will have to do the calculations for three items, so the tutor might as well go along the class in order of seating, allocating the items in consecutive sets of three.

After that, each student should remove the item slips from their envelope and distribute them on the desks of the other class members according to the sequence of item allocation. (This process can lead to some temporary confusion unless it is made very clear which student is responsible for which items, so the allocation process has to be very definite.) By the end of this stage, every student should have all the judgement slips for the items for which he or she is responsible; for each item, they should check that there are as many slips as there are student judges, before commencing the calculations. (Note: it sometimes happens that item slips go astray, are illegible, or have no judgement recorded on them; to save delay and complications, enter such missing values in the modal or most common category.)

The class will now proceed to plot and calculate the medians and SIQ values for each item. At this stage, mistakes will come to light. For example, on a given item with values clustered around 8 and 9, there will be one or two slips with a 3 or a 4 on them: clearly a case where the decision about direction of favourability of the continuum has not been obeyed. Or someone will fail to halve the difference between the 25th and the 75th percentile and produce some huge SIQs. As they complete their calculations, students should enter the item statistics on the blackboard in the tabulation prepared by the tutor. Once again, the faster students may be encouraged to help the slower ones.

CONSTRUCTION OF THE FINAL SCALE. This process has already been explained under the heading of Second laboratory session.

SCORING. If the scale is to be used in an actual research project, then the text will have to be reproduced and a scoring procedure developed. In any case, the tutor should go over these steps with the class.

Our exercise will have yielded a set of, say, 11 items finally chosen to make up the scale. For each of these items we have a median, which constitutes the scale value of the item; however, it is obvious that when we give the scale to groups of respondents, these scale values will be omitted. The chosen items will be reproduced in random order, together with two columns headed 'agree' and 'disagree' (not a five-point Likert format), and respondents will be asked to read each item and then mark the appropriate column.

The score for each respondent will be the median of the scale values of all the items marked 'agree' (usually not more than two or three items, each with its scale value which is not known to the respondent). Items not marked, or marked 'disagree' are ignored. The rationale for this procedure is that, if the scale is well-constructed and if the respondents are consistent, they will agree only with the few items that most nearly represent their own position on the attitude continuum, and will disagree with all the items that are too extreme, or that express the opposite point of view.

Discussion

SUMMARY OF FINDINGS. The main yield of the exercise will be the creation of a Thurstone scale, that is to say, a set of attitude statements chosen from a specially constructed item pool, judged accurately to represent points at regular intervals along an attitude continuum, and which can be scored for each respondent, to indicate a position on that continuum, from most favourable to least favourable to the topic of the scale.

The effort that has gone into the scaling procedure is meant to ensure that such a scale is in important ways superior both to a single attitude question in an interview/questionnaire, and to a miscellaneous collection of attitude statements that have not been through the scaling procedure. The scale is expected to be superior for three sets of reasons:

* because it is based on an item pool which itself has been carefully assembled to cover all, or most of, the relevant aspects of the attitude in question;
* because a scale, as opposed to qualitative or arbitrary devices, has characteristics which should ensure that it is more reliable, and potentially more valid, as well as reflecting more accurately the views of the respondents;

* because the scale can yield a quantitative score, making reliable group comparisons possible.

However, not everyone agrees that attitudes are best represented by straight lines, or that a respondent's personal attitude to a given issue is adequately represented by a point on such a line. Nor is the Thurstone method the only, or necessarily the best, method of attitude scaling. As so often in science, theory and method interact: different attitude theories and problems require different types of measurement, and improved measurement techniques will elaborate, change or falsify attitude theories. The student-researcher is therefore faced with a choice: since no single method of attitude measurement combines all the virtues, our selection must be based on the appropriateness of the measuring technique to our problem and our theoretical orientation.

In this exercise students will have obtained first-hand experience of the construction of an attitude scale. They must now be shown how such a scale may be evaluated, and what kinds of research questions it may help to answer.

SCALE EVALUATION. Taking first the purely measurement viewpoint, the criteria for scale evaluation will be

* unidimensionality
* reliability
* validity
* scores and norms

as described in the handout. The class will note that, in Thurstone scaling, the choice of dimension is based on pilot interviews but is essentially subjective; that its linearity is assumed; and that its division into 11 equal categories symmetrically disposed around a neutral point is arbitrary, but convenient. Unless the exercise is extended, the class will not be able to compute a reliability coefficient (Thurstone reliability coefficients tend to be around 0.80 or better), but different methods of calculating reliability can be discussed, as well as the possibility of developing two parallel scales from the same item pool. Likewise, the class will not be in a position to calculate any validity coefficient (see Introduction), but problems of validation should be discussed in relation to different types of validity (Thurstone scales initially only have face validity until they can be related to other measures). The scoring procedure should also be discussed: for example, the loss of information by not scoring the 'disagree' responses.

LIMITATIONS OF DESIGN AND PROCEDURES. The procedure is subject to all the limitations caused by being a student exercise: lack of sufficient open-ended and exploratory interview material; inadequate conceptualization of the attitude domain; inexperienced item writers; too few item judges, possibly not of the same background as the respondents for whom the scale is intended; item analysis based on inadequate numbers; no opportunity to improve the items and rescale them; no applications which would yield estimates of reliability, validity and sample norms; and no evidence of unidimensionality.

In addition, the procedure is limited by various aspects of attitude scaling generally, as well as by the disadvantages of this particular scaling method. The class might address itself to the overtness and obviousness of any measurement method using language; to the culture-bound nature of attitude statements; to the many possible sources of bias in the judges; to assumptions about linearity and equal-appearing intervals; and to the lack of subtlety in dealing with such emotional and complex human attributes.

Finally, the whole exercise is affected by the state-of-the-art of attitude theory. For example, if we knew more about the way in which attitudes somehow combine knowledge, beliefs, feelings, reasoning and emotions, we would be in a better position to design suitable measures. For the same reason, we need to know more about the way in which attitudes form patterns (value orientations/philosophies of life) within each person. We also know too little about less overt, inadmissible and subconscious attitudes which may require quite different measurement methods. The relatively unformed attitudes of children are another important problem. Last but not least, too

little is known as yet about the many complex and indirect ways in which attitudes relate to behaviour.

POSSIBLE APPLICATIONS. The class may now consider what kinds of psychological questions this type of scaling procedure could answer, as follows.

1. Scaling comes into its own not as a form of individual measurement (such as an IQ test) but for the study of group differences. With the aid of attitude scales we can compare different countries or regions and so on. Or, using the opposite approach, we can give the scale to a large population and then compare and contrast groups who score high, medium and low on our scale. Or again, we may be studying particular groups (e.g. certain political parties, minority groups, parents versus teachers) and wish to obtain measures of their attitudes. In most such applications there will be considerable overlap between the group distributions, and our interest will focus on the significance of mean differences. For example, are young people on average more hostile to authority figures than older people? Are teachers in favour of streaming or tracking? Do people with strong hostility to aircraft noise also score high on a neuroticism scale?

Sometimes we study such group differences for _practical_ reasons; for example, why do some people _not_ take up the welfare benefits to which they are entitled? Sometimes we study them for more _theoretical_ reasons; for example, are theories of anomie correct in postulating a cluster of interrelated attitudes of powerlessness, normlessness, and so on?

2. The Thurstone scaling procedure is particularly useful in situations where we need to measure attitude _change._ Thus, if we are conducting a group experiment or an effects study with a before-and-after design, then we shall wish to measure the attitudes of the same respondents twice: before and after the manipulation. If we were to administer the same attitude scale twice, we might get some distortions because respondents will recognize the items and may try to be consistent with their previous responses, or perhaps will try to

react differently on the second occasion. However, the Thurstone method can, under favourable circumstances, yield two parallel scales: that is, two sets of different items which yet measure the same dimension. In before-and-after designs, the Thurstone method therefore seems particularly appropriate.

3. Scaling procedures are useful in attitude research: that is, in situations where we wish to examine the composition, ramifications and patterning of certain attitudes for theoretical reasons. We may, for example, be studying such broad attitude complexes as authoritarianism, or political conservatism, perhaps as these express themselves in different countries. Or we may be studying parental attitudes, or 'modernism' in developing countries. We may be engaged in testing certain theories about such attitude patterns, or in trying to establish construct validity. Factor analysis is often used to find the underlying components of a set of scales or items. For example, in a study of self-esteem, are self-love and self-hate each other's opposites, or are they independent, so that each respondent should have a score on both, perhaps with an 'ambivalence index' as well? Factor analysis can guide us here.

4. Attitude scales can be used to study links with personality and other internal variables such as emotions, perception and thought processes. For example, we might wish to study the links between the tough-tender aspect of political attitudes, and neuroticism. Or we may be exploring the connections between religious attitudes and internal/external locus of control. In children, we might study the development of certain attitudes in relation to cognitive complexity.

5. Finally, attitude scales can help us when we try to study the complex links between attitudes and behaviour. We may be seeking an explanation for observed behaviour, such as a consumer decision, or a political act, or we may seek to predict a certain kind of behaviour: for example, the rejection of members of an outgroup, or the use of contraception. Fishbein's (1967)

work has shown some of the steps that are necessary to build effective models of such processes, with the aid of attitude scales.

During the discussion the class might be given some illustrative published examples of the use of attitude scales in both practical and theoretical research.

TO SUM UP: students should now be able to discuss the following questions and answers.

* Why scale at all? Why not just use single attitude questions? The answers here have to do with the differences in subtlety and complexity between factual questions and attitudinal ones which involve beliefs, knowledge, feelings and values. The use of language in single attitude questions tends to lead to a great deal of unreliability and lack of validity; when properly applied, scaling techniques usually have good reliability, and yield quantitative measures which can be validated. However, they are relatively crude measures, and are based on some questionable assumptions.
* Is the particular scale we have built any good? The answer must lie in its relevance or appropriateness to our research problem, and in the technical qualities of the scale: that is, its calculated reliability, validity, unidimensionality and scoring procedures.
* How does Thurstone scaling compare with other scaling procedures such as Likert scales, factor-analytic scales, Guttman scales, multidimensional scaling, projective techniques, and so on? Likert scales and Guttman scales offer better assurances of 'purity' - that is, of unidimensionality - especially when factor analysis is applied to Likert scales. Likert scales also make it possible to include some more speculative, less 'obvious' items, and do not require a judging procedure. On the other hand, these scales do not produce equal-appearing intervals, and they do require substantial pilot samples as well as a more complex statistical analysis. Projective techniques and multidimensional scaling usually deal

with covert or inadmissible topics, whereas Thurstone scales are overt: it is obvious what they are 'getting at'. Unless special steps are taken, only Thurstone scales can yield two parallel scales from the same item pool.

By way of oversimplification we may say that Likert scales (with the aid of factor analysis) are best used in exploratory studies, and where comparatively large pilot samples can be obtained. Thurstone scales come into their own in well-known attitude domains, if no computer is available, if equal-interval scoring is important, and where parallel scales are needed: for example, in effects studies.

* How can we use it? What do we get out of it? Some of the answers to this question have been given under Possible applications.
* When should we not use this procedure? When there is much doubt about the dimension, its linearity or its constituents; when the only judges available differ markedly from the groups to which the scale is to be applied: for example, university students acting as judges for a scale to be used with factory workers; when respondents may have language or literacy problems; when measures are needed of covert or inadmissible topics; or when we are dealing with topics to which only a few people have attitudes.

Conclusions

What are some of the lessons that students may learn from this exercise?

* The advantages of scaling procedures over single-question type attitude items, in terms of reliability, purity or unidimensionality, potential validity, and meaningful quantitative scoring.
* The need for self-critical application of scaling techniques, since each procedure has weaknesses as well as strengths; all of them are relatively crude, and may not do justice to the more covert or subtle aspects of attitudes.
* That choice of scaling technique is a matter not of overall superiority, but of appropriateness to the research problem.
* The need to continue to question the various assumptions underlying both attitude theory and attitude scaling procedures.
* The fact that many attitude scales reach adequate standards of reliability and other evaluation criteria, and are widely used in large-scale studies as well as in laboratory research.
* Students will gain some appreciation of the current state of attitude theory in social psychology, and of the links between attitudes and various kinds of group membership, between attitudes and personality attributes, and between attitudes and behaviour.

REFERENCES

Fishbein, M. (1967) Readings in Attitude Theory and Measurement. New York: Wiley.
Oppenheim, A.N. (1968) Questionnaire Design and Attitude Measurement. London: Heinemann.
Shaw, M.E. and Wright, J.M. (1967) Scales for the Measurement of Attitudes. New York: McGraw-Hill.

Further reading

Bynner, J. and Stribley, K.M. (1978) Social Research: Principles and procedures. London: Heinemann.
Lemon, N. (1973) Attitudes and their Measurement. New York: Wiley.
Moser, C.A. and Kalton, G. (1979) Survey Methods in Social Investigation (2nd edn). London: Heinemann.
Open University (1979) D. 304: Research Methods in Education and the Social Sciences. Open University Press.
Rokeach, M. (1968) Beliefs, Attitudes and Values. San Francisco: Jossey-Bass.
Summers, G.F. (1970) Attitude Measurement. Chicago: Rand McNally.

APPENDIX (to form basis of handout for students)

The Thurstone scaling method

In this particular exercise, we shall go through the steps of creating an attitude scale according to the Thurstone scaling method. Thurstone and his colleagues developed this method in the early 1930s and it has found very wide application since then. His main concern was with the problem of obtaining equal (or rather, equal-appearing) intervals along a linear continuum. To do this, he first designed a considerable number of attitude statements, all dealing with the topic of the scale but in varied and different ways (the item pool). After that, he submitted each of these statements to a number of 'judges' (that is, to ordinary people who were similar to those for whom the final scale was intended, and who were asked to 'judge' each statement according to its meaning): did the statement indicate a positive attitude, a strongly negative attitude, a mildly negative attitude or a neutral attitude? Usually, several dozen judges were used in order to give stability to the findings. He then assembled all the judgements for each statement, and used these to choose the best items from the pool for use in the final scale.

Now let us look at this procedure in more detail. In a separate section we have discussed the creation and composition of an item pool, and the art of writing good attitude statements. Students will be asked to agree in class on a topic for our scale, and then to write and hand in a number of attitude statements. These statements will be put on item slips and, during the first laboratory period, each member of the class will be asked to make a judgement on every item in the item pool.

How will this be done?

The tutor will draw a straight line on the board, to represent the attitude continuum. The line will be divided into 11 intervals, and the tutor will agree with the class which end of the continuum will be 'favourable', and which will be 'unfavourable'. Category 6, in the middle, will represent the 'neutral' category. Students will first read through all, or most of, the attitude statements and will then begin to make their judgements. This is not unlike a sorting procedure. The student, acting as an item judge, will read the statement, decide whether a subject's 'agreement' with the statement indicates a favourable or an unfavourable attitude, and to what degree; accordingly, the student will judge the item to belong in category 3, or 10, or 5, or whatever, and will place the item slip in the space reserved for the category. In doing this, students must ignore their own attitudes, and not judge the statements in terms of their own agreement or disagreement. As more judgements are made, students may change their original judgements and place the items in different categories until they are quite satisfied. When all the items have been judged, the students will write (in the right-hand margin, and as clearly as possible!) the category number in which each item has been placed. There is no need to have equal numbers of items in each category; each item should be placed where it seems to belong.

When all judgements (category numbers) have been written on the item slips, the students will be asked to shuffle the item slips back into their original order, according to the item numbers in the left-hand margin.

The tutor will now explain the next part of the procedure. This involves using the students' judgements to choose the 'best' items for the scale. We shall need to be able to place each item precisely where it belongs on the favourable-unfavourable continuum, but not all the judgements will coincide for every item; in fact, for some items there may well be quite a lot of disagreement or 'spread' among the judges. Obviously, items that cause a lot of disagreement are not very useful for measuring people's attitudes, and so they have to be eliminated. The easiest way to do this is to draw a frequency distribution curve for each item, using all the judgements. Some items will have tall, thin curves: these are useful items on which the judges mostly agree with one another; other items will have low, wide curves: such items have to be left out, because there is too much disagreement among the judges.

Once we only have items left with tall, narrow distribution curves, it becomes an easy matter to locate them on our scale continuum. We can work out a kind of average (the median) for each item; thus an item with a median of 3.4 will belong somewhere between point 3 and point 4 on our scale; it will be mildly favourable (or mildly unfavourable, depending on the scoring decision at the beginning of the session). If our purpose now is to build a set of 11 items, one for each point on the scale, then we shall select the items with medians nearest to each scale point, something like this: 1.1; 1.9; 3.0; 4.2; 5.1; and so on.

In the second half of the first laboratory session you will each be made responsible for a small number of items. The tutor will show you how to work out the 'spread' and the median for each item with a minimum of calculation, and where to put these figures on the board. After that, the class and the tutor together will, in the second laboratory session, decide which items to eliminate because they have too much spread, and which items lie nearest to the interval points on the continuum. These will be chosen to make up your own Thurstone scale.

Creating an item pool

Without doubt, the composition of the item pool is the most important step in the attitude scaling process. All subsequent stages amount to little more than item analysis and item selection from among the items in the pool, and no amount of clever scaling or statistical manipulation can produce a good scale from a poor item pool; you cannot make a silk purse out of a sow's ear, even with the aid of modern computers! We must make this point with great emphasis. Every scaling attempt will be preceded by a review of any exisiting scales and relevant background literature. After that, we must conduct several dozens of extended, free-style or 'depth' interviews (recorded on tape), to give us the necessary insights into the ways in which other people think and feel about our topic, what sub-domains there are, and what will be the probable links with neighbouring attitudes; this will enable us to conceptualize the nature of the topic which we are trying to

measure. The importance of this early, sensitive and intuitive stage cannot be overstated. In addition, the interview tapes will yield idiomatic and expressive phrases which can readily be turned into attitude statements; most, if not all statements in the pool should come from these interviews.

In principle, the item pool will consist of a number of attitude statements (some 60 or 70, or more) which each try to 'get at' the topic of the scale in a different way, much as different items on an arithmetic test are designed to measure the child's arithmetic achievement in different ways. Each attitude is likely to have a number of sub-domains, and these should all be represented, more or less systematically, to produce a varied item pool with good 'coverage' of every aspect. Throughout we should bear in mind the assumption that each item can be placed on a linear continuum running from a positive extreme (i.e. in favour of the topic of the scale), through a neutral area, to a negative extreme (i.e. hostile to the topic of the scale). It helps, therefore, to try to 'translate' every statement into the form 'I like X' or 'I hate X'. When editing an item pool, there should also be a rough, approximate balance between the number of positive and negative items.

The writing of good attitude statements is something of an art. Some help can be given to beginners by suggesting faults that should be avoided. For example, statements should be brief, should not use proverbs or common sayings, should use simple, direct language, should not be too 'intellectualized' and should not be 'double-barrelled'. Thus, the statement 'I like a man to be strong, silent and a hard worker' is virtually useless because it is 'multi-barrelled', for how would respondents answer if they agreed with 'strong' and 'silent' but not with 'hard worker': that is, if they agreed with only part of a complex statement?

A typical error made by many students is to produce a great many descriptive statements, of the kind 'Policemen wear uniforms' or 'Some policemen stop people on suspicion'. The trouble with descriptive statements is that they do not unambiguously express an attitude; they require us to make an inference (which may, or may not, be warranted). Thus agreement with the statement 'Policemen wear uniforms' may suggest a favourable attitude to the police only if we can be sure that the respondent thinks that uniforms are something admirable or good. Likewise, if some respondents agree that some policemen stop people on suspicion, what does this tell us about their attitudes to the police? Very little, unless we can be quite sure that stopping people on suspicion is something of which the respondents disapprove or approve, so that agreement with the statement would indicate an unfavourable (or favourable) attitude to the police. (It stands to reason, of course, that in some descriptive statements the intended inference is obvious, e.g. 'I think the police are marvellous'.)

Perhaps a useful test for the inclusion or revision of any statement is to see if it can really be translated to mean either 'I like/approve of X,' or its opposite. Even so, it is best to avoid the descriptive and cognitive-belief kind of statements because, after all, they are not attitude statements, in that they are not warm, personal, perhaps emotional expressions of feelings! It also helps to avoid generalizations, by making statements more personal. Here are some examples of attitude statements about the police.

* 'I always feel better when I see a policeman.'
* 'I think the police nowadays throw their weight about far too much.'
* 'If I had a son who wanted to join the police force, I would be very proud.'
* 'I sleep more safely at night because our police are the best in the world.'

Ideally, after agreement has been reached about the central topic for the attitude scale, the class should conduct a series of individual interviews with randomly selected respondents in order to generate attitude statements that come 'from the horse's mouth'. For students this may not be practicable and so - contrary to what has just been said - members of the class will be asked to interview each other or their friends, or sometimes just examine their own feelings about the topic in order to produce attitude statements. By whatever means, they should each write, and hand in anonymously, some half-dozen attitude statements by a given date, to be included in the item pool.

If possible, members of the class should first look at some books or articles that contain examples of attitude scales, or collections of attitude scales (see Further reading).

4

Interactional analysis: the observation of individuals in a group setting

Hugh Foot

Specification notes

AIMS. The exercise is designed to teach students some of the problems associated with observing and recording social interaction. Students are trained in the use of a modified version of Bales' Interaction Process Analysis and they use the system to analyse interactions in conflict and non-conflict problem-solving discussion groups.

DURATION. Two three-hour sessions are recommended: the first for training and data collection, the second for data analysis. If training is omitted, the exercise can be compressed into one session of three hours.

RESOURCES. The essential requirements are a tape-recorder, stop-watch, blackboard and duplicated problem sheets and response forms. An overhead projector is optional.

LOCATION. Any large classroom (preferably carpeted) that is not tiered.

PRIOR KNOWLEDGE ASSUMED. Little prior knowledge of social psychology is required; some basic grounding in non-parametric statistics is helpful.

SPECIAL REQUIREMENTS. None.

Introduction

Studies of groups and of individuals within groups are legion. This is hardly surprising in view of the difficulties of encapsulating all the essential facets of group life within the confines of a single study or series of studies. The wide variations in the methods and levels of analyses adopted, therefore, reflect the richness of the data which it is possible to extract.

One of the first analytical attempts to create a general purpose descriptive and diagnostic tool designed to produce theoretically important measures for all kinds of small groups was the technique of Interaction Process Analysis (IPA), developed by Robert Bales in the late 1940s and 1950s (Bales, 1950a, 1950b, 1958; Bales and Strodtbeck, 1951). From a historical perspective, IPA was grounded in the group-dynamic tradition with emphasis upon the functional and structural properties of small face-to-face problem-solving groups. Its special application to problem-solving groups was based upon their dynamic, task-orientated nature in which 'phase patterns' can be differentiated as the groups proceed from problems of orientation to problems of solution. Thus the technique is particularly suitable for plotting changes in the quality of the group's activities as it progresses through time towards solving a problem.

Initially Bales used his system of analysis for studying the activities of Alcoholics Anonymous groups, but in practical terms the groups to which IPA can be applied are very diverse (Bales, 1950b). They include: (i) groups concerned primarily with problems external to their own process, such as planning groups, policy forming groups, boards, panels, seminars and classroom groups; (ii) groups concerned with their own procedure or with their own interaction and interpersonal relations, such as training groups in human relations skills, family groups, social and recreational clubs, children's playgroups and adolescent gangs; and (iii) groups concerned with the personal situation or experience of their individual members, such as therapy or counselling groups. Although specifically designed for on-the-spot recording of group situations, IPA can be applied post hoc to a video or sound recording or to a written transcript of the proceedings. Inevitably the lack of visual cues will to some extent impede the accuracy of the system. The size of group to which IPA can be applied may vary between two and about twenty, but it is important that they are groups where the attention of members tends to focus in turn upon individual speakers rather than groups where more than one person may be talking at once.

Despite the longevity of IPA as a tool for analysing group process, it has aged comparatively well: it is still of value in relation to more recent theories of social structure, social differentiation and attribution, and it is still being used practically and commercially as a training device in management and human relations. It has, for example, been used prescriptively to train how groups 'should' go about solving problems successfully. It is also used as a vehicle for giving feedback to individual group members concerning their effectiveness, or lack or it, in promoting the group's objectives. Some modification of the technique has occurred over the years (cf. Bales, 1970) and it formed the basis for other more expanded systems (e.g. Borgatta, 1963; Borgatta and Crowther, 1965). Methods of scoring and analysis have, of course, developed greatly since the technique was first devised.

Bales' and Cohen's (1979) Systematic Multiple Level Observation of Groups (SYMLOG) represents a package of methods for the processing and analysis of data including computer programmes.

For the purposes of the present exercise, data analysis is kept very simple; more sophisticated treatment would be possible, should the tutor wish to undertake it. Inevitably, IPA has certain limitations which will become clear as the exercise described in this chapter unfolds. Nevertheless, as a training device for teaching students to observe what goes on in groups and to relate the ingredients of social interaction to relevant theoretical dimensions of group process, the exercise has many merits.

Specific background to the exercise

IPA is a method of observing and recording the specific actions of a group of people which go to make up the flow of interaction. 'The heart of the method is a way of classifying behavior act by act, as it occurs in small face-to-face groups, and a series of ways of analyzing the data to obtain indices descriptive of group process and derivatively, of factors influencing that process' (Bales, 1950b). Essentially then, IPA is a structured observational approach which provides a pre-established system of categories to be used to classify every interaction that occurs in the group. Bales developed 12 categories which seemed to encompass most of the kinds of social acts that are likely to be emitted in problem-solving groups. Each item of behaviour, whether a verbal comment or merely a sigh, a shrug or a laugh is classified in one of these 12 categories. For each such item or 'act' the person initiating it and the person (or persons or group as whole) to whom it is directed are recorded. Bales' original category system (cf. Bales, 1950a) has been reproduced and is easily found in many social psychology texts (e.g. McDavid and Harari, 1968). Twenty years later Bales (1970) modified the labels attached to several of the categories to encourage wider use of them. For example, his rather extreme categories of 'showing solidarity' (category 1) and 'showing antagonism' (category 12) became 'seems friendly' and 'seems unfriendly' respectively to allow for milder expressions of positive and negative social feeling. This modified version of the scale is given in table 1 and is also found in many social psychology texts (e.g. Hollander and Hunt, 1971; Secord and Backman, 1974). Bales also developed a method for eliciting the interpersonal perceptions of group members.

The question of what constitutes a single codable act is, of course, crucial, and this has to be confronted in briefing and training the observers. Bales does not really describe the division rules to be employed; he sees it as a purely pragmatic problem. The amount of verbal or non-verbal behaviour necessary is that which permits the observer to make a classification. In his own words he defines the basic unit of observation as 'the smallest discriminable segment of verbal or nonverbal behavior to

which the observer, using the present set of categories after proper training, can assign a classification under conditions of continuous serial scoring' (Bales, 1950a). In practice, a string of sentences all aimed at asking a question may constitute a single act, and a brief exclamation or raised eyebrow might equally do so: in terms of the analysis of the interaction, they would carry equal weight.

It is clear that much depends upon the interpretation of acts by the observer: a comment or gesture in one context, or made in a certain way, may be deemed as meaningless and therefore ignored; in another context, or made in another way, it might be highly significant and be assigned to a category which attributes the perceived intention of the initiator. Bales tried to minimize subjective inferences by instructing the observer to interpret the act in terms of the act that immediately

Table 1. Bales' 12-category system and the modified eight-category system used in the exercise

	Bales' 1970 categories	Function	Modified categories
Positive social-emotional area	(1) seems friendly	integration +	(1) acts warmly
	(2) dramatizes (jokes)	tension +	
	(3) agrees	decision +	(2) agrees
———————	(4) gives suggestion	control	(3) gives suggestion
Task area (neutral)	(5) gives opinion	evaluation	(4) gives direction
	(6) gives orientation	communication	
	(7) asks for orientation	communication	(5) asks for direction
	(8) asks for opinion	evaluation	
	(9) asks for suggestion	control	(6) asks for suggestion
Negative social-emotional area	(10) disagrees	decision −	(7) disagrees
	(11) shows tension	tension −	(8) acts coldly
	(12) seems unfriendly	integration −	

preceded it, but this may still lead to some subjective bias. It is also possible that a single act may be classified in more than one way: an act of agreement may also be an act that reduces tension, or giving an opinion may also be an act of rejection. It is hardly surprising that a month or more is advocated as the time necessary for thorough training in using the method. Through training quite high reliability coefficients are typically reported, in the order of 0.90 for categories that occur with high frequency reducing to 0.60 for categories with lower frequency.

The 12 categories are subsumed within two main classes of behaviours: those concerned with social-emotional activities of the group members and those concerned with task-related activities. The social-emotional behaviour itself divides into positive acts: being friendly, dramatizing (joking), agreeing; or into reciprocal negative acts: being unfriendly, showing tension or disagreeing (see table 1). Basically these reactions are associated with the organization of the group involving the maintenance or destruction of harmony, the management of personal tension and group integration or disintegration. Task-related activities divide into questions and attempted answers with differentiation between asking/offering suggestions, asking/offering opinions and asking/offering information. These activities are emotionally neutral and are geared towards pursuing task goals: defining the task situation, developing shared value systems, attempts at control and progress towards solutions.

The categorization of social acts may have an inherent structural utility but is of little functional use unless consistencies in the patterns of activity can be related to dimensions of group process or social evaluations. The main predictive interest vested in the use of IPA involves the stages in the problem-solving sequence and the dimensions of group interaction. The typical sequence of activities in problem-solving groups starts with an initial information-assertion stage where the emphasis is on problems of orientation, defining the task, stating the objectives and sharing information. The second evalu-

ation stage involves a concern with attitudes and opinions: what attitudes should be taken towards the situation, and what values are to be accepted? This is the in-group formation stage and it may be characterized by higher initial amounts of disagreement followed (if the group task is to be successfully completed) by higher amounts of agreement. The third solution stage has its emphasis upon problems of control: deciding what action should be taken.

The other main line of research has focussed upon the dimensions of social evaluation with particular reference to the emergence of leadership. Three such dimensions of evaluation have been identified: power, likeability and contribution to the task. Power refers to the degree of perceived dominance or prominence that a person has over the other group members. Likeability refers to the degree of pleasant or unpleasant feeling aroused by that person, and contribution to the task concerns the leader's task-related activities. These three dimensions are taken to be the primary dimensions by which people judge one another. They should be thought of as unrelated to each other; thus knowing someone's position on one dimension does not predict that person's position on the other two. Put into concrete terms the group member who is emotionally supportive and popular does not necessarily help the group in completing its tasks. This itself has led to interesting speculation about the composition of groups and the characteristics of leaders. In theory the 'great man' concept of a leader is of one who achieves high ratings on all of these three social dimensions. Such men and women are comparatively rare; in practice there is a greater likelihood that people highly rated on task-orientated leadership are poor in terms of the emotional support thay give the group, and vice versa. It can be argued that the success of many long-term 'traditioned' groups lies in the balance of leadership roles within those groups; one member, the task specialist, taking the lead in relation to group activities, another, the social-emotional specialist, constantly bolstering morale and cementing interpersonal relations.

The exercise

The purpose of the exercise is to explore some of the properties of a problem-solving group as identified by Bales and to examine the behaviour of individuals within the group. In terms of a learning experience for students, the exercise is particularly useful in teaching the applications of a structured observational approach and it raises many of the problems associated with classifying social acts or units of purposeful interactive behaviour. Little prior knowledge of social psychology is needed on the part of students, but it would be useful if they had a grounding in basic inferential statistics.

In the specific background to this exercise some stress was laid upon the problems of classifying the behavioural units to be recorded and upon the normal training period which Bales' experienced observers are typically required to undergo. In the interests of simplification the full 12-category system has been collapsed into eight categories, which should give students a slightly easier task (see table 1). The rationale for collapsing certain categories has been arrived at purely on grounds of expediency. The categories 'seems friendly' and 'dramatizes' have been combined into 'acts warmly' which is intended to encompass any act which serves to integrate or reward the group or bolster the status of others. Conversely, 'shows tension' and 'seems unfriendly' have been combined into 'acts coldly' to convey the sense of antagonistic, critical acts likely to lead to increased tension within the group. In the task-related area 'gives/asks for opinion' and 'gives/asks for orientation' have been combined into 'gives/asks for direction'. Whilst there is a distinction between opinion and orientation (information), the distinction is sometimes blurred in practice and particularly in the role-play situations used in the problem tasks in this exercise where group participants may have to 'invent' some of the background details to the scenarios described. There is an inevitable loss to the analysis of the data resulting from this simplified category system, especially in terms of plotting changes in group process through time from problems of orientation to problems of evaluation and solution.

Method

DURATION. The exercise is very flexible and can largely be tailored to suit the time available. Typically it can last over two laboratory sessions of three hours each or it can be compressed into one session. The essential difference between running it over one or two sessions lies in the inclusion of a training session which can be omitted, although it is desirable. For the purpose of providing full details the exercise is treated here as being of two sessions' duration, and the question of omitting the training stage will be addressed later.

Session 1 is devoted to training and data collection and Session 2 to data analysis.

SIZE OF CLASS AND DIVISION OF ROLES. Again flexibility is a hallmark of this exercise and it is suitable for class sizes between six and forty. Since the class is divided up into a group (or groups) of 'discussants' and 'observers', the minimum number of discussants per group is three and the corresponding minimum number of observers is three, one for each discussant. In practice it is desirable to have four or five class members in the discussion group(s) and then all the remaining members are observers, with up to seven or eight allocated to observe each discussant. Up to a point the more observers there are recording the interactions of each discussant, the more unbiassed their pooled data should be.

In the exercise to be described one group of four discussants is employed: the same discussants are used for the 'training' problem, the 'practice' problem and the two 'test' problems. There is no intrinsic objection to using different groups of discussants for each problem, but the advantage of the same group members is that by the time they reach the test problems, they are suitably warmed-up to talking in front of the rest of the class, and comparisons of their profiles can be made between test problems 1 and 2.

If the class is really large and the tutor has the assistance of post-graduate demonstrators, and two rooms are available for use, the whole class can be divided in half, giving two groups of discussants and observers working through the problems in parallel. Comparisons between the styles of the two groups in tackling the same problems are then possible.

Some attention should be paid to the composition of the discussant group(s), and much depends upon the nature of the problem tasks selected: test problem 2 (see Appendix 2b), which involves role-playing a family, requires father, mother, son and daughter roles to be enacted. There is some merit in deciding, prior to the commencement of the exercise, who in particular to allocate as discussants, rather than just seeking for volunteers: one criterion at least should be to .select students who are not too reserved, or lacking in self-confidence; otherwise discussion may flag seriously.

LOCATION. The exercise can be conducted in any reasonably large room or laboratory. In the interests of congeniality and the comfort of the discussants it may be preferable to use a carpeted tutorial/seminar room, rather than a stark laboratory. After initial briefing by the tutor the seating has to be rearranged such that the discussants are seated round a table in the centre of the room and encircled by the observers who must occupy positions which give them a clear view of the discussants.

RESOURCES AND MATERIALS. Apart from the provision of a stop-watch, tape-recorder, blackboard and, optionally, an overhead projector, the only materials needed are duplicated problem sheets, and response form matrices for collecting the group data, to which specific reference will be made in the procedure section. It should be emphasized that the problem sheets are exemplary and individual tutors may wish to modify the content of these or indeed substitute their own problems entirely. The discussion problems and the 'training' and 'practice' discussions are relatively immaterial; the guiding principles in relation to the selection of suitable problems for the two 'test' dis-

cussions are: (i) that solutions are possible in the sense that a consensus can be achieved; (ii) the problems are inherently debatable requiring discussants to state their opinions and not requiring much factual information outside that provided by the brief; (iii) the problems are intrinsically interesting to allow a sufficiently motivated discussion; (iv) the brief for one problem is divisive in the sense that it sets the scene for a conflict of interests rather than a uniformity of interests.

It may also be useful for the tutor to have an assistant who may ideally be a post-graduate demonstrator, or else a member of the class designated for the purpose.

Procedure

SUMMARY OF PROCEDURE: SESSION 1. Training and data collection. In brief the sequence of events may be summarized as follows.

1. A general introduction by the tutor to the analysis of interactions and the Bales' technique in particular.
2. The division of the class into discussants and observers and the re-arrangement of the class and the seating.
3. Discussants engage in their first 'training' discussion problem which is tape-recorded.
4. Training response forms are distributed to the class; categories of interaction to be recorded are explained by the tutor, while an assistant (post-graduate demonstrator or undergraduate) transcribes the first part of the taped discussion on to the blackboard or an overhead slide.
5. The tape-recording is played back to the class act by act. Class members classify each act independently until a sequence of exchanges has been completed.
6. This sequence is then played back again to the class, and class members vote on the way they classified each act. Differences of opinion are revealed and ironed out.
7. A second sequence of acts is similarly

classified, first independently by class members and then, after replay, a consensus is taken. This training procedure may be repeated several times.

8. Discussants are then sent out of the classroom briefly; response forms for the two test problems are distributed to observers, who are briefed in their use before being allocated to observe a particular discussant.

9. Discussants are then recalled to the classroom and given the 'practice' problem; any further classification problems experienced by the observers are subsequently aired.

10. Discussants then undertake 'test' problems 1 and 2 with observers recording the interactions.

SESSION 2. ANALYSIS OF RESULTS AND GENERAL DISCUSSION

11. Observers pool their data by averaging the frequency of emission of each category of social act.

12. Group data are entered into matrices on the blackboard.

13. The tutor provides a thorough briefing about individual and group profiles of interaction and phases of group discussion.

14. The tutor suggests the forms of analysis to be undertaken on the basis of hypotheses or questions generated.

If time demands that the exercise be compressed into one practical session, then the steps associated with the training problem (steps 3-7 inclusive of Session 1) may be omitted. In this event the tutor should introduce the class to the coding categories and response forms after step 2, provide an explanation of their use and then proceed with the practice problem (step 9). While observers are not in any sense trained, they will have some opportunity to air and share views about difficulties they experience in assigning codes.

The procedure in detail: Session 1

1. GENERAL INTRODUCTION BY THE TUTOR. Little prior explanatory information should be provided, at least as far as the members of the discussion group are concerned. Although it is feasible to send discussants out of the room while observers are being initially briefed and trained (steps 1, 4-7), these students would be deprived of much of the didactic function of the exercise. In the light of experience it does not much matter if the discussants know that their utterances and behaviour are to be coded in certain ways, nor does it matter if they even participate in the training exercise by coding their own interaction during the training problem. Expulsion from the classroom during these phases of the procedure carries its own problems in terms of creating disengagement from the exercise and a sense of feeling threatened and exposed when participating in the discussion tasks. Self-awareness is also likely to be heightened during the tasks and this, to some extent, would detract from the involved and motivated discussions which are required for the test problems.

What does matter is that discussants should not have specific information about the nature and quality of their own contribution to the group, such as what types of reactions may be regarded as having positive emotional or negative emotional value, or how a group is typically supposed to proceed from the setting of its objectives to solution (see Introduction). From this it should be clear that the tutor's initial briefing of the class must be kept short and on a very general level, explaining in broad terms what the overall purpose of the exercise is as a training device for the students and what kinds of general use such interactional analysis may have. Where Bales' scale or the modified version of it is introduced in step 4, the tutor's explanations should be confined purely to definitions of particular categories, not to interpretations of the value of social acts.

2. ARRANGEMENT OF THE CLASS. The tutor then nominates the four class members to act as discussants, bearing in mind the comments made at the end of the section on size of class and division of roles. It is advisable to have the names of one or two other suitable discussants in reserve in

the event of absence or genuine reluctance to participate. The discussants are seated around a table in the centre of the room; their positions are marked by large free-standing labels, A, B, C and D. The other class members are designated as observers and they take up positions in a rough circle around the edge of the room. Specific allocations of observers to discussants is not carried out until after training (step 8).

3. TRAINING PROBLEM. With no further briefing discussants are given their training problem which is a soluble arithmetic problem (see Appendix 1). Each discussant is presented with a card which contains one piece of information. The information from all the cards has to be shared before a solution can be worked out. To facilitate oral exchange discussants are instructed to keep their information card in front of them, not to write anything down, and not to share or pool cards. The question card is placed in the middle of the table for all to see. Once discussants have their respective information cards and know the question, they are asked to start the discussion speaking as clearly as

possible and not addressing anyone outside the discussion group. The tape-recorder and stop-watch are started. Discussion may be permitted for up to about eight minutes and it does not matter if it is stopped before the solution is reached.

Observers are instructed to remain as silent as possible and merely to watch the activities of the discussion group.

4. OBSERVERS' TASK. After discussion of the training problem has ended, the class is given training response forms (see table 2) which relate to the simplified eight-category system used in this exercise.

The tutor takes the class through the categories and attempts to define them in turn and gives examples. Guiding students on definitions is not altogether straight-forward and a few points are worth making.

* It is necessary, for coding purposes, to say what constitutes a single unit of interaction (act): it may typically be a sentence or a part-sentence, but in practice several sentences in sequence by the same interactant could consti-tute a single unit if they are all

Table 2. Training response form

Categories	acts														
	1	2	3	4	5	6	7	8	9	10	11	12	13	14	15 ...
1. acts warmly															
2. agrees															
3. gives suggestion															
4. gives direction															
5. asks for direction															
6. asks for suggestion															
7. disagrees															
8. acts coldly															

For each act the observer places a tick (or ticks) in the appropriate row/column(s).

directed towards the same purpose; that is, giving a piece of information, asking a question.

* An act does not have to be a meaningful verbal utterance: it could be an exclamation, a sigh, a laugh, a gesture or any form of significant non-verbal response. For the purposes of training, only the auditory information provided by the tape-recording can be utilized, but observers must be made aware that, for test problems 1 and 2, non-verbal cues may also merit recording.

* Categories of acts are not necessarily mutually exclusive. A single act may be recorded in two categories simultaneously. Thus, in giving a suggestion, a discussant may also be disagreeing with what has just been said.

While the tutor is discussing the categories of acts with the class, the assistant (post-graduate demonstrator or student) takes the tape-recorder into an adjacent room, replays the tape and makes a transcript. Fifteen minutes should be allowed for this, and at least the first 20-30 units of interaction need to be transcribed. The transcript should then be written on to the blackboard or on to an overhead slide. The speaker's identification is irrelevant.

5. OBSERVER JUDGEMENTS. Once observers have had the interaction categories explained to them, the tape-recording is played back act by act and the class follows the transcript on the blackboard. After the first act has been played, class members make independent judgements about how it should be classified and tick the appropriate row under column 1 on the training response form. The tutor plays the second act on the tape, and the class members again make their independent judgements, ticking the appropriate row under column 2. This sequence continues for the first ten acts.

6. GROUP VOTING. The tape is rewound and the interaction is then played back again; on this occasion class members indicate by a show of hands how they coded each act. Differences of opinions are discussed and an attempt is made to reach a consensus on each act.

7. REPETITION OF TRAINING. This procedure is repeated with the next set of ten acts, class members first making independent judgements and then, on replay, voting publicly. By this time class members should have a clearer idea of how the category system is to be used and should be responding in increasingly substantial agreement. A third sequence of ten acts (if they have been transcribed) can be presented in like manner if time permits. This training procedure is rather time-consuming but it serves to increase inter-observer reliability considerably as well as familiarizing observers with the categories they have to use, so its inclusion in the exercise is strongly recommended.

8. ALLOCATION OF OBSERVERS. Once the tutor is satisfied that the observers are well accustomed to using the categories with some confidence, the four discussants are briefly sent out of the classroom. A similar number of observers are then specifically assigned to each discussant and positioned so that they have a clear view of their target person. The tutor draws the observers' attention to the response forms and the way in which they are to tabulate their recordings. The response forms (see table 3) require observers to identify to whom acts are directed by the discussant they are observing. For simplicity the observer enters a tick against the category of act emitted in the column corresponding to the discussant to whom it is directed. If the interaction is directed to several of the discussants or at the group as a whole, then the tick is entered in the column for the group. The emission of each type of act is thus represented by a series of ticks.

9. PRACTICE PROBLEM. The discussants are then recalled to the classroom and given the practice problem which can be any kind of open-ended discussion task. One particularly suitable kind of problem, for example, is a design problem: the group is instructed to discuss the planning of a new shopping precinct, a new traffic system, the layout of an exhibition, and so on.

Table 3. Response form for test problems 1 and 2

Discussant observed ....

| Categories | To whom addressed | | | | | | | | | |
| | A | | B | | C | | D | | Group | |
	1st half	2nd half	1st half	2nd half	1st half	2nd half	1st half	2nd half	1st half	2nd half
1. acts warmly										
2. agrees										
3. gives suggestion										
4. gives direction										
5. asks for direction										
6. asks for suggestion										
7. disagrees										
8. acts coldly										

For each act initiated by the discussant under observation a tick is entered in the column corresponding to the discussant addressed and in the row corresponding to the perceived act.

Group members may be supplied with different pieces of information or with the same piece of background information. The discussion may last up to 10 or 12 minutes.

This problem provides an opportunity for observers to become practised in using the categories and response form. Any further difficulties in categorizing interactions or using the response forms are finally discussed.

10. TEST PROBLEMS. Discussants are then briefed to start the two test problems. Test problem 1 (see Appendix 2a) is construed as a non-conflict discussion situation in which the discussants are to role-play probation officers and social workers in reaching agreement about how to advise a juvenile offender. Test problem 2

(see Appendix 2b) is designed as a conflict discussion situation: discussants role-play the members of a family who, in the circumstances described, have competing interests. In order to assess changes in the style of the discussion, it is suggested that the discussion periods for test problems 1 and 2 be divided into halves: recordings of acts initiated during the second half cumulate in separate columns to those initiated during the first half. The time allotted for each discussion should be identical: between 10 and 15 minutes. This gives sufficient time for a reasonable amount of data to be collected without the discussants losing interest in the topic. It is important that they should be told in advance how long the discussion will last; it helps them pace their rate of progress. Observers can easily be informed unobtrusively when half-time has been reached.

It is also important that the two test problems should be given at the end of Session 1 and not held over to the start of Session 2. Much of the benefit of the 'warm up' for the discussants and training for the observers would be lost if the class came back 'cold' to the test problems at the second session. Session 1 finishes after completion of the two test problems.

Session 2

11. POOLING OF OBSERVERS' DATA. Assuming that all the data have been collected, the session starts with the tutor directing observers to gather into groups in the classroom, according to which discussant they observed in Session 1. To pool their data class members should simply summate and then average the frequency with which each category was recorded as having been used by the discussant in interaction with each other discussant and with the group as a whole. Thus for each test problem the observers of discussant A generate an average number of 'asks for suggestion' acts directed at B, C and D in turn, and at the group. Separate frequencies are generated for first and second halves of each discussion. For the purpose of analysis the average frequencies based on the pooling of individual observers' scores form the basic data. Despite the lack of precision in requiring that averages are rounded to the nearest whole number, they do take account of differences in observer group sizes.

12. INTERACTION MATRIX. The averaged data from groups are then collected by the tutor (or assistant) and transcribed in matrix form on to the blackboard (see table 4). There is a separate interaction matrix for each of the two test problems, and first and second half frequencies are entered in separate cells in the matrix. The matrix enables the display of acts initiated by each discussant towards each other dis-cussant and towards the group.

13. BRIEFING BY TUTOR. On the assumption that the tutor has given very little information about the exercise at the outset of Session 1, this is a suitable stage

at which to address the class in more detail about the Bales technique and group processes, drawing from the Introduction of this chapter. More can also be said about the general purpose of the exercise in terms of the problems associated with classifying social acts. 'Eyeball' inspection of the matrices on the blackboard should enable the tutor to make some comment about the relative contributions of discussants to each problem, about the roles which discussants played within the group and about differences in the types of social acts between problems and between first and second halves of the discussion.

Data analysis and discussion
There should be sufficient data for a variety of detailed analyses of individual categories of social acts. However, the main analyses are outlined below. From the interaction matrices, the total number of acts addressed by each discussant to each other discussant and to the group as a whole should be calculated. These subtotals can be summed to yield an overall total for each row of the matrix which represents the total number of acts initiated by each discussant. Similarly, column totals represent the number of acts each receives from others. The 'total participation' of each discussant is represented by the total number of acts initiated plus the total number received.

With these data a number of questions and hypotheses can be examined based mainly upon the recurrent findings of Bales' own research.

1. The overall amount of participation of each discussant remains the same for each problem. This is particularly interesting to explore in the light of the differences in the type of problems, one essentially non-contentious and the other essentially contentious.

2. The amount of interaction initiated by one discussant towards a specific other discussant tends to be of the same order of magnitude as the amount the second discussant addresses to him/her. More accurately, the lower of the two participators addresses a little more to the higher participator than the higher participator

Table 4. Interaction matrix: for collection of group data

Test problem........................

Initiated by	To whom addressed									
	A		B		C		D		Group	
	1st half	2nd half	1st half	2nd half	1st half	2nd half	1st half	2nd half	1st half	2nd half
A										
B										
C										
D										

Average number of each type of act initiated by each discussant to each other discussant. A simple code system can be devised to denote each type of act: for example, 5A+ might denote five 'agrees'; 2S– might denote two 'asks for suggestions', and so on.

addresses to him/her. If discussants are rank ordered in terms of the number of acts they initiate and the number they receive, there is generally a high correlation between these rank orders.

3. The higher participators tend to address proportionately more of their initiated acts to the group as a whole rather than to specific individuals. Indeed, in many groups the amount the highest participator addresses to the group as a whole exceeds the total that person addressed to all the individual discussants put together. Conversely, the amount that the lowest participator addresses to the group as a whole tends to fall short of the amount that person addresses to any individual discussant.

4. Upwards and downwards mobility within the group can also be detected, according to Bales: if lower participators address more of their acts to the group than to the other individual members, they are taken to be trying to move upwards; if higher participators address more of their acts to other individual members than to the group, then they are taken to be attempting to move downwards.

Analysis of these questions rests upon looking at overall rates of participation. Rather more interesting is the analysis of types of acts engaged in, which requires scrutiny of discussants in terms of task-related and social-emotional contributions to group process. At a fairly holistic level it may be possible to tell if the two complementary types of group leader that Bales has identified (task specialists and social-emotional specialists) actually emerge in the two discussion groups by examining the patterns of acts.

5. From the interaction matrices it is possible to gauge roughly the power position of each person by counting the number of agreements they receive relative to the number of disagreements. This may not give the full picture, of course, because many statements or directives may be made by 'powerful' members which meet tacit, and consequently unrecorded, agreement.

6. Power may also be measured in terms of types of acts initiated: high contributors attempt more solutions and provide more information, low contributors ask more questions and provide less information.

7. Task specialists typically play aggressive, tough-minded, ideas-orientated roles; social-emotional specialists (usually the best-liked members of groups) play more passive roles and concentrate on reducing tension and giving rewards. Such individuals may be identifiable from the interaction matrix.

In addition to representing the data numerically in the interaction matrix, the contributions of discussants can be plotted graphically in an interaction profile, which is an array of the rates of activity in each category. This can be plotted for the group as a whole or for individual members, and it is based upon the percentage of the total acts initiated that fall into each category. Profiles can also be plotted for acts received. This is a particularly useful way of making comparisons of group activity between problems, and comparisons within problems of group activity from the first half of the discussion period to the second half. It is also another means of comparing individual contributions to the group.

8. On the basis of the types of discussion problem chosen, more negative social-emotional acts (disagreement, tension) should be generated in test problem 2 than in test problem 1.

9. If the group is close to a decision on either or both problems, then the first half of the discussion period should be characterized by information asking and giving, and by disagreement; the second half should be characterized by directives, agreement and tension release.

It should be noted that profile norms for Bales' 12-point category scale are published (cf. Bales, 1958, 1970) and can readily be used for comparison purposes after suitable adjustment to take account of the collapsed categories used in this exercise.

The sophistication of the statistical analyses to be employed may vary according to the progress of the students. Simple descriptive statistics in terms of averages, totals or percentages may be used; alternatively a range of nonparametric tests such as Chi Square and Spearman's rho may be appropriate for handling particular parts of the data.

A final observation should be made concerning the collection of subjective data. Bales has laid great emphasis upon the various dimensions of social evaluation mentioned in the Introduction to this exercise, and he has devised methods for collecting evaluative data on group members' likes and dislikes for each other, their opinion about who had the best ideas and who showed the most leadership. There is no reason why the tutor should not seek to obtain subjective reports from the discussants in particular about their perception of their roles and the roles of the other interactants. Such data could usefully be matched up with the quantitative data derived from the observers. Our discussion may give the impression that the amount of total participation by individual members is in some real sense a measure of their group effectiveness. Clearly this is not necessarily so because quantity of acts does not imply quality. Over-talkative group members may well be over-represented on all the quantitative measures. There is not space to address this question here, other than to offer it as justification for collecting subjective data and to ensure that it is not overlooked by students. A concise discussion of this issue is to be found in Bales (1958).

Conclusions

As mentioned earlier, IPA represents a structured observational approach, and its strength as an exercise lies in teaching students some of the problems associated with classifying social interaction and interpreting the meaning and function of various social acts within the group. The exercise can, of course, be taken out of the classroom and into the field, where students may gain valuable insights into the proceedings of real decision-making groups. Students might have an opportunity to do this through clubs and societies to which they belong within their own institutions: they may sit in on committee meetings, working parties, discussion groups and so on. Alternatively, at a civic level and within local authorities, there may be public meetings of the bodies concerned, for example, with education, housing, environmental health, social services, transport and highways, which would provide opportunities for some kind of interactional analyses. In groups that have highly formal and stylized structures (making formal reports and permitting little open discussion) IPA would not be appropriate, but where open discussion is permitted it is an excellent means of exploring group processes and differentiation within the group.

REFERENCES

Bales, R.F. (1950a) Interaction Process Analysis: A method for the study of small groups. Reading, Mass.: Addison-Wesley.

Bales, R.F. (1950b) A set of categories for the analysis of small group interaction. American Sociological Review, 15, 257-263.

Bales, R.F. (1958) Task roles and social roles in problem-solving groups. In E. Maccoby, T. Newcomb and E. Hartley (eds), Readings in Social Psychology (3rd edn). New York: Holt, Rinehart & Winston.

Bales, R.F. (1970) Personality and Social Behavior. New York: Holt, Rinehart & Winston.

Bales, R.F. and Cohen, S.P. (1979) SYMLOG: A system for the multiple level observation of groups. New York: Collier Macmillan/Free Press.

Bales, R.F. and Strodtbeck, F.L. (1951) Phases in group problem solving. Journal of Abnormal and Social Psychology, 46, 485-495.

Borgatta, E.F. (1963) A new systematic observation system: behaviour scores system (BSc. system). Journal of Psychological Studies, 14, 24-44.

Borgatta, E.F. and Crowther, B. (1965) A Workbook for the Study of Social Interaction Processes. Chicago: Rand McNally.

Hollander, E.P. and Hunt, R.G. (1971) Current Perspectives in Social Psychology (3rd edn). New York: Oxford University Press.

Liggert, J. and Cochrane, R. (1968) Exercises in Social Science. London: Constable.

McDavid, J.W. and Harari, H. (1968) Social Psychology. Individuals, groups, societies. New York: Harper & Row.

Secord, P.F. and Backman, C.W. (1974) Social Psychology (2nd edn). Tokyo: McGraw-Hill.

APPENDIX 1

Training problem: soluble arithmetic task

Information distributed among discussants.

1. Graham is 5' 8" tall and is half-way between Derek and Clive.
2. Clive's height is exactly half-way between that of John and Derek.
3. Robert is 2" shorter than Derek.
4. John is 4" taller than Robert.

Question: how tall are John, Robert, Derek and Clive?

Answer: John 5' 9½"
    Robert 5' 5½"
    Derek 5' 7½"
    Clive 5' 8½"

Taken from Liggert and Cochrane (1968).

APPENDIX 2

(a) Test problem 1

Information items

1. John is 16 years old; he works as an apprentice tool-maker in a heavy engineering firm; he has held this job for three weeks having spent six months on the dole since leaving school; he likes his work and is anxious to keep his present job.

2. John is the youngest of three brothers; his two brothers (22 and 20) have both been in trouble with the police; his eldest brother was jailed for two years at the age of 19 for assault and grievous bodily harm; both brothers are unmarried and live at home rarely holding a job down for more than a few weeks at a time.

3. John lives at home with his mother who never exercised any control over her three sons; his father was a drunkard who, when the children were younger, used to beat up his wife frequently; since John was ten, his father has lived away from home and his mother had to bring up the boys on her own and manage on what little earnings they brought into the house.

4. John has never been in trouble with the police before; apart from engaging in a few wild exploits at school, he was never in serious trouble with the school authorities; he was by no means a bright pupil but took his school work seriously and has an ambition to get on in life.

Problem

John has been caught red-handed, aiding and abetting his brothers in a warehouse robbery; since it is his first offence he has been put on probation for two years. You are probation officers and social workers and are considering what advice should be given to the boy and his mother after leaving the custody of the court. Come to some agreement about the advice you would give.

(b) Test problem 2

Information items

1. You are Dad: you are 48 years of age and the owner and manager of a small grocery shop in the suburbs of a large city in the north of England; you like mixing with other people, enjoy football and the pub, and never go into the countryside except for occasional picnics and holidays; you don't much like the countryside and only go at all to keep your wife happy.

2. You are Mum: you are 45 years of age. You were raised on a farm in a rural part of northern England and love the countryside; since you married and moved into the town to raise a family you never had much opportunity of going into the country except occasionally at holiday-time or for picnics; now the children have grown up and can fend for themselves you would dearly like to move into the country again.

3. You are Roger: you are 18 years of age and living at home; you are about to take A levels at a Technical College and have applied for a place at an Agricultural College; you take after your mother and are very keen on the land and farming; you have spent all your school holidays down on your grandparents' farm helping out, and your ambitions are to own a farm of your own.

4. You are Sally: you are 19 years old, also living at home and helping your parents in the shop; you are engaged to be married to a local boy; your interests are mainly social - you like dancing and going to the pictures or theatre - and you have no real knowledge of the countryside.

Problem

Dad's uncle has just died, leaving to Dad and his family a large country house (in good condition) standing in about four acres of rough, rocky ground on the south-west coast of Scotland, about 180 miles from where they live. The house passes to the family on the understanding that they keep it in the family for at least 40 years. The family is gathered together just after they have heard the will read in order to decide what they are going to do with the house.

5

Ethogenic methods: an empirical psychology of action

Rom Harré

Specification notes

AIMS. This chapter includes four exercises in the interpretation of documents, three of which are printed as appendices to the chapter. Appendix 1 is a record of a medical consultation; Appendix 2 is a conversation in which a schoolboy explains bullying; and Appendix 3 contains a record of a discussion between family members, together with an analysis of the markers of the social force of the speech units involved, developed from that family's own interpretations. The fourth exercise involves documents created by the students themselves.

RESOURCES. No special equipment is required for these exercises and the work can be done in an ordinary classroom. Students should each be provided with copies of the appendices. Each exercise is designed to occupy one normal laboratory session of approximately three hours. Since negotiation of interpretations of the material is an important part of each exercise students should be grouped in threes, though the initial analytical work should be done individually.

Introduction

There are two ways of defining psychology. Recent tradition has assumed that human actions are the effects of causes, and that psychology is the science devoted to discovering the mechanism by which such causes operate. On this view human beings as persons are presumed to be essentially passive. Advances in psychological theory have drawn attention to an alternative conception of psychology, according to which human beings are thought of as active beings concerned with the fulfilment of their plans and intentions and thinking out what to do. The methods outlined in this section are intended as an introduction to some of the techniques that are needed to study human actions according to the second of the above conceptions of psychological science.

To grasp the significance of adopting the ethogenic methods of investigation, a student needs to have some understanding of the background discussions of the nature of psychology which have led to their development. Shotter's book (1975) is an excellent introductory survey of the main theories of psychology that are in contention. For more detailed discussions Harré and Secord (1973) or Hollis (1977) could be consulted.

Four exercises are included in this chapter. This first three are intended to introduce the student to the idea of looking behind what is said and done for social meanings, and to learn to negotiate with other people - including, ideally, the original actors - about the interpretations of the material. Each of exercises 1, 2 and 3 should take about three hours, and any two would serve to introduce a student to the flavour of ethogenic methods. The fourth exercise is intended to be introduced at the beginning of the academic year, and to culminate in a three-hour analytical session towards its end.

Since the exercises suggested here utilize documents already prepared, they require no special equipment and can be carried out in an ordinary classroom. Each student needs a copy of the material in the appendices.

There are no routine procedures in ethogenic psychology. The aim of an analytical and interpretative exercise is to develop the art of grasping how the world of social action is viewed from the point of view of some other person, perhaps from that of a radically different community from one's own. The material presented in the exercises attached to this section could be supplemented by documents (written or recorded by audio and video equipment) which have been collected by the students themselves concerning social processes of interest to them.

In studying human action there are two kinds of matters we might wish to find out. We could ask what someone must know in order to be able to carry on some well-defined activity; for example, for someone to be able to play chess adequately a person must know the rules governing the moves of each of the pieces. But just having these resources does not make someone a competent chess player. They must know how to use their knowledge on particular occasions when they are actually required to make a move. In ethogenic psychology we treat the problem of discovering and presenting what someone must know (their resources for action) as separable from the problem of discovering how they use those resources to act (their procedures or performances). Different methods are required to discover a person's resources for social action from those needed to uncover the ways performances are actually brought off.

A scientific investigation begins with the realization that there are patterns in the phenomena. Crystals have regular shapes: the forms of family quarrels repeat

themselves. The patterns may not be immediately obvious to the untutored eye. The identification of patterns depends in part upon the deployment of an adequate conceptual system or analytical model to help them to stand out from the background of social action we take for granted. The impulse to science derives from the perception of patterns and the puzzlement that is engendered in the scientifically minded by wondering how those patterns came to be. In human social interaction there are very many examples of patterned behaviour, some readily available to untutored common sense, some requiring sophisticated analytical models to be identified. Fundamental to the methodology as set out in this chapter is the thought that there are at least three sources of patterned behaviour in human interaction.

The first source is genetic endowment and biological necessity. There may be cases where there is a direct preprogramming of a pattern of interaction which can be identified with psychological structures related immediately to some inherited patterns of genes. Direct preprogramming seems to be very rare in human social actions and feelings. The fact that men find women with large pupils more attractive than those with small may be an example (Harper, Wiens and Metarezzo, 1978). These are exploitations of patterns of behaviour that derive indirectly from a genetic endowment through the cultural exploitation of a biological necessity. For example, there is a biological necessity to eat but, as has been demonstrated amply by anthropologists, meals are more than a mere ingestion of nourishment; they are used as ways of displaying social status and hierarchy. They are endowed with meaning (Douglas, 1972).

Other patterns of behaviour seem to be the product of habits ingrained during a person's upbringing, training and so on. Like those rare cases where there is an obvious relationship to physiological preprogramming, habits are realized in action without conscious attention being paid to the process of an appropriate action. For example, Collett and Marsh (1974) discovered a pattern of stance and body posture by which people pass in the street that is different for men from that displayed by women. This pattern is probably not the result of genetic endowment or biological necessity, though people are not conscious of the regular way in which they adjust their body posture to one another. My guess is that a pattern of this sort is best understood as a habit acquired during early life and is comparable, for example, to the ability to ride a bicycle.

These kinds of semi-automatic patterned behaviour could be investigated by something like the naïve experiment in which an action is construed as the outcome of the causal operation of environmental conditions. Breaking down the event into variables and manipulating one against the other does not seem an unreasonable way of proceeding. One cannot, of course, conclude that the discovery of a pattern of cause and effect reveals a universal human tendency. For example, the experiments on gaze, so fashionable a few years ago, showed that there were patterns in the ways people looked at each other. But the patterns of gaze are different in different cultures (Harper et al, 1978). The apparent universality which accrues from the acultural air of an experiment is an illusion.

Most human social activity is unlike either of the cases at which we have so far briefly looked. The sources of patterned behaviour that dominate most social episodes are the rules, conventions, demands, exemplars, interpretations, legal requirements, codes of honour and so on that differentiate one culture from another at a much higher level of conceptual sophistication and cognitive processing than occurs in the case of patterns sustained by habit. It is to the study of the third and most prevalent kind of social pattern that the ethogenic methodology is directed. In most cases, when people are acting in accordance with the requirements of their culture, exemplifying their knowledge in proper behaviour in pursuit of their projects, they are rarely conscious of the process by which that knowledge is transformed into action. However, it is clear from the investigations which will be mentioned later in this chapter that (i) they once were conscious of these intentions, and (ii) they can be made conscious of them again at any time.

The upshot of these introductory considerations is the realization that there is a small place in the corner, as it were, for the naïve experiment but that to investigate the most prominent process by which human beings create social order a dual methodology must be employed. There must be a way of finding out what people know of the rules, conventions, and so on, of their society and a way of finding out how they utilize these moment by moment in performing appropriate actions. In short, there must be an investigation of people's social resources and there must be an investigation of the processes by which their social resources are utilized.

How to study resources

The basis of the method is the analysis of the accounts that actors give of the actions in which they have taken part. There are also accounts directed to actions that have not yet been done. Fortunately, the way social life is actually lived involves a good deal of challenge to and doubts about what is going on in the social episodes of daily life. Actors are then ready, if challenged, to provide interpretations and justifications for what they have been doing. These are accounts. Empirical investigation of accounts has shown that they include interpretative schemata for making clear what an action means, as well as indications of the rules and conventions of proper action (Lyman and Scott, 1970). Accounts not only serve to keep social life running smoothly, but they reveal bits and pieces of an actor's knowledge of how social life ought to run.

1. Account analysis is the first step, then, in the investigation of the knowledge and beliefs which actors bring to their social life. Account analysis yields material which represents the resources of actors. But the exigencies of social life are such that actors may not produce on a particular occasion the resource material which was actually involved in the production of a particular action. Perhaps to do so would have left them exposed and vulnerable to criticism. It is no part of the ethogenic methodology to suppose that the contents of accounts and the resources employed are coincident moment by moment in day-to-day social activity. But it is the

central ethogenic hypothesis that they are coincident **in the long run.** Studying accounts of a mode of social interaction for considerable periods of time, and relative to as many of the interactors as possible, will yield an adequate representation of their resources. However, even with this reservation it is clear that we should not expect account analysis to give a complete picture of all the rules, conventions and meanings involved. There will be many fragments of knowledge relevant to the action and which perhaps have been deployed by an actor without coming up for criticism and without being consciously referenced, and in these circumstances individual actors will not be aware of the principles of their action, since no defence has been requested. Account analysis must be supplemented by further techniques.

Kelly's repertory grids can be used to explore particular features of the resources of competent actors which are insufficiently detailed in their accounts (Fransella and Bannister, 1977). Furthermore, use of the Kelly grid and of directed interrogation of actors requires that we use a theoretical instrument, which we would call a schedule of ideal resources, representing the knowledge a perfectly competent actor would have at his disposal. This idea comes from de Waele and Harré (1979), who have developed inventories of ideal forms of knowledge for persons in particular social categories. Comparison of the results of account analysis with a de Waele schedule controls the second phase of account analysis, which is a directed interrogation to pull out the material which has not been explicitly produced in defences and explanations in real life. De Waele has shown that there are people who, though they are required to act in certain kinds of milieu, lack the knowledge of the ideal competent actor. Ignorance of what is proper conduct may lead to all kinds of disturbed and violent reactions in social situations for which people are not conceptually prepared.

2. Observer attributions; outsiders, adopting the stance of anthropologists 'looking in' at the life of a strange tribe, have their own accounts to offer of events for which the 'natives' have offered theirs.

It is an essential part of the ethogenic methodology that actors' interpretations and observers' interpretations should be given equal weight initially and negotiated one with the other. Actors can supplement outside observations often in startling ways. For example, women's rituals among the Trobriand Islanders, mistaken by Malinowski for an economic activity, were seen to be relevant to the preservation of tribal honour when Annette Weiner talked to Trobriand women (Weiner, 1976). Observers as outsiders can supplement actors' understanding by making functional hypotheses available about certain kinds of social events. Actors are, of course, authoritative on the question of local meanings and the structure of interaction rituals, but observers may have a viewpoint which allows them to inform actors on such matters as patterns of unintended consequences, which may have much to do with the actual survival of a culture. However, observers' outsider attributions require explicit analytical models if they are to be scientific. Naïve empiricist methodology worked on the quite unfounded assumption that there was some 'real' behaviour which would be the foundation of all observations. The absurdity of such a doctrine has been amply demonstrated in theoretical discussions of epistemology in recent years (Walsh, 1972), so we need not detain ourselves with any critical commentary upon that old error. Analytical models are required to control the conceptual apparatus, in terms of which the identification and classification of features of action can be made. Just as Robert Boyle formulated a conceptual system for analysing the behaviour of gases, explicitly on the basis of an analogue with the behaviour of springs, so social psychologists who aspire to be scientific ought to be as careful as Boyle in laying out their analytical models. Ethogenic work has emphasized the utility of four models, and no doubt there will be many more. These are:

* dramaturgical model: treats episodes as if they were stage performances, yielding concepts like role, script, setting, costume, etc.;
* the liturgical model: treats social events as if they were rituals,

yielding concepts like action, conventional upshot, etc.;
* the game model: treats social events as if they were rule-bound competitions with conventionally defined winnings and losings, yielding concepts such as social strategy and social tactics, social success and social failure;
* the work model: treats social events as if they were the production of social products, yielding such concepts as the production of the means of production of social events, symbolic capital, and so on.

Each of these models casts an oblique light on different aspects of a complex reality. If we are to follow the natural sciences in their triumphant unravelling of the secrets of nature, we must resist any attempt at setting up a descriptive vocabulary for analysing social episodes which is not specifically rooted in a well-articulated set of analytical models.

The results of these model-controlled analyses must then be co-ordinated with the results of account analysis. Ideally, the analytical models employed by an outside observer ought to emerge as the very models that were in use amongst actors to create the social event in question, and which were reflected in their accounts. Then we would have a fully co-ordinated system. In the event of lack of co-ordination, and unless there is positive evidence to the contrary, we must suppose that a disparity between observers' analyses and actors' accounts shows that the reality with which we are dealing is complex. In no circumstances are we permitted to say that the account analyses are false or defective, since they are authoritative as to the moment by moment interpretations that actors put upon events in face to face interaction; therefore, if the actor intends to insult someone and the interactor interprets the actor's actions as insulting, no outsider's reinterpretation can take away the fact that a public insult has occurred.

EXAMPLE: 'FOOTBALL AGGRO'. The work of Peter Marsh (Marsh, Rosser and Harré, 1978) in investigating the social psychological factors and processes involved in the violence which seems to break out at football matches amongst the fans is a good exemplar of the ethogenic method at work in the investigation of resources. The project does not pretend to explain how particular football fans on particular occasions use their knowledge to put on performances, but rather reveals the kind of knowledge, the kind of interpretations of meaning, beliefs and so on which the fans share as competent members of their group.

Accounts appear on two different kinds of occasions. When the fans themselves are discussing 'aggro' within their own scheme, their accounts include quite distinctive rules for regulating action, for defining what is proper within the conventions of their micro-society. Those who break the rules, including the rules governing the interpretation of an action, are told the rules and then punished for breaking them. By investigating these accounts, Marsh was able to provide a systematic representation of members' knowledge, up to a certain point. Accounts were also produced in a second way, when Marsh himself asked fans to give their version of events. Typically, these accounts gave a version of events different from that which had appeared in the national press. Marsh's own 'outsider's analysis of 'aggro' depended on the employment of the model of social ritual, and of a career structure within the micro-society which was ordered by the outcome of the ritual events which the fans construed as 'fights'. Marsh's interactions with the fans took the form of a negotiation between himself as outsider proposing analytical models, and the fans as insiders dialectically relating their accounts to his. It turned out that accounts by other outsiders - particularly the descriptions of events in newspapers - were something yet again. They were best seen as social actions which themselves needed interpretation, forming a further and more complex framework in which the fans' actions were treated as part of a wider social activity in which other citizens, the police and little old ladies were engaged.

But the knowledge that was patently being deployed by the fans in categorizing members of their own and other groups into different social classes, relative to the aggro events which were the centre of the whole business, showed that some further investigative technique was required. To understand the way in which costumes were read as symbolic representations of social status, Marsh constructed a Kelly repertory grid to explore the code of interpreting different items of clothing. This yielded a very specific symbolic system which had perhaps never been explicitly formulated by any fan, but was patently operating as a social semantics throughout their activities. Stages in their careers were marked by the addition of scarves, boots, rosettes, and so on; symbolic accoutrements which, as their personal fame grew, were quietly dropped.

Two models were at work in the organization of this investigation. A general dramaturgical model controlled the way in which events were analysed on the larger scale: drawing our attention to specific settings for action, to the existence of a 'script' and to categories of persons who see to it that the script is realized in the proper fashion, and to the use of distinctive costume to identify particular social categories of actors. A liturgical model drew attention to the ritualistic aspects of much of the activity. The interpretative procedure by which fans themselves talk of these events as 'fights' is a device which is shared with the newspaper reporters, who use a similar language. But use of the liturgical model suggests a closer look at what constitutes a fight, bringing to the attention of the observer the symbolic nature of much of the action.

The final story of football aggro is, then, essentially complex and the yield from the kind of ethogenic investigation undertaken by Marsh is a representation of the ideal resources required by a fan perfectly competent in football aggro.

How, then, should the yield from such an investigation be structured? Other work has suggested that such systems of knowledge ought to be organized in the following way.

* The most general distinction is that between socially differentiated situations. For example, a football fan is capable of recognizing a distinction between a confrontation with the members of another club and that of the retrospective accounting in the pub after the game. Relative to distinct situations there are distinctive systems of conventions controlling the interpretation of action and propriety of conduct (Argyle, Furnham and Graham, 1981).

* Each situation has its arbiters of proper action; these are usually distinctive people, whose reactions are noticed by the others and used as a guide to correct behaviour.

* It has emerged from studies by Rosser (1977) and others that part of the resources needed by a competent social actor is a knowledge of the forms of self-presentation appropriate to particular situations. Should one appear shy, retiring, soft-spoken and biddable, or hard, abrasive, testy and counter-suggestible? Each kind of situation calls for a distinctive personal display, and part of the resources of a competent actor is a knowledge of the conventions governing such display.

How to study performance

Before we turn to detailed examples of methodologies for studying performance, it would be as well to remind ourselves of the basic theory of how actions are produced. We suppose that an individual actor, say a child squabbling over possession of toys, sets, or is set, a goal conceived within the demands of the social situation as seen by the child, who then conceives means to realize that end. But these means will generally involve intermediate ends, each with their own means. This creates a means-end hierarchy which could be represented graphically as in figure 1.

In some cases the relationship between the overriding end and the intermediate ends will be isomorphic with the distinction between the act or acts achieved in a social interaction and the actions by which they are performed. Each action can be seen as an accomplishment for which there are appropriate movements as means. So the structure of the means-end hierarchy ought to reflect the result of the analysis of the conduct of the persons engaged in the action in terms of the three-fold

Figure 1. A means-end structure

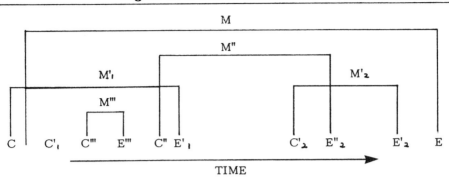

Key   C = cause
      M = means
      E = ends

1,2 ... = successive causes, means and ends
', ", ''' = levels of subordination

distinction, movement, action, act. In general, this theory takes on a cybernetic cast because the means-end hierarchy is further structured by the existence of feedback and feedforward loops so that goal setting can be continuously revised.

It is natural to interpret the nesting of the means-end structure as representing two different relationships between ends and intermediate ends. One relationship is that to which I have already alluded between acts, actions and movements, which may have no relation to any layout of 'thoughts' in real time and could be of classificatory significance only. On the other hand, there are many incidents and activities in which the intermediate ends temporarily precede the ultimate end and the graphical representation of the hierarchy can also be thought of as representing the time span controlled by particular goals, so that a long-term end can be linked to the terminology current in phenomenological psychology. I shall call the representation of long-term ends <u>projects</u> and the representation of short-term ends <u>intentions.</u> Means for realizing both projects and intentions may be very varied and be represented by items as different as rules, conventions, habits, manuals, prayerbooks, exhortations of shamans, and so on.

How one devises a method for studying the way in which means-end hierarchies are formed and the role they play in the pro-

duction of action as a real process depends upon the distinction drawn above between projects and intentions. Projects are relatively permanent features of a person's life and the kind of investigation that one would undertake to find out about them would be very similar to account analysis and its dialectic with observer's attributions that has been illustrated earlier. Projects have something of the same character as the permanent resource structure of social knowledge that an actor draws upon in performances. The most powerful method that has so far been devised for studying projects is the de Waele assisted autobiography, in which by a systematic analysis and augmentation of an individual's recollections, the investigator and his team are able to tease out various themes that are present in a particular life course. Some of these themes are sufficiently clearly directed towards goals to serve as the representation of projects. To become a competent violinist, or be a graduate or a taken-for-granted member of the upper-middle class, would all be projects in this sense.

It is more difficult to develop a methodology for studying means-end hierarchies as they exist in the production of real actions. The problem that has to be solved derives directly from the feature most prominent in real human action, namely the direction of attention to the goal and away from the means by which it is realized.

People become so absorbed in the action that they pay little attention to the means-end hierarchies that theory suggests they are generating in order to perform it. We need a method for studying intention/rule-of-realization pairs which are actually in use at a particular moment in real time. It should be quite obvious that the use of account analysis cannot assist in the study of performance and its mode of production. There is no particular reason to think that a person in normal circumstances would be able to give a moment by moment description of how he or she set intermediate goals, ran over their existing knowledge of appropriate means, chose from various alternatives that which was most suitable for the occasion in question and then followed it. It would be very surprising indeed if a person in normal circumstances maintained conscious attention to such processes. Indeed, it might be the case that if one were to do so, action would be paralysed. Fortunately, there is a psychological phenomenon, the exploitation of which has permitted the development of a methodology to study the production of action in real time. It has been observed by linguists and others that when the system (whatever it might be) that an individual is using to produce a speech or some other kind of public performance is on the point of breakdown, there is a hesitation in the smooth flow of the action. At these points research has shown that the individual actor has become momentarily conscious of the means-end hierarchy, or some portion of it in use at that time. Perhaps this is an adaptive psychological device by which breakdown is dealt with and smooth action restored. By taking an actor back over a recording of a performance to those moments where there are marked hesitations in the action, the momentary conscious representation in the intention-rule pair in play at that moment can be made available for report.

Two distinct methodologies have been developed from this phenomenon.

*   By examining a number of parallel cases and looking for different points of breakdown in similar kinds of action, production, recording, and playing back for the actor, it is possible

(at least in principle) to cover a considerable amount of the production process in so far as the random distribution of accidents allows one to investigate it from beginning to end. But one can hardly rely on accidents to achieve overall coverage. Indeed, there is some evidence that there are certain nodal points around which accidents tend to cluster. However, it is still worth the attempt and the work of Hacker (1982) has demonstrated that, at least for certain short action-sequences, the recording, playback and investigation of hesitation phenomena do pay off in that the actor can report having paid attention to a fragment of the means-end hierarchy.

*   But conscious representation of means-end hierarchies would be a far more powerful method if the breakdown could be controlled. Considerable success has been achieved by Von Cranach and his team in setting up relatively realistic social events in which there is a continuous breakdown achieved by subtle choice of task and actor (Von Cranach and Harré, 1982).

EXAMPLE: 'WRAPPING A PRAM'. Von Cranach's most successful attempt at contriving continuous breakdown depended upon choosing actors to work together on projects that were already known to involve disagreements as to how to proceed. In these circumstances he was able to demonstrate that there was practically continuous breakdown of automatic, smooth-working means-end hierarchies. In some cases almost every step was queried and each means-end element negotiated. The task was complex. A married couple were asked to wrap a pram in paper and string. Various kinds of material were available, including strong but ugly paper, rope, ribbon and so on, as well as fragile but decorative wrapping material. In some cases the husband and wife team shared a very large proportion of the goals and intermediate goals that were involved in the process. In those cases there was very little breakdown and little access to consciously represented means-end structures. But in some cases the goals were sufficiently different from the start to produce continuous breakdown. For instance, in some cases the husband wished to wrap the pram strongly without particular attention to aesthetics, while the wife was less interested in security and more in appearance. In those cases every step was negotiated and every move queried. Von Cranach was able to record these negotiation processes and to discover a large part of the means-end hierarchy.

This methodology is comparatively new. It has been used in Eastern Europe for the study of industrial processes, and has yielded much the same kind of result (Hacker, 1982). It is clear that the production of action does involve means-end hierarchies and that a good deal of the goal setting is available to conscious representation if difficulties occur.

However, not all means-end hierarchies involve conscious or unconscious cognitive goal setting and a search of our resources of knowledge for the appropriate means of realization. We have already noticed that there are occasions on which the actions performed by human beings in co-ordinative episodes are more like habits, and even sometimes pre-programmed routines. In such cases one can use experiments of the traditional kind, identifying dependent and independent variables and testing for relationships by manipulation. But this simple methodology can work only if we are justified in presuming that each habit or routine is independent of other parts of the action; that is, that the action sequence is not structurally integrated in such a way that the meaning that each element has depends upon its location in the structure. It is clear that relative to the act-action-movement distinction reflected in the structure of means-end hierarchies, the level at which experimental manipulation will work is that of the lowest subroutines, since they can be shifted from episode to episode as wholes. A kiss is an osculation, whether given by Judas Iscariot or the President of France. It is only when we rise to the level of action and act that the structural limitation on experiments becomes crucial. Since all our taxonomies must be 'top down', that is, we must use acts to identify actions and actions to identify relevant movements, the simple experiment can find a place in empirical

social psychology - and indeed various other branches of psychology, industrial, developmental, and so on - only as the very last stage of an empirical investigation. It is called for only when we think we have analysed a means-end hierarchy so finely that we have reached the subroutines which are common to a very large number of different structures.

However, this work must be associated with developmental studies to attempt to identify the origins of subroutines in order to distinguish between those subroutines which are physiologically based and derive more or less directly from genetic endowment, and those which are the product of social phenomena like training, education and so on. Bruner (1973) has shown that in many cases it is a combination of these conditions, genetic pre-programming and socially determined educational practices, that builds up a complex routine out of subroutines. Shotter (1975) has described this as the acquisition of personal powers on the basis of natural powers.

How to test one's hypotheses
Keeping in mind the methodology of the natural sciences, which has proved so successful, one should check an analysis by recreating the original entity. What would be an analogue of this traditional test procedure in the analysis of the psychological phenomena which generate social activity? We already have an institution found in almost every society in which syntheses of social reality are routinely performed, namely drama. The playwright and the actor, working with a producer, are concerned to reproduce a version of a slice of life. Of course, there are all kinds of different projects involved in the performance of drama, ranging from mere entertainment to religious ritual and symbolic representations of universal truths. For our purposes we need pay attention to only one feature of drama, namely that aspect in which the events that are the staged simulations of social episodes are like or unlike, convincing or unconvincing representations, of naturalistic episodes of social life (Ginsburg, 1979).

It turns out that there are two distinct ways in which the relative naturalism of a performance deliberately staged is tested. Some systematic work on this has been done by Coppieters (1977) and Mixon (1972). In their investigations they each demonstrated a different way in which verisimilitude is testable. Coppieters studied audience reactions very closely. At different times after a performance he compared an audience's expectations, moment by moment experiences, and remembered reactions. He was able to demonstrate that people have strong intuitions as to the social and psychological authenticity of the staged performance.

It is hardly surprising that audiences have strong intuitive judgements as to whether or not a social event as simulated is a reasonable representation of real life. More interesting still is the result that Mixon first demonstrated, and has since been amply confirmed (also by Coppieters). Actors themselves become emotionally involved in the action as if the events were real (Zimbardo, 1973). Mixon's classical study of the Milgram experiment involved hypotheses as to the rule systems, means-end structures, etc., that were involved in the various reactions to Milgram's instructions to deliver dangerous electric shocks. By asking the actors - in this case ordinary folk recruited as actors - to take part in several playlets whose scenarios were various versions of the rules, interpretations and means-end hierarchies thought to be involved in the original 'Milgram' experiments, Mixon was able to demonstrate that even though the actors were fully aware that what was occurring was a mere simulation of the real events, they nevertheless experienced genuine emotions and strong intuitions as to the plausibility of reconstruction. In this way, by using the results of the two methods outlined above, the intuitions of the folk can be used as a direct test of the plausibility of the proposed rules and interpretations. This parallels exactly the use of native speaker's grammatical intuitions to test the correctness of grammar by using them to construct trial sentences.

The exercises

The methodology outlined in this chapter does not lend itself to short, simple, practical studies. Ethogenic investigations are aimed at uncovering the social knowledge and skill required for some fairly substantial form of life, such as the intimate culture of a family, the modes of adaptation to life in a monastery, football violence, and so on. For the purposes of this manual three documents have been chosen, representing typical social episodes culled from specific ways of life. Only certain limited aspects of the actual events that took place are recorded in the documents. Appendix 1 is a transcript of a commonplace episode with which most people are familiar at first hand. But more is going on in the consultation than the exchange of symptoms and cure. The second document (Appendix 2) records an accounting session directed to episodes which take place off-stage, so to speak, and of which we, as analysts, have no direct record. In the third exercise (Appendix 3) a record of an episode and of an account of this episode are both presented. The fourth exercise uses documents prepared by the students themselves. Copies of the documents to be studied should be made available to each student.

In each case the exercise involves the analysis of written records of the speech and other social performances which formed part of a social episode. Written records or documents are objects of interest in their own right. For instance, one can ask how they are created out of the material available and how the selection and presentation of material is related to the interests of the person who wrote the document. It is well established that grammatical form may be a poor guide to the social force of the speech: for instance, the sentence 'Why don't we have supper now?' is not really a question. The documents presented here could be quite misleading as to the social processes of structured interactions they purport to represent if we took account only of their obvious linguistic features. To overcome such difficulties involves a highly skilled technique, which students will be able to test for themselves in exercise 3.

Each individual student is expected to offer a tentative analysis of each document. A useful method for coding one's results is the Social Cognitive Matrix in which the social knowledge of each participant involved in the episode, described and manifested in their speech and action, can be set out systematically (table 1).

Empirical studies have shown that individual people know a great many such systems of rules and interpretations, sometimes as many as 13 or 14.

The cognitive resources of each person involved in an episode should be coded in this form. Further detail could be elicited by the use of Kelly Repertory Grids to amplify particular 'cells' (cf. Fransella and Bannister, 1977) had we direct access to the original participants.

This matrix representation allows for the systematic analysis of episodes which consist of more than one phase of social interaction, where the situation may be redefined, and the rules and personality display thereby changed. It also allows for the possibility that each interactant may see the social forces and meaning of the episode differently, so that each actor may yield a different matrix.

Discussions among the student group members, subsequent to the preparation of an analysis of participants' social knowledge, can serve not only to sharpen the students' analytical skills but may also help to open up for the students the idea that any social episode may be in reality a complex and multifaceted entity, which is capable of several complementary analyses,

each of which is true. It is not at all uncommon for several different social events to be going on at once, all within the same episode.

Ideally exercises of this sort should be carried out on material created by the students themselves, using video and audio recording, and supplemented with their own observations. Only in a 'multi-media' approach are the ways people create and manage everyday life likely to be reasonably comprehensively represented.

All four exercises are aimed at discovering social resources; that is, the knowledge of rules and interpretations competent actors require. Real-time performance studies are more difficult. Techniques for studying the use people make of means-end hierarchies in bringing their resources to bear on their conduct can be found in Von Cranach and Harré (1982).

Exercise 1
This exercise involves analysing a documentary representation of a social episode to detect the social meaning of the actions performed - for instance, whether what someone says is a plea, a request, a reprimand, and so on - and the means by which the occasion is used as a platform or stage on which to show to others the kind of person one wants to be seen to be. By answering the following questions students should begin to 'get a feel' for the kind of analysis involved.

Table 1

Person A

Knowledge unit	Social situation as defined	Rule system presumed to be operative	Personality displayed	Arbiter of social propriety
1 (Specimen entry)	Informal: tea party as friendship ritual in college hostel	Guest served first, milk in, sugar offered, etc. Topic for talk rules, etc. Arrival and departure rules, etc.	Solicitous, formal; symbols: skirt? tie?	Imagined presence of parent
2	Situation 2	Rules 2	Personality 2	Arbiter 2
(etc.)				

* What was the ostensible or official goal of the interaction?
* By what speech forms (e.g. questions and answers) was it carried forward? What vocabulary did it employ; for example, everyday, technical, typically male, and so on?
* What was the 'actual' goal of the participants in interacting the way they did? If different from the official goal, by what signs are alternative goals manifested?
* By what speech and action was the project to achieve an unofficial goal carried forward?
* Describe the personalities of the various interactants. Identify any specific speech forms in which those personalities were particularly clearly presented.
* Who 'makes the running', so to speak?

Findings should be set out as three sets of 'rules':

* rules for defining the meaning of the events that took place; for example, how is reassurance achieved?
* rules for controlling the development of the episode; for example, how are diversions cut off?
* conventions for the display of personality and social role; for example, the use of 'we' rather than 'I' by those in authority.

For a discussion of more detailed analyses of the social meaning of pronouns, see Kroger (in press).

Exercise 2
A common task for account analysts is to identify a complex hierarchy of definitions with which a certain category of actions is being managed in justificatory talk. For instance, by studying apologies one might be able to build a classification of insults. One might start by differentiating verbal insults from insulting gestures. Were insults based on physical failings treated differently from those based on character defects? Are any categories of insults so deadly that no apology would possibly repair the social damage they inflict?

In the relevant document (Appendix 2) a schoolboy gives an account of what bullying means to him. The account is also a social action in itself. It must be seen as a production for the ears of the investigator, aimed at displaying what the speaker conceives to be an appropriate personality. Students should first use this document to set up a hierarchical classification scheme for acts of bullying, and then relate the justifications for bullying, implicit in the account, to that scheme. Students should be reminded that their classification schemes are a reflection of the document. It was produced for a complex of social purposes. The second stage of analysis involves identifying some of those purposes. Can any of the features of any of the definitions of bullying that are offered be related to those purposes? In a full-scale study of bullying this definitional study would be related to studies of episodes defined as bullying which are actually occurring in a school playground, and to the moment by moment commentary on those sequences provided by victim and aggressor.

There is no special reason for using the particular document printed in Appendix 2 as the material for this exercise. Students (and tutors) may find it profitable to create their own documents representing occasions on which someone provided a commentary on a social event. In no circumstances ought this way of creating documents be called 'data collection'. The document is the datum, not that which it purports to describe. The document is a text, for which the students must provide an interpretation.

Exercise 3
A social episode is created by the interactions of two or more actors. In the course of an episode various social effects are brought about, such as change of an actor's status. Sometimes the actors have similar and sometimes dissimilar projects. To understand an episode we have to try to find out what projects the actors might have, so that our study can be directed to the way actors go about realizing their aims and plans. This is what Goffman (1969) has called the 'strategic' aspect of an interaction.

But to work all this out one must first be able to identify the social force of what the actors have done or said, and what they have said about what they have done, are doing, or are about to do. This involves an assignment of meanings to the events that make up the episode. For practical reasons the exercises in this chapter have to be confined to unravelling the meaning of a reported conversation. Real life involves much more. But even to read a conversation you must be able to 'hear' it, so to speak. To facilitate this students are asked to practise the skill of reading for social meaning by running through the following excerpt and underlining the words which they think would have been stressed by the speaker. This should be followed by a second run through in which stress is placed on different words. Students should test their intuition by asking themselves and their fellow students whether this new stress pattern alters the interpretation of the social force of what the actors are saying.

Stress markings should be checked against those suggested by Kreckel in the second extract in this section: her stress markings are derived from a discussion with the family amongst whom the conversation took place as to the social force of the speeches and the means by which this force was indicated and understood (Kreckel, 1982). They represent the actors' account of how they conducted a family discussion.

Using one of the stress-marked versions of this conversation, specific social interpretations of speech incidents should be identified, using common-sense categories such as plea, complaint, and so on. These interpretations are hypotheses which can be tested by following the conversation through to pick up later speech incidents that seem to be dependent on particular interpretations of earlier remarks. At this stage the structure of the episode can be set out in terms of the categories that have been tested in interpreting the social force of the speeches recorded. Regularities, say between complaints and counter-complaints, can be expressed as rules.

Two hypothetical conversational fragments could now be constructed, using common-sense categories such as those used to analyse the example above. One fragment should preserve the overall social force of the conversation and one should change it. These abstract structures can be fleshed out in imagined speech. Thus, if Complaint-Remedy appears as a regularity, it could be fleshed out as 'Why don't you take any notice of what I say?' 'Sorry, I was thinking of something else.' The technique of creating a dialogue from speech-act categories is required in the construction of plausible scenarios to test the intuitive reasonableness of the structures one has built up on the basis of hypotheses about the rules followed explicitly or implicitly by the actors (for more details see Harré, 1979, chapter 3).

The imagined conversations should be tested on other students for 'naturalness'. In this way intuitions of social propriety can be used to test hypotheses about the expressive techniques used by speakers to convey social force.

Exercise 4

Ceremonial sequences: among the items of social knowledge a competent actor must have access to are the rituals by which social relations are transformed from one stage to another. We are all familiar with formal rituals, such as marriage and degree giving. But there are also informal rituals. For example, it has been suggested (Douglas, 1972) that different forms of hospitality can be used to mark successive stages in a relationship. Since the events in question are usually spread out over some considerable time students undertaking this exercise should have been asked to keep a 'friendship' diary for two or three months. In this diary they would record the sequences of invitation to coffee, meals, etc., through which a relationship was built up and ritualistically ratified. There has been some controversy about how far such rituals permeate the whole of society. Students might care to compare their results with the sequences set out by Douglas in her article 'Deciphering a meal' (Douglas, 1972).

Strengths and limitations of ethogenic analysis

The method of studying the way people talk

about and justify their actions to one another, coupled with the use of analytical models such as the dramaturgical analogy, is meant to be used to investigate a whole form of life. The actors are conceived as knowing what is required of them, though that knowledge may be divided amongst the members of a group. The basic psychological process involved in social action is taken to be expressed in the cybernetic model, here called a means-end hierarchy. In practice this will often be experienced by an actor as following a rule or convention to realize some intention or other. What is intended is thought of as part of what is required to carry out some project, such as acquiring a hoped-for social status.

The method is not addressed to the study of those smaller-scale units of human behaviour that have been referred to here as 'routines'. The study of how someone puts together a complex sequence of movements into a hand shake or a deferential retreat or something of that sort would require quite different methods. There are also limitations on how far one can generalize from the way reasoning presents itself to someone as he or she is consciously working something out, the process assessed by the methods of Von Cranach, to the structure of non-conscious 'information' processing. In the former case the conventions and mode of organization of one's native language play a central part, but it is not at all clear how to understand the processes involved in the latter.

Acknowledgements

I am grateful to David Pendelton, Andrew Ockwell and Marga Kreckel for the use of material from their researches which forms the documents printed in the Appendices.

REFERENCES

Argyle, M., Furnham, A. and Graham, J.A. (1981) Social Situations. Cambridge: Cambridge University Press.

Bruner, J. (1973) Organization of early skilled action. Child Development 44, 1-11.

Collett, P. and Marsh, P. (1974) Patterns of public behaviour: collision avoidance on a pedestrian crossing. Semiotica, 12, 281-289.

Coppieters, F. (1977) Theoretical recollections: a psychological study. Doctoral dissertation, University of Antwerp.

de Waele, J.-P. and Harré, R. (1979) Autobiography as a psychological method. In G.P. Ginsburg (ed.), Emerging Strategies in Social Psychological Research. Chichester: Wiley.

Douglas, M. (1972) Deciphering a meal. Daedalus, Winter.

Fransella, F. and Bannister, D. (1977) A Manual for Repertory Grid Technique. London: Academic Press.

Ginsburg, G.P. (1979) The effective use of role-playing in social psychological research. In G.P. Ginsburg (ed.), Emerging Strategies in Social Psychological Research. Chichester: Wiley.

Goffman, E. (1969) Strategic Interaction. Philadelphia: University of Pennsylvania Press.

Hacker, W. (1982) Objective and subjective organization of working activities. In M. Von Cranach and R. Harré, The Analysis of Action: Recent theoretical and empirical advances. Cambridge: Cambridge University Press.

Harper, R.G., Wiens, A.M. and Metarezzo, J.D. (1978) Non-Verbal Communication: The state of the art. New York: Wiley.

Harré, R. (1979) Social Being. Oxford: Blackwell.

Harré, R. and Secord, P.F. (1973) The Explanation of Social Behaviour. Oxford: Blackwell.

Hollis, M. (1977) Models of Man. Cambridge: Cambridge University Press.

Kreckel, M. (1982) Communicative Acts and Shared Knowledge in Natural Discourse. London: Academic Press.

Kroger, R. (in press) Explorations in ethogeny: with special reference to the rules of address. American Psychologist.

Lyman, S.M. and Scott, M.B. (1970) A Sociology of the Absurd. New York: Appleton-Century-Crofts.

Marsh, P., Rosser, E. and Harré, R. (1978) The Rules of Disorder. London: Routledge & Kegan Paul.

Mixon, D. (1972) Instead of deception. Journal for the Theory of Social Behaviour, 2, 145-174.

Rosser, E. (1977) New directions in social psychology: the ethogenic approach with special reference to adolescent perceptions of the social world. B. Litt. dissertation, Oxford University.

Shotter, J. (1975) Acquired powers: the transformation of natural into personal powers. In R. Harre (ed.), Personality. Oxford: Blackwell.

Von Cranach, M. and R. Harré (1982) The Analysis of Action: Recent theoretical and empirical advances. Cambridge: Cambridge University Press.

Walsh, D. (1972) Varieties of positivism. In P. Filmer et al, New Directions in Sociological Theory. London: Collier Macmillan.

Weiner, A.B. (1976) Women of Virtue, Men of Renown. Austin, Texas and London: University of Texas Press.

Zimbardo, P.G. (1973) The mind is a formidable jailer: a Pirandellian prison. The New York Times, 8 April 1973.

APPENDIX 1 (document for exercise 1)

Doctor (DR) seated at desk; knock at the door.

DR Come in.

Mother (M) and daughter (D) enter.

M	Morning.	
DR	Morning, hello, sit yourselves down.	Smiling, gesturing to chair.
M	(to D) What have you got to say?	
DR	(to D) Hello.	Still smiling.
D	Hello.	Generally, not looking at anyone.
DR	Sit yourself down.	
M	I haven't had time to read it yet. I was going to read it on the way down. What does it say? Tell me.	
DR	What?	Still smiling.

Patient starts to read anyway so no reply given. Patient reading while removing daughter's coat. Reads for approximately nine seconds.

DR	Don't let it worry you.	
M	It needn't worry me?	
DR	No.	
M	Oh all right.	Immediately looks up.
DR	Now what can I do for you?	Waves hand.
M	We've got boils on our backside ... again.	
DR	Again?	Looks away at notes.
M	(to D) Stand up. Can you stand up?	Picking her up.
DR	Let's have a look.	DR has been sitting back in chair looking at mother up to this point. Now starts looking at daughter.
M	(to D) With your back to Dr S. That's a good girl. Stand up there and we'll show him your bum. There's a good girl.	
M	(to DR) Now they haven't really cleared up and gone away sufficiently but I've now got to the stage where I think that something really ought to be done about it.	
DR	Uh huh. Are these the same ones that she's had or do they keep on ...	Examining bottom.
M	Oh no ...	
DR	Keep on ...	
M	You can see all down her leg look.	
DR	Uh huh. See, all right.	Reassurance to daughter whilst stroking affected area with finger. Daughter twisting to look.
M	(to D) Stand up nice and straight.	

DR Yes, they're leaving little lumps aren't they?	
M Yes ... and on the other side you see. But it's only round ...	
DR It's only inside the ...	Strokes relevant area.
M Yes, but you see she's dry at night now.	
DR She's quite dry ... yes.	DR moves away, looks at mother again.
M I mean fair enough she wears a nappy because I don't want her ... not to wear a nappy until after we've moved in, in case we sort of go back a step and then it will be ... you know but er ... she's dry, completely dry at night.	

Note that the gaze pattern changes at this point to a regulative question and answer pattern.

DR Has she had a cold at all? A runny nose or anything.	
M No.	
DR And she's been alright in herself?	
M Yes apart from a cold she had. Yes alright.	
DR And you saw, well, Dr H. ...	Looking at notes.
M Dr H I think was the last one we saw.	
DR About four months ago wasn't it?	
M Yes, well, maybe. I didn't think it was as long as that but perhaps it would ... Yes it might be.	
DR Oh.	Continues looking. Keeps mother talking.
M And, er, we bought some Sizal soap?	
DR Uh huh.	
M And, er, we washed with that but you know it didn't seem to ...	
DR Uh huh ... OK. No sort of runny nose or crusting in the nose or anything like that or so on?	
M No.	
DR All right.	
	Looks away and changes seating position completely. Moves to leg and feet under the desk. This changes the phase of the consultation? Takes out pen.
I think if it's persisting like this er ... In fact I saw you before that didn't I?	Looking away reading notes.
M Yes well, she's had them for I should think about a year now.	
DR Uh huh.	Still writing.

M	Well I mean, I don't know but ...	
D	Go in Rober.	
M	You're going back in the Rover, yes.	
DR	Uh huh.	Still writing.
M	Show off.	Laughs.
DR	Uh huh. What?	Still writing. Laughs.
	Oh yes.	Moves head from side to side, sharing in the joke.

Pause

DR	I'll give you some er ... some penicillin. You should give her one spoonful three times a day, for a week alright? I think you should carry on ...	
		Changes posture/seating position. Looks at mother from this point.
	with some antiseptic baths ...	
M	Yes.	
DR	I mean it is just a superficial er ... sort of skin infection.	
M	I tell you the stuff that cleared it up last time that you gave me was the stuff I put in the bath.	DR looks away. Starts up.
DR	Uh huh.	Still writing.
M	Whatever that was.	
DR	Hibitane.	Still writing.
M	Er ... but that cleared it up.	
DR	Do you remember how big the bottle was?	Reaching for a form.
M	Only a little one. An ordinary ...	
	ordinary medicine size.	Gestures to show size but DR not looking. Laughing.
DR	Yes.	Looks at mother. Laughs.
		Takes book for reference.
M	You sort of know that ...	Gestures again to show size. DR looking at book.

Long pause while mother looks at child, looks around room. DR consulting book and begins writing prescription.

DR	Er ... It's a big bottle. I had a letter from er ... I can't remember who it was now ...	Still busy with papers.
M	(indistinct)	
DR	T.	
M	(indistinct) Yes.	
DR	Er ... They're supplying all the ...	Adjusts seating position to look at mother.
M	Yes, I've given up ... I mean I've ...	Looks away.
DR	Mm.	

M   Especially I ... you know I ...
I started my period last night.
That just about did it. Ha. And
er ... I can't really ... Can't
be bothered with my ... You know
... If ... If I knew ... that I
was going to ...

      Gestures.
      Still looking away.
      Looks at doctor.

    ... happen within a year, then
fair enough. Do you know what
I mean?

DR   Mm.

      Nods, still looking at her.

M   Er ... I don't ... I've got to
the stage where I can't even talk
about it.

      Attempts to compose herself. Adjusts seating
      position. Puts down child. Looks away,
      fumbles with paper, deep breath, straightens
      skirt, shakes head, waves hand, stands up.

D   Are you coming?

M   Er ... I'd better go.

      Stationary.

DR   Do you want to talk about
it? I mean ...

M   Not really ...
Not really er ...

      Waves hand.
      Standing obliquely to DR.
      Raises hand to lips (obviously on the point
      of tears).

    Because I feel such an idiot.

    Er, I don't want to talk about
it.
Oh dear.
I can't walk out like this, can
I? 'Bye.

      Brushes hair with hand, turning even more
      away from DR.
      Heading for door, sniffs, takes door handle,
      stops.
      Sniffs.

DR   Do you want to come and talk about
it some other time when you're
not ...

M   No it's hard to get rid of ... I
won't let go you see.

DR

M   Cheers anyway. Thanks very much.

DR   Alright. 'Bye.

      Laughs.
      Laughs.
      Laughs.
      Exits.
      Looks away.

End

APPENDIX 2 (document for exercise 2)

Paul (P)   What do you mean 'bully'?
Interviewer (I)   Well that's for you to decide. You tell me what you think bullying is.
P   What, picking on other kids, or smaller ones or bigger ones?
I   Well, that's for you to say.
P   Depends on what you call bullying. Some people just pick on 'em or beat 'em, you know, hit them. Some people tease 'em. There's a lot that goes on around here now.
I   There's a lot of ...
P   More of a joke really. Most people do it. More of a laugh.
    Some people take it serious, some don't.
I   Do you think it's possible that sometimes if you mean it as a joke, it's not taken as a joke by others?
P   It means you're word powerful. If you say summat and they get offended but you say it as a joke. They say 'Oh Miss they are bullying me.' Some of them go running to teachers all the time.
I   Who gets bullied?
P   Mainly the Pakis. Mainly.
I   Why's that?
P   Well, for what they are.
I   Why do you think that, then?
P   I don't really like them, but ... I don't really pick on them.
I   What about the chap outside? (Referring to tall, easy-going Pakistani kid)
P   Well, he's all right. He's our pal. Get on well with him.
I   Well, he's a Paki, isn't he?
P   He's a Paki, but I still don't like them.
    I don't like many blacks, but some are all right. Some in't.
I   What about F? (Referring to black kid known to be P's closest mate)
P   Well, he's all right. I go around with him. Some blacks get on my nerves.
I   Don't some whites get on your nerves as well?
P   Oh yes. I mean, if someone causes trouble they can look for trouble. And they don't. Mainly black v. white. What it usually is, anyway.
I   The thing I don't understand, Paul, is that you say it's mainly black v. white, but one of your best mates is black. And you just said it's Pakis that get picked on. And I said 'Well, what about the one outside?', and you said 'Oh no, well, he's a good bloke.'
P   Depends if you know 'em. I mean I know him. We get on all right. But you get some other kid, third or fourth year or summat you don't know. You always as they come past say 'Paki' or 'Greasy git' or summat. It's so common. Everyone says it. Even the girls say it.
I   Don't you think some kids might be hurt by that?
P   Some of them are. Some of them go around the corner and call you all sorts of names.
I   Doesn't it matter to you that they are hurt by this?
P   Depends who it is. Some of my friends. Probably yes. I think about it and won't do it again. Someone I don't know when you cross the road and you never seen them before, wouldn't care.
I   What sorts of people would you have as your friends?
P   A lot of people I know. Mainly from this school. I mean D, and other people I never knew them before I came to this school. We have our arguments. But it's all in a joke way. Some take it serious and some don't.

APPENDIX 3 (document for exercise 3)

<u>Note:</u> the first transcription of the conversation between Marian and Tom is printed in the way it would appear in a novel. But to rid ourselves of our normal ways of understanding printed conversations our usual ways of representing conversation must be eliminated. Comparison between the ordinary (the first) representation and the stress-marked (the second) unpunctuated version of the conversation should make this clear.

Throughout the episode Marian is eating.

T   Important are they?
M   ... to me they are. To you they probably don't mean a bloody thing, but there you are.
T   Such as?
M   One, for a start, get the main one over with ...
T   Marriage.
M   Yes.
T   Well, what did I tell you what was it, about two ...
M   I know what you told me - you told Mum different.
T   I see ...
M   You told Mum different.
T   I told ... What I told your mum love is only what I told you a few weeks ago.
M   You never told me you'd never marry me, that's what you told Mum.
T   I see .. that's it ... we've had this out with your mum already, love. I didn't say I wouldn't marry you.
M   Nobody bloody includes me.
T   Because I tell you, I said I didn't fancy getting married just at the moment, not just yet.
M   Why not?
T   I want to wait until we've been in the flat right?
M   I don't want to go in the flat again.
T   I just ... hang about ... see, you won't hear me out.
M   Go on then. Go on.
T   I want to wait until we've been in the flat, right?
M   Yes.
T   Been in there a couple of months, got the place all done out, get all the knick-knacks in there, right?
M   It don't want much doing to it, and we ain't got many knick-knacks.
T   But I mean ... I tell you what ...
M   So that is a poor excuse, I'm afraid, and if you can't come up with something better than that then you know what to do.
T   Well I told you about the 27th of April and that yous made that date up between yous, didn't yous?
M   If it was left up to you to do any arranging at all you'd never bloody get it done.
T   Course I would.
M   Arseholes.
T   Well, I just don't like ... outsiders, people, lot of people interfering.
M   Well bloody do it yourself then, other people wouldn't interfere now, would they? You made a promise to me and you're bloody ...
T   All right, then, all right then, fair enough then. I'll get a place, I'll get a place to my liking, and that, and get married then.
M   Oh to your liking then? Doesn't matter about me.
T   All right, then, our liking then. You can't move in just like that. Can you?
M   We've got most of it anyway.
T   Such as?
M   We've got paper for a start. That's a good start that is.
T   What paper's that?

M Wallpaper, dear.

T What - them five rolls what you got down at your Gran's or something? Well, where will they go? What will they cover?

M I don't know. I mean you could put something on one wall and have a contrast on the others. It don't cost much for a tin of paint. At least that's something done. It don't cost much for a tin of paint, does it?

T No, it doesn't.

M Well, there you are, then. We're halfway there already with it decorated.

T Oh you are.

M Don't you laugh at me, mate.

T I'm not. I've always got a smile on my face. You know that.

M Arseholes.

T I have.

M You have not, you have not.

T I have, I'm always happy.

M Arseholes. So you're going to name a date then?

T Yeah. But it won't be in the next two months, though - two or three months.

M Why not?

T I don't want to get married in the next two or three months.

M Why not?

T I just don't want to.

Stress markers: Kreckel (1982)

T <u>important</u> are they

M to <u>me</u> they <u>are</u>

to <u>you</u> they probably don't mean a bloody thing but <u>there</u> you are

T <u>such</u> as

M <u>one</u>

for a <u>start</u>

get the <u>main</u> one over with

T <u>marriage</u>

M <u>yes</u>

T well what did I <u>tell</u> you

what was it <u>about</u> two

M I know what you told <u>me</u>

<u>you</u> told Mum <u>different</u>

T I see

M <u>you</u> told Mum <u>different</u>

T I told

what I told your <u>Mum</u> love is only what I told you a few <u>weeks</u> ago

M <u>you</u> never told me you'd <u>never</u> marry me

that's what you told <u>Mum</u>

T I see that's <u>it</u>

we've had this out with your Mum <u>already</u> love

I didn't say I <u>wouldn't</u> marry you

M nobody bloody includes <u>me</u>

T because I <u>tell</u> you I said I didn't fancy getting married just at the <u>moment</u> not just <u>yet</u>

M why <u>not</u>

T I want to wait until we've <u>been</u> in the flat <u>right</u>

M I don't <u>want</u> to go in the flat <u>again</u>

T I

just <u>hang</u> about

<u>see</u> you won't hear me out

M go on then go on
T I want to wait until we've been in the flat right
M yes
T been in there a couple of months
   got the place all done out
   get all the knick knacks in there right
M it don't want much doing to it and we ain't got many knick-knacks
T but I mean
   I tell you what
M so that is a poor excuse I'm afraid and if you can't come up with something better than
   that then you know what to do
T well I told you about the 27th of April and that yous made that date up between yous
   didn't yous
M if it was left up to you to do any arranging at all you'd never bloody get it done
T course I would
M arseholes
T well I just don't like outsiders
   people lot of people interfering
M well bloody do it yourself then other people wouldn't interfere now would they
   you made a promise to me and you're bloody
T all right then
   all right then
   fair enough then I'll get a place
   I'll get a place to my liking and that and get married then
M oh to your liking then
   doesn't matter about me
T all right then
   our liking then
   you can't move in just like that
   can you
M we've got most of it anyway
T such as
M we've got paper for a start
   that's a good start
   that is
T what paper's that
M wallpaper dear
T what them five rolls what
   you got down at your Gran's
   or something
   well where will they go
   what will they cover
M I don't know
   I mean you could put something on one
   wall and have a contrast on the others
   it don't cost much for a tin of paint
   at least that's something done
   it don't cost much for a tin of paint does it
T no it doesn't
M well there you are then
   we're halfway there already
   with it decorated
T oh you are
M don't you laugh at me mate
T I'm not

```
        I've always got a smile on my face
        you know that
M       arseholes
T       I have
M       you have not
        you have not
T       I have
        I'm always happy
M       arseholes
        so
        you're going to name a date then
T       yea but it won't be in the next two months though
        two or three months
M       why not
T       I don't want to get married in the next two or three months
M       why not
T       I just don't want to
```

Part two Technique applications

6

Speech style and employment selection: the matched-guise technique
Peter Ball and Howard Giles

Specification notes

AIMS. This exercise demonstrates a method used to study speech in interpersonal evaluation. Actual speech rate and pronunciation feature among manipulations, and perceived speech rate and pronunciation feature among measures. Several points of methodology are introduced to students, besides research areas concerned with language, attitudes and person-perception, and potential applications in education and business.

METHODS AND ANALYSIS. In the first experiment of the exercise, subjects hear someone talking about a job application, and rate the candidate on four evaluative scales. Next, they receive information about his/her success or failure when interviewed for the job, and are required to estimate retrospectively several features of his/her speech. These data are analysed for evidence of a retroactive 'halo' effect on the perception of speech style.

The foregoing forms a practice trial for the main experiment, and facilitates establishing subject groups matched for evaluative response set. Subjects then play the role of Jobcentre officers and listen to a job interview, different groups actually hearing the same speaker as candidate, but in matched-guises which differ in pronunciation and speech rate. Open-ended responses, in the form of written advice to the candidate and about him/her to another employment officer, are content-analysed. These data, and ratings of the candidate's competence, pleasantness and suitability for selected types of work are subjected to analysis of variance, or other suitable statistical treatments.

PRIOR KNOWLEDGE ASSUMED. No prior knowledge of social psychology nor language/communication studies need be assumed by the prospective students. In fact, naïvity can only facilitate the value of this exercise which can be conducted in the traditional laboratory setting.

RESOURCES. The only materials or resources necessary are a tape-recorder (preferably of good quality), stimulus audiotapes, and questionnaires, with the preparation time being minimal. Prior to running the exercise for the very first time, two sets of short stimulus recordings need to be prepared carefully with the aid of three speakers, one of whom should be able to modify realistically his/her accent so as to make it more standard as well as more regional (or urban) than 'normal'. With the aid of appended transcripts, the recording session should take no longer than half an hour to an hour to produce satisfactory results and thereafter, of course, they are available for all future occasions. Five pages of response sheets in total need to be duplicated for each sub-ject, again according to the specifications laid out in the appendices, before the exercise is embarked upon each time.

DURATION. The entire exercise should be completed comfortably within a three-hour practical session, but this could be re-duced significantly should three assistants and three tape-recorders in three small, nearby rooms also be available (at least for the first hour).

Introduction

This exercise illustrates the investigation of the contribution of speech style to em-ployment selection by means of the Matched Guise Technique (MGT), originally devised by Lambert, Hodgson, Gardner and Fillen-baum (1960), with, as an extra feature, a demonstration of the same social inference process in reverse: the ascription of speech style on the basis of information about a person's success or failure in seeking employment. Several pedagogical aims can be achieved hereby, including introducing students to the following meth-odological aspects of social psychology:

* manipulation of individual social cues as independent variables in laboratory experiments - in this case, speed of speech and pronunciation - with ex-perimental control over materials;
* rating scales and content analysis as alternative measurement techniques;
* matching of subject groups on possible contaminating factors;
* checking the success of manipulations carried out;

and the following content areas:

* the influence of small social cues on decisions which have profound implica-tions for the courses of people's lives;
* halo effects in social judgement;
* stereotyping of social and ethnic groups;
* social perception as an active process of assimilating new information to existing cognitive structures.

Speech style and social relations

Knowledge of the social significance of speech styles in interpersonal and inter-group relations has advanced rapidly in recent years (Shuy and Fasold, 1973; Giles and Powesland, 1975; Giles and St Clair, 1979; Scherer and Giles, 1979; Ryan and Giles, 1982). Speech varieties of dominant and ethnic groups have been shown to carry advantages for their speakers in terms of impression-formation, particularly as far as impressions of ability are concerned. In bilingual Canada, for example, Lambert (1967) observed that both English- and French-speaking Canadians ascribed greater intelligence, dependability and ambition to English than to French speakers. Similar differences in favour of speakers of Re-ceived Pronunciation (RP, commonly known as 'BBC English') were reported by Giles (1970, 1971) in Great Britain, while Ryan and Carranza (1977) reported that Hispanic-accented speakers elicit low-ability stere-otypes in the USA. However, the socio-linguistic advantages do not all lie with the dominant groups, since it has also been found that subordinate groups exhibit 'loy-alty' to their own speech varieties, where judgements of social attractiveness, warmth and generosity are concerned (Lambert, 1967; Strongman and Woosley, 1967; Giles, 1971), their views being shared, to some extent, by members of the dominant groups.

Intergroup theory (Tajfel, 1978) sug-gests that individuals define themselves in terms of comparisons between their in-groups and relevant out-groups, attempting to maximize their distinctiveness on di-mensions which afford favourable intergroup comparison. If frustrated in this, they may adopt strategies of 'social creativity', devising new dimensions of intergroup com-parison, or just reversing their evaluation of dimensions yielding unfavourable com-parisons with out-groups (e.g. 'black is beautiful'). Speech is commonly used as a dimension of intergroup comparison in this way (Giles, Bourhis and Taylor, 1977), with emphasis on language (Taylor, Bassili and Aboud, 1973) or accent (Bourhis, Giles and Tajfel, 1973) as part of minority group members' identity. Individuals are also observed to change their styles of speech, accentuating their distinctiveness from the out-group, when their identity is threatened (Bourhis and Giles, 1977; Bourhis, Giles, Leyens and Tajfel, 1979), so that when members of a subordinate group are trying to join the dominant group from below, and members of the latter are creatively engaged in continual invention of new in-group markers, a 'sociolinguistic pursuit race' may ensue. Ryan (1979) has answered the question of why, given the social disadvantages they impose, low-prestige language varieties continue to exist. She argued that their speakers simply do not wish to give them up because of the latter's contribution to their sense of social group identity. Nevertheless, even if they did relinquish such speech characteristics they would be likely to find themselves merely speaking a new low-prestige variety, as the dominant group sociolinguistically decamped to re-establish its distinctiveness.

A theory of speech accommodation has been developed to explain strategies of linguistic style-shifting in interpersonal encounters (Giles, 1973; Giles and Smith, 1979; Thakerar, Giles and Cheshire, 1982). People generally modify their speech to make it more like that of the person addressed (convergence), especially when trying to create a good impression. This may be seen as intuitive application of similarity-attraction theory (Byrne, 1971) and the initiation of a social exchange transaction (Homans, 1961). When people perceive an encounter as hostile, or wish to make it so, they are likely to increase interpersonal dissimilarities (divergence) on one or more linguistic levels (dialect, lexical diversity, etc.) as an intergroup strategy of accentuating distinctiveness. Since language varieties differ in prestige, accommodative shifts may be upward or downward on the status continuum. There is a perceptual side to this as well, with the listener interpreting convergence or divergence favourably or otherwise, according to the evidence for a friendly, hostile, or ingratiating motive, or the presence of external coercion. Thus, Simard, Taylor and Giles (1976) found that French-Canadian listeners responded more positively (i) to non-converging English-Canadian speakers who were known to have been forbidden to converge than to those who could have had they wished to do so, and (ii) to speakers who were shown voluntarily to have made a convergent choice than to those instructed to converge.

People's attitudes to speech varieties are of practical consequence and this has implications in applied fields like education and employment which will be referred to below. In second language learning, too, attitudes have been shown to contribute to motivation, and thereby towards proficiency (Gardner and Lambert, 1972; Gardner, 1979). Second-language learners have also been observed feeling their social identity threatened by increasing competence in their new language, and trying to reaffirm it by reintroducing non-native markers into their speech: that is, even retreating from an already-attained proficiency in their second language in order to maintain psychological distinctiveness (cf. Lambert and Tucker, 1972).

MGT

Some of the most important research leading to the foregoing theoretical ideas has been conducted using Lambert's MGT (Lambert et al, 1960). MGT is among a number of methods termed 'verbal guise' techniques by Agheyisi and Fishman (1970) when they reviewed research methodology in language attitudes. Verbal guise techniques all involve recorded speech being presented to listeners who are required to estimate the speakers' capabilities, personalities, emotional states, and various other social or linguistic characteristics. Speakers normally read a standard piece of prose, in order to maintain control of speech content and emotive impact, but naturalistic dialogues are also sometimes prepared. Stimulus recordings differ from each other in some aspect of speech which is being manipulated as an independent variable, usually language itself (i.e. with a translated passage) or accent, and the listeners' judgements are analysed statistically to establish whether the linguistically contrasted 'guises' convey significantly different impressions of the speakers.

MGT differs from other verbal guise techniques in that the guises are matched for extraneous vocal variables, such as 'breathiness' and fundamental voice frequency, by all being produced by the same speakers, specially chosen for bilingual or bidialectal skills. 'Buffer' stimuli, recorded by other speakers in their natural voices, are commonly interspersed between the experimental stimuli in studies with repeated measures in order to reduce the likelihood of listeners recognizing successive presentations of the same speakers. Because of the tight control it provides, with materials skilfully produced and thoroughly checked for authenticity, MGT is an extremely powerful research tool. In fact, it has been the most fruitful technique so far used to study social evaluation through speech characteristics.

Advantages notwithstanding, MGT has attracted criticism (Tajfel, 1962). Robinson (1972) suggested that guises merely help listeners identify speakers as members of social groups, to which they then apply the same stereotypes as traditional elicitation with group labels (e.g. Katz and Braly's 1933 procedure) would elicit. However, differences between stereotypes obtained with MGT and mere labels have been found (Ball, 1980), so the former may be specifically sociolinguistic in nature. Lee (1971) raised three objections to MGT: spurious inter-guise contrasts resulting from stimuli of identical verbal content, decontextualization of stimuli, and arbitrary selection of rating scales which are of unchecked reliability. Giles and Bourhis (1973), replying, stressed the corroboration of matched guise results by various methods free of Lee's first two criticisms, the selection of rating scales through often-unreported pilot studies, and the consistency of results between comparable British MGT studies which involved different materials and subject samples. It is also arguable that the most usual data analysis in such research effectively builds-in a reliability check in the error-term, so that genuinely unreliable measurement would lead to statistically insignificant results. What has enabled MGT to withstand the foregoing criticisms is probably less the arguments of its advocates than its sheer productivity in accumulating information useful in building theories about social evaluation and speech.

Naturalistic adaptations of verbal guise techniques
Although verbal guise techniques have

mainly been used in laboratory research of a very decontextualized sort, they are increasingly being adapted for use in everyday life decision-making situations, so that subjects take the tasks more seriously and find them more meaningful. Extrapolation from the laboratory to the outside world also has practical consequences. For example, Seligman, Tucker and Lambert (1972), using unmatched verbal guises (children cannot usually be expected to produce matched guises), showed voice cues to predominate over physical appearance and actual schoolwork in trainee teachers' assessments of Canadian schoolchildren's abilities, a finding recently corroborated by the work of Eltis (1980) with Australian children. In a different social domain, Fielding and Evered (1980) reported an MGT study with an independent-groups design on the significance of the patient's accent in a simulated medical consultation. They found that the same symptoms were more likely to be attributed to psychosomatic than physical causes by medical student listeners when presented in RP, as opposed to a British regional accent.

A number of investigators have used verbal guise techniques to study speech style in the employment interview. Hopper and Williams (1973) presented a simulated job interview to personnel officers, reporting that semantic differential factor scores derived from ratings of the recorded speakers strongly predicted hiring decisions for high-status, but not low-status, jobs. However, in this aspect of their study, the contribution of speech itself to the predictor variables in the multiple regression analysis used is unclear: individual judges' hiring decisions were significantly related to their assessments of speakers on the semantic differential factors, but it is likely that this would be so whatever means of stimulus presentation were used. The same writers also reported another part of their study in which the effect of ethnic speech was assessed, and whether speakers were Black-American or Southern-White accented did not affect hiring decisions. Nevertheless, Giles, Wilson and Conway (1981) found that an ethnic, non-standard accent (Welsh) elicited judgements of higher suitability for low-status jobs, and lower suitability for high-status jobs, than RP. This was from a matched-guise experiment (with accent and lexical diversity manipulated factorially) involving university students who were asked to act as personnel officers after hearing recordings of supposed job interviews. High lexical diversity was judged indicative of unsuitability for low-status work. In Canada, Kalin and Rayko (1978) reported that foreign-accented speakers (Italian, Greek, Portuguese, West African and Slovak) were rated more suitable for low-status, and less suitable for high-status, jobs than English-Canadian speakers, using similar procedures with un-matched verbal guises. Kalin, Rayko and Love (1980), extending this work, reported judgements of job-suitability for four other foreign-accented types of speaker in Canada: for high-status employment, the (descending) order was English/German/South Asian/West Indian and this was reversed for low-status work. Moreover, de la Zerda and Hopper (1979) showed, using MGT, that hiring decisions in Texas were affected by degree of Mexican accentedness (though pronunciation may have been confounded here with speech-rate, hesitancy and other variables genuinely predictive of job capacity).

In all these studies, apart from Hopper and Williams (1973), non-standard or non-native speech appeared to handicap speakers at the upper levels of employment. Another study of Black and White American English by Hopper (1977), using MGT modified to exclude repetition of verbal content, produced an interaction between speaker ethnicity and speaker-standardness: Black standard speakers were more likely than all others to be hired. Black speakers were all at an advantage where supervisory or sales, but not technical, positions were concerned. Hopper's results (Hopper and Williams, 1973; Hopper, 1977) are somewhat at variance with the rest of the findings in this field, and with intuitive expectations, indicating that Black or White American ethnicity alone is not a major determinant of employability in Texas, though it may be in interaction with actual speech characteristics. Results obtained from such research in the future, crossing non-speech and speech characteristics factorially,

will probably manifest further inconsistencies according to local community relations and their on-going changes. This will demand sophisticated theoretical treatment, drawing upon intergroup theory and applying it extensively to employer- and applicant-tactics in the job interview.

Distorted perception of speech style
Everything mentioned so far has concerned inferences about people's non-linguistic qualities from how they speak, but another recent departure in research examines how listeners perceive speakers' speech styles in relation to other information about them. One of psychology's most replicable phenomena has been the 'halo' effect (Thorndike, 1920) which refers to individuals' tendencies to allow their general positive or negative impressions of others to influence their ratings of specific traits on attributes; three recent studies have demonstrated it in impressions of speaker-style. Ryan and Sebastian (1980) found that standard American-English speakers described as lower class were reported to be easier to understand and make listeners feel more comfortable than when the same recordings were attributed to middle-class sources, whereas perception of Hispanic-accented speech was unaffected by this manipulation. The former result is almost the opposite of what would be expected, and was indeed found for non-speech-related measures, and the authors suggest that it arose because standard speakers given high social status sounded affected to listeners, while the discrepancy between the actual speech and listeners' expectations of lower-class speakers made ratings more favourable. Thakerar and Giles (1981) showed that a halo effect in speech perception can also operate retrospectively, with an experiment in which listeners received information about a speaker's academic performance after hearing him and just before making their ratings; when described as highly successful, he was recalled as speaking faster and with more standard pronunciation than when described as unsuccessful. This has been replicated by Ball, Byrne, Giles, Berechree, Griffiths, McDonald and McKendrick (in preparation), using a female speaker discussing a job interview and informing

listeners that the speaker had, or had not, been offered the job. The same authors also found that a 'general Australian' (Mitchell and Delbridge, 1965) speaker was perceived as more 'foreign sounding' when described as belonging to a Greek immigrant family rather than an Anglo-Australian family. These studies illustrate the complex process by which new information is assimilated into old, with distortion of either or both, as the social perceiver constructs an understanding of events and people stable enough to be acted upon. Information flows in all directions in this, with speech characteristics being both a primary source of information, conveying impressions of social attractiveness and competence (which in turn determine decisions to employ, convict or diagnose), and itself perceptually affected by information about status, employability or ethnicity.

A two-part laboratory demonstration

As indicated in the opening paragraph, this exercise demonstrates the use of MGT in research on the role of speech in the employment interview and combines it with illustrating a halo effect in the perception of speech style. Through this, students are familiarized (i) with the matching of subject groups as a means of experimental control, (ii) with experimental manipulation of single social cues, (iii) with two contrasting types of dependent variable, and (iv) with several different content areas in social psychology, including social markers in speech, impression formation and stereotyping. With imaginative adaptation to local resources and circumstances, the exercise should prove fertile training in experimental social psychology, stimulating abler students to design more advanced experiments on related matters for themselves. It is readily modifiable in many ways, besides those suggested here, so that a dossier of variations on the theme may be accumulated with successive cohorts of students.

The exercise has two parts, Experiment 1 on the retroactive halo effect in the perception of speech style forming a warm-up trial for the second, which is about the effect of speech style itself on impression formation. On the basis of previous evi-

dence we hypothesize, with regard to the first part, that somebody described as a successful job-seeker will be recalled as sounding more competent, but not more socially attractive, having spoken faster, more grammatically, with more standard pronunciation, and in a more easily understood way than someone described as an unsuccessful applicant. In the second part, Experiment 2, we hypothesize that an applicant who speaks with a standard accent will be rated more favourably on competence than one who does not, but not on integrity or social attractiveness, and will be judged more suitable for high-status but less suitable for menial work. Similarly, a faster-speaking applicant will be perceived as more competent and suitable for high-status employment, but less suitable for low-status employment, and no more socially attractive or trustworthy than a slower-speaking applicant. The predictions regarding speech rate are the only ones which do not follow straightforwardly from findings already discussed, and the basis for making them is a series of studies by Brown and his colleagues (Brown, Strong and Rencher, 1973, 1974; Smith, Brown, Strong and Rencher, 1975; Brown, 1980) which show competence judgements to be positively related to speech rate, but indicate a more complex relation between speech rate and 'benevolence' ratings, perceived 'benevolence' peaking at intermediate speech rates.

Method

Sample materials and instructions intended to be usable as they stand are appended to this chapter and will be referred to from time to time in this section.

Subjects

The exercise, as described, requires 40 or more student subjects which may be impossible in one laboratory class. If the class is not as large as this, each student might recruit one or more fellow-subjects from elsewhere. Alternatively, one independent variable might be omitted from the experimental design, or the data from several classes could be combined with a consequent delay in full analysis until all classes had participated. An absolute minimum of 10 subjects per cell of the main experiment, all unfamiliar with this research field, is recommended for a viable demonstration.

Resources and materials

TIME. The experiments and data analysis can be conducted within a three-hour laboratory period.

SPACE. Four rooms, each accommodating a group of subjects who can hear the stimulus recordings and make ratings undisturbed, are desirable. Otherwise, groups might be run successively in one room, or simultaneously in a language laboratory or a large room with group listening stations.

ASSISTANCE. With three assistants aiding the tutor, simultaneous running of all subject groups in the four different locations and speedy matching for evaluative response set is simple. Otherwise, subjects themselves can assist in assigning each other to groups, presenting recordings, and preparing data for analysis.

INSTRUCTION AND RESPONSE BOOKLETS. Separate booklets are needed for the two experiments, so that the first can be used for group-matching before Experiment 2 begins. Suggested scales for Experiments 1 and 2 are found within Appendices 4 and 5 respectively. If alternative scales to these examples are used, the tutor should bear in mind the scales employed in previous experiments, the desirability of sampling social judgements extensively, and the research hypotheses. Including scales to validate the experimental manipulations (successful/unsuccessful for Experiment 1 and fast/slow speech and standard/non-standard pronunciation for Experiment 2) is vital. Suitability for work of differing prestige should be included, but ensure that all the jobs are compatible with the interview content. Rating scales should be randomized for positional response set, and enough space should be given for the open-ended responses.

SCRIPTS AND RECORDINGS. These should be adapted to local circumstances and

available skills and be prepared, of course, prior to the practical class assembling. Assuming that the speech community exemplifies an accent prestige continuum, two speakers at neither high nor low extreme are desirable, and a third who can shift realistically and noticeably across the range. This speaker plays the candidate role in the interview of Experiment 2. Recordings should ideally be made by individuals with some acting experience, and checked for authenticity by establishing their non-discriminability from recordings of genuine spontaneous speech.

The examples scripts in the appendices (1 and 2) were prepared by editing transcripts of spontaneous speech obtained through role-play, a procedure recommended if scripts are written from scratch and transcripts of real interviews are unobtainable. Editing should not correct grammar, remove hesitation, etc., as this reduces authenticity.

Recordings must be made under noise-free conditions, with high-quality tapes. If students have to present stimuli themselves, cassettes with the two experiments on different tracks, and with verbal instructions recorded too, will be fairly foolproof.

One speaker records the Experiment 1 script (see Appendix 1) speaking normally, and the others the Experiment 2 script (see Appendix 2) four times, with the employer speaking normally and the candidate varying his style to produce all four combinations of high and low prestige accent and fast or slow speech. Special care is needed over the following: (i) keeping employer speech constant between recordings (particularly avoiding unintended convergence upon the candidate's speech); (ii) controlling aspects of the candidate's speech which are not factors in the experimental design (especially avoiding projection of popular stereotypes); and (iii) achieving orthogonal manipulations of the independent variables (i.e. both fast guises should be equally fast, both non-standard guises equally non-standard, etc.). Speech rate may be checked with a stop-watch and versions of the Experiment 2 recordings, with each speaker erased in turn, may be pre-tested on a panel of raters for equivalence of accent and extraneous variables, as judgements of one speaker can be influenced by contrast with his or her interlocutor (Ball, Giles, Byrne and Berechree, in press). Hardware permitting, the employer's speech could even be held completely constant by recording it only once and editing it together with the candidate's answers to make up the dialogues.

Procedure

Although set out here as two separate experiments, the exercise is meant to be presented to subjects as a single experiment with a warm-up trial.

EXPERIMENT 1. Subjects should be assigned at random to two treatment groups, balanced for sex, at the start of the laboratory session. The tutor then presents the verbal instructions in Appendix 3 as response sheets (Appendix 4) are passed round, instructions uppermost. These printed instructions are read aloud by the tutor and any questions are dealt with publicly in front of the group before the recording is played. Immediately after the recording, subjects complete section A of the response sheet (which contains evaluative scales for later matching purposes), turn it over, read Further information (which accomplishes the experimental manipulation) and complete section B. They then hand in their sheets and take a short break while allocation to groups for Experiment 2 is done.

ALLOCATION OF SUBJECTS TO MATCHED GROUPS FOR EXPERIMENT 2. Teaching purposes can be met by nothing more elaborate than totalling each subject's ratings on the section A scales (of Appendix 4) taking account of positional reversals of evaluation - and assigning subjects to four groups of equal size so that the group means are as similar as possible. One way is to arrange response sheets in rank order of evaluative totals and distribute them in rotation to four piles, beginning each rotation on the last pile of its predecessor to prevent accumulation of differences between piles (i.e. labelling piles P, Q, R and S, the ranked sheets would be distributed thus: P, Q, R, S; S, P, Q, R; R, S, P, Q; Q, R, S, P, etc.). This scoring and matching procedure should take no longer than 15 minutes.

EXPERIMENT 2. Subjects are assembled as four experimental groups in their separate locations, ostensibly because they are to hear excerpts from different employment interviews, and are handed their final set of response sheets (see Appendix 5). The experimenters (i.e. tutor and assistants in each location) read aloud their printed instructions, ask for questions, and present one of the four stimulus recordings. Subjects then make their ratings of the candidate and provide open-ended reports to him and another employment officer, before response sheets are collected.

DEBRIEFING. The tutor may begin by asking subjects what they imagine to be the aims and hypotheses of the exercise adding, if necessary, the question 'Was there perhaps more to it than met the eye?' This should establish how transparent the experiments have been and how valid the data are, before subjects gain the benefit of hindsight. The tutor can then explain the aims and retrace the course of the experiments to show how the hypotheses were brought to test. If any non-psychology students have been subjects, it may be useful to separate the 'talking down' from subsequent class discussion and study of results, releasing them after the first of these, but for psychology students debriefing flows naturally into an examination of design, control, analysis and ethical issues.

Analysis and results

Using response sheets like the examples appended (i.e. Appendices 4 and 5 for Experiments 1 and 2 respectively), data are in numerical form and need no transcription before analysis. Data-processing facilities will determine the most appropriate analyses among those suggested below.

Experiment 1

If analysis can proceed while Experiment 2 is in progress, some results should be available when it finishes.

SECTION A. Although the subject groups of Experiment 2 are matched for evaluational response set, those of Experiment 1 are not, so possible intergroup differences should be checked for with a t-test on section A evaluation totals (or separate ones for individual scales).

SECTION B. The main aim is to establish whether groups receiving interview-success and interview-failure information rated the speaker differently on these scales. t-tests for independent samples may be computed for individual scales. If analysis of the section A data shows a group difference in evaluational set, analysis of covariance, with it as covariate (or individual section A scales as multiple covariates), will control statistically for this. Another approach altogether, if no difference in set obtains, is to take all the section B scales together in a multivariate analysis of variance, combined with discriminant function analysis, to establish how distinguishable by their ratings the treatment groups are, and how the various scales contribute towards discriminability.

Since only two groups are compared in this analysis, results can adequately be presented in one table, with a row for every scale and a column for each of the treatment means, t, the degrees of freedom (if they vary, through occasionally missed scales), and the probabilities. The profile of each treatment group over all scales can be shown in a graph, plotting scale means vertically against scales horizontally. With discriminant function analysis, scale poles could be marked as points along the function separating the two treatment groups.

Experiment 2

Analysis of these data concerns whether the standard and fast-speaking guises elicit more favourable judgements than the non-standard and slow guises on competence and suitability for high-status work, but not social attractiveness or integrity, as indicated by scale ratings and the content of free-response reports. The data comprise a 2 x 2 factorial design with independent groups. From the section A data of Experiment 1, mean evaluative response set may be computed for the four groups to demonstrate the success of matching, but no further analysis is necessary. If no matching has been done, a one-way analysis of

variance on evaluative response set will establish whether it is contaminating treatments in Experiment 2 and, if so, its effect can be statistically nullified by making it a covariate in the analyses.

Separate 2 x 2 analyses of variance for all scales are the most straightforward way of treating the rating data, displaying the results in one table, with columns for the four treatment means and the F values for pronunciation, speech rate and their interaction, indicating probabilities with superscripts, and drawing graphs for significant interactions. Multivariate analysis is again possible, leading to graphic portrayal of the treatments and scales against two discriminant functions.

Subjects should act as judges for content analysis of the free-response data and can proceed with this while the rating scales are analysed. Reports addressed to the candidate and a fellow Jobcentre officer must be scored according to predetermined content categories and the scores subjected to the same type of analysis as the ratings, or appropriate distribution-free tests if parametric assumptions are grossly violated.

Messages may be scored for innumerable content categories, but concern here is mainly with evaluative impact. In scoring materials, allowance is necessary for message length (in words), which itself should be analysed as a dependent variable, since longer messages indicate favourability towards the recipient (Giles, Baker and Fielding, 1975). Reports for the candidate and the fellow-officer may be combined or separated for analysis, the latter providing for examination of potentially interesting differences in what the messages say.

An overall index of favourability is obtainable by applying to each report the formula

$$\text{favourability} = \frac{100 \times (\text{total } a - \text{total } b)}{\text{length of message in words}}$$

(where a = number of positive terms and b = number of negative terms)

weighted, if desired, to allow for intensifiers and de-intensifiers ('very', 'highly', 'slightly', etc.). Scoring could be done separately for competence, social attractiveness, and so on. Since content scoring is a slow process, half the class might score reports to the candidate and the others score those to the fellow-officer, possibly as a supplementary task to be done out of class hours for later analysis. Statistical analysis is best based upon composite scorings from all judges, but inter-judge consistency should be estimated with a suitable reliability measure.

Numerical values may be given to subjects' suggestions regarding suitable and unsuitable work for the candidate, using a standard index of occupational status, and statistical analysis may then be applied.

Discussion

To recapitulate the predictions, Experiment 1 is expected to show subjects forming a more favourable impression of the competence, but not the social attractiveness, of a speaker described as successful in a job interview than of the same speaker when described as unsuccessful. The 'successful' speaker will also be recalled as speaking faster, and in a more socially approved manner. Experiment 2 is likely to show more favourable impressions for the standard-than for the non-standard-accented candidate on competence-related scales, but not on integrity or social attractiveness. The standard-accented applicant will be judged more suitable for high- but less suitable for low-status work, and more likely to be offered the job after the recorded interview. The same positive pattern of results was predicted for the fast as opposed to the slow speaker. These results should be corroborated by those from content analyses of free-response data.

For both experiments, scales included to check the success of manipulations should produce appropriate group differences (successful/unsuccessful in Experiment 1; standard/non-standard pronunciation and fast/slow speech in Experiment 2). Without these differences, failure to obtain significant differences on other measures means nothing. Regarding Experiment 2, note here that, if orthogonality of the two manipulations has been confirmed, as suggested

earlier, a significant interaction would imply interdependence between perception of pronunciation and speech rate.

Whether or not results uphold predictions, the four methodological aims listed at the beginning will have been achieved, but the findings themselves will influence the impact of subject-matter introduced to classes by this exercise. However, the importance of speech characteristics in social encounters will inevitably be highlighted. That the connection between speech cues and human qualities exists in the mind of the hearer, and not necessarily in the objective state of affairs, is demonstrated by the use of the same recording throughout Experiment 1 and the same speaker in Experiment 2. Nevertheless, it is also necessary to emphasize that interpersonal perception is more than simply bias and distortion, which are inevitable by-products of a finite cognitive system, integrating varied sources of information (including memory) into a basis for action in the social world. The human mind seems to be designed to respond not to unique stimuli directly, but via systems of categories into which experiences are sorted by means of inferences which 'go beyond the information given' (Bruner, 1957); that is, it responds to interpretations of stimuli. This gives social perception a heuristic character, highly efficient most of the time, but susceptible to, among other things, oversimplification (e.g. halo effects) and distortions whereby erroneous inferences can be sustained through false validation provided by other people (e.g. in the form of social stereotypes). It is important for students to recognize bias and distortion in social perception as richly informative about its normal functioning, and research into these phenomena as the scientific way of exploiting this, and not just the exposure of human naïvety and illogicality.

Experiments like these advance knowledge about reactions to speech, and the kinds of behaviour likely to result, contributing thereby to an understanding of social interaction in general, but the results also suggest applications in business, education and other spheres. Industrial personnel officers and employment agencies need a more informed analysis of their intuitive, everyday decision-making to counter bias in worker-selection, besides improving their use of speech cues as legitimate sources of information. There are also lessons to be learnt by job-seekers about the realities of the workaday world and the value of self-presentation skills, both sociolinguistic and non-verbal, without which they cannot expect to receive full credit for whatever competence, reliability and trustworthiness they actually possess. Research towards an applied science of how to win friends and influence people, in which school leavers and adults can be systematically trained, has already begun (Trower, Bryant and Argyle, 1978), but has not yet taken advantage of theoretical developments in research on speech, even though it is sound theory, not isolated facts, which is needed to stimulate effective applications.

A good experiment is characterized not so much by the absence of limitations as by their being clearly delineable. These two experiments deal with speech in a static fashion, whereas current research interest has progressed to its dynamics and reactions to them. These would be more complicated to demonstrate in the classroom, however, and the results would be less foreseeable. The sampling of subjects here is limited to students, and caution is needed in extrapolating findings to the rest of the community, though in the case of employment interviews it is needed less than one might expect (Bernstein, Hakel and Harlan, 1975). Other independent variables could be employed in extending the scope of these experiments, using ethnic or religious information about the speaker or some kind of information about the situation (e.g. its formality) in which the recording was made, for Experiment 1, and foreign, or more native accents, besides other speech variables like lexical diversity, grammatical complexity or idiomatic characteristics in Experiment 2. Alternative dependent variables, in the form of other rating scales and sorts of free responses, various behavioural and physiological measures, would also be possible in both experiments. Thus the sampling of manipulations and measures, although restricted in these experiments, is extendable if required. Finally, as a laboratory exercise,

this one is open to the commonly misapplied criticism of artificiality which, if anything, is less applicable than usual here, since the materials and procedures are designed to create in subjects a vividly realistic experience of involvement in employment selection practices.

The fact that subjects are likely to take the task seriously highlights the ethical issue of deceiving subjects by leading them to believe they are hearing genuine job interviews in the exercise. It is an extremely limited and non-distressing deception, and the explanation that the exercise is about impression-formation in employment selection is, of course, accurate. Students are unlikely to object to being thus misled in their own educational interests, but something may be gained from discussion of the ethnical issue and comparing this exercise with 'third degree' research like that of Bjerg (1968) or Milgram (1974). Furthermore, students might be encouraged to establish in discussion, with reference to the ethical policies of professional and academic psychological bodies, principles which distinguish between tolerable and intolerable deception in social psychological research.

Conclusion

From this laboratory exercise, students can gain an acquaintance with the role of linguistic factors in social life, particularly in interpersonal perception, and an appreciation of several finer points of methodology in experimental social psychology, relating to control over stimuli, equation of samples on potentially contaminating factors and confirming the success of manipulations, among others. They should also be sensitized to the types of information, other than verbal content, which flows to and fro during interpersonal encounters, the capacity such information has for eliciting socially stereotyped impressions, and the way in which even their awareness of these cues can be coloured by externally-derived information, thereby acquiring more appreciation of the active and assimilative nature of social perception and the types of error to which it is vulnerable.

REFERENCES

Agheyisi, R. and Fishman, J.A. (1970) Language attitude studies: a brief survey of methodological approaches. Anthropological Linguistics, 12, 137-157.

Ball, P. (1980) Stereotypes of Anglo-Saxon and non-Anglo-Saxon accents: some exploratory Australian studies with the matched guise technique. Mimeo: Psychology Department, University of Tasmania, Hobart, Australia.

Ball, P., Byrne, J., Giles, H., Berechree, P., Griffiths, J., McDonald, H. and McKendrick, I. (in preparation) The retroactive speech stereotype effect: some Australian data and constraints.

Ball, P., Giles, H., Byrne, J. and Berechree, P. (in press) Situational constraints on accommodation theory: some Australian data. International Journal of the Sociology of Language.

Bernstein, V., Hakel, M.D. and Harlan, A. (1975) The college student as interviewer: a threat to generalizability? Journal of Applied Psychology, 60, 266-268.

Bjerg, K. (1968) Interplay analysis: a preliminary report on an approach to the problems of interpersonal understanding. Acta Psychologica, 28, 201-245.

Bourhis, R.Y. and Giles, H. (1977) The language of intergroup distinctiveness. In H. Giles (ed.), Language, Ethnicity and Intergroup Relations. London: Academic Press.

Bourhis, R.Y., Giles, H., Leyens, J.-P. and Tajfel, H. (1979) Psycholinguistic distinctiveness: language divergence in Belgium. In H. Giles and R. St Clair (eds), Language and Social Psychology. Oxford: Blackwell.

Bourhis, R.Y., Giles, H. and Tajfel, H. (1973) Language as a determinant of Welsh identity. European Journal of Social Psychology, 3, 447-460.

Brown, B.L. (1980) Effects of speech rate in personality attributions and competency evaluations. In H. Giles, W.P. Robinson and P.M. Smith (eds), Language: Social psychological perspectives. Oxford: Pergamon.

Brown, B.L., Strong, W.J. and Rencher, A.C. (1973) Perceptions of personality from speech: effects of manipulations of acoustical parameters. Journal of the Acoustical Society of America, 54, 29-35.

Brown, B.L., Strong, W.J. and Rencher, A.C. (1974) Fifty-four voices from two: the effects of simultaneous manipulations of rate, mean fundamental frequency and variance of fundamental frequency on ratings of personality from speech. Journal of the Acoustical Society of America, 55, 313-318.

Bruner, J.S. (1957) On going beyond the information given. In J.S. Bruner and E. Brunswik (eds), Cognitive Approaches to Psychology. Cambridge, Mass.: Harvard University Press.

Byrne, D. (1971) The Attraction Paradigm. New York: Academic Press.

De la Zerda, N. and Hopper, R. (1979) Employment interviewers' reactions to Mexican American speech. Communication Monographs, 46, 126-134.

Eltis, K.J. (1980) Pupils' speech-style and teacher reaction: implications from some Australian data. English in Australia, 51, 27-35.

Fielding, G. and Evered, C. (1980) The influence of patients' speech upon doctors: the diagnostic interview. In R. St Clair and H. Giles (eds), The Social and Psychological Contexts of Language. Hillsdale, NJ: Erlbaum.

Gardner, R.C. (1979) Social psychological aspects of second language acquisition. In H. Giles and R. St Clair (eds), Language and Social Psychology. Oxford: Blackwell.

Gardner, R.C. and Lambert, W.E. (1972) Attitudes and Motivation in Second Language Learning. Rowley, Mass.: Newbury House.

Giles, H. (1970) Evaluative reactions to accents. Educational Review, 22, 211-227.

Giles, H. (1971) Patterns of evaluation in reactions to RP, South Welsh and Somerset accented speech. British Journal of Social and Clinical Psychology, 10, 280-281.

Giles, H. (1973) Accent mobility: a model and some data. Anthropological Linguistics, 15, 87-105.

Giles, H., Baker, S. and Fielding, G. (1975) Communication length as a behavioural index of accent prejudice. International Journal of the Sociology of Language, 6, 73-81.

Giles, H. and Bourhis, R.Y. (1973) Dialect perception revisted. Quarterly Journal of Speech, 59, 337-342.

Giles, H., Bourhis, R.Y. and Taylor, D.M. (1977) Towards a theory of language in ethnic group relations. In H. Giles (ed.), Language, Ethnicity and Intergroup Relations. London: Academic Press.

Giles, H. and Powesland, P.F. (1975) Speech Style and Social Evaluation. London: Academic Press.

Giles, H. and St Clair, R. (eds) (1979) Language and Social Psychology. Oxford: Blackwell.

Giles, H. and Smith, P.M. (1979) Accommodation theory: optimal levels of convergence. In H. Giles and R. St Clair (eds), Language and Social Psychology. Oxford: Blackwell.

Giles, H., Wilson, P. and Conway, T. (1981) Accent and lexical diversity as determinants of impression formation and employment selection. Language Sciences, 3, 92-103.

Homans, G.C. (1961) Social Behaviour: Its elementary forms. New York: Harcourt, Brace & World.

Hopper, R. (1977) Language attitudes in the employment interview. Communication Monographs, 44, 346-351.

Hopper, R. and Williams, F. (1973) Speech characteristics and employability. Speech Monographs, 40, 296-302.

Kalin, R. and Rayko, D.S. (1978) Discrimination in evaluative judgements against foreign-accented job candidates. Psychological Reports, 43, 1203-1209.

Kalin, R., Rayko, D.S. and Love, N. (1980) The perception and evaluation of job candidates with four different ethnic accents. In H. Giles, W.P. Robinson and P.M. Smith (eds), Language: Social psychological perspectives. Oxford: Pergamon.

Katz, D. and Braly, K.W. (1933) Racial prejudice and racial stereotypes. Journal of Abnormal and Social Psychology, 30, 175-193.

Lambert, W.E. (1967) The social psychology of bilingualism. Journal of Social Issues, 23, 91-109.

Lambert, W.E., Hodgson, R.C., Gardner, R.C. and Fillenbaum, S. (1960) Evaluational reactions to spoken language. Journal of Abnormal and Social Psychology, 60, 44-51.

Lambert, W.E. and Tucker, G.R. (1972) Bilingual Education of Children: The St Lambert experiment. Rowley, Mass.: Newbury House.

Lee, R. (1971) Dialect perception: a critical review and re-evaluation. Quarterly Journal of Speech, 57, 410-417.

Milgram, S. (1974) Obedience to Authority: An experimental view. New York: Harper & Row.

Mitchell, A.G. and Delbridge, A. (1965) The Speech of Australian Adolescents. Sydney: Angus & Robertson.

Robinson, W.P. (1972) Language and Social Behaviour. Harmondsworth: Penguin.

Ryan, E.B. (1979) Why do low-prestige language varieties persist? In H. Giles and R. St Clair (eds), Language and Social Psychology. Oxford: Blackwell.

Ryan, E.B. and Carranza, M.A. (1977) Ingroup and outgroup reactions to Mexican American language varieties. In H. Giles (ed.), Language, Ethnicity and Intergroup Relations. London: Academic Press.

Ryan, E.B. and Giles, H. (eds) (1982) Attitudes towards Language Variation: Social and applied contexts. London: Edward Arnold.

Ryan, E.B. and Sebastian, R.J. (1980) The effects of speech style and social class background on social judgements of speakers. British Journal of Social and Clinical Psychology, 19, 229-233.

Scherer, K.R. and Giles, H. (eds) (1979) Social Markers in Speech. Cambridge: Cambridge University Press.

Seligman, C.F., Tucker, G.R. and Lambert, W.E. (1972) The effects of speech style and other attributes on teachers' attitudes towards pupils. Language in Society, 1, 131-142.

Shuy, R.W. and Fasold, R.W. (eds) (1973) Language Attitudes: Current trends and prospects. Washington, DC: Georgetown University Press.

Simard, L., Taylor, D.M. and Giles, H. (1976) Attribution processes and inter-personal accommodation in a bilingual setting. Language and Speech, 19, 374-387.

Smith, B.L., Brown, B.L., Strong, W.J. and Rencher, A.C. (1975) Effects of speech rate on personality perception. Language and Speech, 18, 145-152.

Strongman, K.T. and Woosley, J. (1967) Stereotyped reactions to regional accents. British Journal of Social and Clinical Psychology, 6, 164-167.

Tajfel, H. (1962) Social perception. In M. Argyle and G. Humphreys (eds), Social Psychology through Experiment. London: Methuen.

Tajfel, H. (ed.) (1978) Differentiation between Social Groups: Studies in the social psychology of intergroup relations. London: Academic Press.

Taylor, D.M., Bassili, J. and Aboud, F.E. (1973) Dimensions of ethnic identity: an example from Quebec. Journal of Social Psychology, 89, 185-192.

Thakerar, J.N. and Giles, H. (1981) They are - so they spoke: non-content speech stereotypes. Language and Communication, 1, 255-261.

Thakerar, J.N., Giles, H. and Cheshire, J. (1982) Psychological and linguistic parameters of speech accommodation. In C. Fraser and K.R. Scherer (eds), Advances in the Social Psychology of Language. Cambridge: Cambridge University Press.

Thorndike, R.L. (1920) A constant error of psychological ratings. Journal of Applied Psychology, 4, 25-29.

Trower, P., Bryant, B. and Argyle, M. (1978) Social Skills and Mental Health. London: Methuen.

Useful introductory reading for students

Fishman, J.A. and Giles, H. (1978) Language in society. In H. Tajfel and C. Fraser (eds), Introducing Social Psychology. Harmondsworth: Penguin.

APPENDIX 1: EXPERIMENT 1 SCRIPT

Uh ... well I thought they'd be a good firm to get a job with, because they're quite big, they got offices ... all over the country and they've got some in America and Europe as well and I'm interested in travelling and I thought that they'd be ... that would be a good opportunity ... if I worked for them long enough I'd possibly get posted overseas, probably my best ... opportunity for travelling. I've got a friend that's worked for them for a couple of years and she said they're a good lot to work for and ... that the people are friendly in the office ... and um the job seems, really, to be um ... right up my alley because ...

APPENDIX 2: EXPERIMENT 2 SCRIPT

Employer: Well now let me see, your school report and your exam results are quite satisfactory. I get the impression you really enjoyed school. I don't suppose this stemmed purely from the academic side? ... Tell me, what other activities did you get involved in?

Interviewee: Um ... Oh, plenty of things really. My mates and I used to play football a few days a week ... you know, during lunch break and after school and all that. Oh, er ... and in my last year I was in a production of 'Macbeth'. I didn't have to <u>say</u> anything; I just had to appear on stage as a ghost ... I only did that really because they needed eight people all the same height ... Uh ... we just happened to be the right height. Well ... I mean, I was the same height as seven other guys. I ... er, I quite enjoyed it ... er ... it was the first time I'd ever been in a school production ... uh ...

Employer: Uh-huh ... anything else?

Interviewee: Um ... I was on the organizing committee for school dances. I got elected on to that and I did it for two terms, but then exams came up an' so I handed over to someone else because it would have taken up too much of my time you see ... um ... apart from that, I don't think I did much else at school - apart from work ... To be honest the football used to take up most of my spare time - I used to play most Saturdays.

Employer: I see ... since you left school, do you still play?

Interviewee: Well ... I sometimes play here, but I don't play anywhere <u>near</u> as much as I used to. I've got more interested in hiking now y'see.

Employer: Oh really? ... Are you a member of a club then ... or do you just go off by yourself?

Interviewee: Oh no ... I mean 'no' I don't go hiking by myself ... but I'm a member of the YHA and I go with some friends. We did the Pennine Way last summer.

Employer: Well, perhaps we should move on from your hobbies, 'cos I do a bit of hiking myself - and if we start on about that, we'll be here all day.

Interviewee: Mmm.

Employer: Er, ... well now ... tell me, did you have any jobs while you were at school ... during holidays?

Interviewee: Oh yeah ... um ... I used to work every summer. In the ... fourth year I think ... yeah yeah fourth year, I had a part time job stocking the shelves in Sainsbury's. They used to take me on for a few days before Christmas. I did that every year ... until I left school.

APPENDIX 3: EXPERIMENT 1 VERBAL INSTRUCTIONS

Interviews for jobs are important encounters, because of their effects on the subsequent courses of people's lives. This experiment is about the employment interview and in a few minutes I'd like you to listen carefully to part of one, but before that we shall have a practice run, to get you used to the kind of task you have to carry out.

It's important that we all go through every stage of the experiment in the right order, paying full attention all the time, so don't start examining the material until I tell you, but listen carefully to what I say. Otherwise you may get into a muddle.

Take the sheet of paper headed 'Practice Trial' and, without turning it over, quietly read the printed instructions. If you do not understand anything, raise your hand, but don't discuss them. In fact, from now on, please don't talk at all, because it is important that everyone does the task independently. I'll quickly run through the instructions with you as well now (i.e. instructions on Appendix 4).

... Any questions? (Questions dealt with publicly.)

Then let's begin the practice run now, but remember that even the practice must be taken seriously if it is to be useful.

APPENDIX 4: EXPERIMENT 1 INSTRUCTIONS AND SCALES

Practice trial

You are going to hear someone talking about a job vacancy. Listen carefully and try to imagine what the speaker is like, just as you might if you were talking to a stranger on the telephone, overhearing a conversation behind you on a bus, or hearing somebody on the radio. Different people form different impressions, of course, and there are no 'right' or 'wrong' answers here.

Over the page is a set of rating scales, on which you will be asked to give your impression of the speaker. When you are told to do so, <u>but not before,</u> please turn over, go through the scales in their printed order, and circle the numbers which best represent your opinions: for example:

Unbalanced   1 ② 3   4   5   6   7   Balanced

The rating shown would indicate that the speaker was regarded as quite, but not extremely, unbalanced. If you think the speaker sounds completely neutral with respect to a scale, or you have no opinion at all, you may use a rating of '4' to indicate this.

Make your decisions carefully, but quickly. Long deliberation does not enhance the quality of judgements.

Do not omit any scales. If you have to make any alterations, make it quite clear which rating is being deleted and which is meant to remain.

If you do not understand anything, please ask now.

LISTEN TO THE RECORDING, THEN BEGIN

Section A

The speaker appeared to be:

Untrustworthy	1	2	3	4	5	6	7	Trustworthy
Incapable	1	2	3	4	5	6	7	Capable
Unkind	1	2	3	4	5	6	7	Kind
Dull	1	2	3	4	5	6	7	Lively

NOW TURN OVER AND CONTINUE

The speaker you have heard was one of three applicants interviewed for the job concerned. None of them was considered suitable, so the post has been re-advertised.

OR

The speaker you have heard was one of 12 interviewed, out of a field of 60 applicants for the job concerned. He was offered the post, but decided to go to university and study law instead.

Section B

The person on the recording spoke with:

Non-standard pronunciation	1	2	3	4	5	6	7	Standard pronunciation
A slow speech rate	1	2	3	4	5	6	7	A fast speech rate
Monotonous intonation	1	2	3	4	5	6	7	Expressive intonation
A narrow vocabulary range	1	2	3	4	5	6	7	A wide vocabulary range
Bad grammar	1	2	3	4	5	6	7	Good grammar
A hard style to understand	1	2	3	4	5	6	7	An easy style to understand
An articulate manner	1	2	3	4	5	6	7	A hesitant manner

The speaker gave the impression of being:

Unambitious	1	2	3	4	5	6	7	Ambitious
Unsympathetic	1	2	3	4	5	6	7	Sympathetic
Unintelligent	1	2	3	4	5	6	7	Intelligent
Unkind	1	2	3	4	5	6	7	Kind
Unsuccessful	1	2	3	4	5	6	7	Successful
Not dependable	1	2	3	4	5	6	7	Dependable
Unsure	1	2	3	4	5	6	7	Confident
Insincere	1	2	3	4	5	6	7	Sincere

Now write here your AGE ( ), SEX (   ) and NAME ....

FINALLY, CHECK THAT YOU HAVE NOT MISSED ANYTHING OUT

APPENDIX 5: EXPERIMENT 2 INSTRUCTIONS AND SCALES

Now that you are familiar with rating impressions of recorded speakers, you are going to hear part of an actual interview for a job as a government office clerk. It is one of four for which the employers and the candidates have given their consent for the recordings to be made for research and teaching purposes.

Imagine that you are a Jobcentre Officer who has to advise the candidate about his prospects and self-presentation, and to prepare a short report about him for another officer. Normally, this would be done following an interview conducted by the Jobcentre Officer him- or herself, but quite similar to one conducted by an employer. Study the job applicant's behaviour in the interview and then carry out ratings as you did in the practice run, but this time thinking of them as ratings intended to form part of reports to be given to the candidate and the fellow-officer. After completing the ratings, elaborate your views on the two forms also provided, Form 'A' for the candidate, and Form 'B' for the employment officer, trying to indicate especially your opinions on aspects not covered by the rating scales. If you have any questions, ask them now.

LISTEN TO THE INTERVIEW, THEN TURN OVER AND BEGIN

The candidate gave the
impression of being:

Poor at communication skills	1 2 3 4 5 6 7	Good at communications skills
Insincere	1 2 3 4 5 6 7	Sincere
Unintelligent	1 2 3 4 5 6 7	Intelligent
Bad at working in a team	1 2 3 4 5 6 7	Good at working in a team
Irritable	1 2 3 4 5 6 7	Easy-going
Unambitious	1 2 3 4 5 6 7	Ambitious
Untrustworthy	1 2 3 4 5 6 7	Trustworthy
Impolite	1 2 3 4 5 6 7	Polite
Not dependable	1 2 3 4 5 6 7	Dependable
Unlikely to be offered the job	1 2 3 4 5 6 7	Likely to be offered the job

How suitable do you think the candidate was for the following jobs?

THIS JOB (GOVERNMENT OFFICE CLERK)

Very unsuitable   1 2 3 4 5 6 7   Very suitable

SHOP ASSISTANT

Very unsuitable   1 2 3 4 5 6 7   Very suitable

CLEANER

Very unsuitable   1 2 3 4 5 6 7   Very suitable

SECONDARY SCHOOL TEACHER

Very unsuitable   1 2 3 4 5 6 7   Very suitable

ACCOUNTANT IN A BUSINESS

Very unsuitable   1 2 3 4 5 6 7   Very suitable

How did you find the applicant's speech during the job interview?

                     Slow   1 2 3 4 5 6 7   Fast

      Non-standard
        pronunciation   1 2 3 4 5 6 7   Standard pronunciation

Form 'A': Advice to be given

Indicate both strengths and weaknesses, make constructive suggestions about upgrading qualifications and self-presentation and list the kind of openings the candidate should seek, as well as making any other comments you consider relevant.

_____

----

etc.

Form 'B': Jobcentre report

Indicate candidate's strengths and weaknesses, most suitable and most unsuitable types of work, any special considerations to be noted in future interviews with the client, and any precautions thought appropriate.

_____

7

Recreational use of the street by boys and girls: an observational and developmental study

Antony J. Chapman and Frances M. Wade

Specification notes

AIM OF EXERCISE: this is an observational exercise in which information is collected as to how boys and girls of various ages use streets for recreational purposes. A simple category system is used for classifying activities. The underlying problem is an important and salient one associated with everyday activities: it is how to account for child pedestrian accidents, and for the marked variation in accident rates associated with age and sex of children: five to nine year olds, especially boys, are involved in most accidents. Specifically the study examines whether trends in published statistics are a function of different amounts or types of street usage, with respect to (i) boys versus girls and (ii) five to nine year olds versus older and younger children.

PRIOR KNOWLEDGE ASSUMED: the exercise is suitable for students at the start of their course. It assumes little theoretical knowledge and only rudimentary expertise in descriptive and inferential statistics. From raw data, frequency counts are taken relating to the number of children of each age and sex category engaged in the following activities: running, walking, standing, sitting, talking, eating/drinking, active playing and passive playing, and location on the pavement or road. The ratio of observed boys to observed

girls is compared to the resident population in order to assess the extent to which the sex difference in accident rates is reflected in the disproportionate use of the street by young boys. Percentage scores are used for examining age and sex differences in behaviours: graphs are constructed and inductive analysis is by means of Chi Square tests. Students may perform further analyses: for example, they can relate age and sex distributions of pedestrians to vehicle density for particular streets. It is valuable to have knowledge of reliability and validity concepts, and ethical issues raised by the technique of observation can be discussed generally as well as in relation to this particular study.

DURATION: two three-hour sessions are required. The first session incorporates 60-90 minutes of fieldwork conducted outside school hours (perhaps in school holidays: e.g. half-term). Between sessions students enter their data on collation sheets so as to facilitate the analysis and discussion of pooled data in the second session.

LOCATION: a briefing session, and the data analysis and discussion, all take place in a laboratory or lecture theatre. The collection of data is undertaken in residential areas. Students are assigned predetermined routes to patrol, and the routes are within a locality in which the child population is known: hence a locality may be congruent with an electoral ward.

PROCEDURE SUMMARY: some observers (Type A) are first assigned to observe children systematically. They patrol a predetermined route and, for each child encountered, the following information is noted on pre-printed data sheets: sex, age (estimated), whether the child is on the road or the pavement, activity of the child according to eight prescribed categories, and street name. The remaining observers (Type B) first collect data relating to the traffic density of the streets in the study area. Type A and Type B observers are paired, one with the other, though they do not in fact accompany one another for much of the time: roles are switched half-way through a patrol.

REQUIRED RESOURCES AND FACILITIES: no hardware apparatus is required. Each student is issued with an annotated map and four types of printed sheets for data collection and collation (see appendices 1, 2, 3 and 4). An overhead projector or blackboard is useful for the final session. Conceivably some funding may be required to transport students to their field locations.

Introduction

Child pedestrians tend to use the streets near their homes for three sets of reasons: for journeys to and from school, for running errands, and for general recreational activities. In recreational activities streets serve as playgrounds and meeting places. For this exercise information is collected about recreational use as a function of age and sex. Children are observed in selected streets and their activities noted. The extent of street usage is assessed by relating the number of observed children to the number of resident children, the resident child population having been obtained from school registers or census records. Students are introduced to an observational technique and to a simple classification system for coding observed behaviours. Their attention should be drawn to possible observer influences

and to the difficulties of categorization, as well as to a variety of issues relating to reliability, validity and the nature of data.

The exercise is an example of research within the field of applied social psychology. As far as the broad aims of empirical enquiry are concerned, applied research and theoretical research are often discussed as though they are at opposite ends of a continuum. Polarized in this way theoretical research emphasizes the accumulation and synthesis of knowledge about principles of behaviour, while applied research emphasizes the solving of problems. Applied social psychology is social psychology orientated towards problem solving. Ultimately social psychology seeks to provide a fuller understanding of social behaviour and experience, and applied social psychology seeks to ameliorate social problems. But inevitably any such polarization is misleading; research is not either theoretical or applied: most contributes to both knowledge of principles and solutions to problems.

The social problem of interest to us is child pedestrian accidents, and the ultimate goal of research along the lines of this exercise is to reduce accidents through understanding how, when and why children use streets. From description we move towards theoretical models and policy recommendations. For example, it is commonly held that children cause road accidents by dashing heedlessly into the road, giving drivers no chance to take effective evading action (cf. Chapman, Wade and Foot, 1982). We might expect, therefore, to find that children often run in the course of their street activities. But if running were rarely observed then our theories about accidents, and our opinions about how legally to apportion blame for accidents, would require substantial revision.

Like much applied social research, this exercise is conducted in an everyday setting: naturally occurring public events are observed systematically. Observational methods have been defined by Weick (1968) as 'the selection, provocation, recording, and encoding of that set of behaviors and settings concerning organisms "in situ" which is consistent with empirical aims'.

By design his definition is all-embracing and it blurs any distinction between observational and experimental methodology on the grounds that only on a few dimensions do observation and experimentation differ from one another. Crano and Brewer (1973), for example, identify three principal dimensions: viz. participant-nonparticipant, structured-nonstructured, and response restriction dimensions. These are outlined below in the course of introducing the present exercise.

In practice there is wide variation in observers' participation in the social situations from which the behaviours under study emanate. Participation ranges from complete membership of a group to distancing in time and/or space from those being observed. Hence in 'participant observation' the observer might be accepted as a member of the group: obtaining membership for research purposes may be achieved either openly, and the observer's status as a researcher is then common knowledge, or covertly, and the observer's research function then remains unknown to other group members. Of course an observer's presence may interfere with the natural course of events; but this interference can be minimized by various methods, the most extreme of which is concealment. Total concealment implies a form of nonparticipant observation but, short of that, the concealment can be partial or subjects may falsely believe that others in the group, and not themselves, are the focus of enquiry (cf. Weick, 1968).

In a thorough review of the issues in observational research, McCall and Simmons (1969) noted that participant observation is a blend of methods and techniques characteristically employed for studying informal groups (e.g. factory workers and deviant sub-cultures), complex organizations (e.g. hospitals, unions and industrial corporations), social movements, and communities. It can include both formal and informal interviewing and collecting documents. It invariably involves some direct recording (or tape-recording) of events, although there can be a time lapse between the occurrence of those events and the creation of any permanent record. As regards the choice of measures, participant

observation studies are often open-ended with the range of measures perhaps narrowing as studies unfold over weeks or months. Hence participant observation is characterized by McCall and Simmons as a research enterprise in which several methods are combined in the pursuit of a broad objective, namely an 'analytic description', and that is a form of description which excludes, for example, journalistic reports.

Where this project lies on the participant-nonparticipant dimension is a moot point. (It is also an esoteric point of no practical consequence: any label – for example, 'a participant observation' – does not in itself offer any practical insights into an issue under investigation.) Observers, in independent pairs, patrol selected streets on foot, passing close to child pedestrians whose activities are surreptitiously recorded using prescribed categories: one member of a pair records the children's activities as the other records traffic density. The method thereby resembles a typical participant observation in several respects: first, it involves direct observation of events; second, some principal events are recorded (immediately) subsequent to, rather than during, their occurrence; third, the observers are visible to the observed and there is interaction to the extent that pedestrians (observers and children) comply with rules to limit or avoid social and physical encounters with strangers. If observers did not resemble ordinary pedestrians, other kinds of interaction might be solicited: for example, passers-by might ask what an observer was doing, or they might initiate what they considered to be appropriate conversation having first assigned him or her to a particular role (e.g. market researcher). The project also entails the consultation of documents to establish the sex and age profiles of the population in the study area: the documents can be school attendance registers or volumes containing census data obtained from the local council or public library. As in nonparticipant observation, subjects are not interviewed and there is no intention that the study should evolve over days, weeks or months: there are precisely formulated short-term procedures and a small set of possible outcomes.

Turning now to the 'structured-nonstructured' dimension: on the structured end data are tightly systematized using coding schemes which focus on a limited number of precisely defined behaviours: the behaviours are determined primarily by the hypotheses under investigation. At the non-structured end of the continuum observers supposedly conduct their research with no theoretical preconceptions as to the patterns that their data will eventually take. Again, for convenience of discussion, we are tending to introduce a non-existent polarization, and therefore we should re-iterate that the various techniques lie on a continuum of structuredness and that there is no dichotomy. The more structured approaches allow for reliability checks and for data analysis through inductive statistical procedures, whereas neither reliability assessment nor inductive analysis is usually feasible when data are collected through unstructured observation. Inevitably the researcher is confronted with a trade-off or series of trade-offs: for instance, it may be judged that statistical precision should be sacrificed in the interests of data richness, or vice versa. A decision to record the frequency of specific behaviours (within a set time period and for a particular target group), as here, implies that one has opted for an intensive enquiry into a particular set of behaviours, rather than an extensive enquiry in which an attempt is made to detail all group events.

With many coding systems the decision to record a behaviour is a binary one: the behaviour is judged to have occurred or not to have occurred. Additionally, however, some systems require the observer to judge the intensity of the behaviours: for example, a category such as 'walk' might assume three values: slow, medium and fast. Other systems incorporate items which are measured with standard laboratory equipment such as stop-watches or sound-level meters; but problems about judging the onset of behaviours, for example, can remain in an essentially identical form, and their solutions can be just as arbitrary (e.g. how loud must a noise be before it is recorded as present by the researcher?).

The data in this project are restricted to a small pre-determined set of activities, including 'walking', 'running', 'sitting', 'standing', 'playing' and 'talking'. As already noted, we are thereby embarking on an intensive enquiry vis-à-vis the classification of behaviours into these few categories. Yet, because the categories of behaviours are in fact broadly defined, the enquiry can be said to be extensive with regard to street usage: all aspects are coded. As outlined the system requires a simple frequency count of behaviours observed within samples of subjects. No rating scales or duration measures are used.

The 'response restriction' dimension identified by Crano and Brewer relates to the constraints placed upon subjects' behaviours by the environment within which the observations are made. Towards the more restricted end of this continuum are studies which make use of specifically designed settings and props to elicit or facilitate particular types of responses. In some of our research, for example, children have been brought to a mobile laboratory equipped as a play-room where they watch cartoon films (cf. Chapman, Smith and Foot, 1980): responses are videotaped via concealed cameras and microphones, and the tapes are subsequently transcribed by small groups of independent judges using a computerized event recorder. This project lies towards the opposite end of the continuum: the physical setting is neither designed nor manipulated for the research, and the observers endeavour to exert no influence over the variety of subjects' behaviours.

Specific background to the exercises

We turn next to the specific background behind this research. In Britain the problem of child pedestrian accidents is readily inferred from government statistics published annually (e.g. Department of Transport, 1980). Invariably there are marked age and sex trends in the statistics: it is alarmingly plain that five to nine year olds are especially vulnerable to road accidents, and that the rates for boys in this age range are about twice those for girls. The trends may result from a combination of factors, but on the face of it the most plausible causes are age and sex differences in exposure to traffic hazard and age and sex differences in behaviour: perhaps young primary schoolchildren, and boys particularly, are out-of-doors more, and perhaps some forms of behaviour (e.g. playing football) engender more serious conflict with vehicles than others (e.g. skipping with a rope).

Research on children's road safety is surprisingly sparse and it is also rather fragmented and atheoretical. Nevertheless, it can at least be said that a full gamut of techniques has been tried. A few of the more pertinent studies are mentioned below and all are cited in the book by Chapman et al (1982). From observing children on their journeys to and from school Howarth and colleagues (e.g. Routledge, Repetto-Wright and Howarth, 1974) have reported that exposure to traffic risk increases with age and that there are developmental changes in crossing strategies; but no corresponding sex differences have been noted. Playing outdoors has been investigated using survey, interview and observational methods. In a survey of accidents in Manchester and Salford, Preston (1972) found that more boys than girls were injured at play, and from interviews of mothers Sadler (1972) and Newson and Newson (1976) have reported that boys play more than girls in the street. Sandels (1975) observed more five and six year olds than younger children playing in places which she regarded as unsuitable; but there were no sex differences regarding either the suitability of play locations or their distances from home. In our own observational work (e.g. Chapman, Foot and Wade, 1980) we have witnessed substantially more boys than girls using streets for recreational purposes, but boys and girls have exhibited few differences in their choices of activity.

As a training device this exercise serves to draw students' attention to several clusters of issues. It illustrates many of the problems routinely encountered in using virtually any category system for recording behaviour. In this system, in combination with a number of mutually exclusive and specific categories (e.g. running and walking), are some less objective categories (viz. active play or passive play). The two types of classification provide something of a contrast and the

tutor may find that the latter are evaluated harshly or dismissively (e.g. on the specious grounds of being 'unscientific'). These evaluations should be channelled into critical discussion; on the specific level, about tailoring the definitions to suit the research aims; and, on the general level, about the nature of 'science' and 'scientific progress'. The demand for unambiguous and discrete categories should be emphasized. The desirability of training observers should be raised too: for example, after a period of training at the present task, observers claim that they are increasingly able to focus their attention and to allow irrelevancies to stream past them. The exercise can be used to draw attention to problems of observer interference and bias. Even in the freedom afforded by a street, the observers may sometimes find that they have become entangled with their subjects. They may find that they have become an obstacle, perhaps causing pedestrians to step into the road. It is essential that observers are not biassed in their choice of subjects. In particular, when there are many child pedestrians in sight, it is obviously vital to avoid any tendency to concentrate on those who are engaged in unusual or easily coded behaviour: the simplest means of minimizing this form of potential bias is to observe the child, previously unrecorded, who is nearest.

At all stages of the project students handle data for themselves: they enter tally marks on the data sheets, they convert those marks into numbers, they compile class data, and they perform statistical analyses (inferential and/or descriptive). This continuity aids the students' understanding of how the data are transformed, and it helps them to extend the analysis for themselves. Two distinct types of data are yielded: nominal data (frequency scores) from the use of behaviour categories, and ratio data from the head counts undertaken in calculating the sizes of the sub-samples (for sexes and age groups). Of course, the nature of measurement changes as studies are 'shaped' on the structuredness dimension; and, by pointing to the ways in which increasing the structure of the categorization alters the type of data obtained, the exercise can be used to review the characteristics of nominal, ordinal, interval and ratio scales of measurement. The use of simple binary-decision categories yields nominal data, as here, but if the design were to incorporate rating scales (e.g. of running speed) and duration measurements (e.g. of time spent running) the exercise would yield ordinal and ratio data respectively.

To recapitulate, this project investigates children's recreational use of streets, and hypotheses relate to the 'differential exposure to hazard' and 'heedless behaviour' explanations of the age and sex patterns in pedestrian accident statistics. Prediction 1 is that boys' exposure to traffic hazard is greater than that of girls: specifically, it is predicted that excluding school journeys the ratio of observed : resident children (the Observation Ratio, OR) is higher for boys than girls. Prediction 2 is that boys more than girls engage in heedless behaviours; namely, running, active play and activities in the roadway. Children in three age groups are observed (up to four years of age; five to nine; and ten to fourteen) and predictions are made (corresponding to Predictions 1 and 2) consistent with children's accident rates being higher for five to nine year olds than for other children. Hence, Prediction 3 is that OR is higher for five to nine year olds than older children; and Prediction 4 is that heedless behaviours are seen more commonly in five to nine year olds than older children. These two predictions are not extended to children under four because children in this age range are usually accompanied by adults.

Method

Roles and deployment of student observers
The project is conducted over two consecutive practical sessions. A standard lecture theatre or a laboratory of almost any description will suffice for plenary meetings; that is, when the tutor outlines the procedures and when the class data are collated and discussed. In the first session half the students in the class begin by observing children (Type A observers) and half begin as observer-enumerators of traffic (Type B observers); the two types of observer are paired, and individuals switch roles half-way through their patrol. Each observer pair is allocated a small sector of streets and only infrequently do members of a pair find themselves together in the one street (see below). There is no overlap of sectors and they should in combination comprise all streets in a geographical area whose resident population can, with relative ease, be ascertained.

The main resource is a set of sections of a large scale map (e.g. an ordnance survey map) divided into sectors, the number of sectors equalling the number of observer pairs. The tutor annotates the sections with sector boundaries and route directions. With a small class it may be possible to place all sectors on one large copy. However, there is much to be said for each observer pair receiving a unique map, with a single sector displayed and annotated; for example, observer pairs then have no excuse for encroaching upon another pair's sector, in part or in whole! But if this practice is followed, the tutor may nevertheless wish to produce a single map of the study area (by combining the various uniquely annotated maps): this would be useful for class discussion in the second session and hence would assist students in writing their practical reports. Additionally, for collecting data, each observer pair requires five or six Pedestrian Data Sheets (Appendix 1) and two Traffic Density Sheets (Appendix 2): extra sheets will be necessary for the practice session. For processing their own data students require a Pedestrian Collation Sheet (Appendix 3) and a Traffic Density Collation Sheet (Appendix 4). Clip-boards are useful but they do increase observer conspicuity. A handout, to be read after the observation and before the second practical session, should provide the rationale for the study, the hypotheses, and a reading list. If some or all of the sectors are outside a comfortable walking distance from the teaching department it may be necessary to underwrite student fares on public transport or to have access to a minibus. The second session involves pooling observers' collated data, for which is required a standard blackboard, or whiteboard, or overhead projector with acetate plates and pens.

Unless the first session is scheduled during school holidays (e.g. half-term), it should include an afternoon. This is because children are observed on streets and specifically <u>not</u> on school journeys (when, for example, boys and girls would of necessity be present in approximately equal numbers). Observations are made in residential areas during the late afternoon of the first practical session, when children are on the streets after returning home from school. It is desirable that all observation routes should start within a short walk from the initial briefing session. Prudency and expediency dictate that the project is run when weather and light conditions are likely to be good; this is not only for the observers' comfort and safety but because otherwise the streets may be virtually deserted. The project commends itself to placement early in the students' teaching year because the statistical procedures can be relatively unsophisticated if preferred.

Prior to the first practical session the tutor should undertake several tasks. First, using the map, the selected study area is divided into the sectors. All else being equal, it is recommended that a sector comprises about one mile of streets so that it requires approximately 30 minutes to patrol one. When feasible, long shopping streets, having many pedestrians, are divided into two or more segments and then shared between adjacent sectors; and, in general, arrangement of sectors should be such that they all include quiet and busy streets. Each observer pair should be issued with a map of the area (or copy) with a single sector clearly delineated. Having completed observations in certain streets at the start of their patrol, it is possible that observers may subsequently need to pass along some of those same streets again in order to gain access to others: therefore the directions of patrols should be marked on the students' maps, with care given to minimizing the amount of unnecessary walking. Crossroads and junctions serve as useful boundary markers for sectors. Within the constraints just outlined, it is usually possible to arrange patrols so that few, if any, main roads have to be crossed.

Choice of study area and subjects

For ease of obtaining population information (i.e. the numbers of resident boys and girls in the three age groups), the geographical study area is chosen to be congruent with an electoral ward or primary school catchment area. Conveniently the National Census, like the road accident statistics, is organized such that there is separate information for the age groups under four years, five to nine years and ten to fourteen years; and census data for electoral wards are publicly available from local councils and libraries. Alternatively, schools are usually very co-operative in research of this nature and enthusiastically supply details about catchment boundaries and ages and sex of children on their registers. The youngest age category (under four) would clearly have to be omitted if school registers were used but, as we have said earlier, these children are rarely outdoors unless accompanied by adults. Naturally some children from neighbouring wards or catchment areas will intrude into the study area, and resident children will also migrate into those neighbouring regions. For this exercise it is reasonably assumed that there are no systematic imbalances in these movements with respect to either boys/girls or children in the three age groups. The tutor also has to prepare four sets of data sheets for distribution to all students at the start of the exercise. These are shown in the appendices.

Temporal arrangements

During the opening part of the first session the tutor (i) gives the background context to the project, (ii) issues the maps and data sheets, and (iii) briefs students to be observers/observer-enumerators. Members of the class then disperse in pairs to their designated sectors. It is strongly recommended that they undertake a practice period of at least 15 minutes prior to the onset of the observation. It is important (see above) that formal observations should not begin until after children have arrived home from school. Afternoon school is usually finished by four o'clock (in Great Britain) and primary schoolchildren generally accomplish their homeward travel within 20 minutes (cf. Routledge et al, 1974): therefore, to allow for stragglers, it is recommended that formal observations should start at half-past four. There is no necessity for students to return to the tutor when they have fulfilled their observational duties. However, at the end of the session (or at least between sessions), individual observers should each enter their own data on the Pedestrian Data Sheet (Appendix 1) and Traffic Density Sheet (Appendix 2). During the second practical session the data for all students are pooled (through the tutor), and analyses are carried out by individual students.

Briefing of observers

The pre-observation briefing focusses on observational techniques, the category scheme and procedures to be adopted by the observers. As far as possible the specific hypotheses are not discussed, the objectives being expressed in very general terms: this is an attempt to reduce observer bias. Observers begin their observations at, say, half-past four, starting their patrols at the points indicated on the maps. Each pair follows its prescribed route with observers using three criteria for selecting subjects: first, they are children estimated to be aged 14 years or younger; second, they are pedestrians; and third, they are not accompanied by an adult. To be regarded as 'pedestrians' they are required to be on the pavement or road, either on foot or sitting or lying down; they do not qualify as pedestrians if they are riding, or are mounted on, bicycles or other wheeled toys/vehicles (such as scooters, roller skates and skateboards). This operational definition includes as pedestrians any children who are seen standing with bicycles, etc., or who are pushing rather than riding them.

Type A observers proceed at a casual walking pace watching the activities of the nearest boy/girl who is under 14. They look away to record information as unobtrusively as possible on a Pedestrian Data Sheet, and then the next subject is sought as their patrol is continued. Information is classified following the row headings, left to right, in Appendix 1. As an observer moves into the various streets the street names are listed in turn. Having noted the sex

and age of an observed child, the row entries are continued by the making of a single entry in one of the four primary information categories: a tally mark is placed under 'run', or 'walk', or 'stand', or 'sit'. These mutually exclusive behaviours are defined as follows:

* 'run' (to include athletic behaviours such as those commonly called 'jumping', 'gambolling', 'cartwheeling', 'somersaulting' and 'skipping' without rope): forward, backward or sideways motion of the legs during the course of which both feet are sometimes off the ground simultaneously;
* 'walk': forward, backward or sideways motion of the legs in which at no time are both feet off the ground;
* 'stand': no regular motion of the legs, and the body weight is borne primarily or exclusively by the feet;
* 'sit' (to include actions commonly termed 'kneeling' and 'lying'): the body weight is borne principally by parts of the anatomy other than the feet and there is no change of body location.

Data recording for the one subject continues with secondary information being entered in the same row. In the 'road/pavement' column, the letter R is entered if the subject is in the roadway (or in the centre of the road on a raised, kerbed area); while the letter P is entered if the subject is on the pavement (being defined as a raised and kerbed strip at the side of the roadway).

Other secondary information relates to playing, eating/drinking, and talking. 'Play' is defined as interaction with a person or object (excepting drinkable and edible items) and is subdivided into 'active play' (which potentially involves the child moving more than two metres) and 'passive play' (which involves less movement, perhaps no noticeable movement). Examples of active play are fighting and playing ball games. Examples of passive play are handling snails and cradling dolls. Clearly subjective judgements are demanded for this classification. Hence observers may find it helpful, and it may be more reliable, to note play behaviours in 'longhand' (as illustrated in Appendix

1), and then introduce the active/passive subdivision at the end of the observation period. 'Eating/drinking' are defined by the process of placing food or drink in the mouth and swallowing; and 'talking' (which includes shouting or singing) is defined in terms of discernible vocal sounds or, for more distant subjects, displays of lip movements. Having completed this classification, the (Type A) observer moves to the next subject and the next row on the Pedestrian Data Sheet. This procedure continues to the halfway stage in the observation session when, at a pre-arranged point on the route, Type A observers meet their Type B partners and exchange roles. With just a little practice most observers, as they approach a small group or procession of subjects, are able to register the activities of those subjects with ease; they readily develop a knack of committing their observations to paper without calling attention to themselves. It is vital that observers try not to record any child twice: children are disregarded if they reappear on an observer's route. From traffic observations, the density classifications (quiet or busy: see Appendix 2) are later transferred to the Pedestrian Data Sheet in a segment of the first column for each street.

Although they start from the same points and tread common routes, Type B observers, as traffic enumerators, proceed at an irregular pace, and they conduct their traffic counts independently of Type A observers' activities. As already indicated individuals switch Type A and Type B duties half-way through the observation period, having rendezvoused on their prescribed route. In their traffic enumerating role, students record three-minute traffic counts of vehicles (including bicycles) travelling on five or more roads in their sector. (By standing at intersections and junctions - marked on their maps by the tutor - they can usually undertake counts for two or more roads at one time.) For each of these roads information is entered under the first two headings of the Traffic Density Sheet illustrated in Appendix 2: these headings are 'street name' and 'number of vehicles in three minutes'. 'Vehicles per hour' (the third column) is calculated by multiplying the observed three-minute number

ber (i.e. the figure in the second column) by a factor of 20. In the final column is entered a Q (for quiet street: 0-120 vehicles per hour) or B (for busy street: 121 or more vehicles per hour). Entries in columns three and four can usually be made in quiet moments during the observation, but they can be deferred until the observation period is terminated.

Data tabulation
Before the second practical class each observer transfers his or her pedestrian data to the Pedestrian Collation Sheet illustrated in Appendix 3. This groups data according to subjects' ages and sex. Taking each row in turn from the Pedestrian Data Sheet, the student places a tally mark in each appropriate cell in the collation sheet. For example, from Appendix 1, the first observation is of a seven-year-old boy running and talking while playing football on the road; hence tally marks are placed on the collation sheet in the row for 'Boys 5-9' under the columns headed 'run', 'R', 'active play' and 'talk'. The street (York Road) has been classified as 'quiet' (Q) (see below). Football is classified as 'active play' because potentially it involves more than two metres of movement: had this child been 'standing', his activity would still be classed as 'active play'. The collation process is straightforward, the single possible uncertainty residing in the active/passive play classification. In Appendix 3 numbers have been entered (instead of tally marks) to illustrate how the collation progresses. Thus, **1** (in bold print) refers to the first subject, **2** to the second subject, and so on to the final (twelfth) subject. Next the numbers of subjects, corresponding to the age and sex categories, are entered in the first column, headed 'N'. The grand total equals the number of all children observed (12 in this illustration). Finally, the tally marks are summed in the other cells and entries made beside the tally marks. In Appendix 3 these totals are shown in bold print: in the student's sheet only one number would be entered in any one cell.

As enumerators the student observers, in their enumerator roles, use the Pedestrian Data Sheet to record traffic density for each street. By this point the density data have been condensed to two categories, giving two classes of street: Q = 'quiet'; B = 'busy'. On the Pedestrian Data Sheet a Q or B is entered (shown in Appendix 1) for each of the streets listed. Entries are also made in the Traffic Density Collation Sheets (Appendix 4), indicating the numbers of boys/girls in each age group who are observed in busy and quiet streets. In Appendix 4 the traffic density collation exercise has been completed from the data given in Appendix 1; again numbers have been used to represent each subject, and the bold numbers are cell totals. We would recommend that where there is bold print in Appendices 3 and 4 students should use a second ink colour, or circle the numbers. Some internal checks on collation accuracy are available: each of the sub-sample sizes, and the grand totals, remain constant from the Pedestrian Collation Sheet (Appendix 3) to the Traffic Density Collation Sheet (Appendix 4).

Data collection, analysis and results

Analyses of data pooled from all students (i.e. for the entire study area) are recommended, rather than analyses for individual students (i.e. for sectors or half-sectors). Hence data for the class are pooled in the opening part of the second practical session. Six student-clerks are appointed - one for each of the age/sex categories - to pool data from Pedestrian Collation Sheets: and six more clerks are appointed to collect the traffic density information. Each clerk has a master collation sheet (or acetate sheet for an overhead projector, with rows and columns already labelled), on to which are transferred the various cell totals from each student. For example, one clerk collects scores for boys under four, a second collects the data for five- to nine-year-old boys, and so on. Students visit each clerk in turn until all the data have been pooled, including the clerks' own data. Each clerk then enlists the assistance of other students to sum the scores within each age/sex category and for each activity. The accrued information relates to child pedestrians in the whole observation area, with behaviour frequencies given

for the six age/sex categories. The next step is to transfer the clerks' summed scores to a large board (or to project them on to a screen), so that students can note down the class data.

Testing predictions

PREDICTION 1. The first prediction states that higher exposure to traffic hazards for boys is reflected in a higher OR for boys than for girls. Ratios are derived by dividing the number of children observed by the number of children resident in the area, calculating each age group separately. Hence:

$$\frac{\text{Five- to nine-year-old boys observed}}{\text{Five- to nine-year-old resident boys}} = \frac{48}{144}$$

Therefore, OR = 1:3 (which is 33.33 per cent)

$$\frac{\text{Five- to nine-year-old girls observed}}{\text{Five- to nine-year-old resident girls}} = \frac{23}{118}$$

Therefore, OR = 1:5.13 (which is 19.49 per cent)

Hence OR is numerically higher for boys than for girls. In other words, proportionally more boys than girls were observed to use the streets.

PREDICTION 2. The second prediction states that, relative to girls, boys run more, play more active games, and are found in the roadway more. For the pooled data in the Pedestrian Collation Sheet (i.e. for the class as a whole), a percentage is calculated for each of the 'run', 'active play' and R cells by dividing the observed number in the cell by the number of subjects in the sub-sample and then multiplying by 100. These percentages should be entered on a blank Pedestrian Collation Sheet (or written directly on a blackboard or overhead projector). Taking each of the three activities separately, statistical associations and the statistical significance of sex differences can be established using Chi Square tests.

PREDICTION 3. The third prediction is that OR is higher for five to nine year olds than for older children. Hence ratios are compared for five to nine year olds and ten to fourteen year olds.

PREDICTION 4. The fourth prediction is that five to nine year olds exhibit more heedless behaviours than older children. This prediction is examined in similar fashion to Prediction 2. Taking 'run', 'active play' and 'R' separately, frequency scores are cast in three tables for Chi Square statistical analyses.

FURTHER PREDICTION. The traffic count data can be used to investigate sex differences in exposure to traffic. From pedestrian accident statistics, it might be ex-

pected that more boys than girls would be observed in 'busy' streets (i.e. those with more than 120 vehicles per hour). This prediction is tested in much the same way as the others: percentage scores for boys and girls in quiet and in busy streets are subjected to Chi Square tests.

Presentation of data
The salient features of the data can be brought out pictorially as in figure 1, for example, which depicts sex and age trends in running and active play. (Note that the data represented in figure 1 are fictitious pooled data and are not derived from the fictitious data in appendices 1-4.)

Figure 1. Age variations in boys' and girls' (a) running and (b) active playing

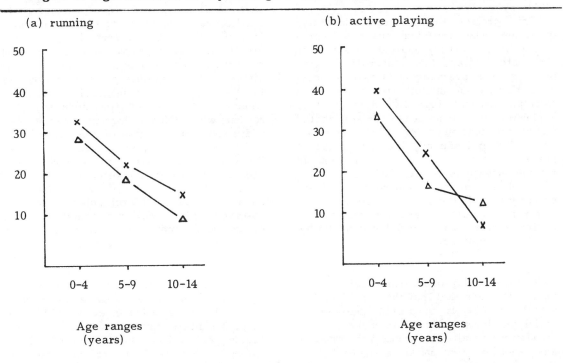

(a) running

(b) active playing

Age ranges
(years)

Key: Boys ✗

Girls △

Note: the data depicted above are not based upon the data given in the tables.

Discussion

From our own research (e.g. Chapman et al, 1980) we expect support to be gleaned for all four predictions. Almost certainly boys will be found to use streets for recreational purposes to a greater extent than girls. Sex differences in 'heedless' behaviours are likely to be found for some of the age groups, showing more 'heedless' activity for boys. However, it is unlikely that all these differences will be statistically significant, especially if subsamples are small. Some trends may even run counter to prediction: that is, girls may be observed to engage in some heedless behaviours more than boys. Regarding age trends, running and active play will probably be found to decrease as subjects' ages increase, while walking and talking will probably be more prevalent in older children.

This project raises three conceptual questions. The first concerns how appropriate it is to study routine behaviour in the context of accident analysis. In extrapolating from everyday behaviour to accidents there is an implicit assumption which warrants critical appraisal: namely, that accidents and routine behaviour are located on the one continuum (cf. Chapman et al, 1982). But it could be, for instance, that patterns of sex differences observed in routine situations reveal little or nothing of consequence about abnormal, accident situations; and thus, having little or no external validity vis-à-vis accidents, exercises such as this may be of negligible practical significance.

Let us take it that the exercise is indeed valid and move to the second question which is to do with statistical significance. We have said that the aim of applied social research is to provide answers to social problems and then to make recommendations to alleviate those problems. In any research which has a bearing on practical issues the question of statistical significance assumes full importance. If large sex differences were observed in the so-called 'heedless' behaviours - say, boys engaged in much more running and active games - policy makers might be tempted to suggest that boys should be presented with more road safety training, perhaps through informal bodies like scout troups and youth clubs. The onus on the social scientist under these circumstances would be as far as possible to ensure through empirical means that there was a true sex difference: that is, to demonstrate beyond reasonable doubt that the findings were not due to empirical artifacts or to sampling error. To err on the conservative side, before committing themselves, researchers might choose to set the statistical confidence level at a more stringent level than conventionally set (i.e. above 0.05). Then again, before making any recommendations having far-reaching consequences, the observational exercise described here might be considerably elaborated and conducted in various towns and cities and under various temporal and environmental conditions.

The third issue concerns the temptation to impute accident causality to exposure factors. If a sex difference in exposure to traffic hazards is inferred, it remains logically unsound to assert that accidents are 'caused' by exposure to traffic hazard per se: at most one can merely suggest that differences in exposure probably contribute to the sex difference in accident rates. It cannot be emphasized too much that the reasons why accidents happen have not been addressed in the course of this procedure.

There are two major design limitations. One concerns the assumptions underlying the use of the Chi Square test, and the other concerns the reliability of the method. Chi Square requires that each subject has been observed only once, but sometimes this consideration may not be met in full. In the main, this is because children may cross sectors and because, within each sector, students share the observation-of-children duties. The extent of the problem can be estimated by trailing subjects in the style of Routledge et al (1974): it would be interesting to know the time and course of journeys, the number of sectors entered, and the number of observers encountered en route.

The reliability of any coding system is primarily dependent upon category discriminability within the classification scheme and upon the efficacy of coder training. In this project these aspects of reliability can be both assessed and optimized. Estimating age and sex can be problematic, especially when children are wearing unisex clothes, coats with hoods, and so on. For a major project, observers lacking experience with children should spend some time beforehand in nursery and primary schools. Short of that, it helps inexperienced observers to see films and photographs portraying children in their various age groups. Some reliability estimates can be gained by having observers within pairs independently assess the ages (and/or sex) of particular children, and then make comparisons of their assessments. The efficient use of the category system is readily improved through prior training and practice. The reliability of its use can also be evaluated, again by comparing observers' categorizations for particular children.

Finally, it should be noted that subjects are observed without their (or their caretakers') knowledge or consent. This practice is contrary to the basic principle of informed consent, whereby subjects understand the nature and extent of their participation and freely consent to it. This principle may be considered particularly important when the subjects are members of the community who are especially vulnerable to exploitation by others: for example, children. Psychologists are divided in their opinions about the necessity for unobtrusive observation of naturally occurring behaviours. Most psychologists regard the practice of concealing observations as acceptable when behaviours are public and/or when the settings are open to public scrutiny. However, a minority regard any form of unaware participation in research as an intolerable invasion of the individual's right to privacy. Clearly what is taken to constitute 'public behaviour' is intrinsic to the debate. Even though some settings obviously permit public observation, the issue of privacy remains when individuals in those settings do not expect to be observed, or perhaps expect not to be observed.

Conclusion

Through this exercise students become aware of several key factors relating generally to the choice and use of observational techniques. They are introduced to the participant-nonparticipant dimension; they contemplate the degree of structure in the classification scheme and the necessary compromise between an intensive and extensive scheme; they analyse the extent to which behaviours are restricted by the observer bias and observer interference; and they debate the ethics of unobtrusive observation. In addition they gain some insight into the extent to which validity and reliability can be established in relation to this particular applied social problem. The exercise also provides an opportunity for illustrating how changes in the design of a study lead to different scales of measurement and different kinds of data.

REFERENCES

Chapman, A.J., Foot, H.C. and Wade, F.M. (1980) Children at play. In D.J. Oborne and J.A. Levis (eds), Human Factors in Transport Research, Volume 2. London: Academic Press.

Chapman, A.J., Smith, J.R. and Foot, H.C. (1980) Humour, laughter and social interaction. In P.E. McGhee and A.J. Chapman (eds), Children's Humour. Chichester: Wiley.

Chapman, A.J., Wade, F.M. and Foot, H.C. (eds) (1982) Pedestrian Accidents. Chichester: Wiley.

Crano, W.D. and Brewer, M.B. (1973) Principles of Research in Social Psychology. New York: McGraw-Hill.

Department of Transport (1980) Road Accidents Great Britain 1978. London: HMSO.

McCall, G.J. and Simmons, J.L. (eds) (1969) Issues in Participant Observation: Text and reader. Reading, Mass.: Addison-Wesley.

Newson, J. and Newson, E. (1976) The Seven Year Old in His Home Environment. London: Allen & Unwin.

Preston, B. (1972) Statistical analyses of child pedestrian accidents in Manchester and Salford. Accident Analysis and Prevention, 4, 323-332.

Routledge, D.A., Repetto-Wright, R. and Howarth, C.I. (1974) A comparison of interviews and observation to obtain measures of children's exposure to risk as pedestrians. Ergonomics, 17, 623-638.

Sadler, J. (1972) Children and Road Safety: A survey amongst mothers. Report SS450. London: HMSO.

Sandels, S. (1975) Children in Traffic. London: Elek.

Weick, K.E. (1968) Systematic observational methods. In G. Lindzey and E. Aronson (eds), The Handbook of Social Psychology (2nd edn), Volume 2. Reading, Mass.: Addison-Wesley.

APPENDIX 1. PEDESTRIAN DATA SHEET

Street name and classification	sex	age	Primary information				Secondary information			
			run	walk	stand	sit	road/ pavement	active/ passive play	eat/ drink	talk
Q York Road	M	7	/				R	football		/
Q York Road	M	7		/			P	football		/
Q York Road	F	14		/			P		/	
Q Hollow Lane	M	6		/			P			/
Q Hollow Lane	M	4			/		P			/
Q St Martin's Road	F	10		/			P			
B Nantucket Avenue	F	10		/			R	stilts		
B Nantucket Avenue	F	14		/			R			/
B Nantucket Avenue	M	14		/			R			/
B Nantucket Avenue	M	8				/	P	photographs		/
B Penhill Road	F	8			/		P	photographs		/
B Manor Road	M	9			/		R	photographs		/
Pascoes Avenue										

APPENDIX 2. TRAFFIC DENSITY SHEET

Street name	Number of vehicles in three minutes	Vehicles per hour	Street classification
York Road	1	20	Q
St Martin's Road	3	60	Q
Hollow Lane	3	60	Q
Manor Road	6	120	Q
Penhill Road	80	1,600	B
Nantucket Avenue	8	160	B

APPENDIX 3. PEDESTRIAN COLLATION SHEET

Subject group	n	Primary information				Secondary information					
		run	walk	stand	sit	R	P	active play	passive play	eat/ drink	talk
Boys 0-4	1			5 1			5 1				5 1
Boys 5-9	5	1 1	2,4 2	12 1	10 1	1,12 2	2,4,10 3	1,2 2	10,12 2		1,2,4,10,12 5
Boys 10-14	1		9 1			9 1					9 1
Girls 0-4											
Girls 5-9	1		11 1				11 1		11 1		11 1
Girls 10-14	4		3,6,7,8 4			7,8 2	3,6 2	7 1		3 1	8 1
Grand total (N)	12										

Note: cell totals and sample sizes are in bold print.

APPENDIX 4. TRAFFIC DENSITY COLLATION SHEET

Subject group	n	Quiet	Busy
Boys 0-4	**1**	5 **1**	
Boys 5-9	**5**	1,2,4 **3**	10,12 **2**
Boys 10-14	**1**		9 **1**
Girls 0-4			
Girls 5-9	**1**		11 **1**
Girls 10-14	**4**	3,6 **2**	7,8 **2**
Grand total (N)	**12**		

Note: cell totals and sample sizes are in bold print.

8

Social skills training: the need for a knowledge of social behaviour
Paul Robinson and Peter Trower

Specification notes

AIMS OF THE EXERCISE: to demonstrate how relatively small changes in individuals' social behaviour can dramatically affect their ability to have normal social interactions.

PRIOR KNOWLEDGE ASSUMED: it is assumed that the students will have little or no knowledge of looking at elements of social behaviour. A basic knowledge of experimental method and statistical analysis is assumed (including familiarity with the use of semantic differential scaling, although this can be omitted if it is new to the students).

DURATION: the exercise is expected to last approximately three hours with a final discussion of results at a later date.

LOCATION: one large room or several smaller ones depending on group size and equipment available.

RESOURCES: as many of the following as are available: stop-watches, event recorders, audio- and videotape-recorders. Variations are given for differing equipment availability.

SPECIAL REQUIREMENTS: none.

Social behaviour is arguably the most central and important characteristic of human beings, and yet social behaviour as such remained a relatively neglected subject in psychology and related disciplines until recent years. In the last two decades or so, however, researchers have focussed increasingly on the topic, and today there is a substantial body of scientific information. From this information a striking picture emerges of Man possessing social skills of extraordinary complexity and sophistication (Argyle, 1978). As research progresses, the components and processes of interpersonal relationships are unravelled and understood to the point where we can now identify scientifically some of the complex behaviour patterns involved in friendship, love, domination and other psychological qualities in social interaction (Argyle and Trower, 1979). A natural and vital extension of this work is to analyse the behaviour of people with problems (including psychiatric patients) and devise ways of helping them to acquire more effective social skills (Bellack and Hersen, 1979).

In this chapter we present an exercise designed to show participating students something of the psychological power and complexity of elements of social behaviour, and to demonstrate just how handicapping a deficit in one or more elements of social skills can be for an individual. Thus we aim to show how one branch of psychology can have important relevance in an applied setting, and the way this has developed in clinical psychology can be followed up in the literature (e.g. Trower, Bryant and Argyle, 1978).

Introduction

Social behaviour is a wide field and as such has benefitted from analysis by a variety of different specialists including sociologists, anthropologists and linguists as well as psychologists. The basic model behind social skills training and its approach to social behaviour is that of a skills learning model (Argyle and Kendon, 1967). This is centred around the idea that human behaviours are mostly learnt and can be developed by means of structured learning opportunities. In discussing the learning and training of these skills we shall take an eclectic position, and will not be arguing for any particular theoretical model.

What then are the important aspects of social behaviour? The first and most obvious answer is that social behaviour does not occur in a vacuum, but rather as part of an interaction and a context. First, an interaction has a purpose or goal, whether it be loosely stated as in two old friends reminiscing over the past, or more clearly stated as in, say, a marriage ceremony. If this purpose is to be attained then the individuals involved in the interaction must perceive the cues given by the others involved with regard to which behaviour it is appropriate for them to show. These cues may indicate other people's expectations, attitudes or feelings, or refer to unwritten rules of conduct generated by the social community (Scherer and Giles, 1979).

Second, the individual must show appropriate behaviours for the situation. These must be such that they not only allow the person to achieve their particular aim in the interaction but also conform to the rules of the situation and the needs of others involved. For example, in a chat between friends, one purpose of which is to maintain and perhaps extend the friendship, it is unlikely that one individual doing all the talking will be seen as acceptable behaviour by the other person.

Finally, if individuals are going to act as self-correcting systems, they must be aware of the feedback that they receive from others in the social setting. Equally importantly, they must also provide feedback for the others in the interaction, so if an individual is enjoying a conversation with a friend then adequate cues of this fact should be provided.

The exact summary of these stages depends on the model one is using. Thus the Argyle and Kendon (1967) model labels these stages perception, translation, performance and feedback. A behavioural model labels them antecedents (or setting conditions), behaviour, and consequences (or social reinforcement/punishment). Which model is chosen is not crucial. The important point is to realize that an interaction can break down due to problems at a variety of different stages: for example, people may behave inappropriately due to lack of skills in their repertoires or because they have misperceived the cues in the situation.

It can be seen that, although we normally take the execution of social behaviour for granted, it consists of a large number of complex skills. The task of research is partly to examine social behaviour closely and discover what elements it consists of and what constitutes 'normal' behaviour under a variety of conditions (e.g. Siegman and Feldstein, 1978).

To take an illustrative example, the amount and patterning of eye gaze have been shown to play a variety of important roles (Argyle and Cook, 1976). In normal two-person interactions between peers it has been shown, for example, that the person speaking looks at the listener less than the listener at the speaker, such that as the individuals change role so they change their gaze time. Roughly the speaker looks at the listener for about 30 per cent of the time spent talking and the listener 50-80 per cent of the time spent listening. Furthermore, the speaker tends to look at the listener at the end of his/her turn (i.e. as he/she finishes speaking and changes to become the listener) and so it often functions as a 'hand-over' cue.

By deviating markedly from the normal pattern for one's cultural group an individual affects the interaction in striking ways. Let us take an imaginary pair of people, John and Rachel. They meet for the first time at a party and Rachel starts talking to John. All the time they are talking John never once looks at Rachel. This makes Rachel feel very uncomfortable, since she feels that John is not interested in her or what she has to say, or that John is very 'shy'. Whatever explanation she uses, she does not find the interaction rewarding, and is likely to keep it quite short and to move on to someone else.

What would Rachel's reaction have been if John had behaved at the opposite extreme, namely 100 per cent eye contact? She starts a conversation and finds that John, who is a stranger to her, never takes his eyes off her. She is likely to consider him rude and offensive, and possibly even sexually offensive due to her interpretation of his behaviour in comparison to normal male behaviour in these circumstances. She might also wonder whether something dreadful had occurred to her make-up/hair/wig, etc. ('What on earth is he staring at me like that for?'). The interpretation she makes will affect her emotional reaction. In the first place she is likely to get annoyed and in the second place embarrassed. Either way she is likely to end the interaction quickly and move on.

These examples demonstrate how a change in a single element of behaviour can radically affect social interactions, and how the other person's interpretation of the behaviour will also have a major effect. Furthermore, it illustrates the importance of the context of the behaviour. If Rachel and John were lovers it would be perfectly acceptable to Rachel for John to stare into her eyes for five minutes continuously whilst softly saying 'sweet nothings'. Similarly, a long pause in the conversation is likely to be felt as very awkward on a first meeting, but quite normal between two lovers.

Another example of a behavioural component bound by normative rules is the question. Too many precise questions ('Who are you? Where do you live? What do you do? What do your parents do?' etc.) which allow only short answers fired off in rapid succession will make the person feel interrogated rather than chatted to; appropriate perhaps in an interview but hardly between potential friends. A normal interaction uses a few introductory questions to establish identity and a common area of interest from which a general conversation is developed. Contributing unequally to the interaction will create difficulties: either individuals are seen to be hogging the conversation and only wanting to talk about themselves or, at the other extreme, they appear shy and withdrawn with nothing to say for themselves.

The number of behavioural elements is considerable, and in the non-verbal domain alone includes gaze, facial expression, gesture, posture, proximity, touching, vocalization, and physical appearance (Argyle, 1975; Knapp, 1978). Such elements do not occur in isolation but are organized in many complex ways (Argyle, 1969); for example, we can look at the frequency of questions, the timing of disclosures, the pattern of pauses, interruptions and the turn-taking 'system' (Duncan and Fiske, 1977). In the following exercise we shall focus mainly on a few of these specificable and quantifiable behaviours. Participants may also like to look at the more interpretive aspects, however, in ways to be suggested later.

The exercise
The exercise will be attempting to show how altering one or two of the basic behaviours can have major effects on interaction as discussed in our imaginary examples with John and Rachel above. It is to be hoped that this will bring students' attention to a variety of points. It should sensitize them to the complexity of social behaviour and the possibilities of fine-grained analysis. It should also illustrate how handicapping it might be for an individual to exhibit social behaviour which deviates too far from the normal. This type of approach helps clinical psychologists and others to identify those aspects of an individual's behaviour which might be contributing to a problem, and help to train that person in a more socially acceptable manner.

Method

The main activity is a role-play by two students which is observed by other students. The role-play is carried out under a variety of different conditions. As such, the exercise allows a large amount of flexibility, being suitable for a group of four or five students or a large group. A large group is either split into several smaller autonomous groups or excess numbers used as observers to record a wider variety of behaviours. In order to be more consistent throughout the chapter a group size of about 30 will be assumed. This is then split into four groups of seven or eight students each, so that each group provides two students as role-players (henceforth called the 'actors') and five as observers. (More than one pair within each group could be actors if time allows a complete repeat of the exercise.) In this way four sets of observations are obtained which can then be pooled for analysis (to be discussed later).

Resources
Basic resources can be minimal: two chairs facing each other for the actors, paper and pencil for recording by the observers and a minimum of two stop-watches (or at least a clock with a sweep second hand). However, the availability of other equipment, in particular more stop-watches or event recorders, audio- and/or video-recorders, allows a greater degree of refinement in data collection. Ideally then, a video- or audio-system is set up to record the interaction and these provide a record against which observations can be checked, or new observations made afterwards.

Using the standard class (outlined above) split into four groups, it might be easier if four separate rooms are available to minimize noise interference between groups. However, given a reasonably large room this need not be a major problem. Should video equipment be available, it is likely that the groups of students will have to use the equipment in rotation so only one location will be required.

Basic procedure
The tutor introduces the background to the exercise and the general aims behind it (as outlined in the Introduction). Then the class forms into groups and actors chosen by volunteering or election. Unless the sex balance of the class deviates severely from 50/50 we suggest making each pair of ac-

tors a mixed-sex pair, otherwise the effects of sex role on behaviour may mask other effects. Equipment is handed out, the actors given scripts, and the measures to be taken are discussed. The groups then separate to carry out the exercise. After completing the exercise and any further data analysis decided upon (using audio- or videotape-recordings) the groups are brought back together so that the data can be pooled and methods of examining the data outlined. A general discussion of the findings and of the difficulties of the exercise can then be embarked upon. This discussion session could take place at a later time or date if more than one slot has been timetabled for the exercise.

Pre-class preparation
Before the class the tutor will need to prepare an introduction to the basic aims of the exercise, and a set of scripts for the actors. It has been found that actors in a role-play often find it easier if they are given guidelines before they carry it out. These scripts need to contain a description of the situation which is to be role-played, general guidance on how individuals might react in such situations and the specific alterations of behaviour required during that particular role-play.

For the sake of simplicity it is suggested that only one context is used and the variations made to elements of the actors' behaviour. However, more ambitious participants can hold the elements of behaviour constant and vary the context in order to examine situational effects on behaviour (e.g. Ginsburg, 1979).

As order effects may well occur due to practice (as actors become better acquainted with their roles) it is suggested that the order of each group's variation is staggered. With four groups and four variations this could be done according to table 1.

The situation chosen should be one that the students are likely to be familiar with, so that they will be acquainted with the normal pattern of interaction in the situation. For example, an initial meeting at a party, with introductions by host or hostess or self-introductions; sitting in a bar or coffee bar where you are introduced to a stranger and left to talk to him or her.

Table 1. Possible arrangement of behaviour variations to allow for order effect

Student group	Behaviour variations			
I	A	B	C	D
II	B	A	D	C
III	C	D	A	B
IV	D	C	B	A

Table 2. A selection of possible variations in behaviour

1. Overlong pauses before replying: for example, always count to eight before starting a speech.

2. Unclear hand-over (finishing speaking to become listener): for example, always finish speech with an 'um' or 'er'.

3. Abnormal eye gaze: for example, 0 per cent or 100 per cent.

4. Body proximity: moving closer to the other person than you feel is correct, continually moving body towards them, touching them whenever there is a suitable opportunity (the sex of the individual carrying out this behaviour will affect its outcome).

5. Using many questions which only allow for a short answer, such as 'Where do you live?' 'What do you do?' 'What do your parents do?' 'Do you have a car/motor bike?' 'Don't you think this place/party is awful?' If the person replying seems about to extend their answer you should try to interrupt with another question.

6. Giving only brief answers to any questions asked, aiming to be monosyllabic and expressing few, if any, views on subjects.

Variations in behaviour can be selected from the list in table 2, but normal (non-deviant) behaviour by both the actors should always be included as one of the variations.

Thus a possible set of four combinations could be:

A Actor 1: normal behaviour
   Actor 2: normal behaviour

B Actor 1: abnormal eye contact (0%)
   Actor 2: normal behaviour

C Actor 1: normal behaviour
   Actor 2: overlong pauses

D Actor 1: unclear hand-over
   Actor 2: close body proximity

This selection can be done by the teacher when preparing the script and kept secret from the class until after the completion of the exercises. In this way the students can see whether they are able to identify the variations in the actors' behaviour. Also it means that their measures are not likely to be biassed by observer expectancy effects.

The teacher will, therefore, have to prepare eight scripts (A1, A2, B1, and so on) and have four copies of each, one for each of the actors in the four groups. Each script might look something like this.

1. SETTING: you are sitting in the Students Union coffee bar and are introduced to a stranger by a mutual acquaintance who then leaves and you try to carry on a conversation with the stranger.

2. GUIDELINES FOR YOUR BEHAVIOUR: ask a few questions to find out some background information on the other person and then try to establish some common interest, or play it by ear in your usual way.

3. BEHAVIOUR ALTERATION REQUIRED: whilst trying to act in the same way as you normally would, avoid all eye contact with the other person. It does not matter where you look as long as you don't look at their face. The same

principle applies to the other altered behaviour: act in your normal way except for the specified behaviour.

Measures

A considerable variety of measures of social behaviour have been taken. There are two distinct categories: objective and subjective measures. Our emphasis is on objective measures of behaviour and this is reflected in the suggestions we give here. However, we are also including a suggestion for a subjective measure should this be desired. After all, in normal everyday life we all refer to our social interactions in subjective and emotional language and this method of measuring will help organize the 'impressions' that the students gain of the interaction.

OBJECTIVE MEASURES. The suggestions given here have been chosen on the basis of ease of measurement and analysis. The amount and type of equipment available is also a factor in choosing the measures, and we have therefore put this information, together with the list of measures, in table 3.

Two of the basic types of objective measures are frequency counts and duration. For frequency counts we add up each occurrence of the behaviour of each interactant over a specified period of time. We suggest a period of five minutes starting from the beginning of each interaction. The period chosen is arbitrary, the main essentials being a defined starting point, that it is long enough to get a reasonable sample of

Table 3. A selection of measures and the equipment they require

Type of measure	Behaviour to be measured	Equipment					Minimum number of observers
		Clock with sweep second-hand	Stop-watch	Event counter	Audiotape recorder	Videotape recorder	
F	Questions	x	/	/	/		1
F	Turn changes	x	/	/	/		1
F	Smiling	x	/	/		/	2
F	Posture shift	x	/	/		/	2
F	Eye gaze	x	/	/		/	2
D	Speech		x		/		1
D	Smiling		x			/	2
D	Eye gaze		x			/	2
D	Gesturing		x			/	2

For full definitions of behaviours and explanations of the table see text.

Key: F = frequency count
D = duration
x = essential
/ = extra equipment which it would be advantageous to have

behaviour, and that it is kept constant for each interaction both in the student group and between groups (for ease of analysis, see below).

There is also the problem of what constitutes one occurrence of the behaviour chosen. Although we could provide definitions we feel this would sacrifice an important part of the learning involved in having to decide on definitions prior to observations. No one definition is necessarily a correct one: different researchers may, and do, use different definitions, although they may try to use the same ones for consistency and ease of interpretation of results between studies. The question of definitions, then, is left open for discussion with the class but we give some guidelines below.

Questions are reasonably easily defined, but how will two different pieces of information requested in one sentence be counted: one question or two? Turn changes are also often clearly distinguishable but what if the speaker stops, there is a pause during which the other person makes a noise (e.g. 'er', or 'um') but does not say any words, and the original speaker starts again? A clear definition can help avoid these problems although it may not cover every circumstance. A taped recording can be particularly useful here to allow for analysis afterwards. The recording can be stopped and replayed in order to check how a particular instance fits with the definition decided upon. Similarly, with smiling, posture shifts and eye gaze, it can be difficult deciding if a short break has occurred to make one long occurrence into two or three shorter ones. Again, a recording for later playback can help overcome these difficulties.

The number of occurrences can be noted either by using a prepared record sheet on which a tally count is kept or by using an event recorder. The second method is preferable, especially with potentially high frequency behaviour such as eye gaze, as it can be done more quickly and without the observers having to take their eyes off the subjects.

Another problem in measuring frequencies is that some behaviours may be exhibited by both subjects simultaneously (e.g. smiling). This is reflected in the column for 'minimum number of observers' in table 2. Clearly, to get an overall total for, say smiling, it is necessary to have two observers each watching separate actors. Interesting information can be found by analysing the behaviour of each of the actors separately, but as this can lead to a massive amount of analysis we suggest combining both subjects' totals into a single score.

The duration measures require similar considerations to those outlined above. They will consist of a total duration of occurrence within a given period (i.e. the same five minutes of interaction). Definitions of when the behaviour is occurring or not will have to be decided upon (are within-speaker pauses to count as speech or not?). The recording procedure will involve a cumulative stop-watch which is started and stopped at the same time as the behaviour with totals for each actor being combined to provide a single figure.

One final point on recording is that the number of observers suggested is the bare minimum to obtain a result. Due to the difficulty in recording these types of behaviour it is desirable at least to double the number of observers for each behaviour. In this way it is possible to check the accuracy of the observation. It is also possible to calculate such things as inter-rater reliability coefficients, although we do not consider this is essential here as there is likely to be quite enough information for analysis. It is suggested, though, that if two or more observers differ markedly they re-observe the behaviour on the video- or audiotape-recording. If this is not possible, or the discrepancy is small, the mean figure can be taken. This requirement highlights one value here of a tape-recording (either audio or visual) in that it allows analysis of any number of other behaviours at leisure after the interaction has occurred and permits any one observer to check his/her own (intra-rater) reliability.

SUBJECTIVE MEASURES. For a subjective measure we suggest the use of a semantic differential such as that used by Trower, Bryant and Argyle (1978), which is shown in table 4. This is used in the normal way with raters scoring each interaction on a seven-point scale for each adjective pair. Each actor, at least, should fill in the semantic differentials for him/herself and separately for the other actor. This gives scope for comparing judgements of self with those of the participant observer. Discrepancies between the two will help highlight the fact that subjective judgements about self often differ in significant ways from the judgements of others. In addition, observers can rate each actor, thus permitting further comparisons to be made.

Table 4. General ratings

Cold	- - - - - -	Warm
Assertive	- - - - - -	Submissive
Socially anxious	- - - - - -	Calm
Happy	- - - - - -	Sad
Rewarding	- - - - - -	Unrewarding
Poised	- - - - - -	Awkward
Socially skilful	- - - - - -	Socially unskilful

We therefore suggest the following procedure. After each interaction has been role-played the actors are each given two copies of the semantic differential to complete before they start the next role-play.

Exercise organization
As there are a large number of tasks to be carried out when the role-plays take place, groups of students will need to get well organized before they start. If video- or audiotape-recording facilities are available they will have to be set up and checked for quality (particularly of the sound and lighting). A standard shot of two people in the same frame, orientated at about 45⁰ to each other, is quite sufficient without panning and zooming: it should not be necessary to have all the students acting as film crew!

One person can be in charge of timing the five minutes from the start of interaction and signalling it to the observers. (A simple call of 'time' would also mark it on the tape.) The two actors would have their scripts in the pre-arranged order and simply have to act to them when requested,

stop at the five-minute signal, fill in a semantic differential (if used) and get ready for the next role-play. The remaining four students (using the standard group of seven outlined above) can then record the various measures decided upon. Given that we suggest doubling up on the minimum number of observers this means that two behaviours having a minimum requirement of one observer can be observed and checked or only one behaviour having a minimum requirement of two observers. Clearly, this emphasizes the advantage of a tape-recording facility. For example, if only an audiotape-recorder is available it will be possible to have the four students observing and recording eye gaze during the 'live' interaction and then measuring three behaviours from the audio-tape (i.e. frequency of questions and turn changes and duration of speech). Indeed, with a bit of ingenuity they might manage to measure both frequency and duration of eye gaze by holding a stop-watch in one hand and event recorder in the other. They will then have to press both when eye gaze starts and only the stop-watch when it finishes (or it might be easier always to press both and divide the resulting frequency by two). In this way the four observers could measure five elements of behaviour and the actors would also produce a semantic differential for each role-play.

Data analysis

Each group of students should have collected a set of measures on each of four role-plays (under varying constraints) which lasted five minutes each. For each measure they should preferably have two results which can be averaged provided they are reasonably close. If not close they should be re-measured or, if this is impossible, an average will have to be accepted but recognized as being of doubtful validity. The method of analysis will be the same for each measure so we will only refer to one set of data from now on.

Once the group members have finished collecting their results they can be allowed to see the actors' scripts for a debriefing. Then they should graph their results for each measure. Thus they will have four points with the differing role-plays (A, B, C, D) along the x-axis and the amount of the behaviour (either frequency or duration) along the y-axis. Similar sketch graphs can be drawn for each of the adjective pairs in the semantic differential, with one for each of the actors.

For the next stage all groups should pool their results. This then gives four values for each measure under each condition and an analysis of variance can be carried out. (This is the reason for requiring consistent definitions and timings across groups.) A similar approach can be used with each adjective pair of the semantic differential, although eight values will be available as the pair of values obtained from each actor pair should be kept separate rather than averaged. (For this analysis an extra factor could be used of self-ratings versus participant observer ratings.)

In this manner an analysis of variance will be carried out for each measure taken and the results of these analyses will show whether or not variations in observable behaviour have occurred under the differing situational constraints. The analysis of results from the semantic differential will show a similar effect for subject impressions.

Discussion

The above exercise is designed to demonstrate that a relatively small change in behaviour from that which is socially 'normal' can have a striking effect and indeed even seriously impair social interaction. We would expect a considerable change on subjective impressions between the no-construct role-play (situation A) and the other three (B, C and D). We would also expect variations in observable behaviour although, depending on the behaviour change specified and the measures used, this may not show up so clearly. One of the important points which we hope will emerge is the difficulty in pinning down subjective impressions of impaired social beha-

viour in terms of changes in observable, quantified behaviours.

Given that variations in behaviour can lead to impaired interactions, it is important that we have an understanding of what constitutes 'normal' behaviour if we are to help those with difficulties in social interactions. This type of difficulty (i.e. impaired social skills) has been implicated in a wide variety of social problems, and there has been a considerable upsurge of interest and literature in using social skills training to help overcome such problems.

The behaviour changes and suggested measures were chosen with this body of knowledge in mind to demonstrate some of the important variables in social behaviour. They were also chosen as being some of the simpler behaviours with which to work. However, we expect that students may find difficulties in working with these behaviours and this would demonstrate the complexity of the problem. This is likely to be particularly true where video equipment is unavailable; students will realize just how many different types of behaviour are occurring but they can only focus on one or two at a time.

When a videotape-recording has been made, students might like to replay it and notice how various other behaviours are used in a social interaction, and how they fit together to form a system. Using the turn-taking system as one example, the observer may find some or all of the behaviours in the Appendix listed.

The complexity of a social interaction has meant that, for this exercise, we have had to limit ourselves to easily specified and easily observed behaviours. More complex analysis requires a greater familiarity with observing social behaviour, plus sophisticated methodology and equipment. Nevertheless, we would expect this limited analysis to demonstrate our basic point clearly, namely that it only requires small variations in social behaviour from the 'norm' to affect an individual's interaction significantly, which can result in serious social problems.

REFERENCES

Argyle, M. (1969) Social Interaction. London: Methuen.

Argyle, M. (1975) Bodily Communication. London: Methuen.

Argyle, M. (1978) The Psychology of Interpersonal Behaviour. Harmondsworth: Penguin.

Argyle, M. and Cook, M. (1976) Gaze and Mutual Gaze. Cambridge: Cambridge University Press.

Argyle, M. and Kendon, A. (1967) The experimental analysis of social performance. Advances in Experimental Social Psychology, 3, 55-98.

Argyle, M. and Trower, P. (1979) Person to Person - A Guide to Social Skills. New York and London: Harper & Row.

Bellack, A.S. and Herson, M. (eds) (1979) Research and Practice in Social Skills Training. New York: Plenum Press.

Duncan, S. and Fiske, D.W. (1977) Face to Face Interaction. New Jersey: Erlbaum.

Ginsburg, G.P. (1979) Emerging Strategies in Social Psychological Research. Chichester: Wiley.

Knapp, M.L. (1978) Nonverbal Communication in Human Interaction (2nd edn). New York: Holt, Rinehart & Winston.

Scherer, K.R. and Giles, H. (eds) (1979) Social Markers in Speech. Cambridge: Cambridge University Press.

Siegman, A.W. and Feldstein, S. (1978) Nonverbal Behavior and Communication. New Jersey: Erlbaum.

Trower, P., Bryant, B. and Argyle, M. (1978) Social Skills and Mental Health. London: Methuen, and Pittsburgh: University of Pittsburgh Press.

APPENDIX

Turn-taking signals

HANDING OVER. Meaning: 'I've finished; over to you'
    Asks question and continues looking. Leans forward
    As A finishes talking, looks at B and then looks down or away
    Stops gesturing
    Changes voice pitch on last word or two
    Uses concluding phrase
    Doesn't start new phrase

TAKING UP. Meaning: 'Please finish; I want to speak'
    Prepares other that he or she is going to speak
    Withholds any response until other stops speaking, and then takes up conversation
    Uses simple reflection, picking up a word or phrase, but then keeps the floor
    Interrupts and speaks strongly, avoids speech errors and keeps talking
    In group, gets speaker's attention by body shifts and orientation
    Interrupts B during pause for thought

SUPPRESSING A TURN CLAIM. Meaning: 'I'm carrying on'
    As A reaches a point, doesn't pause, doesn't look back at other, continues gesturing, talks louder

RESISTING A HAND-OVER. Meaning: 'You carry on'
    Uses a listener response and keeps looking at other
    Asks question to turn other's question round, then continues looking at other

(Adapted from Trower et al, 1978.)

9

Person perception
Mark Cook

Specification notes

AIM OF EXERCISE: to acquaint students
with some of the methodological problems
encountered in measuring accuracy of person
perception; to allow students to compare
their opinions about someone else's personality with an outside criterion; to test
simple hypotheses about factors affecting
accuracy of person perception.

PRIOR KNOWLEDGE ASSUMED: some knowledge of statistical analysis is desirable,
although instructions and a formula for
calculating rank order correlations are
given. The class tutor should have some
understanding of the concepts of reliability, validity and error of measurement in
psychological tests.

DURATION: about two hours in all; in the
recommended format, the personality tests
are given the week before, requiring 10-15
minutes of the previous week's class. The
exercise can, however, be done all in one
week if desired.

LOCATION: any room will do, preferably
one conducive to a group discussion. The
exercise can be done as a field study if
required.

MATERIALS: personality tests (Eysenck
Personality Inventory - EPI - suggested),
scoring keys, forms (supplied), name

badges, pencils, calculators, statistical
tables.

SPECIAL REQUIREMENTS: none.

Introduction

The aim of this exercise is to demonstrate
a way of measuring individual differences
in the way people perceive each others'
personalities, and to show that differential accuracy is being measured, rather
than stereotype accuracy. The exercise
must be designed therefore to avoid the
numerous methodological and statistical
artifacts that can arise in the study of
the accuracy of person perception.

The significance of the accuracy of
people's judgements of each other is three-
fold. It has obvious practical relevance,
in that people are constantly forming opinions of each other, and acting on those
opinions. A person who habitually forms
wrong impressions of others will find life
difficult as a consequence. Consider, for
example, the decisions to: accept the offer
of a lift late at night; ask someone to
marry you or accept such an offer made to
you; ask someone to help you get a job by
writing you a good reference; intervene in
a quarrel between two friends. A similar
range of decisions occurs in professional
contexts where an individual may have to
decide whether to employ this person or

152

that; release this person from prison or not; accept this person's plea for special treatment or reject it.

More generally, 'person perception' is one of the starting points of social psychology. Talking to someone, joining their group, staying in their group, leaving their group, conforming, bargaining, persuading; all presuppose you have perceived them, summed them up, judged them, and formed an impression of them. It is a truism that people react to the world as they see it, not to the world as it really is; yet is a very important truism, for the discrepancy between the seen social world and the real social world is often very great.

More generally, accuracy of person perception is relevant to a broad class of theories of social psychology. Phenomenological theories emphasize heavily the point that people react to what they see; therefore the way people see the world is the most important issue, if not indeed the only issue, in psychology. Since the most important things people perceive are generally other people and their moods, intentions and thoughts, accuracy of person perception is a key issue. Historically, examples of phenomenological theories include Kurt Lewin's field theory, and Snygg and Coomb's 'phenomenal field' theory. Currently popular versions include Kelly's personal construct theory, and aspects of the 'new look' in social psychology (Harré and Secord, 1972).

Trait rating studies and their problems

The history of the study of accuracy of person perception falls into three phases: the period of 'naïve empiricism', the period of disinterest, and the period of revival. The date of the ending of 'naïve empiricism' can be given precisely as 1955; the date of the revival of interest might be more vaguely set in the early 1970s. Before 1955, numerous studies of accuracy of person perception appeared, the majority using one of two favourite paradigms: 'trait rating' and 'empathy'. In a trait rating study, the judge expresses an opinion of the subject using a multi-point scale; thus Taft (1956) required his judges to rate each other on five-point scales for persuasiveness, social assertiveness, so-

ciability, carefulness, drive, and conformity. The judges' ratings were then compared with a set of criterion ratings, and difference scores calculated. The smaller the summed difference between a particular judge's ratings and the criterion ratings, the more accurate a judge of others that person was taken to be. There are two main snags with this paradigm, one obvious, one more subtle. The obvious snag is the criterion; what is the 'correct' value of the subject's social assertiveness, drive, and so on? Taft used 'expert opinion'; other researchers used self-ratings by the subject, or some form of group consensus. All, however, are obviously themselves judgements of the subject, and there are no grounds for supposing they are any better than the judge's opinion.

The less obvious snag arises from the use of difference scores, which prove to be statistically complex and potentially very misleading. These statistical complexities have come to be known as 'Cronbach's components'. Cronbach's (1955) paper analysed difference scores based on ratings of a number of traits across a number of subjects; this yields seven 'components', but the simpler case of ratings on one trait yields three components. These are 'mean', 'spread', and 'correlation'.

MEAN OR 'LEVEL'. If the mean of a judge's ratings is higher or lower than the mean of the criterion scores, the difference score will be higher, and apparent accuracy consequently lower; if a constant error were subtracted from, or added to, all the ratings, the judge's apparent accuracy would be improved. The constant error is an artifact of the use of numerical scales, and may not reflect the judge's accuracy of perception. The judge may match the mean of the criterion ratings by chance, or may match them through a more or less conscious decision to use the middle of the scale, as opposed to actually thinking about the target person's personality, as the experimenter intends.

SPREAD. The spread of a judge's ratings may correspond to the spread of the criterion scores, or it may be greater or smaller. If the judge's spread is greater than the criterion spread, the judge's difference score will be greater, and the accuracy score correspondingly lower. Again, the judge may match the spread of the criterion ratings by chance or by semi-conscious strategy rather than by a conscious decision about the subjects' personalities.

CORRELATION. The judge's ratings may correlate with the criterion scores. That is, the judge may have correctly perceived which subjects score higher than the mean, and which subjects score lower than the mean. In other words, the judge may have placed the subjects in an approximately correct order of possession of the trait being judged.

Cronbach's analysis was very valuable and penetrating, but its scope has tended to be over-estimated. His observations apply only to trait-rating studies, and not to other ways of studying accuracy of person perception. The problem arises in trait-rating studies because the judge is required to express an opinion in terms of an arbitrary numerical scale; different judges may represent the same estimated level of, for example, extraversion by different numbers. This is a fault of numerical rating scales, and has been noted in the study of personality and attitudes for years. For example, Vernon (1953) observed that 'the outstanding defect of this type of scale is the variations in standard and distributions adopted by different raters'. (In fact the same problem exists in most school and college marking systems, and is dealt with, by some, by careful comparison of samples of papers marked by different examiners.)

'Empathy' studies and their problems
In the 'empathy' paradigm, the judges predict how the subjects complete a personality questionnaire; the criterion - how the subject actually completed the questionnaire - looks sound but is not. The difficulties arise from 'stereotype accuracy' and 'assumed similarity'. When asked to say whether the subject agrees that 'his/her mother is (or was) a good person', the judge may not consider that subject as an individual, seeking evidence that he/she seemed to think well of his/her mother; the judge may attempt instead the easier tasks of deciding either how most people would

answer such a question (stereotype accuracy), or how the judge would answer such a question (assumed similarity). In the former case, the judge is in effect giving an opinion about the questionnaire item - most people would say their mother is (or was) a good person - and in the latter case the judge is giving a personal opinion: yes, my mother was a good person. But in neither case is the judge doing what the experimenter actually wanted, which is thinking about the subject. These problems are termed collectively 'response set artifacts'.

Such artifacts arise in any study of the accuracy of person perception that uses a multiple-choice format, not just those that use personality questionnaires. Whenever judges have to choose between two or more outcomes, they can 'cheat' by considering which of them is the more generally likely, not which of them the particular subject chose. Thus recently devised tests of the accuracy of person perception include Schroeder's filmed binary choice procedure in which the judge has to decide which of two responses the subject will make (e.g. break a light bulb or water a pot plant) and Fancher's 'programmed case' method, in which judges decide, retrospectively, what choice the subject made at a crucial moment in his/her life; for instance, at the outbreak of the Second World War, did he/she join the army, go to college as planned, or become a journalist? In both these tests, as in any multiple choice test, the possibility exists that one response will be more likely than the others, and that some judges will be able to use this information to get higher scores, without considering the subjects as individuals.

Similarly, the judge can 'assume similarity' and choose, as the subject's choice or outcome, the judge's own choice or outcome; there is evidence from a wide variety of tasks that judges commonly do precisely that. Byrne and Blaylock's (1963) study of married couples found that they assumed considerably more similarity of opinion - to the extent of husband/wife correlations of 0.69 and 0.89 - than was justified by the actual similarity of their opinions, represented by correlations of 0.30 and 0.44.

The ranking method as a solution to artifacts

Cronbach's (1955) revelations of complicated and seemingly intractable problems in apparently straightforward experiments so disheartened researchers that they largely abandoned the topic and came, by what one suspects was a process of rationalization, to consider it unimportant or even non-existent. The issue is, however, a real and important one, and there are ways of studying it that are not methodologically suspect.

Various attempts have been made to avoid the problems created by 'Cronbach's components'. Data can be analysed more carefully, separately identifying Cronbach's components; several complex methods of analysing trait ratings have been devised (see Cook, 1979, chapter 7). Alternatively, correlations can be calculated between the judges' ratings and the criterion ratings; a correlation necessarily eliminates the 'level' and 'spread' componments of the accuracy score.

However, these methods do not solve the response set artifact problem, and in any case only apply to rating studies. The response set problem can only be solved by altering the judge's task in such a way that the judge cannot use response sets. The experimenter can do this by altering the questions asked; Dymond (1954) eliminated any item in her empathy test where more than two-thirds of the subjects checked the same response. More drastically, the experimenter can alter the structure of the task itself, and use matching or sorting methods (Cook, 1979). Another way of restructuring the task is to require the judges to give their opinions in rank order form. This eliminates Cronbach's 'level' and 'spread' effects, and gives a single score representing each judge's ability to distinguish between the subjects. Requiring judges to give their judgements in rank order form also eliminates response set artifacts. The essential point of such artifacts is that the judge makes an informed guess (or an uninformed but lucky guess) about what most subjects will say or do or think. If judges are required to rank order the subjects, they are forced to differentiate between them, and cannot assume all or most sub-jects are like themselves, or that all or most will make the usual or socially desirable response.

The rank order method was used in several early studies of accuracy of judging intelligence but was later replaced by rating methods. Ranking has also been used in sociometric research, and in research on marriage. Cook and Smith (1974) employed the rank order technique with groups of friends, and with class groups, and found judges able to rank order their groups according to extraversion, but not for neuroticism. (For both traits, the criterion was score on the EPI.) Judges could not rank order each other for intelligence, but could rank order for authoritarianism, where an adequate spread existed.

The present exercise is essentially a replication of the class groups part of Cook and Smith's research, so the hypotheses are:

* subjects will be able to rank order members of a group according to some personality dimensions;
* subjects can rank order for extraversion better than for neuroticism;
* subjects can rank others better where there is a wide range of individual differences in the dimension concerned.

Method

Overall organization
This study requires about two hours of class time, and may be divided into five phases as described below.

OBTAINING THE CRITERION DATA. An inventory, such as the EPI, is completed by every student in the group, and scored by the tutor (NOT the students).

COMPOSING THE EXPERIMENTAL GROUPS. The data from the personality inventory are used to set up experimental groups, each consisting of between seven and 14 people.

GROUP DISCUSSION. Each group discusses a standard topic for 30-60 minutes, to ensure every group member has some acquaintance with every other group member.

RANK ORDER JUDGEMENT. Each group member places every member of the group, including him/herself, in order of perceived possession of the personality trait(s) being studied.

ANALYSIS AND DISCUSSION. The criterion rank order, derived from the inventory data, is made available, and compared with the perceived rank orders by means of rank order correlation. Treating these rank order correlations as scores, further analysis according to trait being judged, sex of subject, or personality of subject is then possible.

As suggested before, in the interests of saving time, the first two phases can be completed prior to the start of the exercise proper.

Materials and resources required
This study does not need very much in the way of materials and facilities (and indeed can be conducted, if necessary or desired, as a field study, using no laboratory facilities at all). However, like all social psychology experiments, it does require a number of people as subjects, the minimum requirement being one group of at least seven people.

Conducted as a laboratory class, the study has the following requirements.

A sufficient number of copies of a suitable personality questionnaire should be available with scoring key, information about reliability, and student population mean and standard deviation. The EPI, which measures extraversion and neuroticism, and contains a short social desirability scale, has proved very suitable. Other inventories and tests that can be used include the Wilson-Patterson Attitude Inventory (formerly the Wilson Conservatism Scale), the Lee and Warr (1969) version of the California F scale, and the Rosenzweig Picture Frustration Study. An intelligence test can also be employed if the tutor is confident that some spread of ability exists in the class; Cook and Smith (1974) employed the AH5 test of high grade intelligence but found students unable to rank each other for intelligence, probably because there was insufficient spread in the criterion data. (The rest of this chapter assumes EPI extraversion and neuroticism are studied, so tutors who use different traits and measures will have to rephrase the instructions accordingly.)

There should also be a supply of 'Perceived Rank Order' forms on which subjects record their perceived rank orders for the trait(s) being studied, and a supply of Criterion Rank Order forms, giving the 'true' rank order, and space for calculating a rank order correlation (see tables 1 and 2 for samples of these forms).

A supply of badges to be worn by subjects is also required; alternatively, cards may be placed on the table in front of them, so that subjects can identify and refer to each other during the judgement stage of the study. Subjects should be identified by letters A-N; numbers should not be used as they will create confusion during judgement and scoring. Subjects' names or initials should not be used, to avoid the risk that one subject might learn what another subject has said about him/her.

A room must be provided in which each group can hold its discussion. The judgement and scoring phases of the experiment should also be done in this room. It is important that the room should be the right size, and have the right atmosphere. A large laboratory fitted with benches is not suitable, and tends to inhibit the group discussion. A seminar room, which the subjects can fill without overcrowding, is more suitable. A table for the subjects to sit around is optional, but is useful to work on while writing and scoring the estimated rank order.

Hypotheses
In the basic class version of the study the tutor assumes complete control of design, composition of experimental groups, choice of trait(s) to be studied; the subjects remain unaware of the design, and of the purpose of the study until the judgement phase (the fourth phase) is reached. Some suitable inventories have been listed above. Group size should not exceed 14, nor be less than seven; if too large, the group ranking task will be too difficult and cumbersome, and if too small, the correlation will be unreliable and hard to interpret.

Employing the EPI, several hypotheses may be tested:

1. that extraversion will be perceived more accurately than neuroticism (Cook and Smith, 1974);
2. that no sex difference will be found. Sex differences in reaction to others' emotional expressions are reliably found, women reacting more (Hoffman, 1977); sex differences in other tests of accuracy of person perception are not reliably found (Taft, 1955; Cook, 1979);
3. that extravert judges will be more accurate judges (Taft, 1956) while neurotic judges will be less accurate (Taft, 1955). (These two hypotheses are only weakly supported by previous research.)

Other variations are possible within the basic design: for example, the length of the experimental discussion can be varied. Unpublished work by Cook and Buckley found no difference in accuracy when ten-minute filmed interviews were compared with three-minute interviews. (This manipulation obviously presupposes that subjects do not know each other already.)

The range of the criterion available within the group can also be varied. Across 11 groups Cook and Smith (1974) found a 0.55 correlation between average accuracy of ranking and spread of authoritarianism in the group. (It could be argued that showing that subjects cannot do an impossible task - ranking each other on a dimension where they do not differ much - is uninteresting, were it not that one of the failings of research on accuracy of person perception has been that subjects would always get a proportion of the answers right through the operation of the artifacts described in the Introduction. Proving that subjects cannot perform the task under certain conditions thus has some value. This variation in the design is also a useful stand-by should the distribution of criterion data prove limited.)

Finally, the topic of conversation can be varied. Evidently a discussion of student social life forms a useful basis for judging extraversion; perhaps a discussion of the problems and difficulties of being a student would form a more useful basis for judging neuroticism. (The tutor should bear in mind the possibility that groups may not keep to the specified topic.)

Procedure

The criterion data are collected first so that the groups can be composed using the inventory scores. The tutor should aim to include the largest possible spread of criterion scores in the groups, bearing in mind that if there is little or no range of criterion scores, the task becomes very difficult. The tutor should also break up existing pairs of friends as far as possible, so that judgements are made only on the basis of acquaintance formed during the group discussion. (For the same reason, it is desirable to conduct this study early in the course, before students have got to know each other too well.)

Tutors can adopt one of two systems of collecting criterion data and composing the groups. They can administer inventories at a previous class, perhaps as an exercise in itself, and compose the group(s) at their leisure during the intervening week. This may create a problem with students who did not attend the previous week, and who have not therefore contributed criterion data. Alternatively, they can adminster inventories at the beginning of the class, collect them, score them, and compose the groups. This has the advantage that friends can be separated into different groups more readily, working on the principle that they will tend to be found sitting next to each other. It will take some 15 minutes to score the inventories and compose the groups, so the tutor will need to contrive some activity or call a tea break to fill in this interval. The first method is generally better because the completion of the inventory and the person perception task are clearly separated in the minds of the subjects, and because class time is not taken up completing inventories and composing groups. It should therefore be used, unless attendance is particularly irregular.

To compose the groups the tutor should score the inventories, then tabulate the results, including the subjects' (code) names. Having decided how many groups to use and of what size (which depends obviously on the size of the class), the tutor selects subjects for each group to ensure as far as possible a wide but even spread of extraversion, a wide but even spread of neuroticism, no correlation between extraversion and neuroticism scores within the group, and the separation of friends. (Depending on the sex distribution in the class, and tutor's preference, the tutor may balance sex within each group, use all-male and all-female groups, or ignore sex of subjects as a factor.) Tutors may find this stage easier if they write each subject's details on a file card, and physically sort them into groups.

The published norms for the EPI (Eysenck and Eysenck, 1964) will enable the experimenter to decide if groups have a 'wide and even distribution'. The mean and standard deviation of extraversion for a student population are 11.10 and 4.54, so that 68 per cent of scores will fall within the range of 6.6. to 15.6, and 95 per cent within the range 2.02 to 20.2. Corresponding mean and standard deviation for neuroticism are 10.01 and 5.01, and the corresponding 68 per cent and 95 per cent ranges are 5.00 to 15.02 and 0 to 20.03.

Two difficulties may be encountered at this stage: high social desirability (lie scales) scores, and poor command of English. High lie scale scores are fortunately rare when the EPI is completed for research purposes by students. A student whose command of English is poor may have difficulty completing the inventory, and may even misunderstand sufficient items to give a false result. The tutor or an assistant should help such students complete the inventory.

Briefing and instructions

COLLECTING THE CRITERION DATA. The inventory is distributed and completed according to its own printed instructions, and requires no further comment by the tutor. Subjects may preserve their anonymity by using code names if desired.

COMPOSING THE GROUPS. Inform the class that (N) groups have been set up according to a principle that will be revealed later. Avoid drawing the subjects' attention to the personality dimensions

being studied.

GROUP DISCUSSION. Lead each group to its discussion room, ensure that subjects are comfortable, then tell them to discuss 'student social life' for (N) minutes. Each group should have the tutor or assistant present at the beginning of the discussion. To help the discussion get started, and ensure that every group member speaks at least once, the 'leader' should ask each person in the group to say in turn what he or she thinks about student social life. Once the discussion is under way, the leader should withdraw. It does not particularly matter if the discussion strays from the subject of student social life, so long as it keeps going.

When (N) minutes have passed, stop the discussion, distribute the Perceived Rank Order forms (table 1), and read out the instructions printed at the top of the form.

The tutor should circulate among the students while they complete the Perceived Rank Order form to answer questions, and ensure the instructions have been understood. (This is particularly important because an undetected error in the ranking makes the subject's entire data uninterpretable.)

When all subjects have completed the Perceived Rank Order form, and the tutor has checked that they have been completed correctly, collect the badges or cards with the identifying letters. (This should be done before the criterion data are distributed in order to make it more difficult for subjects to relate the criterion data to actual persons.) Then distribute copies of the Criterion Rank Order form (table 2), and read out aloud the instructions printed at the top of it.

The tutor should again circulate to answer questions and ensure the students have understood the instructions. A transparent copy of the Perceived Rank Order and Criterion Rank Order forms projected on an overhead projector will help students at this stage.

When all the students have finished scoring their data, explain the way in which the criterion rank order was derived. The tutor should emphasize at this point that the personality data were collected

Table 1. Perceived Rank Order form

'Decide who is the most extravert person in your group, then enter the number 1 against his/her letter on the list below. Decide who is the second most extravert, and enter the number 2 against his/her letter at rank position 2. Extraversion may be defined as a combination of sociability and impulsiveness. Continue this process until every person in the group has been given a rank position. Include every member of the group in the rank order. Remember to include yourself in the rank order. Ties are not permitted; that is, you may not put two or more persons down as, say, third equal. You may start at the other end of the rank order if you prefer, deciding who is the least extravert, second least extravert, and so on. Or you may adopt any other strategy you like. Repeat the procedure for neuroticism, which may be defined as a general tendency to become anxious or upset about things.'

```
Subject A [____]
        B [____]
        C [____]
        D [____]
        E [____]
        F [____]
        G [____]
        H [____]
        I [____]
        J [____]
        K [____]
        L [____]
        M [____]
        N [____]
```

NB. For neuroticism, use a similar list, but on a separate sheet, or reverse of this sheet, to prevent subjects comparing rank orders.

Where the group size is less than 14, and the tutor has insufficient time to prepare sheets with the correct number of rank positions, surplus subjects' ranks should be crossed out at the bottom of the list.

for research purposes, and do not represent any sort of diagnosis of individual subjects' actual personalities. The tutor could at this point explain or recall the concept of test reliability, and point out that the reliability of the EPI exraversion and neuroticism scales are 0.82 and 0.84 respectively, so that subjects might obtain scores as many as four points different on one in three re-tests. Tutors will need to use their judgement at this stage to decide if any subjects have been worried by limited revelation of their personality involved in the study, and how much reassurance, if any, is required. Obviously students whose scores placed them at the extremes of less socially desirable traits are most likely to be worried.

Alternative design as a field study
In this version, the students act as experimenters and study pre-existing groups of friends that they go out and find and test. Evidently the procedure in this version is quite different. The tutor starts by explaining the hypothesis and method to the students, then supplies each student experimenter (or group of experimenters) with copies of the inventory, and the Perceived Rank Order form. The student experimenters obtain criterion data and perceived rank orders, and return to the class to score the inventories and construct the criterion rank order before calculating the rank order correlation and performing any further analysis. This version of the study requires an intervening week during which the students collect the

Table 2. Criterion Rank Order form

'Line up the edge of the form against your list of perceived rank order positions, so that the set of (N) criterion ranks is alongside the set of perceived ranks. For each person in the group, subtract the perceived rank from the criterion rank, and enter the result in the second column, headed D. Square each D score, and enter the result in the third column, headed D^2. When you have done this for every person, you are in a position to calculate a rank order correlation between the criterion rank order, and your perceived rank order, using the formula $1-(6\Sigma D^2/(N^3-N))$. Then repeat the whole procedure for neuroticism using the other side of Criterion Rank Order form.'

Criterion rank	Subject	D	D^2
2	A		
5	B		
1	C		
9	D		
11	E		
10	F		
4	G		
8	H		
3	I		
6	J		
12	K		
14	L		
7	M		
13	N		

(Extraversion)

NB. The neuroticism rank uses the same layout.

---

data, making it a two-week class; alternatively the students may be briefed the week before. It would, however, be suitable for classes that were too small to constitute experimental groups with a reasonable spread. It would also be suitable perhaps for more able and enthusiastic students.

Data collection and analysis

Each subject will have (i) a rank order correlation for each pair of perceived and criterion rank orders, and (ii) a set of perceived rank orders for each trait. These data are collected and collated for the whole class, then distributed for further analysis.

From each subject, therefore, the tutor should collect: (i) (code) name, sex and age (if required), a rank order correlation value for each trait studied, and (ii) the set(s) of perceived ranks.

These are collated for each group and, if appropriate, for the whole class (depending obviously whether the tutor wants students to analyse their data within groups, or to compare groups).

The tutor then draws up two matrices, for each group. The first lists subject's number (arbitrary 1-N), sex and age, EPI extraversion and neuroticism scores, and correlation coefficients for predicting extraversion and neuroticism (table 3).

The second matrix lists subject's number (again arbitrary but corresponding to the number in the first matrix), sex and age, and his/her perceived rank order of the whole group for each trait studied (table 4). (Sex and age data may be omitted if desired, and should be omitted if they could identify particular students, e.g. the one male 'mature student' in the group.)

Table 3. Layout of Table A, for tabulating main personality and accuracy data

Subject number	Sex	Age	EPI		Accuracy	
			E	N	rE	rN
1						
2						
3						
4						
5						
6						
7						
8						
9						
10						
11						
12						
13						
14						

Table 4. Layout for analysis of consensus on perceived rank order

Rank for subject

Subject numbers	A	B	C	D	E	F	G	H	I	J	K	L	M	N
1														
2														
3														
4														
5														
6														
7														
8														
9														
10														
11														
12														
13														
14														

(Table 4 is only required for subsidiary analyses 5–7 below, so this step may be omitted if desired.)

Analysis

Each student will have one or more personal accuracy score, indicating how successful he/she was in ranking the group members according to their personality scores. Point out to the students the value such a correlation needs to exceed to achieve statistical significance, the limits imposed on such a correlation by the reliability of the personality test, and the demonstrated absence of a general trait of ability to perceive others accurately.

Discuss with the class the information they used to make their judgements, the strategies they used to draw up their Perceived Rank Orders, the procedure's validity as a measure of accuracy of perceiving others, and its relevance for personnel selection.

The class can then proceed to test the various hypotheses outlined in the Introduction, using the tabulated data for whole group, or the whole class, as follows.

1. COMPARING ACCURACY OF JUDGEMENT OF DIFFERENT TRAITS. The accuracy of ranking extraversion is compared with the accuracy of ranking neuroticism across whole groups or the whole class, using the t-test for related groups.

The generality of ability to perceive personality accurately is determined by correlating accuracy scores for extraversion with accuracy scores for neuroticism across the whole group, but first look at the mean and s.d. of accuracy scores for each trait; if, as Cook and Smith (1974) found, subjects' accuracy scores for neuroticism are consistently near zero, no correlation with accuracy scores for extraversion can be obtained.

2. SEX DIFFERENCES IN ACCURACY. Accuracy scores of males and females for each trait are compared, using t-tests for unrelated groups or two-way analysis of variance, with sex of subject as one factor, and trait ranked as the second (repeated) factor (see Kirk, 1968).

3. PERSONALITY CORRELATES OF ACCURACY. This analysis employs the criterion data as a measure of the subjects' personality. This analysis may be performed in one of two ways. Subjects may be divided into two groups according to their extraversion or neuroticism scores and t-tests for unrelated groups, or two-way analysis of variance, calculated as in (1) above. Alternatively, the criterion data may be correlated with the accuracy scores.

4. TOPIC OF GROUP DISCUSSION, LENGTH OF GROUP DISCUSSION. These factors, if included in the design, are compared across groups, again using t-tests for unrelated groups, or two-way analysis variance in which trait is the second (repeated) factor.

Analyses (1) and (4) require only the data obtained for table 3; analyses (5) to (7) require the data obtained for table 4.

5. IMPLICIT PERSONALITY THEORY. For each subject, calculate a rank order correlation (see Siegel, 1956, chapter 9) between the Perceived Rank Order for extraversion, and the Perceived Rank Order for neuroticism. A positive correlation indicates that the subject expects extraverted persons to be neurotic, while a negative correlation indicates that the subject expects extraverted persons to have stable personalities. A zero correlation indicates that the subject sees no link between extraversion and neuroticism; extraversion and neuroticism as personality traits are, in fact, uncorrelated. Unpublished work by Cook and Buckley found a very strong tendency for subjects to expect a high negative correlation between extraversion and neuroticism.

6. CONSENSUS JUDGEMENT. Use the data of a whole group for each trait separately to determine if a group consensus exists; even if subjects are unable to rank each other according to the criterion personality scores, they may agree among themselves about who is most extravert or least extravert, and so on. Kendall's Coefficient of Concordance (see Siegel, 1956, pp. 229-238) gives an index of overall consensus among members of the group. If a significant consensus is obtained (see Siegel), calculate the mean rank attributed to each subject by the group, and examine these means in the light of the criterion data.

7. SELF-RANKING AND SELF-ESTEEM.
Each subject has ranked him/herself on each
trait. Where one end of the trait dimension
is clearly more desirable than the other, a
tendency to give oneself a 'better' than
average rank position might be taken as a
measure of self-esteem.

Discussion

Cook and Smith (1974) found that subjects
could rank each other for extraversion to
the extent of an average correlation of
around 0.50. This held for groups of
friends, for practical class groups, and
in later unpublished research for collections of videotaped interviews. Evidently
sufficient relevant information can be
communicated in the course of a fairly
short discussion for subjects to make an
informed estimate of another's sociability
and impulsiveness.

For neuroticism, however, a different
picture emerged, with correlation coefficients centring on zero, a finding again
replicated across groups of friends, practical class groups, and sets of videotaped
interviews. Evidently the information
needed to assess a person's neuroticism is
not available, at least in a form subjects
can recognize and use, in the type of interaction studied. It was suggested in the
Introduction that discussing a different
topic might make the task easier (although
Cook and Buckley's unpublished videotaped
interview study did include questions about
relations with boy/girl friend, colleagues,
and so on, in the course of an interview
intended to be mildly stressful). This
finding, that neuroticism cannot be assessed from brief encounters, has obvious
practical implications for counselling and
selection interviewing.

If subjects do achieve some accuracy in
ranking more than one trait, it is possible
to determine whether any transfer from one
task to the other occurs; is the accurate
judge of extraversion also an accurate
judge of neuroticism? Previous research has
found no evidence of generality of accuracy, although Cline (1964) did find some
limited transfer where judgement tasks were
all based on the same set of filmed
interviews.

The results of the study should show,
therefore, that people can judge at least
some aspects of personality, while at the
same time finding that they cannot judge
others. This, it may be recalled, can be
taken to show that the ranking method is
free of the artifacts found in other types
of research on accuracy scores without
really thinking about the target people.
Cook and Smith also reported that subjects
found the task meaningful and seemed to
complain less than subjects doing tasks
using rating scales.

The exercise bears some resemblance to
the sort of decisions often made during the
course of selection interviewing in which
candidates are placed in order of perceived
suitability before the lucky one or ones at
the head of the rank order are offered the
position. It is reassuring to know that
such decisions have some demonstrable validity, but the results of the Cook and
Smith experiment also show they have considerable limitations. Some traits cannot
be judged in this way with above chance
accuracy, and even the results for extraversion show only a limited accuracy.

The results also incidentally provide
some evidence of the validity of the
personality measures. If the personality
measures were unreliable or lacking validity, judges' rankings would presumably bear
no resemblance to criterion rankings derived from them. It will be recalled, moreover, that judges were not told that the
criterion for their judgements was the EPI.

Limitations of the study
There are two main limitations to this
study: control of the sample of behaviour
used for the judgement of personality, and
the criterion.

The group discussion leaves the sample
of behaviour poorly controlled in two ways:
it is impossible to ensure that every person in the group makes an equal contribution to the discussion, and some may
contribute so little that their silence is
the only information the rest have to judge
them by. It is difficult to ensure the
subjects have no other information about
each other besides that made available to
the discussion. (Also, since each group of
subjects has a different discussion, it is
difficult to generalize across groups, or

to pool data from different groups.) These difficulties are common to all research using small groups whose essential spontaneity makes rigorous experimental control difficult. One possible compromise between control, and richness and diversity of information, is the use of videotape-recordings. It would be possible, for example, to videotape a group discussion, and play back the recordings to as many experimental subjects as required. (Tutors with videotape-recording facilities who wish to try this method will find it useful to prepare still photographs of each person in the film to remind their subjects who was whom.) Cook and Buckley conducted a number of experiments using a pool of individual videotaped interviews that could be assembled in different combinations for different experimental designs. This is time-consuming, and presents serious problems of re-recording videotaped material (which is often very difficult), and also creates a serious difficulty with order effects. The same set of videotaped interviews, shown to the subjects in differing orders, generates slightly but significantly different rank orders.

The criterion of extraversion and neuroticism in this study was the EPI, which imposes two sorts of limitation on the results. The first is simply that judges' perceived rank order correlations cannot, in theory, exceed the re-test reliability of the extraversion and neuroticism scales (0.82 and 0.84 respectively). (Correlations higher than 0.82 or 0.84 will occur by chance, however.)

The second limitation is that the EPI, like other criteria in research on accuracy of person perception, turns out in the last analysis to be just another opinion about other people. The E and N scores derive from the answers the target people gave to sets of 24 questions about themselves; they are in a sense self-judgements or self-perceptions made by the target people which the experiment compares with judgements or perceptions made by the subjects. Depending on one's view of personality, one might see this as an inevitable limitation or just a reflection of the current limits of personality measurement. Obviously many traits are socially defined, and exist only in the eye of the beholder; it would be ab-surd to suppose there could ever be a way of measuring 'politeness' that did not depend somehow on other people's opinions. But if everyone thought a particular person unintelligent, it would be possible to prove them wrong by showing that person had a high IQ. According to Eysenck's theories of the biological basis of personality, it might be possible eventually to measure extraversion or neuroticism by behavioural or psychophysiological methods, without relying on people's opinions at any stage.

Ethical problems

There are three possible ethical objections to this study.

First, it is necessary to keep the subjects in ignorance of aspects of the design and the hypotheses being tested, but not necessary actually to deceive them. Many social psychology experiments are possible only with naïve subjects.

Second, the exercise may reveal to subjects their positions within the group on the traits being studied. The subject may learn therefore that he/she is the most neurotic person in his/her group. Subjects do not learn their actual scores. Tutors who are concerned that such information might worry their subjects can reduce the risk by having one group analyse another group's data, so subjects never learn their position on the criterion rank order. The tutor collects the Perceived Rank Order forms from group A, and gives them to group B, together with the Criterion Rank Order form for group A. Group B thus analyses group A's data, and vice versa. On completion of the analysis, the correlations and perceived rank order (the data of tables A and B) are returned to the original groups. A simpler solution is to omit neuroticism from the design; subjects are not worried by having high or low extraversion ranks.

Finally, the subject may learn what rank order position other subjects have attributed to him/her. This should not happen if code names are used, if subjects keep their own Perceived Rank Order forms, and if potentially identifying sex and age data are omitted.

As a postscript, it may be argued by some schools of thought that the tutor should reveal personality data to the subjects, and should reveal to the subjects what they said about each other. The latter might be justified if all the subjects had genuinely volunteered for a 't-group' type session, but attendance at practical classes is rarely genuinely voluntary, and this exercise is not meant as a t-group session. Revealing to someone that he/she has a high neuroticism score can serve no useful purpose; when one has finished explaining about test reliability and validity, and assuming the subject understands, there still remains the uncomfortable probability that someone with a high neuroticism score actually has a neurotic predispostion. And what can the subject do with this information, except worry about it?

Conclusion

Many people flatter themselves they are very good judges of others; many social psychologists thought the study of such judgements was an easy area to research. Both have been proved wrong. Research on the accuracy of person perception has been beset by methodological problems, so much so that the impression was created in the years following publication of Cronbach's (1955) critique that research was virtually impossible. Indeed, the apparent difficulties led many workers in the field to argue, by a familiar process of rationalization, that the issue was not important, or even that it did not exist. This conclusion was obviously quite false: people do make decisions about each other, and these decisions are often wrong; and furthermore the consequences of such wrong decisions are often substantial. Hence ways of finding out if someone's opinions about others are accurate are vitally needed; refinements in experimental method since Cronbach's critique have provided them. The present study, in a modest way, tries to avoid some of the worst problems pointed to by Cronbach by re-inventing a method used in some of the earliest research on the subject - the rank order - and using psychometric tests as the criterion. The rank order seems quite successful, but the criterion presents problems, containing still a large subjective element.

Assuming for the sake of argument that the present method is a satisfactory test of individual skill in forming judgements of others, it will be apparent that most people are much poorer at this task than they like to think. Judgements of extraversion - a highly 'visible' characteristic after all - have some accuracy, but the average correlation of at best 0.50 accounts for only a quarter of the variance. Attempts to judge people in terms of neurotic tendency generally prove to have little if any validity. Yet consider how often people make such judgements, often wearing a professional or semi-professional 'hat' of one sort or another. Consider the resemblance of the exercise to what goes on at selection interviews, case conferences, in end-of-term reports on school behaviour, supervisor's assessments, and so on. All these types of decisions, usually made with sublime faith in their accuracy, are just as fallible, and just as likely to be imperfectly correlated, if at all, with what the object of them is really like. Besides teaching the students how to avoid some of the worst problems of Cronbach's components, this exercise should teach them to be a little less ready, a little less sweeping, and a little less confident in their assessments of others.

REFERENCES

Byrne, D. and Blaylock, B. (1963) Similarity and assumed similarity of attitudes between husbands and wives. Journal of Abnormal and Social Psychology, 67, 636-640.

Cline, V. (1964) Interpersonal perception. In B.A. Maher (ed.), Progress in Experimental Personality Research, Volume 1. New York: Academic Press.

Cook, M. (1979) Perceiving Others: The psychology of interpersonal perception. London: Methuen.

Cook, M. and Smith, J.M.C. (1974) Group ranking techniques in the study of the accuracy of person perception. British Journal of Psychology, 65, 427-435.

Cronbach, L.J. (1955) Processes affecting scores on 'understanding of others' and assumed similarity. Psychological Bulletin, 52, 177-193.

Dymond, R.F. (1954) Interpersonal perception and marital happiness. Canadian Journal of Psychology, 8, 164-171.

Eysenck, H.J. and Eysenck, S.B.G. (1964) Manual of the Eysenck Personality Inventory. London: University of London Press.

Harré, R. and Secord, P.F. (1972) The Explanation of Social Behaviour. Oxford: Blackwell.

Hoffman, M.L. (1977) Sex differences in empathy and related behaviour. Psychological Bulletin, 84, 712-722.

Kirk, R.E. (1968) Experimental Design: Procedures for the behavioural sciences. Belmont, Ca: Brooks Cole.

Lee, R.E. III and Warr, P.B. (1969) The development and standardization of a balanced F scale. Journal of General Psychology, 81, 109-129.

Siegel, S. (1956) Nonparametric Statistics for the Behavioral Sciences. New York: McGraw-Hill.

Taft, R. (1955) The ability to judge people. Psychological Bulletin, 52, 1-23.

Taft, R. (1956) Some characteristics of good judges of others. British Journal of Psychology, 47, 19-29.

Vernon, P.E. (1953) Personality Tests and Assessments. London: Methuen.

Further reading

Cook, M. (1979) Perceiving Others: The psychology of interpersonal perception. London: Methuen.

Cook, M. (in press) Perceiving others. In M. St Davids and M. Davey (eds), Judging People. London: McGraw-Hill.

10

Intergroup and interpersonal dimensions of social behaviour: the case of industrial bargaining

Geoffrey M. Stephenson and Maryon Tysoe

Specification notes

AIMS: the exercise is designed as a role-play experiment in intergroup processes in negotiation between union and management representatives. Negotiating instructions are varied to increase the salience of intergroup or interpersonal factors in negotiation.

DURATION: two three-hour sessions are required for the full version of the exercise to be implemented effectively.

LOCATION: a small room (or cubicle) is desirable for each dyad, with a table and chairs; otherwise a large laboratory would be necessary.

RESOURCES: cheap portable tape-recorders, tapes and microphones are required for each negotiating dyad; stop-watches, writing paper and pens should also be available. Other negotiating information and scales in the appendices must also be prepared and duplicated in advance.

SPECIAL REQUIREMENTS: none.

Introduction

Objectives of the exercise
This exercise illustrates the usefulness of studying social behaviour from both interpersonal and intergroup perspectives by showing that group decisions vary as a consequence of changes in the relative salience of intergroup and interpersonal orientations. In addition, it (i) introduces students to the experimental technique of the role-playing debate and (ii) illustrates the application of method and theory to problems of industrial relations.

General theoretical and methodological background
Stephenson (1981) proposes that social behaviour may usefully be characterized in terms of both its intergroup and interpersonal significance. For instance, although our interactions with friends may have largely interpersonal import most of the time, they can also have a strong intergroup dimension when our membership of different social groups - families, genders, generations, for example - becomes of significance. Then we may find ourselves having to cope with the fact that our roles as representatives of those groups will impinge on or interact in some way with our interpersonal interests, perhaps in contradiction to them. Consider some of the problems which may arise from the differing intergroup allegiances of a couple who live together. Which of them does most of the housework may reflect intergroup assumptions about what is appropriate behaviour

for men and women, rather than interpersonal understanding about what is appropriate for them in particular; and this intrusion of the intergroup perspective may be highly disruptive. Or, more pertinent to the theme of this exercise, take the case of two workmates, one of whom is promoted to a managerial position. Their friendship is then put under strain because they are no longer just friends, but members of groups whose goals are seen to be in conflict. The intergroup perspective impinges on their interpersonal relationship, probably at some cost to the latter.

Whilst social behaviour generally may usefully be viewed in this way, certain occupations and tasks pose particular problems for the effective reconciliation of interpersonal and intergroup interests. Let us consider the role of a shop steward. Whereas in the previous example intergroup allegiances threatened interpersonal relations between friends, the shop steward may develop friendships with managers which create problems when they bargain as representatives of their respective groups. Nevertheless, Batstone, Boraston and Frenkel (1977) see close relations as a necessary requirement if effective bargaining is to take place:

A balance of power by itself is insufficient. There has also to be a relationship of trust. If the persons concerned are powerful, then they will be more likely to be able to resist pressures to break confidences. But beyond that there has to be a readiness to enter into trust relations. For the 'informal chat', which is central to a strong bargaining relationship, involves a partial dropping of caution, since information private to one's own side is imparted. Both leaders (stewards) and management are very aware of this trust relationship and the fact that it rests upon an acceptance of 'the facts of life', that is, the basic conflict which exists between them.

Of course, those stewards who fail to make a convincing show of the 'basic conflict' with management may find their interpersonal relations with management the source of distrust and accusations of betrayal from their workmates.

The specific research background
The work of Batstone and his colleagues indicates how the development of a 'strong bargaining relationship' may enable shop stewards and managers to deal with one another in a spontaneous way, but without necessarily betraying the trust placed in them by their principals. Such productive relationships in which intergroup and interpersonal interests are effectively reconciled may be comparatively rare, though it is interesting that they emerged where the potential for intergroup conflict was greatest. More typical, in our experience, is an uneasy alternation or compromise between the competing intergroup and interpersonal interests.

Morley and Stephenson (1977) report a series of experiments in which the relative salience of interpersonal considerations was varied by manipulating the medium of communication in which (role-playing) negotiations were conducted. In those experiments, one side (management or union) or the other was given a stronger case (as judged by independent assessors of the background literature used by the role-players) such that, other things being equal, the outcome ought to have favoured the side which had been given the strong case. When subjects, in pairs, negotiated an agreement, it was found that the agreement was more likely to reflect the relative strength of case when subjects negotiated by 'telephone' (audio communication only) than 'face-to-face', regardless of whether the management or the union had been given the stronger case. Face-to-face, the bargainers would usually compromise mid-way between their respective demands. This finding was attributed to the fact that when negotiating face-to-face the interpersonal orientation of the bargainers was stronger than when they were communicating by telephone. In the latter relatively impersonal condition, the emphasis was more upon negotiators' roles as party representatives, and the outcome presumably favoured the side with the stronger case for two reasons: first, increasing concentration on the negotiation issues and relevant arguments should lead to a more objective assessment of the issues in contention; and second, the interpersonal considerations that might otherwise mitigate against exploiting one's advantage are not so much in evidence.

In those experiments, and subsequent replications (e.g. Short, 1974), the interpersonal orientation was varied indirectly by changing the mode of communication, principally 'audio' rather than 'face-to-face'. Other investigators, for example, Milgram (1974) in his studies of obedience, have also used the medium of communication to 'deindividuate' or 'depersonalize' social relationships. In effect, the telephone renders individuals more anonymous than does face-to-face interaction or, indeed, any other medium (e.g. a video-link) which combines both vision and hearing. Advantage can be pursued more thoroughly without too much interpersonal distraction.

The exercise

The exercise to be outlined in this chapter is based on the results of an experiment by Tysoe and Stephenson (unpublished) in which the orientation of the role-players was varied directly via the instructions concerning what attitude to adopt in the negotiation. The facts of the case, and the general instructions about what agreement should be secured, remain the same in both conditions. In the interpersonal condition, however, subjects are told additionally before they start negotiating that at the end of the negotiation they will be required to report on how their opponent responded throughout the negotiation. In other words, they are instructed to be aware of the other person's thoughts and feelings. In the intergroup condition, on the other hand, subjects are instructed to be aware of how their own constituency would respond to what is being said. They are told that when the negotiations finish they will be required to write an account of how they think their fellow group members would evaluate what had happened in the negotiation. The former instructions make salient the interpersonal dimension of the negotiation process, and the latter the intergroup dimension.

Using the material employed in this exercise, Tysoe and Stephenson found that the stronger case (in this instance, management's) prevailed more in the intergroup than in the interpersonal condition. They also discovered that women were more susceptible to the experimental manipulation than were men, a second aspect of the results which may be replicated in the current practical exercise, or at least controlled for in the composition of the groups.

How can you be sure that the 'intergroup' and 'interpersonal' instructions were effective? If subjects have followed their instructions, marked differences in the quality of interaction will occur, which will be reflected in analyses using modified versions of Bales' IPA (see chapter 4) and Morley and Stephenson's Conference Process Analysis (CPA) (see Morley and Stephenson, 1977). In addition it will be found that negotiators are less identifiable as union or management representatives in the interpersonal than in the intergroup condition. If time and experimental conditions permit, similar comparisons may be made between 'all male' and 'all female' negotiation dyads.

Method

Aims of the exercise
All members of the class should be role-playing participants in this exercise on negotiations. The exercise will take the form of an experiment, in which one main factor of intergroup-interpersonal salience is manipulated. The principal hypothesis is that the side with the stronger case - in this instance, management - will do better in the intergroup condition. Expectations concerning negotiation processes and negotiators' perceptions will also be examined. Where possible, a comparison of male and female negotiators may be incorporated into the design.

Timetable
Two sessions are required for the full version of the exercise to be implemented effectively. If only one is available, the analysis of the negotiation process may be excluded. However, role-playing may be completed, and an analysis of agreed

settlements carried out and discussed satisfactorily, in one session. If two weeks
are available, role-playing and transcription from the tape-recordings would
occupy the first session. The following
week, outcomes, questionnaire results and
the 'process' data would be analysed and
discussed.

Required resources
It is desirable for each pair of negotiators to be able to record their discussion. (A cheap portable recorder is
quite adequate for this purpose. Cassette
machines make transcribing more straightforward.) This is necessary if the process
analysis is to be included in the exercise.
If sufficient tape-recorders are not available, then as many of the negotiations as
possible should be recorded, distributed
equally between experimental conditions. It
is also advisable to have separate rooms
(or cubicles) for each dyad, but it may be
possible to house a number of groups in a
large laboratory, in particular if those
groups are not to have their discussions
recorded. In each negotiating room, in
addition to the tape-recorder, tape and
microphone, there should be a stop-watch
placed on the negotiating table for timing
the negotiation, spare writing paper and
pens, and two chairs facing each other
across the table. All participants should
have previously been trained to use the
tape-recorder.

The items in appendices 2-8 should be
typed and duplicated on separate handouts
in advance and, where different versions
are required for different experimental
conditions, these are best coded in some
unobtrusive way.

To increase the realism of the exercise
it is necessary to up-date the wages figures given in the background material. This
can be done simply by adding a percentage
roughly corresponding to the inflation rate
since December 1980. As much of the detailed argument will centre on relativi-
ties, it is not necessary to be pedantic
about this, but it is important that the
wage rates look reasonably realistic.

General procedure
The experimental paradigm to be used in
this practical is called the 'role-playing

debate' paradigm (Morley and Stephenson,
1977). Participants play the roles of
representatives of opposing groups. They
have to negotiate an agreement concerning
disputed issues by unrestricted verbal
communication, and are provided with relevant background information. Morley and
Stephenson have argued that this is a more
appropriate way of studying negotiations
than by using one of the more popular but
simplistic techniques such as matrix games
and the 'Bilateral Monopoly' game (Siegel
and Fouraker, 1960).

Every member of the class may be
expected to take part in this practical
exercise as either a union or management
representative. Allocation to union or management roles is best made according to
performance on Stephenson's management-
union questionnaire (see Appendix 1), preferably administered and scored before the
day of the practical to save time during
it. Otherwise allocation can be random, or
based on personal preference. Random allocation at least disposes of one possible
alternative explanation of differences
which may be obtained between conditions:
that is, an explanation in terms of personality differences. The disadvantage of
this is the reduced face validity of the
procedure.

A further random subdivision of subjects
then needs to be made into 'interpersonal'
and 'intergroup' conditions. So far as is
possible the ratio of men to women should
be kept constant in all four groups (union
interpersonal, union intergroup, management interpersonal and management intergroup) which have been formed.

At the start of the practical the four
groups should meet separately to study
their appropriate background material (cf.
Bass, 1966), a copy of which is given to
each person. This contains:

* Townsford Textile Company: background
  information (Appendix 2);
* negotiating assignment (management or
  union) (Appendix 3);
* issue 1 for bargaining: wages (Appendix
  4);
* issue 2 for bargaining: vacation pay
  (Appendix 4);
* negotiating instructions (interpersonal
  or intergroup) (Appendix 5).

Twenty minutes is generally sufficient for this part of the exercise, including time for the tutor to answer questions about the material. Requests for further information about the company must, unfortunately, be politely refused, although technical terms and information must be explained if required. In order not to weaken the effects of the experimental manipulation (intergroup - interpersonal orientation), general discussion between participants should not be permitted during pre-negotiation preparation.

Homogeneous (i.e. with the same negotiation instructions), same-sex (as previous studies have indicated differences in the orientation of men and women to this type of task) management/union dyads must then be formed. Each dyad should be directed to their assigned position, where both members are given a copy of the negotiating rules (Appendix 6), shown the required equipment (see above), and seated opposite one another at the table. Each dyad is given two final contract sheets (see Appendix 7), one for each of issue 1 (wages) and issue 2 (vacation pay). Once it is ascertained that the negotiating rules have been fully understood, the dyads can be left to themselves to negotiate a 'contract'.

When a dyad has completed its negotiation, one member will notify the tutor who should then ask each member of the dyad to complete the post-negotiation questionnaire (Appendix 8). There should be no discussion or collaboration between the two members of a dyad at this point. The tutor should collect questionnaires and final contracts, clearly record names and experimental conditions, and ensure that all questions have been answered.

Additional procedure for two-week practical

When two weeks are available, the participants should at this stage obtain the necessary transcriptions so that the process of negotiation can be analysed (as well as the outcomes and questionnaire scores) the following week. If only one week is available, then at this stage the class should be reconvened for a group analysis and discussion of the data already available; that is, the agreed outcomes and questionnaire results.

The 'interpersonal' negotiations should differ in character from the 'intergroup' negotiations. Ideally, a full transcript of each negotiation could form the basis of a comparison using a suitable category system like CPA. In this practical exercise just two hypotheses will be tested using a simpler procedure:

* there will be more expressions of <u>agreement</u> in the 'interpersonal' negotiations;
* the role (management or union) of negotiators will be more readily identifiable in 'intergroup' than in 'interpersonal' negotiations.

DATA FOR THE FIRST HYPOTHESIS can be obtained by the dyad replaying their negotiations and each member counting (by use of tally marks) the number of times he or she said something which justifies use of the CPA mode of <u>accept</u> (see Appendix 9 for definition and examples). The average acceptance rate per dyad can then be determined by calculating the average number of accepts per minute of negotiations. This should be done during the first session.

DATA FOR THE SECOND HYPOTHESIS comes from transcribed material. The dyad should be asked to transcribe in detail five minutes' worth of negotiations taken approximately from the middle of the negotiation. Copies of this should be given to the tutor for further preparation and use in class the following week.

During the interval between the two classes, the more enthusiastic participants should be asked to divide their transcripts into CPA acts and code them in terms of CPA categories. (For this purpose, students will need to refer to chapter 10 of Morley and Stephenson, 1977.)

Additional advice on procedure

It is important that adequate time is allowed for mastery of the materials in groups, as some students will initially feel ill at ease with information of this kind. Students generally adopt a sensible and constructive approach, and are usually very involved in the argument and debate. It is, of course, important for the tutor to be fully conversant with the material, and to be prepared to explain and defend the information provided. Some more knowledgeable students occasionally complain that insufficient background financial data are provided. This can be defended on the grounds that it is not feasible to provide more data in an exercise of this sort (and that in any case plant-level negotiators in fact do quite frequently negotiate in comparative ignorance of the true state of their company's financial position). It can also be emphasized that they are free to use their knowledge of the prevailing industrial relations climate in their negotiations.

It hardly needs to be said that the importance of the negotiation instructions (Appendix 5) must be emphasized to the participants.

Results

Common to one-week and two-week practical

1. ANALYSIS OF OUTCOMES: does an intergroup orientation favour the stronger party? The background material, or scenario, was written so as to favour the management side. In particular, the Townsford workers, being only in the middle range of skill, were relatively well paid and had generally been treated well by the company in the past, so that some sympathy for the company's present predicament would not have been amiss. Does management do better in the intergroup than in the interpersonal condition, as has been predicted, and previously demonstrated? That question may be answered by comparing the cost of the final settlement agreed by dyads in the two conditions. The cost should be lower in the intergroup condition. Each dyad should calculate this by adding together the cost of the agreements on issues 1 and 2 to produce total cost scores. Conventional parametric statistical techniques may then be used to test the significance of differences between the conditions. For example, a t-test may be used to test the significance of the difference in total cost of the settlement in the interpersonal and intergroup conditions.

Besides examining the means, it will be fruitful to look for differences in the variability. An intergroup orientation is likely to constrain negotiators, such that a more limited range of outcomes is achieved than in the interpersonal condition where negotiators may feel more at liberty to agree to what seems appropriate to them as individuals. This possibility should be examined. It should be noted that because the two issues are considered together as a package, it is not legitimate to treat each issue separately.

Thirty minutes is adequate time for dyads to achieve an agreement. Deadlocks, however, may occur, and they are more likely in the intergroup condition. They present a certain difficulty. How should the outcome be described in such cases? Following Morley and Stephenson (1977), the most effective strategy is to take the midpoint between the last offers made by each side to represent the final contract. However, it is rare that both issues are not settled, so this stratagem should not normally need to be employed.

The intergroup orientation is likely to lead to a greater intransigence on the part of the negotiators. The highly committed representatives may be moved to reiterate and emphasize their own position and opposition to alternatives, thus prolonging the negotiations. It is appropriate to perform an analysis of the time taken to reach agreement. If all the negotiation groups have come to agreement within the allotted time, parametric statistics should be employed to test the significance of the differences between intergroup and interpersonal conditions, and the t-test may again be used for this purpose. However, when deadlocks occur, negotiations are artificially curtailed, and either some arbitrary time should be assigned (e.g. the maximum permitted negotiating time) or, more satisfactorily, non-parametric statistics should be employed. For example, using Mann-Whitney U, deadlocks may be assigned the highest rank, and the times of the other settlements used to rank order the remainder.

2. ANALYSIS OF POST-EXPERIMENTAL QUESTIONNAIRES: as a quick check on the successfulness of the strength of case

manipulation, the responses to question 7 may be examined. Of course, this check is not perfect because it is likely that those who are seen to have 'won' will be deemed to have had the stronger case. Nevertheless, there should be a general tendency for management to be seen as being in the stronger position, and this is the view expressed by unbiassed judges who do not know which role they will subsequently be asked to take.

If only one week is available, there will be little time in class for further analysis of the questionnaire results, but at this point the data from all the groups should be collated and made available to all participants for analysis (as indicated below) during the week. However, the tutor should at least discuss in class how those in the different conditions should have responded to the other questionnaire items, and how differences might be statistically examined. (If two weeks are available, the analyses can be conducted the following week.)

Whilst there are unlikely to be differences between conditions in the responses to questions 1 and 2 (concerned with general satisfaction), if the experimental manipulation has been successful then there should be marked differences on questions 3-6. Negotiators in the intergroup condition should feel more 'accountable' and 'committed', and have wanted to look 'stronger'. Analyses of scores (from 1 to 9) on each scale, using t-tests, should be carried out separately for those in management and union roles, and for averaged dyadic scores. This is because the general hypothesis (of greater 'commitment' in the intergroup condition) is rather more likely to apply to those given the stronger (management) position.

Similar separate and combined analyses should be carried out for answers to question 6 on each of the scales contained there. There are likely to be overall differences between the interpersonal and intergroup conditions, with greater 'tenacity', 'obstructiveness', and so on in the intergroup condition. However, this is most likely to occur for perceptions by union of management and for management self-perceptions, given management's stronger case and greater likelihood of

holding out for victory.

The analysis of the negotiation process (session 2)

The second session should begin with a consideration of outcomes, as detailed in a previous section, before going on to analyse and discuss the results of the questionnaire. This will provide a good lead into a more detailed examination of the negotiation process. The questionnaire examines participants' perceptions of their behaviour, whereas the process analysis aims to draw conclusions from more or less objective categorizations of that behaviour.

While outlining the 'additional procedure' above we stated two hypotheses; that there will be more expressions of agreement in the interpersonal than in the intergroup condition, and that 'role identifiability' will be greater in the intergroup than in the interpersonal condition. The first hypothesis may be tested simply using the CPA mode categorization agree made by the participants themselves the week before. Methodologically this is not ideal, as the numerical judgements made by participants may be directly influenced by the experimental manipulation. In the context of a practical exercise, however, 'blind' scoring is difficult to achieve. The dyadic agreement rate scores in the intergroup and interpersonal conditions should be compared using a t-test.

For the role identifiability hypothesis to be tested, it will be necessary for the tutor to have prepared material using the transcripts made by the participants the previous week. The four longest (ignoring unsuccessful interruptions) management and the four longest union 'speeches' from each transcript should be typed up in random order separately for each transcript. the experimental conditions and roles (management or union) being coded so as to be unidentifiable except to the tutor. In class, all the 'transcripts' should be judged by each of the participants, every speech item being assigned either to the management or union role. The order in which transcripts are judged should be randomized, and the judges may be informed that the division of items between the roles is even. A score out of eight (representing the number of speeches correctly identified) may then be obtained for each transcript as judged by each participant. An average score for each transcript can then be calculated, and may be used to test for differences between intergroup and interpersonal conditions, using a t-test.

Other analyses may be carried out if time permits. For example, there is the interesting question of sex differences in bargaining. There is evidence (Tysoe, 1979; Tysoe and Stephenson, unpublished) that women may negotiate differently, with respect both to what is said and what is decided. It may well be that women are more susceptible to the intergroup/interpersonal manipulation than are men, and this is a possibility that may be explored if there are sufficient data from the practical class, using all the indices we have so far described.

Further analyses of the transcribed material may also be carried out by students separately, and later brought together for subsequent group analysis and discussion. The intergroup condition is likely to yield a greater concern with what Bales termed task orientation of the 'positive' kind, and social-emotional behaviour of a 'negative' kind than in the interpersonal condition (which should foster more open-ended questioning, and more 'positive' social-emotional behaviour). Suggestions for use of Bales' IPA are given in chapter 4; Morley and Stephenson's CPA may also be employed. CPA was designed especially for use with negotiation groups, but it is more complex than Bales, making explicit some of the distinctions that are implicit and confused in Bales' system (for example, between 'modes', the manner of exchange, and 'resources', what is exchanged), and using special categories derived from analyses of interaction in bargaining. The system and its use are described fully in Morley and Stephenson (1977).

Further design considerations: bargaining teams

Formal wage bargaining normally takes place between teams of representatives, although meetings between individuals may take place privately and secretly. If sufficient numbers of students are available in the practical class, or if sufficient rooms are not available, then bargaining teams of two or three persons each may be formed and employed in place of individual representatives. It is likely that bargaining teams, in contrast to individuals, will most readily adopt an intergroup approach, which may decrease the likelihood that the intergroup/interpersonal manipulation will be effective.

Use of teams will have other consequences. Almost certainly the variability of settlement points will be reduced, because the impact of personality differences between the sides which might otherwise affect the process will be curtailed. Teams are also more likely to deadlock owing to the difficulty each will have with what Walton and McKersie (1965) term 'intra-organizational bargaining'; that is, the process of creating and maintaining ingroup cohesiveness. Use of teams will also raise the question of the appointment of a principal spokesperson for each side. If this is done it would be likely to decrease the risks of deadlock, but probably with detriment to general member satisfaction. Whilst it may not be feasible to examine systematically the effect of negotiation between teams in this practical experiment, nevertheless the use of one or two for demonstration purposes is worth considering. One such negotiation could be video-recorded and used to illustrate issues concerning the interplay of intergroup and interpersonal forces in negotiation.

Discussion

The findings should illustrate the importance of analysing social behaviour according to the interplay of its intergroup and interpersonal components. The experience of coping simultaneously with conflicting intergroup and interpersonal demands, even in role-playing, is one which is frequently found to be personally salutary, and it is worth finding time in general class discussion to allow students to comment on how they felt they coped. It is also a central and neglected problem in social behaviour generally and some discussion of this should be initiated.

There are, of course, limits to the conclusions which may be drawn from such role-playing studies. For example, let us suppose that the results clearly demonstrate that the intergroup condition more frequently elicits victories for the party with the stronger case. Can this result be generalized? Unfortunately, this experimental design gives only management the stronger case. Maybe there is something about the managerial role, or those people who are pro-management, which contributes to this effect. Maybe in real life being truly responsible to a group either heightens the effects we have observed, or conceivably diminishes them. Maybe the concept of 'strength of case' does not apply straightforwardly in real life.

All these objections have some substance but should act only as a spur to further enquiry, both in the field and experimentally. The concept of role identifiability is itself based on analyses of real negotiations (Douglas, 1962; Morley and Stephenson, 1977; Stephenson, Kniveton and Morley, 1977). Similarly, the decision to examine communications systems and 'style' of bargaining was a result of observing remarkably consistent differences in the 'quality' of negotiations in different factories (see Morley and Stephenson, 1977). This means that the theoretical issues examined in this practical are ones of direct relevance to industrial negotiations, although any practical conclusions we might wish to infer must be made ten-

tatively, and be subject to evaluation from political, economic and pragmatic standpoints. There is, however, a legitimate role for social psychology in the analysis of industrial relations problems which has been neglected in the past (see Stephenson and Brotherton, 1979). This practical should illustrate both the potential usefulness of social psychology for industrial relations and, equally important, the contribution that analysis of such real-life contexts can make to theoretical issues in social psychology.

Conclusion

This practical was designed to examine the effects of shifting negotiators' attention from the level of an interpersonal exchange to the role demands of negotiating an agreement on behalf of their parties. By doing so, it demonstrates: (i) the potential _practical_ value of research in social psychology for the understanding of industrial negotiations; (ii) the _methodological_ importance of using a paradigm that makes some attempt to capture the complexity of negotiations between groups in dispute and can, therefore, reveal the operation of such interpersonal and interparty orientations; and (iii) the _theoretical_ importance of distinguishing between the interpersonal and intergroup dimensions in interactions between members of different groups.

Acknowledgements

The authors would like to thank Dominic Abrams and Russell Newcombe for their help with the practical experimental sessions required for the preparation of this chapter.

REFERENCES

Bass, B.M. (1966) Effects on the subsequent performance of negotiators of studying issues or planning strategies alone or in groups. Psychological Monographs: General and Applied, 80, whole no. 614, 1-31.

Batstone, E., Boraston, I. and Frenkel, S. (1977) Shop Stewards in Action. Oxford: Blackwell.

Douglas, A. (1962) Industrial Peacemaking. New York: Columbia University Press.

Milgram, S. (1974) Obedience to Authority. London: Tavistock.

Morley, I.E. and Stephenson, G.M. (1977) The Social Psychology of Bargaining. London: Allen & Unwin.

Short, J.A. (1974) Effects of medium of communication on experimental negotiation. Human Relations, 27, 225-234.

Siegel, S. and Fouraker, L.E. (1960) Bargaining and Group Decision Making. New York: McGraw-Hill.

Stephenson, G.M. (1981) Intergroup bargaining and negotiation. In J.C. Turner and H. Giles (eds), Intergroup Behaviour. Oxford: Basil Blackwell.

Stephenson, G.M. and Brotherton, C.J. (1979) Industrial Relations: A social psychological approach. Chichester: Wiley.

Stephenson, G.M., Kniveton, B.H. and Morley, I.E. (1977) Interaction analysis of an industrial wage negotiation. Journal of Occupational Psychology, 50, 231-241.

Tysoe, M. (1979) An experimental investigation of the efficacy of some procedural role requirements in simulated negotiations. PhD. thesis, University of Nottingham.

Walton, R.E. and McKersie, R.B. (1965) A Behavioral Theory of Labor Negotiations: An analysis of a social interaction system. New York: McGraw-Hill.

APPENDIX 1

Management–union questionnaire

The questionnaire yields two sub-scales of <u>Attitudes towards management</u> and <u>Attitudes towards trade unions</u>. The 16 items should be made up in conventional form in random order, and subjects required to respond to each item on a nine-point scale as follows:

Attitudes towards industrial relations

Please indicate with an X on each scale the extent to which you agree or disagree with each of the following statements:

1. The company should have the unchallenged right to discharge a worker it thinks is unsatisfactory.

    Agree ___ :___ :___ :___ :___ :___ :___ :___ :___ Disagree

2. In negotiations the management side is often rigid and inflexible.

    Agree ___ :___ :___ :___ :___ :___ :___ :___ :___ Disagree

and so on. The full list of 16 items is as follows. Items are grouped according to their pro- or anti-management position, or as pro-union or anti-union.

Items in management–union questionnaires

MANAGEMENT (anti-)

1. In negotiations the management side is often rigid and inflexible.
2. Management is too aloof and remote from day-to-day activity on the shop floor.
3. Management often resists legitimate claims from representatives of workers.
4. It is frequently managerial policy which provokes industrial unrest.

MANAGEMENT (pro-)

5. We need a new Industrial Relations Act to give management the weapon it needs to take the initiative away from trade unions.
6. Most managers are sufficiently concerned about the health and safety of the work force.
7. It is a manager's unquestionable right to manage his or her company's affairs without interference from trade unions.
8. The company should have the unchallenged right to discharge a worker it thinks is unsatisfactory.

UNION (anti-)

9. Unions represent the interests of top union executives rather than the interests of working people.
10. Trade unions have too great a say in the running of the country.
11. Unions rarely adopt a positive attitude, but merely obstruct the intentions of management.
12. Unions are more to blame for inflation than management.

UNION (pro-)

13. Unions should be given equal representation with management on the Board of Directors.
14. Workers have an undeniable right to withdraw their labour in times of dispute.
15. It is only through trade union activity that higher standards of living are achieved.
16. Industrial democracy can only be achieved by the active pursuit of trade union principles.

From responses to the above items, two scores should be derived: (i) for attitudes towards management, and (ii) for attitudes towards unions. In deriving these scores, from items scored on a '1' (disagree) to '9' (agree) scale, remember that negative items are scaled in reverse.

The median should be used to divide the group into those who should unequivocally be management representatives (i.e. those who are pro-management and anti-union) and those who are unequivocally union representatives (being anti-management and pro-union). (If the negotiations of men and women are to be compared, this procedure should be followed separately for both sexes, given that the attitudes of men and women towards industrial relations are likely to differ somewhat.) The remaining subjects can be allocated to roles using combined (total) scores on the two sub-scales (e.g. attitudes towards trade unions minus attitudes towards management). Allocation would have to be random in the case of ties.

APPENDIX 2

Townsford Textile Company: background information

The Townsford Company is a small textile company located in a large northern town. Townsford is respected for the consistent quality of its work in the dyeing and finishing of raw woven fabrics. It employs approximately 100 people, at the middle range of skill for the area.

General business conditions of the town are good, but the financial conditions of Townsford are increasingly unstable. The backlog of orders has fallen, while profits have decreased with the rising costs of raw materials and transport.

The company has raised its prices to cover a recent wage increase, but it is unable to pass full costs on to customers if it is to maintain a competitive position with other sections of the industry. If the union would co-operate with the company in the purchase and manning of more modern equipment, improvements in efficiency would, in the long term, aid the company's financial position. The union has, however, refused any discussion of re-organization and consequent reduction of restrictive practices.

The personnel policies at Townsford are better than those of most plants the same size. The past president of the company, who retired three months ago, valued the reputation of Townsford as a 'good place to work'. His successor intends to continue with the same objectives.

For the last 25 years, a majority of employees have been members of the union. Relations of the union with the company have been quite good, with grievances promptly discussed and settled. The first strike occurred, however, three years ago and lasted 15 days. The workers obtained a sizeable wage-rate increase.

Townsford's wage scale compares very favourably with most other textile firms. It is about five per cent below textile firms which employ workers of a higher level of skill, producing a higher quality product, but ranks higher than firms employing workers of a similar level of skill. Wages in the industry have increased in proportion to increases in other industries and, to a large extent, with increases in the cost of living. With regular wage increases over a period of years, Townsford's workers have remained on a high pay scale relative to that of equivalent workers in other industries.

Unemployment is at an average level in the area: it should not be very difficult to obtain replacements of similar skill. Management is, however, reluctant to dismiss employees of some years' standing. Any wage increase at the present time would, in management's view, necessitate cuts in the size of the labour force in addition to price increases, and increases in the holiday entitlement would merely exacerbate present financial difficulties. Townsford gives seven paid holidays and three weeks of paid vacation to all workers with at least one year of service.

The previous contract has now expired. Negotiations for a further one-year contract broke down in the final week with both sides adamant in their positions. The only agreement reached was that each side would select a new bargaining agent to represent it, scheduled to meet today in an attempt to avert the strike which is due to begin tomorrow.

APPENDIX 3

Assignment as company negotiator

You have been selected by the Townsford Company to represent it in its negotiations with the union. Negotiations for a new one-year contract broke down last week. The union demands for general wage and benefit increases are completely unreasonable.

Employees' hourly rates compare very well with others in the area. If labour costs are increased, it would necessitate further price increases which could seriously damage the company's competitive standing. The union has refused to discuss the introduction of more modern machinery, which would improve efficiency, reduce present restrictive practices and, therefore, lower costs to some degree.

Although no compromises were reached in either side's position it was decided that each side should appoint new negotiators in an effort to settle the contract and halt the strike which begins tomorrow.

Each week on strike would cost the company heavily in lost profits.

You are to do the best possible job you can to get a good settlement on the contract on each of the two issues for the company. The company has a falling backlog of orders and will probably lose its major customers if increased labour costs necessitate further significant price increases. The finances of the company are rapidly becoming a serious source of concern.

It is important to the company that the issues be settled in the given bargaining period. We realize that this involves compromises on both sides, and you are appointed to carry out binding negotiations for us. Remember, your job is to reach a settlement on the issues that is good for the company.

OR

Assignment as union negotiator

You have been selected by the union to represent it in its negotiations with the Townsford Company. Negotiations for a new one-year contract broke down last week. You feel this refusal on the part of the company to grant your demands is another illustration of their failure to understand the difficult problems you face in a time of rapidly rising prices. The management have been obstructive recently, in aiming to introduce more modern machinery which might lead to fewer jobs, when unemployment in the area is already at a high level.

The union is aware of the financial difficulties of the company, with rising costs of raw materials and a decreased level of orders. It is, however, irritated by the company's refusal to grant the workers wage and benefit increases. Although no compromises were reached in either side's position, it was decided that each side should appoint new negotiating agents in an effort to settle the contract and halt the strike which begins tomorrow.

Each day on strike would cost the workers heavily in lost wages and overtime pay.

You are to do the best possible job you can to get a good settlement of the contract on each of the two issues for labour. It is important to the workforce, however, that the issues be settled in the given bargaining period. We realize that this involves compromise on both sides, and you are appointed to carry out binding negotiations for us. Remember, your job is to reach a settlement on the issues that is good for the workforce.

APPENDIX 4

The two bargaining issues

Issue 1 for bargaining: increase in basic wage

PAST CONTRACT: 188p per hour.

CURRENT POSITIONS: union demands an increase of 19p per hour; management refuses outright.

	Increase per hour in pence	Total money value in £ over 1 year
Management aim	00	0
	01	2500
	02	5000
	03	7500
	04	10000
	05	12500
	06	15000
	07	17500
	08	20000
	09	22500
	10	25000
	11	27500
	12	30000
	13	32500
	14	35000
	15	37500
	16	40000
	17	42500
	18	45000
Union aim	19	47500

DATA FROM AN INDEPENDENT COMMUNITY SURVEY (last year): information is given below on Townsford, four other textile plants and averages for non-textile industries in the country. The Moss plant and the Rose plant are the only ones employing highly skilled workers.

	Townsford	Moss	Rose	Baxter	Kraft	Average for other industries in the country
Number of workers	100	300	90	150	300	60
Hourly wage rate	188p	198p	198p	174p	178p	208p

Issue 2 for bargaining: vacation pay

PAST CONTRACT: three weeks' paid vacation for all workers with one year's service.

CURRENT POSITIONS: union wants four weeks' paid vacation for workers with two years' service; management rejects.

	MANAGEMENT AIM					UNION AIM
	3 weeks for 1 year's service	3 weeks for 1 year's service; 4 weeks for 18 years' service	3 weeks for 1 year's service; 4 weeks for 14 years' service	3 weeks for 1 year's service; 4 weeks for 10 years' service	3 weeks for 1 year's service; 4 weeks for 6 years' service	3 weeks for 1 year's service; 4 weeks for 2 years' service
Total money value in £ over 1 year	0	1,200	3,000	4,800	12,000	20,000

DATA FROM AN INDEPENDENT COMMUNITY SURVEY (LAST YEAR): information is given below on Townsford, four other textile plants and averages for non-textile industries in the country. The Moss plant and the Rose plant are the only ones employing highly skilled workers.

	Townsford	Moss	Rose	Baxter	Kraft	Average for other industries in the country
No. of workers	100	300	90	150	300	60
Paid holiday	3 weeks for 1 year	3 weeks for 1 year	3 weeks for 1 year	3 weeks for 1 year	3 weeks for 1 year; 4 weeks for 14 years	3 weeks for 1 year; 4 weeks for 10 years

APPENDIX 5

Negotiating instructions

There are four variations: two intergroup (management and union) and two interpersonal (management and union). They are as follows.

Intergroup management: PLEASE READ THESE NEGOTIATING INSTRUCTIONS CAREFULLY

ATTITUDES TOWARDS YOUR ROLE: it is important that you should know what attitude to adopt towards your role. It is your task to come to an agreement with your opposite number, an agreement that will be binding on both sides. In doing this I want you to be especially aware of the implications of what you are saying for your own party. At the end of the negotiation I shall ask you to say how you think your fellow managers will judge your performance as their representative. Remember that your opposite number is a union representative aiming to get as much as he/she can for his/her own side. You must concentrate on the task you have been entrusted with; that is, to secure the agreement your side wants. Remember, you are accountable to your fellow managers.

Intergroup union: PLEASE READ THESE NEGOTIATING INSTRUCTIONS CAREFULLY

ATTITUDES TOWARDS YOUR ROLE: it is important that you should know what attitude to adopt towards your role. It is your task to come to an agreement with your opposite number, an agreement that will be binding on both sides. In doing this I want you to be especially aware of the implications of what you are saying for your own party. At the end of the negotiation I shall ask you to say how you think your fellow shop stewards will judge your performance as their representative. Remember that your opposite number is a managerial representative aiming to get as much as he/she can for his/her own side. You must concentrate on the task you have been entrusted with; that is, to secure the agreement your side wants. Remember, you are accountable to your fellow shop stewards.

Interpersonal management: PLEASE READ THESE NEGOTIATING INSTRUCTIONS CAREFULLY

ATTITUDES TOWARDS YOUR ROLE: it is important that you should know what attitude to adopt towards your role. It is your task to come to an agreement with your opposite number, an agreement that will be binding on both sides. In doing this I want you to be especially aware of the effect of what you are saying on the other person. At the end of the negotiation I shall ask you to give an account of what happened from his or her personal point of view. Remember that your opposite number is not just a shop steward, but an individual with a job to do. Try to understand how he/she might be feeling about things. Remember, you are both responsible individuals, and as such accountable to one another for the decision you reach together.

Interpersonal union: PLEASE READ THESE NEGOTIATING INSTRUCTIONS CAREFULLY

ATTITUDES TOWARDS YOUR ROLE: it is important that you should know what attitude to adopt towards your role. It is your task to come to an agreement with your opposite number, an agreement that will be binding on both sides. In doing this I want you to be especially aware of the effect of what you are saying on the other person. At the end of the negotiation I shall ask you to give an account of what happened from his or her personal point of view. Remember that your opposite number is not just a manager, but an individual with a job to do. Try to understand how he/she might be feeling about things. Remember, you are both responsible individuals, and as such accountable to one another for the decision you reach together.

APPENDIX 6

Negotiating rules

There are two issues to be negotiated. You can discuss them in any order or at any time. You can agree on both issues at the same time. Thirty minutes is the maximum time allowed for the negotiation. If agreement has not been reached on both issues at the end of that time, a deadlock must be declared.

When you and your opposite agent are ready to negotiate, you can begin. Start the stop-watch when you begin, so you can time your negotiation.

You will see that you have a tape-recorder. Please use it to record your negotiation, beginning your recording as you start the stop-watch and begin the negotiation.

When you reach agreement on an issue, circle the appropriate settlement on the 'Final contract' sheet, and you must both initial the agreement in the spaces provided. Once an agreement has been initialled, you cannot re-open negotiations about it again.

When you have initialled your agreement on the second issue, stop the stop-watch immediately and write down the time taken to reach agreement in minutes and seconds in the space provided on the 'Final contract' sheet for issue 2. If you have not finished by the time 30 minutes is up, you must stop immediately and write 'D' for deadlock in the space provided for time taken to reach agreement.

After you have reached agreement on both issues, or 30 minutes is up, please stop the tape-recorder and summon the tutor.

IF YOU DO NOT UNDERSTAND ANY PART OF THE INSTRUCTIONS AND MATERIAL YOU HAVE BEEN GIVEN, CALL THE TUTOR.

APPENDIX 7

Final contract agreement

(a) Final contract: issue 1

Wages

PENCE INCREASE PER HOUR (circle agreed amount)

00	01	02	03	04	05	06	07	08	09
10	11	12	13	14	15	16	17	18	19

INITIALS OF NEGOTIATORS

Management ....

Union ....

(b) Final contract: issue 2

Vacation pay: put tick in appropriate box:

3 weeks for 1 year's service	3 weeks for 1 year's service; 4 weeks for 18 years' service	3 weeks for 1 year's service; 4 weeks for 14 years' service	3 weeks for 1 year's service; 4 weeks for 10 years' service	3 weeks for 1 year's service; 4 weeks for 6 years' service	3 weeks for 1 year's service; 4 weeks for 2 years' service
☐	☐	☐	☐	☐	☐

Initials of negotiators

Management ....

Union ....

State time taken to reach agreement on the two issues:

APPENDIX 8

Post-negotiation questionnaire

State party represented (management or union):

Questionnaire

Please put a cross in the appropriate space on each scale to indicate how strongly you feel one way or the other about each question.

Do not spend too long over each item.

1. How satisfied are you overall with the agreements reached?

   Dissatisfied ___ : ___ : ___ : ___ : ___ : ___ : ___ : ___ : ___ Satisfied

2. How satisfied were you with your own performance in the negotiations?

   Dissatisfied ___ : ___ : ___ : ___ : ___ : ___ : ___ : ___ : ___ Satisfied

3. How accountable did you feel to the party you were representing?

   Unaccountable ___ : ___ : ___ : ___ : ___ : ___ : ___ : ___ : ___ Accountable

4. How important to you was it to look strong to the other negotiator in the negotiations?

   Unimportant ___ : ___ : ___ : ___ : ___ : ___ : ___ : ___ : ___ Important

5. How committed did you feel to your party's position during the negotiations?

   Uncommitted ___ : ___ : ___ : ___ : ___ : ___ : ___ : ___ : ___ Committed

6. Please describe both yourself and the other negotiator during the negotiations on the following scales. Mark an 'X' in the space best describing yourself on each dimension and an 'O' in the space describing the other negotiator. You have to judge whether the person you are rating lies at one extreme of a scale, or in the middle, or somewhere in between.

   Rigid ___ : ___ : ___ : ___ : ___ : ___ : ___ : ___ : ___ Flexible

   Constrained ___ : ___ : ___ : ___ : ___ : ___ : ___ : ___ : ___ Free

   Influential ___ : ___ : ___ : ___ : ___ : ___ : ___ : ___ : ___ Uninfluential

   Competitive ___ : ___ : ___ : ___ : ___ : ___ : ___ : ___ : ___ Co-operative

   Successful ___ : ___ : ___ : ___ : ___ : ___ : ___ : ___ : ___ Unsuccessful

   Helpful ___ : ___ : ___ : ___ : ___ : ___ : ___ : ___ : ___ Obstructive

Hostile   __ : __ : __ : __ : __ : __ : __ : __ : __   Friendly

Hard   __ : __ : __ : __ : __ : __ : __ : __ : __   Soft

Yielding   __ : __ : __ : __ : __ : __ : __ : __ : __   Tenacious

Productive   __ : __ : __ : __ : __ : __ : __ : __ : __   Destructive

Unemotional   __ : __ : __ : __ : __ : __ : __ : __ : __   Emotional

Strong   __ : __ : __ : __ : __ : __ : __ : __ : __   Weak

Deliberate   __ : __ : __ : __ : __ : __ : __ : __ : __   Impulsive

Formal   __ : __ : __ : __ : __ : __ : __ : __ : __   Informal

Aggressive   __ : __ : __ : __ : __ : __ : __ : __ : __   Defensive

Rejecting   __ : __ : __ : __ : __ : __ : __ : __ : __   Accepting

7. Who did you think had the stronger case? Please put a cross in the appropriate box.

Management ☐   Union ☐   Cases approximately ☐
equally strong

APPENDIX 9

The following excerpt is taken from chapter 10 of Morley and Stephenson (1977). That chapter, entitled 'Conference process analysis', describes in detail how to divide a transcript into 'acts' and to describe each act in terms of its 'mode', 'resource' and 'referent'. The category <u>accept</u> is one of four modes (offer, accept, reject and seek), and is defined as follows:

CATEGORY 2: ACCEPT
Each of the units underlined below is coded as 'accepts': e.g.

U: So I think we are justified in claiming the 100 per cent/.
M: <u>I would agree that in the time if things go as they should do, then this would be a good thing for both company - and the workers/.</u>
U: That requires a direct yes or no/.
M: <u>That's true/.</u>
M: How would you suggest then that we deal with this now/ as a company/? I mean, you're part of the community in this respect/.
U: <u>Yeah/. Yeah/.</u>
U: I would say now that we've got to reach agreement on the exact percentage/.
M: <u>Yes/.</u>
M: We have to think of this before lashing out on 85 per cent/.
U: <u>Well, yes/. I entirely agree with you/.</u>

Part three Problem investigations

11

Gathering eyewitness testimony
Ray Bull

Specification notes

AIM OF EXERCISE: to determine whether males or females are the more accurate eyewitnesses.

PRIOR KNOWLEDGE ASSUMED: little or no prior theoretical knowledge is required but a basic grounding in simple statistics may be necessary.

DURATION: this exercise can be conducted within three hours, or it can be made more complex and thus require two three-hour sessions.

LOCATION: explanation of the study and its data analysis can be undertaken in any teaching room; data gathering is straight-forward and this will be conducted in a public thoroughfare.

RESOURCES: no special equipment or other resources are required.

Introduction

This exercise is designed to examine some of the factors which influence the accuracy of eyewitnesses' recollections and to high-light the problems encountered when attempting to collect and quantify such recall. Though most lay people are of the opinion that they can easily remember

someone, psychologists' field studies have shown that eyewitnesses' recollections can, in many circumstances, be poor. At the present time, legal procedures and court practices are unsure as to the general accuracy of eyewitness testimony. Whilst laboratory-based studies of facial recall have generally observed the subjects to be highly accurate, field studies (out in the street, so to speak) have frequently found much poorer levels of performance. The study described here will not be conducted in the laboratory, but in a public tho-roughfare. Thus not only can this study be considered as a worth-while piece of re-search, it can also be viewed as a useful training exercise in how to conduct 'field studies' and approach members of the public in order to gather meaningful information from them.

Comparisons will be made between the accuracy of male and female witnesses, and it is suggested that the sex of the to-be-remembered stimulus persons and/or the duration of the incident (short versus long exposure) may have an influence on whe-ther females are more accurate witnesses than are males. One of the major reference books on the psychology of eyewitnessing is that by Clifford and Bull (1978). In order to conduct and write a report on the present exercise it is not necessary to consult such a book (of course, those in-terested enough may wish to do so), nor the other references listed at the end of this exercise (nearly all of which are summarized in Clifford and Bull, 1978).

How accurate are eyewitnesses?

In 1972, in response to general disquiet, the Home Secretary appointed Lord Devlin to chair an official committee to examine the laws and procedures on person identification (Devlin, 1976). The former Chief of the Metropolitan Police, Sir Robert Mark, is quoted as saying that, 'If the police, the lawyers and the courts did their jobs properly the most likely cause of wrongful convictions is mistaken identity', and Lord Gardiner that, 'Most wrong convictions were on the matter of identification' (Cole and Pringle, 1974). If such statements are valid then not only may an innocent person be found guilty, but also the true culprit could still be at large. To decide whether such views have any validity is a very difficult problem indeed. However, it is on just this type of question that those people best equipped to study human behaviour scientifically (i.e. psychologists) should have something of value to say.

It has been claimed that 'There is certainly a persuasive argument that the human memory for faces is so fallible that evidence of identification is virtually worthless. It seems likely that most people are quite incapable of remembering a face' (Cole and Pringle, 1974). Upon examination (Clifford and Bull, 1978) it appears that such claims as this are based on what amounts to anecdotal evidence. Now anecdotal evidence may eventually be found to have been correct, but scientifically rigorous studies of the powers of person identification are needed in this very important area of human behaviour.

In this respect Lord Devlin (1976) called for exploration, of a research nature, into 'establishing ways in which the insights of psychology could be brought to bear on the conduct of identification parades and the practice of the courts in all matters relating to evidence of identification'. Even though a few early psychologists (e.g. Munsterberg, 1908) had argued that sense data are fallible, recall is idiosyncratic and eyewitness testimony inherently unreliable, their views were almost entirely ignored by the legal world.

Until very recently jurors, judges and lawyers placed a great deal of faith in eyewitness testimony and only in the last couple of years have books been published (e.g. Clifford and Bull, 1978) and events taken place to counter the claim of Levine and Tapp (1973) that 'Psychologists have had little impact on the Law's unwarranted reliance on eye-witness reports'.

In the light of the evidence and arguments presented to it the Devlin Committee recommended that only in exceptional cases should a verdict of guilty be arrived at when the evidence against the defendant depends solely on the testimony of one eyewitness. Some forms of corroboration of such evidence would usually be necessary before guilt could be proven. Thus, in the last few years, judges have been required to inform jurors about the possible limitations of eyewitness testimony. As a consequence of this, some people now believe that the balance of proof has swung too much upon those wishing to prove guilt. If an eyewitness claims that he or she is sure that the person they are viewing (or hearing) is the one who committed the crime, then is it right that the suspect should be set free due to lack of corroborative evidence? Methodologically rigorous and ecologically valid investigations are obviously needed in this important area of human behaviour.

Laboratory versus field studies

Ecologically valid studies are ones which investigate behaviour in its true context as opposed to an artificial situation (such as a laboratory can sometimes be). For decades psychologists' research on memory blindly followed the 'nonsense-syllable' research tradition of Ebbinghaus. This arid approach was one reason why the Devlin Committee found little of value in its reading of the psychological literature. Until recently the main thrust of psychological research was orientated towards theory-testing, there being a strong emphasis on logical rigour and formal elegance. Socially relevant research on real-life problems tended to be avoided, perhaps because such research is difficult to design, conduct, analyse and discuss. The laboratory-based tradition of research in psychology often suffers 'from too severe control over variables (which results in findings of no practical importance), from the choosing of the dependent variable in terms of convenience rather than importance, and from the presentation of stimuli of an artificial nature in an unrealistic way' (Clifford and Bull, 1978). Much laboratory-based research on people's powers of visual recognition can be said to suffer from these limitations. Though the results of laboratory-based studies seem to support the view that most people have excellent powers of recognition, such a conclusion is not necessarily warranted.

In the laboratory, Shepard (1967) asked people to look at 600 pictures of various objects, landscapes and scenes. They were then shown 60 pairs of pictures where only one of each pair had been seen in the original 600. They were simply asked, for each pair, to pick out the picture previously seen. This situation is quite analogous to going through a series of mugshots. Correct identification was made in 97 per cent of the cases. In a similar type of experiment Nickerson (1965) showed 800 pictures of objects to a group of people and then showed them another set of 400 pictures, and they had to say which of these 400 pictures had appeared in the first batch of photos seen. Nickerson found 92 per cent correct recognition. Standing, Conezio and Haber (1970) showed the staggering total of 2,500 photos of unfamiliar paintings, scenes and magazine photos to a group of students for 5-10 seconds. At the end of about seven hours' viewing the observers still achieved 90 per cent correct identification of photos seen, even with an interval of a day and a half between first seeing and later identifying.

While the power of visual memory seems staggering it could be objected that it is quite easy to distinguish between different objects: a cat is vastly different from an aeroplane. Face recognition may be quite a different story because the pattern of features is very similar across all faces. What are the facts? Hochberg and Galper (1967) asked people to look first at a series of 35 and then at a series of 60 faces. They then presented 15 pairs of photographs - one of each pair having been seen previously, the other not - and asked for identification of the face previously seen. The subjects' recognition performance was better with 35 faces than with 60 faces, but even with 60 faces to store they still recognized them on 90 per cent of occasions. In this study the faces were of females. Yin (1969) observed 96 per cent correct identification of male faces presented as photographs.

The results of these laboratory-based studies could be taken to suggest that eyewitnesses will usually produce high levels of recognition performance. However, it should be borne in mind that in such studies (i) the subjects are aware that subsequently their recognition powers will be tested, (ii) their attention is focussed upon the stimuli to be recognized later, and (iii) each stimulus is static/stationary and is viewed for at least several seconds. In contrast to this, in field studies (which attempt to simulate criminal episodes) the usual procedure is to stage an incident in front of unsuspecting witnesses and then to ask for remembered details of people's actions. This experimental approach is a big advance over static inspection and recognition of photographs in the sense that the action is dynamic, it reproduces real life in content and the subjects are unprepared for becoming witnesses.

In order to study the effects of eyewitness testimony in a somewhat realistic setting Buckhout (1974) staged an assault (located on the California State University campus) in which a distraught student 'attacked' a professor in front of 141 witnesses. The whole incident was recorded on videotape so that objective reality could be compared with the eyewitness reports. After the attack Buckhout and his colleagues took sworn statements from each witness asking them to describe the suspect, the incident and the clothes worn. The witnesses gave very inaccurate descriptions, and they greatly over-estimated the duration of the incident (in this case by a factor of over $2\frac{1}{2}$). The accuracy score for appearance and dress was only 25 per cent of the maximum possible total score. Height and weight were reasonably accurate, but unfortunately Buckhout had chosen a target person of average height and weight, so there were no independent means of assessing whether subjects were perceiving and remembering accurately or merely guessing.

For the purpose of the present experimental exercise a procedure somewhat similar to that of Buckhout will be employed except that no one will be 'attacked'. In a public thoroughfare a colleague (or 'confederate') of the experimenter will stop a passer-by and ask one or more questions. When the confederate has moved on the experimenter will approach the passer-by and will then try to gather some details of recall of physical aspects of the confederate. Both male and female passers-by will be used, the experimental hypotheses being that there will be a significant difference in the recall of female as opposed to male passers-by.

Male versus female witnesses

Most of the research concerning sex differences in eyewitness accuracy suggests that female witnesses may often prove to be more accurate than males. Cross, Cross and Daly (1971) found female observers to perform significantly better than male observers on female faces, with the male observers being equally good on the male and female faces. In a similar way Ellis, Shepherd and Bruce (1973) found that while there was no significant difference between male and female observers for male faces, there was a significant difference for female faces, with women performing better. How can the weight of evidence in favour of women be explained? A number of possibilities exist. Cross et al and Ellis et al explained their findings of female superiority by the greater exposure of females to female faces in magazines and cosmetic literature, and thus the increased opportunity to learn to encode features of faces.

The above sex difference findings have been drawn from studies on schematic and photographic faces. Does female superiority also hold in real-life or simulated crime studies? It appears that it does not. Kuehn (1974) showed that female victims are poorer at giving complete descriptions of assailants, whereas Bahrick, Bahrick and Wittlinger (1975) indicated that in non-emotionally charged atmospheres female superiority does reassert itself in recognition and recall of people who have been involved in interactions. Clifford and Scott (1978) showed that when a non-violent

episode is viewed for later recollection female witnesses are better than males, but when a violent episode is viewed, later recall by males is superior to that of females. Thus females were found to perform poorly under stressful conditions, a finding that supports Kuehn's tabulation of real-life police-elicited recalls from male and female victims. Generally speaking, females are better at recognizing previously seen faces in non-stress situations. Under stressful viewing conditions males may make the better type of witness.

Hypotheses

In the present exercise witnesses are required to recall details about a person who speaks to them. Since the present study is designed to be non-stressful for the witness, the main experimental hypothesis is that female witnesses are more accurate than male witnesses (a one-tail hypothesis). Subsidiary hypotheses can be (i) that the sex of the person the witnesses try to recall has an effect, and (ii) that the length of time for which the witness sees the to-be-recalled person may influence how much they remember. (These hypotheses and their relevant experimental methodology will be discussed towards the end of the Method section, once the basic procedure has been outlined.)

Method

No special equipment or materials are necessary for this study. Students will work in pairs. In a local public place one of them (referred to here as the 'confederate') will approach and ask a question(s) of a member(s) of the public who is walking along. Shortly after this interaction has ceased the other student in the pair (referred to here as the experimenter) will ask the member of the public some prepared questions concerning the physical appearance details of the confederate. If only a little time (e.g. less than one hour) is available for the data gathering, then the data from several pairs of students (working in slightly different localities) can be combined for the subsequent analysis. In total, data from a minimum of at least six witnesses from each sex must be available.

If more than 1½ hours is available to each pair of students, then each pair should be able to gather enough data (i.e. at least six for each sex of witness) for statistical analysis to be performed on their own data.

Should it be desired to expand this exercise by including further independent variables such as that of sex of stimulus person (i.e. confederate), or that of duration of the interaction, or both, more time (between two and four hours) will be required for the data gathering.

Procedure

Since the question of whether female eyewitnesses are more accurate than males seems to depend upon the level of stress or arousal induced during the witnesses' viewing of the to-be-recalled information, a conscious decision needs to be made about the way in which the experimental interaction will take place in the present study. For the purposes of this experiment it is advised that the interaction between witness and confederate be non-stressful for the witness. It is suggested that the member of the experimental team (the confederate) who interacts with each witness asks them a straightforward commonplace question such as 'Could you tell me the time, please?' The main independent variable in the present experiment is that of the sex of the witness and the dependent variable is how well the witness remembers the appearance of the confederate. The confederate should attempt to ensure that the way he or she interacts with each witness is as similar as possible from witness to witness (i.e. that the confederate's behaviour becomes a 'controlled' variable).

It is important to note that only those passers-by who respond to the confederate's questions can act as experimental subjects (i.e. are witnesses). Any passer-by who does not stop when approached and questioned by the confederate will not be asked to recall details of the confederate later.

Experimenter's instructions to subjects (i.e. to the witnesses)

Once the interaction between the confederate and a subject has ceased and the confederate is out of sight, the experimenter should approach the subject and say something like, 'Excuse me, we are conducting a study of how well people can remember a stranger that they have just spoken to. A few seconds ago a friend of mine came up to you and asked you for the time. May I ask you a few questions about his/her appearance?' If the member of the public agrees to this request he/she now becomes a subject and his/her recall accuracy is assessed.

When the experimenter has finished questioning the witness a short debriefing explanation should be given to the subject. The experimenter should briefly describe the aims of the study (i.e. to investigate eyewitness accuracy and to see if females are more accurate eyewitnesses than are males), and should thank the member of the public for participating in the study.

Assessing recall accuracy

Decisions have been made concerning how to assess the accuracy of the witnesses' recall of the physical details of the confederate. Would it be better to ask each witness to describe the confederate in his or her own words or would it be better to ask each witness to answer a structured questionnaire? If the first of these alternatives is used problems of scoring the recall will ensue; for instance, one witness may correctly recall four different and important aspects of the confederate whereas another, say a hairdresser, may correctly recall four details about the confederate's hair but nothing else. Are these two witnesses to receive the same accuracy score? It is therefore suggested that a questionnaire be drawn up before the experiment takes place. This questionnaire can take a variety of forms. A number of questions (say 12) can be asked, each either providing the witness with restricted choice of response (e.g. 'Did he have light or dark hair?') or each permitting the witness to use his/her own words (e.g. 'What was the colour of his hair?'). This second form of question will make the scoring of the recall problematical since, for example, if the confederate had black hair and a witness replied 'brown' how would such recall be quantified (as totally wrong, nearly right, half right)? To overcome such problems it is suggested that a 'forced choice' questionnaire be used and table 1 provides an example of this.

If a questionnaire somewhat similar to table 1 is used each witness's recall can be scored out of 12. Note that the final question (number 12) in the suggested questionnaire asks about the presence of something that, in fact, the confederate was <u>not</u> carrying. This question is designed to examine whether witnesses will infer the presence of something when in fact it was absent (Clifford and Bull, 1978). In connection with question 8 witnesses may say 'yes' more often for male than female confederates. Such response biasses serve to make the gathering of eyewitness recall a complex affair! Furthermore, for question 10 there is the problem of what 'fat' and 'thin' mean to each witness. Would the witnesses' answers to these questions depend on how fat (or thin) they themselves are? (A similar point may apply for question 11.)

Table 1. A suggested questionnaire for use in obtaining information about the witnesses' recall of the confederate

1. Was the person that asked you the question(s) taller or shorter than 5' 8"? (5' 3" for female confederates)?
2. Did he (she) have brown or blue eyes?
3. Was he (she) wearing dark or light trousers?
4. Was he (she) wearing glasses?
5. Was he (she) wearing a jacket or a long coat?
6. Did he have a moustache/beard? (Use 'lipstick' for female confederates.)
7. Was his (her) shirt blue or green?
8. Was he (she) wearing a belt?
9. Was his (her) hair light or dark?
10. Was he (she) fat or thin?
11. Did he (she) have a large or a small nose?
12. Was he (she) carrying a note-pad?

(Note that for questions 2, 3, 5 and 7, one of the two alternatives should, of course, actually have been part of the confederate's true appearance: otherwise the questions should be modified appropriately.)

Summary of method

To summarize the methodology, a confederate (one of a pair of experimenters) will approach and ask a question(s) of a member of the public who is walking along in a local public place. A few moments after this interaction has ceased (and the confederate is out of sight) the experimenter will approach the member of the public and inform him or her that an experiment on the accuracy of memory is being carried out. The member of the public will be asked if he or she is willing to answer a small number of brief questions. (The mention of brevity is likely to increase the rate of co-operation.) If the member of the public agrees he or she then becomes an experimental witness and their recall is gathered and scored for accuracy. If in response to a recall question a witness replies 'don't know', is this as suggestive of inefficient recall as a witness who produces an incorrect response to a question (e.g. says eyes were blue when they were brown)? For the purposes of the present experiment either of the two above forms of error will score zero and each correct response merits a score of one. Students may wish to discuss in their reports the extent to which giving each of the two types of error illustrated above a score of zero is a satisfactory method of quantifying the witnesses' recall.

Analysis

Data from several experimenter/confederate pairs can be pooled for the purposes of statistical analysis of the data. Since the independent variable of sex of witness leads to an 'independent measures' experimental design, a statistical 'test of difference' for independent measures should be used (i.e. either the independent t-test if the data approximate a normal distribution or, alternatively, the Mann-Whitney U test). (For details of these tests see a book on simple statistics such as Robson, 1973.)

Histograms of the raw data can be drawn as shown in figure 1, one for the male witnesses' recall and one for the female witnesses' recall. These two histograms can be compared by eye to see whether or not

Figure 1. Histograms of the recall data

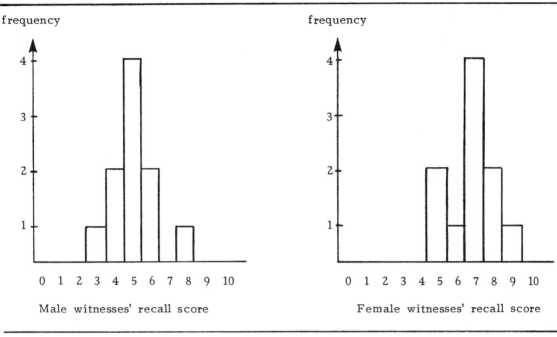

Male witnesses' recall score

Female witnesses' recall score

they suggest a difference between the recall of male and female witnesses. The histograms may also be used as a guide to whether or not the raw data approximate a normal distribution.

Optimal additonal independent variables

For more advanced students the basic, single variable exercise described above can be expanded into a more complex study.

SEX OF STIMULUS PERSON. A second independent variable which can be introduced easily into the design of the experiment is that of sex of confederate (i.e. the witnessed person). This is a variable worthy of investigation since the literature reviewed in the introduction suggests that female witnesses may be most accurate when attempting to recall details of female as opposed to male stimuli.

DURATION OF INTERACTION. If it is not possible, or desirable, to vary the sex of the confederate then an alternative, and very significant, second independent variable can be that of the duration of the interaction between confederate and witness. The confederate can ask half the

witnesses for the time (short duration), but engage the others in a longer-lasting interaction by asking them, for example, some questions about television. (In both duration conditions the confederate would not be carrying a note pad). In this latter (i.e. long duration) condition not one but several questions can be asked of each witness.

For example:

* 'Excuse me, I'm conducting a survey. Do you think there is too much sport on television?'
* 'What is your favourite television programme?'
* 'Why do you like that particular programme?'

The last of these three questions being an 'open-ended' question will usually ensure that this 'long duration' condition will cause the witness to be exposed to the confederate for a longer period of time than in the short duration condition.

The experimental hypothesis for the effect of the independent variable 'short versus long duration' is that the witnesses' recall of details of the confederate will be more accurate in the long duration condition. (Is this a two- or one-tailed hypothesis?) This hypothesis may be thought to be merely going along with what common sense would predict. Psychology is frequently accused of doing this, but we should be aware that psychology has an important role to play for society by scientifically confirming what common sense may suggest. For instance, some previous research (Laughery, Alexander and Lane, 1971) found that the longer the time for which a facial photograph had been viewed the more accurate was subsequent recognition. Clifford and Richards (1977) found that policemen's recall of a person who asked them questions was more accurate for long-term than for short exposure durations. This latter study, however, found that members of the public showed recall that was somewhat poorer under long than under short exposure duration conditions.

If a second independent variable (or factor) is introduced into the experiment (e.g. sex of confederate, or duration of exposure) then there should be an equal number of male and female witnesses in each of the two extra conditions (i.e. an equal number of witnesses in the four experimental conditions as shown in table 2).

The ideal statistical test for the experimental design illustrated in table 2 is a two-way analysis of variance. If this statistical text is beyond the scope of the students then a number of independent t-tests can be used, such as (i) one t-test comparing male versus female witnesses, with the data from male and female confederates being combined together; (ii) one t-test comparing male versus female confederates, with the data from male and female witnesses being combined together; or (iii) a series of t-tests comparing each of the four 'cells' of the experimental design with each of the other cells. In the above two-way design, sex of confederate can be replaced by duration of exposure (short versus long). The use of a two-way analysis of variance is advised since it is less time consuming and more statistically appropriate than a series of t-tests. Furthermore, the analysis of variance permits examination of the 'interaction' between the two independent variables as shown in figure 2.

An 'interaction' signifies that, under one condition (or level) of an independent variable (or factor) the second independent variable has a certain effect (e.g. sex of witness has no effect with male confederates) but it has a different effect under another condition of that independent variable (e.g. sex of witness has an effect with female confederates). Whether or not an analysis of variance is performed on the data, if the experiment contains two independent variables then a diagram such as that illustrated in figure 2 should always be drawn.

The present experiment is also capable of being expanded into a three-way design; that is, three independent variables: (i) sex of witness, (ii) sex of confederate, and (iii) duration of exposure. A three-way analysis of variance should be performed on the data, there being an equal number of

Table 2. The allocation of subjects to conditions if two independent variables are used

Variable 2, e.g. sex of confederate	Variable 1, sex of witness			
	male		female	
Male	S1 S2 S3	S4 S5 S6	S13 S14 S15	S16 S17 S18
Female	S7 S8 S9	S10 S11 S12	S19 S20 S21	S22 S23 S24

Figure 2. Diagrammatic representation of an interaction between two independent variables (or factors)

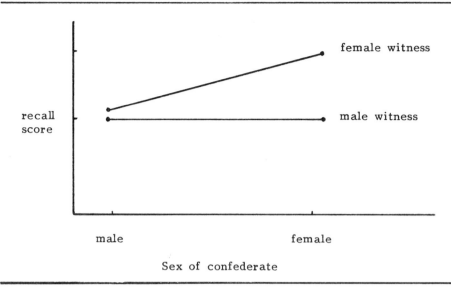

observations (say three) in each 'cell' (or experimental condition) of the design, as illustrated in table 3.

Discussion

This exercise should highlight for the stu-dent some of the problems to be considered and overcome when gathering data not in the laboratory but 'out in the streets'. Also, various ways of assessing witnesses' memory accuracy have been considered and this issue of how best to assess memory performance applies to all types of experimental study of memory performance. The

Table 3. The allocation of subjects to conditions if three independent variables are used

Variable 2 sex of confederate	Variable 3 exposure duration	Variable 1 Sex of witness male female
male	short	S1 S13 S2 S14 S3 S15
	long	S4 S16 S5 S17 S6 S18
female	short	S7 S19 S8 S20 S9 S21
	long	S10 S22 S11 S23 S12 S24

exercise also permits students to see how the design of an experiment can be expanded from the single independent variable case to a design employing two or even three independent variables, whilst keeping other factors constant as 'control variables' (e.g. the confederate's behaviour).

The data gathered in this study will show whether there exists a significant difference in the accuracy of female versus male eyewitnesses. (The effects of the variables of (i) sex of witnessed person, and (ii) duration of exposure of the stimulus person to the witness, may also have been examined.) The overall level of eyewitness accuracy found in the fairly naturalistic setting used in this study can be compared with the levels of accuracy found in the laboratory-based studies of facial photograph recognition mentioned in the Introduction.

The findings of the present study have implications for the debate on whether eyewitness testimony is usually accurate or inaccurate. Legal and police practices and procedures can benefit from the results of research on this topic.

The present study is not a perfect simulation of real-life criminal episodes and in the Introduction it was noted that the amount of arousal induced in a witness may influence whether females or males are better eyewitnesses. This factor needs to be taken into account when commenting on the data gathered in the study. Further,

many aspects of the witness may not have been controlled for (e.g. age, or whether the male witnesses were in more of a hurry than the females). Other factors for consideration are (i) the extent to which the confederate behaved in exactly the same way with each of the witnesses, and (ii) the limitations of the questionnaire used in gaining a score for eyewitness accuracy.

If female witnesses are found to be more accurate than males, is this due to their more efficient sensory input of physical details of the confederate, or to their better memory storage of such information, or to their more efficient retrieval of it from memory (or to a combination of these three factors)? When asked to recall, do some witnesses try harder than others to be 'good witnesses'? Such questions reflect an important consideration: that in psychology, gathering and statistically analysing data takes us only halfway towards our goal; we have then to explain the data.

Conclusion

This exercise is an attempt to determine whether females are more accurate eyewitnesses than are males. Several methodological problems (e.g. how best to assess memory performance) are discussed, as are the problems of conducting experiments not in the laboratory but 'out in the street'.

REFERENCES

Bahrick, H., Bahrick, R. and Wittlinger, R. (1975) Fifty years of memory for names and faces: a cross-cultural approach. Journal of Experimental Psychology: General, 104, 54-75.

Buckhout, R. (1974) Eyewitness testimony. Scientific American, 231, 23-31.

Clifford, B. and Bull, R. (1978) The Psychology of Person Identification. London: Routledge & Kegan Paul.

Clifford, B. and Richards, G. (1977) Comparisons of recall by police and civilians under conditions of long and short durations of exposure. Perceptual and Motor Skills, 45, 503-512.

Clifford, B. and Scott, J. (1978) Individual and situational factors in eyewitness testimony. Journal of Applied Psychology, 63, 352-359.

Cole, P. and Pringle, P. (1974) Can You Positively Identify This Man? George Ince and the Barn Murder. London: Deutsch.

Cross, J., Cross, J. and Daly, J. (1971) Sex, race, age and beauty as factors in recognition of faces. Perception and Psychophysics, 10, 393-396.

Devlin Report (1976) Report to the Secretary of State for the Home Department of the Departmental Committee on Evidence of Identification in Criminal Cases. London: HMSO.

Ellis, H.D., Shepherd, J. and Bruce, A. (1973) The effect of age and sex upon adolescents' recognition of faces. Journal of Genetic Psychology, 123, 173-174.

Hochberg, J. and Galper, R. (1967) Recognition of faces (I). An exploratory study. Psychonomic Science, 12, 619-620.

Kuehn, L. (1974) Looking down a gun barrel: person perception and violent crime. Perceptual and Motor Skills, 39, 1159-1164.

Laughery, K., Alexander, J. and Lane, A. (1971) Recognition of human faces: effects of target exposure, target position, pose position and type of photograph. Journal of Applied Psychology, 55, 477-483.

Levine, F. and Tapp, J. (1973) The psychology of criminal identification: the gap from Wade to Kirby. University of Pennsylvania Law Review, 121, 1079-1132.

Munsterberg, H. (1908) On the Witness Stand: Essays on psychology and crime. New York: Clark, Boardman.

Nickerson, R. (1965) Short term memory for complex, meaningful visual configurations: a demonstration of capacity. Canadian Journal of Psychology, 19, 155-160.

Robson, C. (1973) Experiment, Design and Statistics in Psychology. Harmondsworth: Penguin.

Shepard, R. (1967) Recognition memory for words, sentences and pictures. Journal of Verbal Learning and Verbal Behaviour, 6, 156-163.

Standing, L., Conezio, J. and Haber, R. (1970) Perception and memory for pictures: single trial learning of 2560 visual stimuli. Psychonomic Science, 19, 73-74.

Yin, R. (1969) Looking at upside-down faces. Journal of Experimental Psychology, 81, 141-145.

12

Attribution processes
Mansur Lalljee

Specification notes

The exercise described in this chapter is designed to test Kelley's hypotheses concerning the influence of consensus, consistency and distinctiveness information in making causal attributions within the context of attributions for success and failure. In keeping with much of the research on attribution processes, a questionnaire consisting of brief descriptions of hypothetical events is proposed as a way of pursuing the problem. Two different dependent variables are suggested: rating scales of attribution to personal and situational causes, and the respondents' open-ended explanations about why the event occurred. The main merits of the exercise centre round the methodological problems involved in drawing up the questionnaire and in providing students with some experience of content analysis.

AIMS OF EXERCISE: (i) to teach students how to structure stimulus material and design questionnaires to test hypotheses; (ii) to enable teaching and practice of analysis of variance; (iii) to introduce students to content analysis.

PRIOR KNOWLEDGE ASSUMED: none.

DURATION: 2½-3 hours.

LOCATION: only one room is necessary,

provided that students are able to confer in groups of about four.

RESOURCES/FACILITIES: each student will need a copy of the questionnaire included in Appendix 1 and the coding categories for the content analysis included in Appendix 2.

SPECIAL REQUIREMENTS: none.

Introduction

The explanations that people provide for events have, until recently, received little attention from psychologists. However, explanations have not been neglected by other disciplines, notably philosophy, anthropology and sociology. The philosopher's interest has focussed primarily on the nature of scientific explanation, and anthropologists and sociologists have stressed that different frameworks of explanation are prevalent in different societies and in the same society in different historical periods. The proper study of explanations by the psychologist must be the examination of explanations that are actually provided by people. The tendency to seek explanations for physical events, social processes and human behaviour seems as pervasive a human tendency as any other. An explanation serves to disambiguate an event, to impose a particular sort of stability and predictability upon the world and to enable the individual to act towards it in a systematic manner. To the child a wide variety of events are considered worthy of explanation, and it is apparently easily satisfied with any explanation. A vital part of the process of socialization includes learning what events the adults in the culture consider worthy of explanation and the kinds of explanations they consider acceptable. A child must learn not only the generally acceptable forms of explanation but also how to invoke the appropriate sort of explanation on a particular occasion. It must also learn that different explanations have different intra- and interpersonal effects.

Of course, the area has not been entirely neglected. Piaget's work is an important instance of the way in which different forms of explanation vary as a function of cognitive development. In some of his earlier work on the child's conception of the world and on the development of moral judgement, Piaget attempts to relate the type of explanation the child provides to more general characteristics of cognitive functioning (see Piaget, 1929, 1932). More recently the explanations that children provide have received some attention from Robinson and Rackstraw (1972), who have attempted to examine differences between middle- and working-class children within the context of Bernstein's (1973) notions of elaborated and restricted codes.

In current social psychology, interest in how people explain events can be traced to the work of Fritz Heider (1958). Drawing on Heider's writings a number of researchers have put forward hypotheses about how the layman arrives at attributions of causality and what the consequences of such explanations are. This area, now called attribution theory, has been dominated by two general assumptions: first, it is concerned with causal explanations rather than, for instance, explanations in terms of regularity or categorization and, second, it draws a central distinction between explanations in terms of personal causes and explanations in terms of environmental causes.

The general issue that is explored by researchers concerned with attribution theory can be clarified through an example. Take, for instance, the case of a student doing badly at work. There may be agreement that he or she is doing badly, but there may be considerable disagreement as to why. The unsatisfactory performance could be explained in terms of lack of ability, in terms of not trying hard enough, in terms of emotional stress, a crisis in personal relationships, uncertainty about future employment, the difficulty of the course, bad teaching or in a variety of other ways. Given the wide range of possible causes the next question concerns the systematization or organization of explanations. Attribution theory sees as central the distinction between explanations in terms of personal and environmental causes. Thus explanations in terms of cleverness or diligence are based upon aspects of the person, while explanations in terms of the nature of the task or the quality of the teaching are based upon causes external to the person.

The distinction between attributions in terms of internal and external causes is central to the theory put forward by Harold Kelley (Kelley, 1967, 1973) as to how we arrive at attributions. This distinction will be central to the study suggested in this chapter, which explores some of Kelley's ideas. However, it is important to note that the internal/external distinction by itself is unlikely to be adequate. One of the goals of attribution is to enable the perceiver to make predictions about the behaviour of other people and to assist in detecting the underlying invariances. Indeed some investigators, such as Weiner (1980), have distinguished between explanations in terms of three dimensions: locus (i.e. internal versus external), stability and control. An explanation in terms of a person's intelligence implies a stability which is not implied by an explanation in terms of effort, though they may both be internal explanations. An explanation in terms of a person's mood or emotional state may be less under the individual's control than his intentions. In a sense the goal of the individual's attribution may be to seek out the more permanent dispositions of the other. It should be pointed out that attribution theory has less to say about whether these attributions are correct. It is a theory dealing with how the layman arrives at attributions and what the consequences of these attributions are rather than a theory about whether or not these inferences are accurate. Mischel (1968), amongst others, has argued that the notion of personality traits is frequently misleading, since it implies a generality of behaviour across different social situations which is not supported by the available evidence. The central questions for our purposes here concern how people arrive at attributions rather than whether these attributions are correct or not.

Since the work of Freud, the idea that our opinions of ourselves and others are highly motivationally-biassed has formed a general part of psychological thinking. The work on interpersonal perception in the 1950s and early 1960s, too, stressed notions such as stereotypes and halo effects which emphasized the irrationality and distortions of our thinking about other people. Attribution theory has attempted to correct this imbalance. Rather than see Man as an organism that distorts incoming information in order to satisfy the wishes and needs of the organism, the general model underlying attribution theory is of Man as a scientist, or perhaps an applied scientist, sifting and analysing information in order to arrive at his conclusions. The paradigm case of scientific explanation as far as attribution theory is concerned is that of causal explanation, and the way in which causal explanations are arrived at is by observing covariation between events. Quite simply, if two events are observed to covary, then one is seen as the cause of the other. More specifically, Kelley suggests that in order to make causal attributions people use covariation information with reference to three dimensions: persons, entities and time.

Covariation information with regard to persons he calls consensus information. It is concerned with whether or not other people behave in similar ways towards the stimulus object. Thus, in the example of passing an exam, consensus information refers to the behaviour of other people with reference to that exam. If most people pass the exam, we have an instance of high consensus; if few people pass the exam, we have an instance of low consensus. The

second sort of information that is considered relevant is distinctiveness information. Distinctiveness refers to the behaviour of the person with reference to other relevant entities. Thus if the exam that John passed was a history exam, we might want to know whether his passing the history exam was for him distinctive (i.e. did he pass other exams?). If he did not then his response to the history exam is distinctive; if he did then his response to the history exam is not distinctive. The third sort of information that Kelley claims is important is consistency information: that is, information about the particular actor's response to this particular entity on previous occasions. Does John always pass his history exams? If he does then we have an instance of high consistency; if he does not then we have an instance of low consistency. On the principle of covariation Kelley suggests that in the case where there is high consensus, high distinctiveness and high consistency (i.e. where most people pass the exam, where John fails other exams, and usually passes history exams) the outcome is attributed to the entity (to the history exam) rather than to characteristics of John. It is to this issue that we will return in the experiment described later in the chapter. Before we proceed to the details of the study and its particular background, two other issues should briefly be mentioned.

Attribution theory stresses the rational information processing aspects of forming attributions about the causes of behaviour. Where the attributor has information from multiple observations, information along the three dimensions of persons, entities and time is used. But what of cases where the person does not have such information, where information about only single observations is available and a judgement is required on that basis? This is particularly relevant to first encounters in professional contexts such as interviews. Here Kelley suggests that the person draws on a variety of 'causal schemata', one of the most important of which has been called the 'discounting principle'. Where there are a variety of plausible causes for an effect, the role of any particular cause in producing that effect is discounted. This can be illustrated with reference to a range of well-known experiments. Kelley himself draws heavily on the ideas of Jones and Davis (1965), and a brief description of an experiment by Jones, Davis and Gergen (1961) will serve to illustrate the idea.

The stimulus material for the experiment was a tape-recording supposedly of a selection interview. In one of the experimental conditions subjects listened to a tape-recording of a person apparently being interviewed for the job of an astronaut. Some subjects were told that a good astronaut is supposed to be 'inner-directed': that is, independent, with little need for social contact. Other subjects were given to understand that a good astronaut should be obedient, co-operative and friendly; in short, 'other-directed'. One recording consisted of the interviewee behaving in an inner-directed way. In those cases, subjects were much more confident that the speaker really was inner-directed if they were told that the good astronaut should be other-directed, than when they were told that a good astronaut should be inner-directed.

Conceptually the experiment is simple. If the interviewee behaves in an inner-directed way, there could be two explanations for this behaviour: (i) he or she really is an inner-directed person; and (ii) he or she is behaving in an inner-directed way to get the job. When it is believed that a good astronaut should be inner-directed, both these explanations are plausible. When it is believed that a good astronaut should be other-directed, the second of the two causes above can be ruled out. The perceiver will have more confidence that the behaviour was due to the other person's disposition since in this case there are fewer plausible causes, and consequently more certainty.

The same principle has been used with interesting results in the area of self-perception. In a study by Lepper, Greene and Nisbett (1973), children who enjoyed drawing with magic marker pens were subsequently rewarded for drawing with them. These children showed a decrease in subsequent play with the pens compared with a control group who went through similar experimental manipulations without expec-

tations of reward. Here again the discounting principle is at work. If a person performs some intrinsically interesting act for a reward that person may become uncertain as to whether it was done primarily for the reward or because it was intrinsically interesting. If, however, it was done in the absence of any external reward, the intrinsic motivation is not in doubt. In the former case there are two plausible causes, in the latter case only one. The notion of discounting applies to interpretation of our own behaviour as well as to our interpretation of the behaviour of others.

This discussion has centred around the processes involved in forming attributions. It should be stressed that attributions do have important consequences. Indeed the Lepper et al study on self-attribution demonstrates a behavioural consequence. The children who were rewarded for performing an initially valued activity performed that activity less on a subsequent occasion.

Attributions have also been related to helping. In a field study by Barnes, Ickes and Kidd (1979), student subjects were telephoned a few days before an examination by someone ostensibly in the same class who asked to borrow their lecture notes. The caller explained the inadequacy of his or her own notes in different ways to different subjects. Explanations in terms of lack of ability to take good notes resulted in greater helping than explanations in terms of lack of motivation. Patterns of attribution have also been related to depression (Abramson, Seligman and Teasdale, 1978). Abramson et al suggest that, compared with others, depressed people tend to explain their own successful outcomes more in terms of external causes and their failures more in terms of internal ones.

Let us return to the set of ideas from which we will derive the experiment to be suggested in this chapter. Kelley maintains that when making an attribution of causality to personal or environmental forces, a person draws on information concerning consensus, consistency and distinctiveness. If there is high consensus, high consistency and high distinctiveness a stimulus attribution will be made; when there is low consensus, high consistency and low distinctiveness a person attribution will be made. Both these predictions are based on the principle of covariation. In the first case the effect always occurs when the stimulus is present (high consistency and high consensus) and not when the stimulus is absent (high distinctiveness). In the latter case, the effect occurs when the person is present (high consistency and low distinctiveness) and not when the person is absent (low consensus). Kelley's initial ideas were formulated with reference to covariation along all three dimensions. This is relevant in a number of instances. Take, for instance, the event 'Dr Smith praised Jane's philosophy essay'. Here we can ask whether other lecturers praised Jane's essay, whether Dr Smith praises other work by Jane and whether Dr Smith usually praises Jane's philosophy essays. Kelley's ideas concerning the pervasiveness of these three types of information and their influence on the attribution of causality to forces internal or external to the person have attracted a great deal of attention.

A number of studies have been conducted exploring these ideas. Two main categories of study can be distinguished. The first category includes studies where the information concerning consensus, consistency and distinctiveness are presented and manipulated within a questionnaire. Typically subjects are presented with a brief description of an event as well as consensus, consistency and distinctiveness information, and asked to rate the cause of the event along selected rating scales. For instance McArthur (1972) presented subjects with items concerning the occurrence of an event (e.g. 'John laughs at the comedian') and manipulated the other information presented to the subject through statements such as 'Almost everyone who hears the comedian laughs at him' (high consensus) or 'Hardly anyone who hears the comedian laughs at him' (low consensus). Similar manipulations were made from consistency and distinctiveness information.

The second category of study includes experiments where subjects have typically been asked to make attributions of a target person's behaviour on the basis of information of his or her behaviour as well as information concerning the behaviour of others in the same situation. For instance, Wells and Harvey (1977) asked their subjects to read the report of the procedure of a psychological experiment (such as Nisbett and Schachter's (1966) study on receiving electric shocks) and presented them with information (not always authentic) about how other people had behaved during the experiment. Subjects are then told about how a particular person behaved and asked to make attributions concerning the causes of that behaviour. The results of both sorts of experiments are broadly supportive of Kelley's hypotheses.

However, in many cases people may not have all this information and in many other instances it may not even make sense to require it. For instance, if Jane was popular at the Christmas party, it may make sense to ask whether she is always popular at the Christmas party, and whether she is popular at other parties, but does it make sense to ask if everyone was popular at the Christmas party? Again, if Jane got admission to college, what would count as consistency information? Or if Jane divorced John, we may want to know about how often she divorces her husbands or whether other people have divorced John, but would we want to know if Jane had divorced him frequently in the past?

It seems that for some events only certain kinds of information seem relevant. Even where consensus, consistency and distinctiveness are all relevant a person may not have access to all three types of information. What then if we take each of these dimensions separately? A later paper by Kelley and his colleagues (Orvis, Kelley and Cunningham, 1975) claims that high consensus should lead to more stimulus attributions than low consensus, since the information suggests that the effect always occurs when the stimulus is present, and does occur even in the absence of the particular person. Low distinctiveness should lead to more person attributions than high distinctiveness since the effect is present when the person is present and does occur in the absence of the particular stimulus. Where there is low consistency, the effect cannot be explained in terms of the stable characteristics of either the person or the stimulus, since the effect is not regularly observed even when both are present, and should lead to an attribution in terms of the particular circumstances of the event. The study by Orvis et al provides support for these hypotheses. In the proposed study the influence of consensus, consistency and distinctiveness information will be investigated. In order to simplify the analysis the notions of attributions to stimulus and to the circumstances will be included in the more general concept of situational attributions.

The most rudimentary way to investigate these hypotheses would be to use one event (e.g. 'John got high marks for his history essay') and to present the relevant information (e.g. 'Most people got high marks for the history essay' as compared with 'Few people got high marks for the history essay'). Attributions of causality could be obtained on a seven-point rating scale ranging from 'Entirely caused by the person' through to 'Entirely caused by the situation'. One limitation of such a decision would be the uncertainty as to whether the results obtained are relevant to other events. This particular event has several distinctive characteristics: the agent is a male, the event has a positive outcome, the event is concerned with academic achievement, perhaps even more specifically with academic achievement of a particular sort (history essay). In order to have greater confidence in the generality of our results it is important to use more events. Since there is no general taxonomy of events from which they can be systematically chosen, the events can, for instance, be selected with reference to past literature, with reference to the theories of the investigator (which may be based on past literature) or with reference to a specific practical issue.

In order to introduce variety in the type of event, two subsidiary variables will be introduced. Several studies have shown that success is explained more in terms of internal causes and failure in terms of external causes. It has been argued that this is because we assumed that people embark on ventures in which they expect to succeed (Kelley and Michaela, 1980). This finding has been substantiated with reference to the tasks involving intellectual abilities. Relatively little attention has been paid to interpersonal

tasks. Orvis et al (1975) and McArthur (1972) suggest that interpersonal tasks are seen as depending more on both the agent and the stimulus person than are other tasks. Extrapolating from this we can conclude that the difference in the explanations for successful and unsuccessful outcomes will apply more to intellectual tasks than to interpersonal ones.

Thus the hypotheses to be tested are:

* that high consensus information will lead to more situation attributions than low consensus information;
* that low distinctiveness information will lead to more person attributions than high distinctiveness;
* that low consistency information will lead to more situational attributions than high consistency.

The subsidiary hypothesis is that there will be an interaction between outcome (success versus failure) and type of task (intellectual versus interpersonal) such that success will lead to more person attributions than failure for intellectual tasks; but that the same effect will not be obtained for interpersonal tasks.

Method

General requirements
The exercise to be outlined below can be completed in 2½-3 hours including the calculation of means and standard deviations with an appropriate calculator. Unless a calculator programmed to perform the relevant analysis of variance is available, the complete statistical analysis will have to be done outside class time. The students themselves will serve as subjects for the exercise. Each student will require one copy of the questionnaire in Appendix 1 and one copy of the Content Analysis Coding sheet in Appendix 2. The exercise can be conducted in one room, and for most of the time students can sit at tables filling in the questionnaire, reporting data and commenting on aspects of the exercise. For part of the time students will be asked to confer in groups of about four to discuss aspects of the content analysis. It is assumed that there will be about 30 students

in the class. Smaller numbers will make data collection easier, and the exercise shorter. An alternative format is suggested to deal with larger numbers.

Design

The general structure of the session will be as follows.

* Administration of questionnaire. This will be done in two parts: first the subjects are asked for open-ended explanations; when this is completed they make attributions of causality on a seven-point rating scale of attribution of causality to personal or situational causes.
* Brief exposition of the ideas and background to the study, followed by discussion of the design of the study and the items on the questionnaire.
* Analysis of ratings of the consensus information.
* Introduction to the content analysis, and carrying out content analysis in groups of four.
* Statistical analysis of the results of the distinctiveness items.

The simplest questionnaire could use one intellectual event and one interpersonal event, and manipulate all the information and all the outcomes with reference to these events. For instance, the intellectual event could concern John and his history essay. The successful outcome would be 'John did very well on his history essay' and the unsuccessful outcome 'John did very badly on his history essay'. These two items could be presented with each of the two levels of the three types of information. Thus the basic theme (i.e. John and his history essay) would occur 12 times in the questionnaire. Similarly, an interpersonal event (for instance, Jim impressing or failing to impress Peter) could also be presented with each of the two levels of the three types of information and occur 12 times. These 24 items would have to be presented in at least two different random orders to ensure that the results obtained were not due to different responses on earlier items as compared with later items or to the succession of particular items.

Such a design would be theoretically complete in the sense that the relevant experimental manipulations have been carried out in a controlled way. But problems would remain. Since only one item of each sort is included the problem of generality raised earlier would reappear. Boredom and inattention may affect the subject because of the sheer repetitiveness of the items. Further, since everything else is kept constant, the independent variables may be highlighted and the subjects easily infer the hypotheses. An alternative design would involve preparing multiple versions of the questionnaire. Several instances of intellectual and interpersonal events could be included with one group of subjects receiving a 'success' version of the event and another group receiving a 'failure' version. Similarly one group would receive the item with one sort of information, others with different sorts of information. For instance, group A would receive a questionnaire with 'John did very well on his history essay', and group B would receive a questionnaire with 'John did very badly on the history essay'. Group A1 would get the item with high consensus information; group A2 with low consensus information. Similarly, group B could also be subdivided into two groups with different versions of the questionnaire and so in all four versions would be needed. The questionnaire suggested below attempts to strike a balance for the purposes of a practical class between the simplest design and more complex ones.

The students should be seated such that they can fill in a questionnaire but also be able to divide into groups of four for the content analysis. The instructions to the class and the suggested questionnaire are in Appendix 1. It should be made clear to the students that they should finish Part 1 of the questionnaire (the open-ended explanations) and then pause. They should not look at the second part till the entire class has completed the first part, since knowing that they will be asked to make ratings of attributions of causality to personal or situational causes may influence their own explanations.

The administration of the questionnaire should take about 30 minutes. This should be followed by a brief exposition of the theory and a detailed discussion of the design of the questionnaire. Note that the questionnaire consists of six intellectual and six interpersonal events. The intellectual items are instances of a history exam, a geography essay, a biology practical, a crossword puzzle, an anagram test and a radio quiz. The interpersonal items are instances of attempts to impress, encourage, gain respect, reassure, interest and dominate.

Within each type of item, half were randomly assigned to positive outcomes and half to negative outcomes. All the 12 items appear twice, once with high consensus, high distinctiveness or high consistency information, and once with low consensus, low distinctiveness or low consistency information. The final order of the items in the questionnaire was randomly determined, with the constraint that the two instances of the same event do not occur in succession.

One of the strengths of the design includes the variety of items. Since the type of information appears as high or low for the same item, the comparison of the effects of different levels of information can be securely made. Similarly, using several instances of intellectual and interpersonal tasks strengthens our confidence in any differences found with reference to this comparison. There are, however, difficulties and limitations. For instance, within each type of event the success/failure comparison refers to different items. This could, of course, be taken into account by developing an equivalent questionnaire interchanging the success and failure outcomes. Another difficulty is the lack of control for order effects. The tutor may also question the suitability of different types of items. Only males have been mentioned in the items. Clearly the entire design could be replicated with female agents, and sex included as a between groups factor in the analysis. An item such as 'John gave offence to Jack' may be unclear, since it may have been a successful or an unsuccessful outcome. 'David failed to convince Peter to buy the car' includes an additional element (the car). The class should be asked to suggest items that might have been used and to evaluate their suitability. The background theory and discussion of the design should take about 30 minutes.

Data collection, analysis and results

The class will have two sorts of data: ratings of attributions of causality and open-ended explanations about why the event occurred. Analysis of each type of data should be performed separately.

Data from the rating scales can be used to test the hypothesis concerning consensus information; and data from the open-ended explanations can be used to test the hypothesis concerning distinctiveness information. The effects of outcome and of event type can be analysed in both cases. These analyses can be demonstrated in class, and the data from the consistency information can be used for the students to analyse independently, if this is thought advisable.

Analysis of rating scales

The main hypothesis to be investigated is that when high consensus information is provided, people attribute causality more to situational factors than when low consensus information is provided. Outcome (success and failure) and type of event (intellectual and interpersonal) were also included, and an interaction was expected between these variables. Thus we have three independent variables: information level, outcome and event type, and the design is a 2 x 2 x 2 factorial, with repeated measures across all levels of all the factors. In order to clarify the design, the tutor can put the following broad structure (see table 1) on the board. It will also enable a ready tabulation of the data.

The letter in each column refers to the item on the questionnaire. This makes for easy reference to the relevant material and if the class is about 30 students or less, it is relatively easy to get each student to read out their results and for the tutor to put them on the board. Students can copy the results into their own notebooks as they are being tabulated, and they will therefore have the data to perform their own analysis independently. If there are more than 30 students in the class, tabulation of the data from all the students may not be viable. The class can then be split into two groups and the tutor may want to treat the type of event as a

Table 1

| High consensus | | | | Low consensus | | | |
| Success | | Failure | | Success | | Failure | |
Intell-ectual	Inter-personal	Intell-ectual	Inter-personal	Intell-ectual	Inter-personal	Intell-ectual	Inter-personal
(I)	(H)	(E)	(T)	(R)	(C)	(L)	(G)
S1							
2							
3							
.							
.							
.							
n							

between groups factor. Thus the data from some students can be used for the intellectual items, and the data from other students for the interpersonal items. Thus some data from all members of the class can be used.

The data can be collected and tabulated in about 20 minutes, and some of the students can be asked to calculate the means and standard deviations for each of the main effects and the interactions. If the main hypothesis is confirmed, the scores for high consensus items should be higher than those for low consensus. The interaction between outcome and event type can also be readily examined. The scores for intellectual/failure items should be the highest, those for the intellectual/success the lowest, and the two sets of interpersonal items should be in between.

Analysis of open-ended explanations

The open-ended explanations can be used to test the hypothesis that low distinctiveness information leads to more person attributions than high distinctiveness. The interaction of outcome and type of event can also be examined. The first task with any content analysis is to set up a reliable scheme which can be used to classify the data. The scheme will be guided by the particular hypotheses under investigation. Appendix 2 distinguishes between three types of explanation: explanations in terms

of the person; explanations in terms of the situation and explanations involving both person and situation elements. There are various examples of each type of explanation drawn largely from a coding manual of explanations for success and failure produced by Elig and Frieze (1975).

Students should be divided into groups of four for the coding of their responses. They should first familiarize themselves with the coding scheme in Appendix 2 and then proceed to code their own responses. They should not code their responses on the questionnaire but on a separate sheet, since each questionnaire will be coded by several students. When a student has completed the analysis of his or her own data, the person should exchange the questionnaire with one of the other members of the group, and independently code the responses of that student. Next the two students should discuss the coding of the two questionnaires, checking their level of agreement, and resolving disagreements. This will enable them to have some preliminary practice before they code data that will be statistically analysed. When the pair of students have completed discussion of their own two questionnaires, they should then exchange questionnaires with the other two members of their group. They should independently code the responses of the two questionnaires, and when this is completed, work out the percentage of items on which they agreed. They should then arrive at agreement for the remaining items. This data will be analysed statistically.

The tutor should first enquire how many pairs achieved agreement on at least 90 per cent of the data, and then how many achieved agreement on at least 80 per cent. The causes of the difficulty and limitations of the coding scheme can be considered. This can be done through asking what responses were particularly difficult to code and why.

The data should be examined for the effects of distinctiveness. If the behaviour of the person is not distinctive on this particular occasion then a person attribution is expected. There are various ways of analysing the data, but the simplest would involve dichotomizing the data and performing an analysis of variance. The general format for the analysis is the same as that for the previous analysis. For each relevant item, each student can read out whether or not the explanation was coded as a person explanation. If it was, a score of 0 is entered; if not, a score of 1, and a $2 \times 2 \times 2$ analysis of variance is then calculated on the scores.

Familiarization with the coding scheme and performing the content analysis should take about 30 minutes, and discussing the ensuing problems and tabulating the data should take another 30 minutes (see table 2). If the main hypothesis concerning the effects of distinctiveness information is confirmed, scores for high distinctiveness should be higher than scores for low distinctiveness. The interaction between outcome and type of event is similar to that expected in the case of consensus information.

If desired, the consistency results can be tabulated as shown in table 3.

Table 2

High distinctiveness				Low distinctiveness			
Success		Failure		Success		Failure	
Intellectual	Interpersonal	Intellectual	Interpersonal	Intellectual	Interpersonal	Intellectual	Interpersonal
(B)	(U)	(D)	(A)	(J)	(Q)	(P)	(W)

(The letters refer to the items on the questionnaire.)

Table 3

High consistency				Low consistency			
Success		Failure		Success		Failure	
Intellectual	Interpersonal	Intellectual	Interpersonal	Intellectual	Interpersonal	Intellectual	Interpersonal
(F)	(O)	(X)	(V)	(K)	(M)	(N)	(S)

(The letters refer to the items on the questionnaire.)

Discussion

The study was designed to test a range of hypotheses which will now be reviewed.

* Did subjects make more situation attributions when presented with high consensus than with low consensus information?
* Did subjects make more person attributions for low distinctiveness than high distinctiveness information?
* Did subjects make more situational attributions when presented with low consistency than with high consistency information?
* Was there an interaction between outcome and type of event?

Some other questions which should be examined include whether there were main effects of outcome or of event type, and whether there were any other interactions. The explanations for these results should be considered.

Assuming that the results of the study broadly support the hypotheses, the limitations of the methodology can be discussed. The inadequacy of the particular questionnaire has already been touched upon, but a number of more general questions remain.

The first concerns the presentation of the material. The events were baldly described and information is seldom received in this way. It assumes one step in the processes leading to an explanation, viz. the definition of the event as being successful or as being a failure. This may sometimes be clear enough but on many occasions may be ambiguous. For instance, that John got a particular mark on his essay may be clear, but was it a 'good' mark? There are many instances where a person may get high marks but not consider these good because the person expected to do better; and, conversely, cases where average marks may be considered good for a particular individual. Perhaps these problems of the definition of the outcome of the event are more difficult with regard to interpersonal than with intellectual tasks.

The method adopted also ignores the social context of the question. Why ask 'Why did John do well on his history essay?' unless you expected him to do badly? Explanations are usually provided to particular other people in particular social contexts, and the explanation provided is at least in part guided by the assumptions the speaker makes about the knowledge and expectations of the questioner. These interpersonal factors are neglected by the present approach.

The form of the presentation of the information is also debatable. Rather than present the information in a line of print, it is possible to make up visual material with film to present the relevant information sequentially. Such a method of presentation would be much more realistic, and give us more confidence in the generality of the results.

Finally, the hypothesis may well have received support when consensus, consistency and distinctiveness information are presented to the subject. This tells us about how information is used. It does not, however, tell us about what information a person might seek. In the Introduction it was pointed out that the general model of attribution theory was of Man as a scientist. Lalljee (1981) has pointed out that the model adopted by Kelley is largely that of an inductivist, who approaches nature with no theories, but counts instances of different types of information to arrive at his conclusions. Scientific method also presents us with a different analogy: that of the scientist as a hypothesis-tester. This approach would imply that we usually have some theories about why an event occurred, and look for information that will enable us to test them. It would suggest that we may not seek information about consensus, consistency and distinctiveness except when we do not have specific hypotheses about the event. In order to map the process of information search a different methodology, for instance, inviting subjects to ask questions about the event and analysing the questions, would have to be used.

REFERENCES

Abramson, L.V., Seligman, M.E.P. and Teasdale, J.D. (1978) Learned helplessness in humans: critique and reformulation. Journal of Abnormal Psychology, 87, 49-74.

Barnes, R.D., Ickes, W. and Kidd, R.F. (1979) Effects of perceived intentionality and stability of another's dependency on helping behaviour. Personality and Social Psychology Bulletin, 5, 367-372.

Bernstein, B. (1973) Class, Codes and Control, Volume 1. London: Routledge & Kegan Paul.

Elig, T.W. and Frieze, I.R. (1975) A multi-dimensional scheme for coding and interpreting perceived causality for success and failure. JSAS catalogue of selected documents in psychology, 5, MS 1069.

Heider, F. (1958) The Psychology of Interpersonal Relations. New York: Wiley.

Jones, E.E. and Davis, K.E. (1965) From acts to dispositions: the attribution process in person perception. In L. Berkowitz (ed.), Advances in Experimental Social Psychology, Volume 2. New York: Academic Press.

Jones, E.E., Davis, K.E. and Gergen, K.J. (1961) Role playing variations and their informational value for person perception. Journal of Abnormal and Social Psychology, 63, 302-310.

Kelley, H.H. (1967) Attribution theory in social psychology. Nebraska Symposium on Motivation, 15, 192-238.

Kelley, H.H. (1973) The processes of causal attribution. American Psychologist, 28, 107-128.

Kelley, H.H. and Michaela, J.L. (1980) Attribution theory and research. In M.R. Rosenzweig and L.M. Porter (eds), Annual Review of Psychology, Volume 31.

Lalljee, M. (1981) Attribution theory and the analysis of explanations. In C. Antaki (ed.), The Psychology of Ordinary Explanations of Social Behaviour. London: Academic Press.

Lepper, M.R., Greene, D. and Nisbett, R.E. (1973) Undermining children's intrinsic interest with extrinsic reward: a test of the 'over-justification' hypothesis. Journal of Personality and Social Psychology, 28, 129-137.

McArthur, L.A. (1972) The how and what of why: some determinants and consequences of causal attribution. Journal of Personality and Social Psychology, 22, 171-193.

Mischel, W. (1968) Personality and Assessment. New York: Wiley.

Nisbett, R.E. and Schachter, S. (1966) Cognitive manipulation of pain. Journal of Experimental Social Psychology, 2, 227-236.

Orvis, B.R., Kelley, H.H. and Cunningham, J.D. (1975) A closer examination of causal inferences: the roles of consensus, distinctiveness and consistency information. Journal of Personality and Social Psychology, 32, 605-616.

Piaget, J. (1929) The Child's Conception of the World. New York: Harcourt Brace.

Piaget, J. (1932) The Moral Judgement of the Child. London: Routledge & Kegan Paul.

Robinson, W.P. and Rackstraw, S.J. (1972) A Question of Answers, Volume 1. London: Routledge & Kegan Paul.

Wells, G.L. and Harvey, J.H. (1977) Do people use consensus information on making causal attributions? Journal of Personality and Social Psychology, 35, 279-293.

Weiner, B. (1980) Human Motivation. New York: Holt, Rinehart & Winston.

APPENDIX 1

This study is concerned with how people explain events. The following questionnaire consists of a number of statements which report the occurrence of some event. Following each statement there is in brackets an item of information which applies to the event reported. The study consists of two parts, and the instructions for the second part will be dealt with after the first part has been completed.

Part 1

In the first part of the study your task is to decide, on the basis of the information given, what you think probably caused <u>the event</u> to occur. Please write down your explanation in your own words in the space below the information. Please read each item carefully before answering.

EXAMPLE: EVENT: Dr Smith praised Joe's essay. (Information: Dr Smith praises most people's essays.)

EXPLANATION FOR THE EVENT: that is, why do you think Dr Smith praised Joe's essay?

*   *   *

A. EVENT: Julian failed to gain Steve's respect. (Information: Julian did not fail to gain the respect of many other people.)

EXPLANATION FOR THE EVENT:

B. EVENT: Henry did well in his history exam. (Information: Henry did not do well in his other exams.)

EXPLANATION FOR THE EVENT:

C. EVENT: Robert succeeded in impressing Paul. (Information: few people succeeded in impressing Paul.)

EXPLANATION FOR THE EVENT:

D. EVENT: Nick did badly on the anagram test. (Information: Nick did not do badly on other tests.)

EXPLANATION FOR THE EVENT:

E. EVENT: Peter failed to win a prize on the radio quiz. (Information: most people
   ◯ failed to win a prize on the radio quiz.)

   EXPLANATION FOR THE EVENT:

F. EVENT: Howard successfully completed the crossword puzzle. (Information:
   ◯ Howard usually succeeds in completing the crossword puzzle.)

   EXPLANATION FOR THE EVENT:

G. EVENT: Robin failed to encourage Trevor. (Information: few people failed to
   ◯ encourage Trevor.)

   EXPLANATION FOR THE EVENT:

H. EVENT: David succeeded in impressing Jim. (Information: most people succeeded in
   ◯ impressing Jim.)

   EXPLANATION FOR THE EVENT:

I. EVENT: John got high marks on the geography essay. (Information: most people
   ◯ got high marks on the geography essay.)

   EXPLANATION FOR THE EVENT:

J. EVENT: Chris did well on his history exam. (Information: Chris did well on his
   ◯ other exams.)

   EXPLANATION FOR THE EVENT:

K. EVENT: Tom successfully completed the crossword puzzle. (Information: Tom
   ◯ seldom succeeds in completing the crossword puzzle.)

   EXPLANATION FOR THE EVENT:

L. EVENT: Edward failed to win a prize on the radio quiz. (Information: few people
   ◯ failed to win a prize on the radio quiz.)

EXPLANATION FOR THE EVENT:

M. EVENT: Roy succeeded in arousing Brian's interest. (Information: Roy seldom
   ◯ succeeds in arousing Brian's interest.)

EXPLANATION FOR THE EVENT:

N. EVENT: Frank did badly on his biology practical. (Information: Frank seldom does
   ◯ badly on his biology practical.)

EXPLANATION FOR THE EVENT:

O. EVENT: Hugh succeeded in arousing Graham's interest. (Information: Hugh usually
   ◯ succeeds in arousing Graham's interest.)

EXPLANATION FOR THE EVENT:

P. EVENT: Douglas did badly on the anagram test. (Information: Douglas did badly on
   ◯ other tests.)

EXPLANATION FOR THE EVENT:

Q. EVENT: Charles succeeded in reassuring Andy. (Information: Charles succeeded in
   ◯ reassuring many other people.)

EXPLANATION FOR THE EVENT:

R. EVENT: Bill got high marks on the geography essay. (Information: few people got
   ◯ high marks on the geography essay.)

EXPLANATION FOR THE EVENT:

S. EVENT: Martin failed to dominate Ron. (Information: Martin seldom failed to
○ dominate Ron.)

EXPLANATION FOR THE EVENT:

T. EVENT: Michael failed to encourage Jeffrey. (Information: most people failed to
○ encourage Jeffrey.)

EXPLANATION FOR THE EVENT:

U. EVENT: Alan succeeded in reassuring Gerry. (Information: Alan did not succeed
○ in reassuring most other people.)

EXPLANATION FOR THE EVENT:

V. EVENT: Tony failed to dominate Dick. (Information: Tony usually fails to
○ dominate Dick.)

EXPLANATION FOR THE EVENT:

W. EVENT: Derek failed to gain Larry's respect. (Information: Derek failed to gain
○ the respect of many other people.)

EXPLANATION FOR THE EVENT:

X. EVENT: Adrian did badly on his biology practical. (Information: Adrian usually
○ does badly on his biology practical.)

EXPLANATION FOR THE EVENT:

Part 2

PLEASE DO NOT READ THESE INSTRUCTIONS UNTIL YOU HAVE COMPLETED THE FIRST PART OF THE STUDY.

In the second part of the study we would like you to rate each event along a seven-point scale in terms of how far you think the event described was probably caused by characteristics of the situation and how far you think it was probably caused by characteristics of the person.

1	2	3	4	5	6	7

Caused entirely   Caused about   Caused entirely
by the person   equally by person   by the situation
                     and situation

Beside each event on the questionnaire is a circle. For each event we would like you to indicate, by entering the appropriate number, how far you think the event was probably caused by characteristics of the person or characteristics of the situation. Thus if you think event A was caused entirely by the person then enter the number 1, if you thought it was caused entirely by the situation then enter the number 7, and if you thought it was caused partly by the person and partly by the situation, indicate your judgement about the causality of the event by entering the appropriate number from 1 to 7. Please do this for each item on the questionnaire.

APPENDIX 2

Person explanations

In this category code those explanations that seem to be primarily in terms of the characteristic of the agent.

EXAMPLES: He is an intelligent person
He tried hard
He was in a bad mood
He was afraid of failing
He is interested in people

Situation explanations

In this category code those explanations that seem to the primarily in terms of the situation. This will include the characteristics of the stimulus and of the circumstances.

EXAMPLES: The test was very difficult
He had been badly taught
He was lucky
The room was hot and stuffy
The other person was easily impressed

Person and situation explanations

In this category code those explanations that seem to be about equal in terms of the characteristics of the agent and characteristics of the situation.

EXAMPLES: He knew the material well
He didn't get on well with the lecturer
They were friends
The task was too difficult for him to do
They were equally opinionated

13

An aspect of prejudice
Glynis M. Breakwell

Specification notes

AIM: the aim of this exercise is to introduce students to the experimental investigation of intergroup dynamics; particularly
that aspect of prejudice which is associated with devaluation of an out-group's
products and how this is affected by
manipulation of group memberships.

PRIOR KNOWLEDGE: no prior knowledge
is assumed.

DURATION AND FACILITIES: the experiment can be executed in one hour and
merely requires a room large enough to
house all class members. No special resources or facilities are required.

Introduction

Conflicts between groups are common occurrences. The sorts of groups involved
range from whole nations to coteries of
four or five people, and the hostilities
take many forms from overt physical
violence to subtle propaganda. It is
therefore difficult to produce a single
all-encompassing social psychological
explanation for conflict between groups.
However, over the last 20 years, two
competing explanations have evolved.

The first essentially <u>social</u> psychological explanation of intergroup conflict
came from Sherif (1966). Sherif argued that
hostilities between groups occur as a consequence of a conflict of interests. It is
when two groups want to achieve the same
goal but both cannot have it that hostility
is engendered. In contrast, when two groups
work together to achieve a mutually desirable goal which neither would achieve
without co-operation, hostility will be
squashed. Sherif provided support for this
very pragmatic argument from field studies
in summer camps for boys in the USA. His
studies had three or four stages. In the
first stage, boys would arrive at the camp
and be allowed to grow accustomed to the
place and make friends; at this stage the
boys comprised a single large group. The
second stage involved the arbitrary dichotomy of this initial group and the resulting activities. After these two groups had
settled into their distinctive routines,
the third stage involved the introduction
of competitive activities. This entailed
sporting events in which teams from one
group were matched against teams from
other groups. Sherif hypothesized that
these competitive games, because they
introduced a goal (presumably victory)
which both groups wanted but only one could
have, would instigate hostility between the
groups. In fact, this was exactly what
happened: verbal and physical attacks were
made by both groups on their opponents and
these extended beyond the arena of the
sporting activities (e.g. raids were made

at dead of night into the opponents' territory and havoc wrought). In some of the studies, the initiation of conflict was followed by a fourth stage that was expected to eradicate the intergroup hostilities. This entailed the introduction of what Sherif called a 'superordinate' goal which is a goal that both groups wish to attain but neither can attain without the co-operation of the other. For instance, the boys were faced with the choice of pooling their financial resources in order to hire a film to be shown at the camp; neither of the groups would have enough money to hire the film alone and if they were to get to see the film both groups had to co-operate in the enterprise. Sherif's hypothesis was to some extent supported: intergroup hostilities did decline after the groups had co-operated to achieve a series of superordinate goals, but they were not eradicated.

After Sherif's work, several researchers began to question whether a conflict of interests was a necessary precursor of intergroup hostility. Sherif had shown it to be a sufficient cause for hostility but he had not shown it to be a necessary cause. To put this another way, when a conflict of interests occurs hostility follows, but hostility may occur in the absence of a conflict of interests and, if it does, another sort of explanation is necessary.

The second sort of explanation of intergroup hostility came after a series of experiments had shown that it can arise in the absence of a conflict of interests. These experiments involved the creation of artificial 'minimal groups' in the laboratory. Membership of these minimal groups was on a random basis (sometimes explicitly so) and communication between members was impossible; an individual would not know the identity of other members, and no group goal or purpose would be established. Such groups were effectively a totally arbitrary categorization without a raison d'être. There was no conflict of interest between groups created in this way, yet such groups motivated intergroup discrimination. Faced with the task of allotting rewards to members of their own group and members of the other group, subjects in these experiments gave preferential treatment to members of their own group (Taj-

fel, Billig, Bundy and Flament, 1971). Prejudice in favour of one's own group and bias against the out-group in this situation cannot be explained in terms of conflicts of interest between the groups; there was no objective conflict of interest. The mere fact of categorization, by simply creating two 'groups', seems to activate the potential for prejudice. The burning question is obvious: why should this be so? Prejudice in this context serves no objective end; the individual receives no objective benefits from discriminating against the out-group. However, perhaps it can be explained in terms of the subjective, psychological benefits which accrue.

Tajfel and his co-workers (see Tajfel, 1978) have evolved an explanation for prejudice which centres on the psychological benefits it generates. They argue that a person builds a social identity out of group membership, and that a person will want a satisfying social identity. In order to create a satisfying social identity it is necessary to belong to groups which have a positive image. But groups gain a positive image only through comparison with other groups. An individual knows how well her or his group is doing by comparing it with the performance of other groups (a process similar to the individual social comparisons that Festinger, 1954, described). Emphasizing the distinctions between groups and focussing on those which enable one's own group to come out on top is an essential part of creating a satisfying social identity. The drive towards a satisfying social identity is therefore seen to be at the root of prejudice. It would seem that prejudice bolsters self-esteem (Veblen, 1958; Gergen, 1971) through bolstering group-esteem.

Having looked at the possible general causes of prejudice, it is time to look at the ways in which prejudice can be expressed and the factors which influence its extent.

Prejudice can be manifested in many ways. Obviously, it can involve physical attacks on another group but it is often more subtle. It might involve minimizing contact with the other group, preventing its members from gaining access to important resources (like employment or housing) and the use of propaganda against them. Propaganda is itself a complex phenomenon but it normally acts to deprecate the other group and to justify the in-group. The deprecation of the out-group often involves the development of a negative stereotype of its members. It also frequently involves maligning the skills or abilities of the out-group and devaluing anything its members have had a hand in producing. It is this last aspect of prejudice, the devaluation of the products of the out-group, which will be explored in this exercise.

There have been a number of studies of the devaluation of out-group products. Sherif, Harvey, White, Hood and Sherif (1962) showed that, after competition between groups in their boys' camps, members of one group would under-estimate the talents, capacities and skills of members of the other group. Blake and Mouton (1962) explored this phenomenon in the laboratory with artificially created groups which were asked to produce group solutions to a problem and then asked to rate their own solution and that of another group. Subjects knew that the two groups were in competition and consistently claimed that their own group's solutions were better than those of the other group. Ferguson and Kelley (1964) queried whether explicit competition between the groups was necessary for this sort of intergroup prejudice to occur. They designed an experiment where groups were not in competition and found that subjects still discriminated in favour of their own group's product. They found that a group member did not even have to be involved in the process of production to show this prejudice. They concluded that 'attraction to the group is the crucial factor behind the bias'. Merely being a member of the group encourages the individual to prefer the products of that group. This finding fits nicely with the predictions of self-esteem explanations of intergroup prejudice: the value of the group's products reflects on the value of the group itself and so must be seen as better than those of other groups if the individual's social identity is to be satisfying.

Of course, various circumstances are known to influence the extent of in-group bias. Deschamps and Doise (1978) showed that ingroup bias is actually reduced when individuals have to think in terms of more than one membership simultaneously. In their experiment, subjects were either allotted to a single category and then asked to evaluate members of their own category and members of its antithesis (e.g. males rating males versus females) or they were allotted to a 'crossed category' and asked to rate members of their own and other crossed categories (e.g. young men rating young men versus old men versus young men versus old women). Crossed categorization effectively evoked more than one membership simultaneously. Those allotted to a single category showed greater ingroup bias than those in crossed categories for whom bias was virtually eradicated. The implication is that multiple memberships act to circumscribe prejudice.

The second sort of factor known to influence the extent of prejudice which is important for the current exercise is associated with the objective nature of a group's products. In some situations it is obvious that the in-group's products are objectively inferior to those of the out-group and the distinction cannot be totally ignored. Lemaine (1974) examined how a group would deal with this. He asked two groups to build huts which would then be evaluated by the experimenter and the winning group would be rewarded. He provided both groups with materials to build the huts but one group were deprived of some essential components for a good hut. The hut produced by one group was therefore objectively inferior. He then found that members of the disadvantaged group produced a little garden around their hut and claimed that this should be taken into consideration in evaluating their hut. They were effectively trying to alter the criterion of evaluation. Knowing that they could not gain kudos for the group on the existing criterion, they sought to substitute one on which they could. Lemaine called these redefinitions of the criterion acts of 'social originality'. Objective inferiority motivates a group to change the rules of the game. Given the opportunity, groups will choose dimensions of intergroup comparison which allow them to come out on top.

Aims and hypotheses of the exercise

The objective of this exercise is to take two themes from the research described above and mould a single experiment around them. These themes are the devaluation of an out-group's products and the attenuating effect of crossed categorization on in-group bias.

The form of crossed categorization to be used is not directly comparable with that used by Deschamps and Doise. The design entails bringing representatives of two groups into the laboratory. These groups should be ones that occur naturally and have a meaning for the subjects. Once in the laboratory, one-third of the total in each of the natural groups will be required to leave their original groups and form a third 'mixed' group. Each of the three groups will have to produce an artifact and each subject will be asked to rate the three products on scales provided by the experimenters.

The prime hypothesis is that subjects in the new mixed groups will manifest less intergroup prejudice than members of the other two groups. This hypothesis is based on the assumption that members of the mixed group will have dual allegiances to their original groups and to the new group. It is also based on the assumption that they would not deprecate groups to which they are shortly to return, since that would reflect badly on their self-esteem. A subsidiary hypothesis might be made about the use of rating scales. Following Lemaine, it could be hypothesized that group members will choose to inflate the scores of their own group on scales which refer to qualities that they particularly identify with their own group. This subsidiary hypothesis should become clear as the method is described since it depends on the rating scales adopted.

Method

Precursors to the actual execution of the experiment include:

* choice of groupings to be used;
* choice of task;
* choice of cover story and preparation

of any materials it involves;
* preparation of rating scales;
* materials for the task should be made ready;
* decide on division of labour: that is, who are to act as subjects and who as experimenters. Experimenters should then be briefed by the tutor on the procedure.

The execution of the experiment should take no more than one hour. It falls into six stages and these are described in turn below.

Stage 1: the cover story

Most experiments use 'cover stories'. They are the false explanations for the experiment which subjects are given in order to prevent them from guessing its real purpose. Here the choice of cover story will depend on the sort of groups taking part and the type of task they are asked to do.

If members of the class are unaware of the experimental hypotheses, there is no reason to suppose that they should not be used as subjects. However, subjects could be gathered from outside the class. This might seem impractical if the class numbers are large because it would mean a high proportion of the class would remain inactive during the experiment. In view of this problem, it will be assumed in what follows that class members will take the part of subjects, so some of the class will be subjects while others will act as experimenters. The number of experimenters necessary will depend on the demands of the cover story, which in turn will depend on what groupings are used.

The choice of groupings can be a matter for debate; any two antithetical groups will do, though it is preferable that they should motivate strong allegiance in their members. The two groups could be erected on the basis of sex, academic background (e.g. arts versus science), preferences for different football teams or types of music, adherence to different religious doctrines, and so on. The ways in which students acting as subjects (Ss) can be split into two groups are innumerable. For the sake of illustrating the method below it will be assumed that Ss are divided into two groups on the basis of their academic background.

On most psychology courses, students will have had either prior training in science or arts subjects (e.g. in A levels or O levels). Students with a mixed background could then be excluded from the Ss sample and would naturally form the residue to act as experimenters. Since the arts/science dichotomy is quite strongly reinforced throughout the school system, it seems on an a priori basis quite likely to be a meaningful grouping for those selected.

The task set for the groups can also be a matter for discussion. As long as it involves a product that can be evaluated later, any task can be used. Of course, practicalities should be considered. The task should be interesting, not too time-consuming and should not involve inappropriate equipment. Moreover, the task should be relevant to the dimension around which the groups were created. For instance, the arts and science groups could be asked to produce a tower from materials (like paper, sellotape, wire, etc.) provided.

Having chosen the groupings and the task, the cover story can be created. The central point is that it should be realistic without betraying the real experimental purpose. In the case of the task being to construct the tower, it could be suggested to subjects that the purpose was to observe whether arts and science groups engage in different forms of communication when involved in a creative task. The cover story could then be supported by having experimenters observe the interactions and appear to record them on record sheets specially prepared.

Stage 2: focussing on the two groups
The two groups should comprise equal numbers of Ss and the number in each should be divisible by three. Having been given the cover story, Ss should be told that the two groups are very different and recognized to be different by the experimenters. The object is to make membership of these particular groups uppermost in the subjects' minds. For instance, it can be emphasized in the case of the arts/science dichotomy that people from these two backgrounds seem to have different orientations to creativity and rationalizations for this could be evolved.

Stage 3: creation of the mixed group
One-third of the Ss from each of the two initial groups should then be chosen at random to form the mixed group. Students acting as experimenters should decide whether they wish to find a further cover story for this or to institute it without further explanation. Explanation is preferable since Ss are bound to query this further division. In the example of the arts/science dichotomy where the initial cover story involved the notion that the experiment was set up to explore communication patterns, there is no reason why this original story should not be extended. The creation of the mixed group could be said to be necessary in order to examine communication between members of the two types of academic background when faced with a communal task.

Stage 4: the task
The three groups thus established would then be introduced to the task, given the necessary materials and instructions and be asked to do it. They would remain in the same room but would be asked not to communicate across group boundaries. No explicit instructions to compete should be given. An arbitrary time limit of 15 minutes might be set for the task.

Stage 5: evaluation of the products
Those conducting the experiment should decide on the nature of the rating scales to be used for evaluations. The exact nature of the scales will be a function of the task, but a five-point rating system might be most appropriate. A number of scales said to be relevant to the product could then be constructed and each subject would rate each of the three products on each scale. A sample rating schedule is provided in the appendix; it uses the scales relevant to evaluating the towers produced by arts/science/mixed groups.

Having finished the ratings, Ss should be asked to rank order the rating scales in terms of how important they believed their group would consider each scale. The information on ranking will be used together with information on differential usage of scales to test the second experimental hypothesis.

Stage 6: debriefing
At the conclusion of the experiment, Ss must be told of its real purposes. They should be provided with an opportunity to comment on the procedure. They might be specifically asked if they had guessed the experimental hypotheses.

Results

Collation of data
Collation of data should take no more than 15 minutes. Schedules should be collected from subjects, and schedules from each of the three groups should be kept apart. For ease of description the two initial groups will be called A and B and the mixed group X. The class teacher should collate the data. A grid, like that in table 1, can be used to summarize data. Subject 1 in Group A's product on the first rating scale (which might be 'beauty', for instance) would have that rating entered in the grid at position 'k'. The entire grid would be filled in this way so that it summarizes all the raw data.

Data on the rank ordering of the rating scales in terms of their importance to the group must also be recorded. For each scale the mean ranking that it receives from members of each group in turn should be calculated. This is a way of establishing the group's ranking of the scales.

Analysis of the data
The data can be subjected to analyses at various levels of complexity in accordance with the experience of the class. Whatever analysis is chosen, it should be designed to test the original hypotheses. These were that:

Table 1. Collating the data

			Group products							
			A			B			X		
		Subjects	Scales			Scales			Scales		
			1	2	n*	1	2	n	1	2	n
Groups	A	1	k								
		2									
		3									
		4									
	B	1									
		2									
		3									
		4									
	C	1									
		2									
		3									
		4									

(* The number of scales will vary. The fewer scales used, the simpler the analysis will be.)

* the mixed group would show less in-group bias and outgroup devaluation than the other two groups;
* rating scale usage would reflect how important each scale was perceived to be to the group; scales believed to be unimportant would not be used in order to differentiate between groups.

Given the nature of the data, the most comprehensive test of these hypotheses would be provided by subjecting the data to a 3 x 3 x 3 Analysis of Variance with repeated measures on two factors. This analysis is described in Kirk (1968, p. 299). It would effectively allow the analyst to assess what effects group membership, the origin of the product evaluated, and the scale used had upon ratings. It would also pinpoint the effects of interactions between these three main factors.

The simpler 3 x 3 (groups x products) Analysis of Variance with repeated measures on one factor (products) might be conducted if the differences between scales were ignored. This would involve taking the sum of ratings made by each subject about each group's product across all scales. This would treat the scales as if they were merely a cumulative means of rating the product. It would mean that differences between ratings on different scales would be lost. However, it allows statements to be made about the effects of group membership and the product evaluated on the ratings and includes information on the ways in which these two factors interact. This analysis is described in Kirk (1968, p. 249).

A much simpler way of looking at the data would be to examine mean ratings of each product by each group. Mean ratings would be calculated by taking each rating made on each of the scales by each of the subjects in a group, summing them and dividing by the number of subjects. There would then be nine means in all:

group A on products A, B and X;
group B on products A, B and X;
group X on products A, B and X.

These means could then be represented graphically as in figure 1. The mean

ratings in figure 1 were invented for the purpose of demonstration. They represent the pattern which might be expected from the results if the hypothesis that the mixed group shows less bias were to be confirmed.

The patterns in figure 1 are based on two assumptions.

* That group X does not differentiate between the three products and that the ratings of all fall roughly in the middle of the scales. In fact, it may be that their ratings fall at the bottom of the scale or collect at the top. The actual level of the ratings is less important than their relative ratings of the three products.
* That groups A and B do not discriminate as much against the product of group X as they do against the products of each other. This is an assumption which the experiment will test.

Another type of graphic representation of results might be worth while if it is suspected that different rating scales are used differentially by the three groups. For instance, if group A is a bunch of arts students and group B a bunch of engineers and the scales include one rating of aesthetic properties of the product and one rating of the aerodynamic stability, it may be that arts students employ the aesthetic dimension to differentiate between the two groups' products but ignore the aerodynamic properties of the products. For the arts students aerodynamic properties are unimportant and the product that their group creates does not have to have more of these properties than anyone else's product. Graphs representing mean ratings on each scale independently would show differences of this kind in usage. Figure 2 shows what the pattern might look like. It shows group B treating the scale as unimportant, group A considering it a good dimension for intergroup discrimination and group X considering it important but not engaging in in-group bias. These types of graph for each rating scale would provide some test of the second hypothesis. Of course, data on the ranking of scales in terms of importance would enable the experimenter to

Figure 1. Mean ratings of the three products

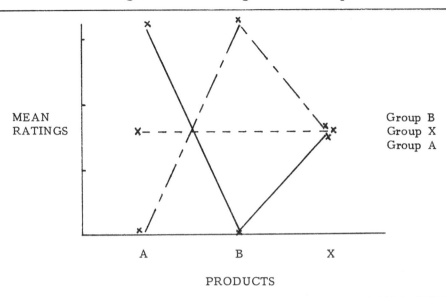

MEAN
RATINGS

Group B
Group X
Group A

A   B   X

PRODUCTS

predict what patterns would occur on each scale.

Before going on to a general discussion, one warning should be given about the simpler sorts of analysis. Mean ratings can be misleading unless they are considered in relation to the standard deviation involved. For instance, a mean in the middle of a rating scale can be an artifact produced by an even split amongst subjects whose ratings are really bimodally distributed. Data should be examined for this kind of artifact.

Discussion

Having collated the data and produced rough graphs of the results during the second hour of the laboratory class, there should be about an hour left to discuss the methodology and the findings.

In fact, the discussion can be rather neatly divided into two parts; one on the methodology and one on the findings. In method, this experiment is typical of an entire genus. It examines group dynamics in a highly simplified and controlled way which is both its advantage and its weakness. It entails the creation of artificial, short-term changes in group struc-

tures, allows a limited range of activities and modes of expressing allegiance and is perfectly tailored to the requirements of the experimenter. Moreover, it only involves small groups (four or five), though they may be drawn as representatives from larger groupings, and it permits only individuals to express intergroup discrimination (groups as a whole do not produce ratings or opinions; the individual is the fundamental source of data). There are obviously severe limitations on the generalizability or realism of results from such circumscribed situations. Nevertheless, this method of choosing one variable, manipulating it and holding other variables constant while the effects are recorded is the central feature of the experimental method. Its strength is that it may indicate something of the power of the variable manipulated to change behaviour; it can pinpoint correlational relationships even if it can never establish causal ones. These small-scale experiments do have a value as long as they are seen to be what they really are. They should not be treated as the foundation for massive generalizations about international relations. Each well-constructed experiment contributes something to our understanding of group dynamics. Taken together and bound into

Figure 2. Mean ratings on one rating scale

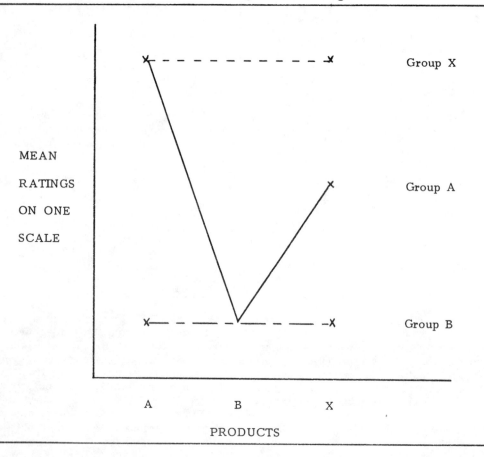

some semblance of order by social psychological theory, they may have something to say about international relations. As yet they are silent.

There are other methodological problems in this type of study apart from that associated with generalizability of results. It is always difficult to know whether the subjects have perceived the experimental manipulation in the way in which they were meant. In this experiment, the manipulation only works if the subjects placed in the mixed group feel that for them a new grouping has been created. If no new allegiance has been created for them, it is unlikely that the hypotheses will be borne out.

This particular problem with the experimental manipulation brings into focus an issue which has been deliberately avoided throughout the description of the exercise.

Central to the exercise is the whole troubled issue of what constitutes a 'group'. There are several comprehensive considerations of this issue in the literature (Cartwright and Zander, 1968, pp. 46-48; Dean, 1969, pp. 217-242); suffice to say here that the term is shrouded in ambiguity. It seems that all sorts of groups can exist along a continuum from the completely concrete (groups with fixed hierarchies, goal structures and communication patterns) to the totally conceptual (groups which exist only in the concept systems of those who believe that they belong). All types seem to have the power to motivate allegiance and intergroup discrimination like that described earlier. On this basis, there is no reason to suppose that the manipulation creating a new group in the experiment by bringing together representatives from the original groups should not work. As long as those allotted to the mixed group believe themselves to be members it should operate as a fully-fledged group.

If the hypotheses were supported the mixed group should show less intergroup discrimination. This could be a consequence of one of two things: either the mixed group is less critical of others or it is more critical of itself. Either way, it implies that creating mixed groups has advantages. It may reduce prejudice across group boundaries and it may reduce the chances of 'groupthink' (Janis, 1976). The ill effects of prejudice are well catalogued; those of 'groupthink' less so. 'Groupthink' is what happens when a group begins to believe that it is invincible and its ideas infallible. Most frequently, this is a totally unrealistic perception of the situation and can lead to dire mistakes (Raven and Rubin, 1976, describe how the Nixon group showed all the signs of groupthink during the Watergate period). A mixed group which has resources of self-criticism may avoid the perils of 'groupthink'.

Of course, in looking at the implications of the results a cardinal rule should be obeyed. The results can only be understood in context. It may be totally inappropriate to jump to the conclusion that because a mixed group in this experiment showed less intergroup discrimination, all mixed groups will do so. The effects of mixed grouping will obviously depend on the exact conditions of mixing, the history of the 'parent' groups and the context in which discriminations might be made. It is equally obvious that other experiments may be designed to shed light on these issues.

Conclusion

Students doing this exercise should gain some knowledge of the social psychology literature on intergroup relations; they should derive some understanding of the limitations and strengths of the experimental methods applied in research on group dynamics; and they should begin to appreciate that the same data can be subjected to analyses at various levels of complexity in order to test the same hypotheses.

It should become clear during the exercise that an experiment of this sort has a stage structure. Experimentation is a bit like gardening: it involves planting, transplanting, pruning, watering and harvesting. It should be viewed temporally and the different stages should not be taken out of order. The stages of the experiment construct the social phenomenon that is to be explored in microcosm.

The other manifest lesson the exercise has to offer is that all experiments of this kind involve a choice of how much room to give the subjects. The experimenter has to decide how much freedom subjects will have to choose the arena of activity, the medium of expression for opinion and the audience for those opinions. In making that decision, it is often easiest for the experimenter to include only freedoms that can be encompassed by the existing theoretical framework. In this way a theory may be tested in a narrow fashion, but it is possible (by restricting the subjects' freedom) to preclude unforeseen responses or reactions. Important data which lie outside the cognizance of the theory are therefore never unearthed and the fundamental tenets of the theory go unchallenged. The point is that experiments which offer the subject minimal freedom of response may test a theory but they are unlikely to advance it.

REFERENCES

Blake, R.R. and Mouton, J.S. (1962) Overevaluation of own-group's product in intergroup competition. Journal of Abnormal and Social Psychology, 64, 237-238.

Cartwright, D. and Zander, A. (1968) Group Dynamics (3rd edn). New York: Harper & Row.

Dean, D.G. (1969) Dynamic Social Psychology. New York: Random House.

Deschamps, J.C. and Doise, W. (1978) Crossed category membership in intergroup relations. In H. Tajfel (ed.), Differentiation Between Social Groups. London: Academic Press.

Ferguson, C.K. and Kelley, H.H. (1964) Significant factors in overevaluation of own-group's product. Journal of Abnormal and Social Psychology, 69, 223-228.

Festinger, L. (1954) A theory of social comparison processes. Human Relations, 7, 117-140.

Gergen, K. (1971) The Concept of Self. New York: Holt, Rinehart & Winston.

Janis, I. (1976) Groupthink. In E.P. Hollander and R.G. Hunt (eds), Current Perspectives in Social Psychology (4th edn). Oxford: Oxford University Press.

Kirk, R.E. (1968) Experimental Design: Procedures for the behavioral sciences. Monterey, California: Brooks Cole.

Lemaine, G. (1974) Social differentiation and social originality. European Journal of Social Psychology, 4, 17-52.

Raven, B. and Rubin, J. (1976) Social Psychology. New York: Wiley.

Sherif, M. (1966) Group Conflict and Cooperation. New York: Routledge & Kegan Paul.

Sherif, M., Harvey, O., White, B., Hood, W. and Sherif, C. (1962) Inter-group Conflict and Cooperation: The Robber's Cave experiment. Norman, Oklahoma: University Book Exchange.

Tajfel, H. (ed.) (1978) Differentiation Between Social Groups. London: Academic Press.

Tajfel, H., Billig, M., Bundy, R. and Flament, C. (1971) Social categorization and intergroup behaviour. European Journal of Social Psychology, 1, 149-177.

Veblen, R. (1958) The Theory of the Leisure Class. New York: Mentor Books.

APPENDIX

The suggested format for the rating schedule outlined below is structured to conform with certain assumptions:

1. that the subjects, when placed in a group, were given a name for that group by which they could identify it;
2. that only five rating scales are in use (in fact any number can be used);
3. that rating is done on a five-point scale;
4. that subjects have just completed the task of building a tower out of material provided (in fact, any sort of task can be set).

Rating schedule format

Which group did you work with? ...

Consider the three towers which the groups have produced.

Now say how good you think they are in terms of the five sorts of qualities listed below. Rate each tower in terms of each quality. Use a five-point rating scale: 5 means that the tower possesses the quality in abundance and 1 means it does not have it at all, so 3 means the tower has that quality to an average extent. Put your rating in the appropriate column.

Qualities	Group A's tower	Group B's tower	Group X's tower
1. Beauty 2. Stability 3. Unusual/originality 4. Usefulness 5. Uses materials efficiently			

Now think about the five qualities. Consider what your group would think were important qualities for the tower to have. Rank order the five qualities in terms of how important your group would think them to be. Put down the most important first, next most important second, and so on.

Most important ....

....

....

Least important ....

(NB. The language in the schedule can be made more or less complicated depending on the audience to whom it is directed.)

14

Co-operation and competition in groups: simulation of crowd panic

Robin Gilmour

Specification notes

AIM OF EXERCISE: to examine some of the determinants of crowd panic behaviour; to see how far it is possible to set up in the laboratory a meaningful experimental analogue of a large-scale social phenomenon.

PRIOR KNOWLEDGE ASSUMED: little prior knowledge on the part of students is assumed. Some basic appreciation of the experimental approach in social psychology would be helpful; the exercise can be used to develop this.

DURATION: the exercise can be conducted within a single three-hour period.

LOCATION: one large room or two smaller rooms would normally be required. The exercise can be carried out using one smallish room if space is limited.

RESOURCES: watches, notebooks, and a reward system such as sweets or money.

SPECIAL REQUIREMENTS: narrow-necked chemistry jars. A number of cones will have to be made for the exercise (see main Resources section of the method for details).

Introduction

This exercise is based on the studies by Mintz (1951) attempting to simulate crowd panic reactions in a laboratory situation and examine the factors influencing such behaviour. Thus one important set of questions raised by the exercise concerns the validity and usefulness of investigating complex social phenomena in the laboratory in what appears to be a highy simplified and very artificial way. At a more specific level the exercise is used to examine some of the factors which may cause group members to behave in a seemingly 'irrationally' competitive way when a co-operative response would be more rewarding. The influence of factors such as different reward structures for the experimental task, communication within a group and emotional arousal of subjects in producing competitive rather than co-operative behaviour can be investigated here.

Background to the exercise
The general background to this exercise comes from the work on crowds and collective behaviour (e.g. see Milgram, 1977). Within this area one of the features of persistent interest to both investigators and the public at large has been that of irrational behaviour. Typically, crowds are seen as behaving in an unpredictable and uncontrolled fashion with a potential for harmful or violent outcomes that is a major

cause for concern. One example here would be football crowds going 'on the rampage': and the general concern has been given even more point by the recent (July, 1981) series of riots in various parts of Britain.

Theories of crowd behaviour, too, ranging from Le Bon's (1903) early psychological analysis through to Smelser's (1963) sociological approach, have tended to focus on the regressive, irrational character of individuals' actions and to use mobs and riots as paradigm cases. Clearly the emphasis given to certain kinds of crowd behaviour, though understandable in terms of its social impact, may produce a limited and distorted picture of crowd phenomena in general and may similarly bias the sort of explanations offered, so that analyses attempt to explain the irrationality of individual and/or group behaviour. Thus the heightened state of emotional arousal observable in some crowds may be suggested as interfering with 'normal' rational behaviour.

This bias in both focus and explanation can be seen in the study of crowd panic which forms the immediate background to the present exercise. Mintz (1951) was concerned with the way groups of people in certain situations appeared to panic and behave in ways which were seemingly irrational and dysfunctional. The particular illustration he used was that of the theatre fire where, instead of remaining calm and leaving the building in an orderly manner which could have been done quickly and efficiently so that everyone escaped safely, people panicked and blocked the exits with the result that a number were trampled or burnt. Earlier explanations of such behaviour should, he argued, have stressed the emotional excitement of the situation interfering with rational adaptive responses. However, it is possible to suggest a more 'rational' model of participants' reaction in terms of their perception of the reward-cost structure of the situation: if everyone remains calm their orderly, co-operative behaviour produces a satisfactory pay-off for the individual (i.e. escape); if, on the other hand, some people stop co-operating and start trying to force their way out, then the reward-cost structure for the remaining indivi-

duals changes and they may see the best chance of their own survival in individual competitive action ('If I don't fight my way out now, others will block the exits and I will get burnt'). In addition, as disorder increases, communication is likely to break down, preventing the re-emergence of co-operative action.

Mintz set out to examine the influence of reward structure and communication on group panic by setting up a laboratory experiment in which a group of subjects were given the task of extracting a number of cones from a glass bottle which had a narrow neck so that the cones could only come out one at a time (see Method section for further details). Unless cones were extracted individually they tended to jam in the neck of the bottle. Thus Mintz attempted to construct an analogue of the theatre fire where co-operative behaviour produced a successful outcome and panic and competition would be non-adaptive. The effects on subjects of rewards and fines for performance could be experimentally studied, as could the influence of communication and emotional arousal. In keeping with his initial hypotheses, Mintz found that emotional arousal had little effect in producing 'traffic jams' in the experiment but that significant effects were produced by changes in the reward structure.

Methodologically, the Mintz experiment is particularly interesting. It is an attempt to apply an experimental approach to a complex social phenomenon and to bring an instance of a large-scale social behaviour into the laboratory, and as such is worthy of consideration however one views arguments about the value of the traditional experimental approach in social psychology (see Harré, 1980). Such a simulation - creating an analogue task that tries to model significant features of the original phenomenon - is one extensively employed in social psychological research, and the Mintz example provides a useful basis for examining this methodological approach since there is such a large apparent difference between the behaviour under investigation and the situation actually being experimented on.

Thus the present exercise based on Mintz's earlier experiment can be put to considerable educational use. As indicated above it can be used to introduce and discuss general issues about experimental approaches in social psychology, and the possibility and value of attempting to bring complex social behaviours into the psychological laboratory. The exercise also raises on a more specific level questions of artificiality in experimental procedure and the validity of data generated by such procedures. On the face of it, pulling cones out of a glass bottle would seem to be too far removed from a crowd panic in a burning theatre for behaviour in the one situation to have much relevance to the other: as Milgram (1977) put it, the Mintz experiment 'stands in relation to actual panic as the game of Monopoly does to high finance'. Yet experience of actually participating in the experimental situation may well modify this view: far from remaining self-conscious about the artificial nature of the task, subjects tend rapidly to become involved in it: it seems to have a fair amount of psychological impact or 'experimental realism' (see Lewin, 1979). This can usefully lead students to take a more careful look at the issue of artificiality in experimentation rather than accepting it too readily as a valid criticism of experiments, as so often happens. Here, as with the other exercises in this volume, students gain important knowledge from their involvement in a practical exercise that is not readily available in other teaching contexts.

In addition, the present exercise raises issues of measurement and analysis that can be pursued because a simple clear behaviour (pulling cones out of a jar) proves difficult to convert into a manageable measure, and obvious and gross differences in results are not easily susceptible to statistical tests of significance (see Results and Discussion). Students should also gain some understanding of experimental design as well as procedure since the exercise allows the control and investigation of a number of variables. Finally, there is perhaps a useful lesson to be learnt in the employment of simple materials in the experiment, in contrast with a view of experimental research as requiring purpose-built, complex and expensive equipment.

Aims and hypotheses

The exercise aims, then, to use the Mintz experiment to look at a number of important features of the experimental approach to social behaviour. More specifically, the exercise is concerned with co-operation and competition among members of a group on an experimental task (extracting cones from a bottle) and permits the examination of a number of variables influencing performance. Following Mintz, it is possible to look at the effect of varying the reward structure by instituting a system of rewards and fines in terms of points or money (or sweets make a perfectly practicable substitute). Similarly, the effect of interfering with communications in the group can be studied as can the influence of emotional arousal. If numbers permit, it is also possible to look at effects of sex differences in the compositions of groups.

To a large extent the number and nature of hypotheses to be investigated can be determined by the tutor and much will depend on the number of subjects available for the exercise. As a starting point it is suggested that the effects of reward structure and communication be examined so that the initial experimental hypotheses are (i) that groups show significantly more 'panic' behaviour (i.e. cone jamming with consequent poorer performance) when operating under a reward structure and (ii) that groups show significantly poorer performance under conditions inhibiting verbal communication. An additional hypothesis would be that conditions of emotional arousal have no significant effect on a group's performance.

Method

To give a general summary first, the exercise involves having groups of subjects perform an experimental task of extracting a series of cones from a glass jar within a specified time. Each group has two sets of ten trials, the first a competitive one with rewards and fines, the second a co-operative one without the reward structure. An additional condition involves having one group perform in the competitive situation in silence and a further condition, involving a group performing in the presence of an emotionally-arousing 'rabble', can be added. Some assistance from a few class members in running the exercise is needed, with the rest of the class acting as subjects, or the exercise may be carried out with outside subjects and class members acting as 'experimenters'.

Resources required

SPACE. It is best if each experimental group works on its own, which requires at least two smallish rooms or a larger room which can be divided up into separate areas. If more groups are being run at the same time further space will be required. Each group will need a clear area of floor (preferably uncarpeted) with a table and some chairs at the side.

SUBJECTS. Class members can themselves be the subjects for this exercise. Each experimental group requires five or six subjects plus two or three 'experimenters', so the number of groups to be run and the number of experimental conditions will vary depending on the size of the class. With a very large class subjects can be run in groups of 10 or 12.

Alternatively, if there is ready access to outside subjects (for instance, class members can be relied on to bring along suitable people) these may be used with class members running the experiment as far as possible, which gives them a useful element of practical research experience. The exercise can be run successfully with a variety of subjects, from children to undergraduates.

EQUIPMENT. Each group will require a heavy glass jar with a relatively wide base and narrow neck (see figure 1).

These are easily obtained from chemistry equipment suppliers (or borrowed from a chemistry department, possibly). With each jar there should be about 15 cones made out of some convenient material such as wood or aluminium and constructed so that the base of the cone is a bit narrower than the neck of the jar (i.e. so that the base of one cone and the tip of another will jam the neck: see figure 1). A hole should be drilled along the length of each cone and a

long waxed string attached.

One variation that Mintz used in his experiment involved having water pour into the bottle to add more pressure to the task since subjects had to keep their cones dry to avoid being fined. If the tutor wishes to copy this then a jar with an appropriate inlet will be required (again readily available from chemistry suppliers) together with a suitable water reservoir, such as a plastic bottle with tap and connecting tubes. Then it is easy to arrange a water flow by placing the reservoir on a table and opening the tap. When this condition is used it helps to have a small sponge pad stuck to the base of each cone to show whether it has been kept dry or not.

Figure 1. Equipment for the exercise: glass jar and cones

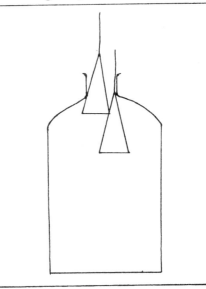

In addition to the above equipment, each group will need a stop-watch, a notebook to record results, cloths or paper towels to mop up spilt water (where water is used) and some system of rewards and fines. As indicated earlier, tutors could try simply awarding points here, but some additional incentive for subjects helps: this could take the form of a points system with a reward for the highest number of points in a group over the whole experiment. Mintz used small sums of money, but unless the tutor has a sizeable fund for disposal here in reasonable amounts, a better alternative which has proved both economical and effective is to use something like sweets (it is surprising how rewarding these are found to be even with final year undergraduates!).

TIME. The exercise described here can be carried out within a single three-hour period.

Procedure
The tutor should first of all decide how many groups will be used in the exercise and what conditions are to be examined given that each group task involves the removal of 10-12 cones from a jar, so that each group should consist of five or six subjects with two cones each, or - with a large class - the tutor can have 10 or 12 subjects with one cone each. As suggested earlier, tutors should try to have at least two sets of conditions, one comparing the presence with the absence of a reward structure within each group, and the other looking at differences between groups when verbal communication is inhibited in one of them. Thus minimally the exercise requires two groups of five subjects, although it is better with two groups of six: and depending on the numbers at their disposal tutors can arrange for two larger groups of subjects, and/or repeat the basic procedure with further groups and/or add further conditions to the experiment. To simplify the rest of this discussion it will be assumed that the exercise uses two groups of six subjects: tutors can modify procedure details appropriately where they depart from this.

Class members who are going to assist with the running of the exercise need some advance briefing so it will be necessary to select a suitable number of them (see Resource section above) beforehand and arrange a briefing session before subjects arrive. It is best to allow about half-an-hour either before or at the beginning of the practical period to check and lay out equipment and brief assistants. If class members are being used as 'experimenters' running groups of subjects it is better to

allow them an additional half-hour to become more familiar with their task, organize their instructions to subjects, and so on. In the briefing, the running of the rest of the exercise should be described (see below) and roles assigned to assistants. For each experimental group it is helpful if one individual is responsible for giving instructions to subjects and timing trials; a second scores performance, noting the number of cones extracted by the subjects in the time allowed for each trial, or the time taken to extract all the cones; and a third holds the glass jar down on the floor to avoid breakages and unjams cones when necessary. Depending on numbers available, the first two roles can readily be combined: and, similarly, the tutor can choose whether to perform one of the roles or to act as overall organizer and have class members handle all the running of the experimental task.

Equipment should then be prepared ready for subjects, with the glass jar in the centre of each group's floor space, and 12 cones in the jar on the bottom with their strings coming out of the jar and spread around it on the floor. Two or three spare cones should be ready in case of breakages, and rewards (where used) should be available on a side table, with a stop-watch for timing and a notebook for recording results.

When subjects arrive they should be assigned by the tutor to groups on a random basis, but without putting people used to working together in the same group if possible. Groups are taken to where the equipment is laid out and introduced to the exercise as one on group performance. Instructions should then be given along the following lines:

The experimental task here is set up as a kind of game in which you have to try to get cones out of the jar there in a given time of 20 seconds. In doing this you can win or lose rewards in the form of sweets (taking this example for convenience here; other reward systems can also be used). For each cone safely extracted within the time limit you will get two sweets, and for each one remaining in the jar after 20 seconds you will lose one sweet. To start with, each of you will be given four sweets to cover any initial losses. Wins and losses will be settled at the end of each trial and if you go into 'debt' this will be noted and set against future winnings.

There will be a number of trials. When I say 'go', try to get your cones out of the bottle. At the end of 20 seconds I'll say 'stop now' and then I want you to stop just where you are. Please try not to pull too hard on the cones because they are fairly fragile.

The 'no communication' group should also be told not to talk among themselves.

After ensuring subjects understand the instructions, the initial 'bank' of rewards should be placed visibly in a separate pile for each subject on a side table so that they can see their subsequent wins and losses. Subjects should then be told to take hold of the ends of the strings attached to the cones and wait for the start of the trial before lifting cones off the bottom of the jar. The signal to start can then be given and the trial ended after 20 seconds are up or all the cones are out of the jar. At this point note should be taken of the number of cones out of the jar or the time taken to get them all out; after which each subject can be rewarded or fined accordingly. After this has been done all the cones should be put back in the jar by one of the assistants to avoid learning cues to the subjects and the trial repeated.

After ten trials subjects should be stopped and new information given for the co-operative condition; in this case all groups get the same instructions along the following lines:

The next set of trials is different. There will be no rewards or fines and what we will be interested in is the performance of this group as a whole compared with other groups doing the same thing, so you should try to co-operate to get as many cones out as possible.

There should be no restrictions on any of the groups now, and again each group will be given ten trials and the number of

cones extracted or time taken on each should be recorded. At the end of the second series of trials subjects should be given their rewards, have the purpose of the exercise explained to them, and be thanked for their participation.

Variations in procedure
One variation that can be used in the competitive condition involves having water pouring into the jar during these first ten trials so that subjects have to keep cones dry as well as extract them, thus putting them under somewhat greater pressure (and extending the analogue with a theatre fire to a small extent).

For this, the additional equipment noted above is required and instructions have to be modified so that subjects are given a different reward structure: for example, two sweets for each cone extracted during the trial and kept dry, one for each cone extracted in time but wet, one lost for each cone not extracted but kept dry, and two lost for each cone not extracted and wet. Procedure, too, is slightly more complicated. Water flow has to be started at the beginning of each trial and stopped at the end by the person giving instructions to the group. It must be noted whether cones are wet or dry (the sponge pad on the base of the cone helps here), and at the end of each trial cones need to be dried off, the jar emptied of water and dry cones put back into the jar. Inevitably some water gets spilt and has to be mopped up, so a suitable floor needs to be used. However, the water input does seem to add more interest to the task and so may well be considered worth the extra trouble.

Another variation in procedure mentioned previously is to add a third 'emotional arousal' condition to the competitive trials. Here groups perform in the presence of class members who attempt to produce an emotionally charged atmosphere in order to examine the effect of this on performance (following earlier explanations of crowd panic). For this a few class members need to be selected and briefed in advance. Their function is to create an emotional atmosphere in some way, for example by cheering, booing, making a noise, and so on during the first ten trials: but it is extremely difficult to do this in any kind of plausible way and certainly some practice will be required. At the very least students involved in this should learn just how difficult in practice the role of experimenter's confederate can be. Given the nature of this experimental condition a separate room will be required.

Results and analysis

At the end of the experiment the class will have available two sets of data for each group; the results of each set of ten trials in terms of the number of cones extracted by the group in each trial, or the time taken to get them all out. Initially these can simply be tabulated by group and by trial and inspected to note improvement over the trials (learning effect), difference between each set of trials, and differences between groups. Typically in the

reward-fine (competitive) condition, groups show some learning effect improvement over trials, but a very marked improvement in performance as soon as they switch to the second set of trials without a reward structure (see table 1) thus supporting the first hypothesis. Typically also, performance in the 'no communication' group is markedly worse than the 'reward-fine only' group for the first ten trials and improves significantly to comparable levels in the second set of trials (see table 1), in accordance with the second hypothesis.

At this point some important questions arise which can usefully be explored by the class. As table 1 shows, groups produce results which look very obvious on simple inspection: the data seem to be clear-cut indicators of performance and show gross differences over experimental conditions: a situation not often found in social psychological research. The difficulties arise

Table 1. Sample of group performance on Mintz-type experimental task

	Trial number	Reward/fine only group		No communication group	
		Number of cones removed	Time taken in seconds	Number of cones removed	Time taken in seconds
Reward/ fines imposed	1	3	20	2	20
	2	5	20	0	20
	3	8	20	2	20
	4	10	20	0	20
	5	6	20	1	20
	6	12	18	0	20
	7	8	20	0	20
	8	10	20	1	20
	9	12	19	1	20
	10	10	20	1	20
No reward structure	1	12	8.5	10	20
	2	12	6	12	11
	3	12	5.5	12	8
	4	12	3.7	12	6.5
	5	12	4.4	12	4.5
	6	12	5.3	12	4
	7	12	3.8	12	4
	8	12	3.6	12	5
	9	12	5.9	12	4
	10	12	3.1	12	4.5

when an attempt is made to look at results in a more rigorous and quantified way. First, while results are clear in behavioural terms they pose measurement problems, switching from numbers of cones per criterion period to a measure of time taken to extract all cones, which makes it difficult to compare performance in a precise way over trials. The situation here provides a good basis for the tutor to raise important questions about measurement in a context which should make them more meaningful to class members. In the first instance one can look at ways of making the existing data more amenable to analysis, such as converting all scores to numbers of cones or time measures in some fairly arbitrary way but, of course, this would be crude and would tend to distort the results. An alternative approach is to consider modifying the procedure to produce more manageable results: for instance, a time measure only could be used, with trials ending when all cones have been extracted. Such a procedure would provide more 'useable' results and would approximate more to Mintz's original experiment but was not suggested at the start of this exercise for practical reasons. Trials would become too lengthy (and too frustrating for some groups who have been known on occasion to break bottles in their attempts to remove their cones), so in order to keep the exercise within manageable proportions the more restricted procedure was adopted. That it results in 'awkward' data is seen as no disadvantage since it provides a good starting point for useful discussion, in keeping with the primary purpose of the exercise as a learning situation.

A similar set of points can be raised in relation to further analysis of results, since the exercise provides results that are 'obviously' significant yet it is difficult to 'prove' this statistically; an interesting problem, and again a good basis for the tutor to develop discussion of the use and problems of statistical tests. As they stand, about all that might usefully be done with the data is to graph rough learning curves for each group: a proper statistical analysis would require constructing for each group regression curves for each set of ten trials and seeing whether these could be collapsed into a single regression curve, which is too complex a level of analysis to be appropriate for use in this exercise. If the experimental conditions were repeated with a second set of groups then it might be possible for results to be analysed using non-parametric methods such as Friedman's two-way analysis of variance (see Siegel, 1956). However, as suggested before, 'official' analysis of results is not important in terms of the primary educational aim of the exercise: here, as elsewhere, difficulties are often more instructive than is successful operation.

Discussion

Generally the results of the exercise should show in a crude but clear way the significant effects of reward structure and communication conditions on groups' performance on the experimental task, in keeping with the initial hypotheses. This is also to some extent in keeping with Mintz's original findings although he lays less stress on the effects of communication than on reward structure.

The findings, then, should tend to support Mintz's argument for the significance of reward structure in group behaviour. However, the exercise - and Mintz's original experiment - is not completely clear on this. The difference between the two sets of trials for each group is not only in terms of the presence or absence of a reward structure; it may also reflect a difference of 'set' induced by other aspects of the situation such as the instructions, which would seem to provide a competitive followed by a co-operative set quite apart from the use of rewards. Tutors might use this opportunity to discuss with classes how the procedure could be changed to examine more carefully the importance of reward structure by itself: for example, by altering instructions for subjects.

Experience of running exercises along the lines of the one described here suggests that inhibiting communication may well have a greater effect than Mintz claimed; and again tutors could use the opportunity to discuss with classes how the exercise could be designed to separate out clearly independent effects of communication and reward structure, perhaps as the start of a more general discussion on developing complex research designs.

An additional point worth mentioning about the design of the exercise concerns order effects. Groups are run first in competitive and then in co-operative conditions when normal good procedure would suggest counterbalancing order to separate out learning effects over trials. However, for this exercise it was felt that experience first of successful performance in the co-operative situation was likely to carry over to such an extent as to mask the influence of other factors.

In terms of the original phenomenon at issue - crowd panic - the exercise raises a number of considerations which should provoke useful discussion in class. Substantively, it can be seen as at least suggesting a more 'rational' explanation of an apparently non-rational behaviour: that 'panic' may be more a function of perceived changes in reward structure for people, or communication breakdown than emotional contagion, say (typically, 'emotional arousal' conditions in the exercise show little effect). The implications of this can be explored both generally in terms of the kind of analysis of social behaviour involved and specifically in relation to the particular phenomenon of crowd panic. Discussion can be further extended by moving from the somewhat limited instance of theatre fires to perhaps more immediately relevant examples of panic buying which share the same essential characteristics and where the results

of an exercise like the present one might have practical implications which the class can be invited to consider (e.g. how might we prevent a situation where a commodity in short but adequate supply - like petrol or sugar, to take recent cases - becomes the object of panic buying such that a real shortage results?).

As has been indicated earlier, the present exercise is particularly interesting for the range of methodological issues raised, as well as providing practical experience of a group experiment. Classroom discussion can focus on questions of measurement and analysis, on experimental design, and on wider issues of meaning and artificiality in experimental approaches to large-scale social psychological phenomena (e.g. 'Is there any psychological meaning in the experimental task used here that is relevant to crowd panic in theatre fires or commodity shortages?').

Conclusions

The lessons to be learnt from the exercise have been outlined above. Briefly, they concern the possibility of applying a more rational economic analysis to apparently irrational group behaviour and of using an experimental laboratory approach meaningfully to investigate 'real life' social behaviours. The exercise described here is interesting as a demonstration of an experimental approach to crowd behaviour but is particularly valuable as a means to explore important questions in experimental social psychology.

REFERENCES

Harré, R. (1980) Causes for pessimism. In R. Gilmour and S.W. Duck (eds), The Development of Social Psychology. London: Academic Press.

Le Bon, G. (1903) The Crowd. London: Unwin.

Lewin, M. (1979) Understanding Psychological Research. New York: Wiley.

Milgram, S. (1977) The Individual in a Social World. Reading, Mass.: Addison-Wesley.

Mintz, A. (1951) Non-adaptive group behaviour. Journal of Abnormal and Social Psychology, 46, 150-159.

Siegel, S. (1956). Nonparametric Statistics for the Behavioral Sciences. New York: McGraw-Hill.

Smelser, N.J. (1963) Theory of Collective Behaviour. New York: Free Press.

15

Norms and roles in the small group
Peter B. Smith

Specification notes

AIMS OF THE EXERCISE: to teach students to inter-relate what they have read about small group behaviour in texts to the behaviour of a particular small group to which they belong; to demonstrate the interconnections between social norms and social roles; and to illustrate how data collection may be used not only to study behaviour but also to create opportunities for changing it.

PRIOR KNOWLEDGE ASSUMED: none essential. Familiarity with Asch-type conformity studies and the use of rank correlation coefficients is an advantage.

DURATION: 2-3 hours.

LOCATION: any room large enough to seat the members of the practical class will suffice.

RESOURCES AND FACILITIES REQUIRED: a blackboard. Copies of one handout and one questionnaire prepared in advance.

SPECIAL REQUIREMENTS: the exercise is best conducted as late as possible in the term or year during which the practical classes occur.

Introduction

Perhaps the most central problem in social psychology is that of how people's behaviour is affected by their reactions to others. When interacting with strangers we must necessarily base our behaviour on generalized assumptions about how others would react to any particular behaviour on our part. These assumptions may be internalized within ourselves in the form of feelings as to what does or does not seem like appropriate behaviour in a given setting, or they may be externalized as feelings that one wishes to please, or to displease, particular others whom one encounters. When a group of people continue to meet one another for some time, opportunities arise to test out these generalized assumptions and to adapt them to the reactions which others in the group do actually have to one's behaviour. In many groups these reactions may not be spelt out very clearly, so there is plenty of scope for misunderstanding and misperception. Nonetheless, with the passage of time, any group which continues to meet one another develops an increasingly unique set of norms about how one should behave in the others' presence.

This exercise seeks to investigate this process in the context of a laboratory practical class. Two specific questions are addressed:

* what is the level of normative consensus in this group?
* what is the relationship between the level of normative consensus and the demographic structure of the practical class?

The merits of the exercise are that it focusses on some very basic central concepts of social psychology, and does so in a manner whereby students should find it easy to make connections between the exercise and their everyday experience of being in the practical class.

Most research by social psychologists concerning group norms has been formulated in terms of the process of conformity. Many researchers have followed the lead of Asch (1956) in seeking to demonstrate that group norms are created through the majority of group members imposing their views on the minority who may initially have different views. In Asch's experiment, small groups were assembled within a laboratory and asked to make judgements of physical stimuli, such as the relative lengths of various lines. All but one of the members of each of these groups were actually in league with the experimenter, and on certain trials they all gave the same incorrect responses. The naïve subject was asked to respond last and it was found that quite often that person did indeed conform to the incorrect previous judgements made by the others. This occurred even though it was actually very easy to make the correct judgements. Although this study provides one of the major landmarks in the development of social psychology, it is easy with 30 years' hindsight to see that it begged more questions than it answered.

The Asch study and its numerous subsequent replications are often cited as 'demonstrating' conformity. In fact, in the original study, about 35 per cent of the judgements made by naïve subjects moved towards conformity with the stooges' false judgements, while the remaining 65 per cent did not do so. Thus one could with equal justice argue that the experiments demonstrate independence from social pressure. A further critique of the Asch study has been advanced by Moscovici (1976) who argues that even in the 35 per cent of cases where conformity did occur, the effect is caused

not by the fact that the majority outnumbered the individual but by the fact that the majority responded consistently with one another. According to Moscovici, in deciding whether or not to accept a viewpoint we are not much influenced by how many others hold it, but we do take a lot of notice of whether the viewpoint is consistently maintained. There is some evidence within Asch's own work which supports this view: for instance, the finding that the amount of conformity obtained was unaffected by how many stooges were employed. In order to test his hypothesis, Moscovici set up studies in which a minority group of two stooges gave incorrect but consistent judgements as to the colours of lights on a screen, while the larger majority group of naïve subjects made their judgements. He found that the consistent minority did indeed influence the judgements of the majority.

Moscovici's findings imply a major reconceptualization of the manner in which a group's norms may be expected to develop. Asch's model implies a unilateral process of influence, whereby the most widespread viewpoints in the group will become the orthodoxy, and those who dissent from them must change their views or leave the group. Moscovici, by contrast, would envisage a more fluid, two-way process of influence. The group's norms will arise out of the persuasiveness and consistency with which various views are advanced. Moscovici's view also makes it easier to imagine the possibility that in some groups there might be no consensus, but rather a state of continuing conflict.

The assumption that consensus in a group or in a society is the 'normal' state of affairs, whereas conflict is either unusual or pathological, has crept into the thinking of many theorists, not least Asch. Indeed his choice of experimental procedures picks out a field - judgement of physical stimuli - in which that assumption is virtually unassailable. If we except the small minority who doubt the efficacy of their own eyesight, our daily experience of the physical world is solidly built on the consensual assumption that others see it the same way that we see it ourselves. However, the norms which develop among a small group of people are rarely concerned with judgements of the physical world. More typically they concern the values and actions of group members and their reactions both to each other and to others outside the group. Allen and Levine (1968) set up Asch-type experiments concerning both physical judgements and social values. They found that the conditions inducing greatest conformity on physical judgements were not the same as those inducing greatest conformity on social value judgements. In particular, on physical judgement tasks, the addition of a subject who gave correct answers virtually eliminated conformity to the majority stooges' judgements. On social value judgements, the effect of the additional subject depended upon the position which he took. In other words, the experiment supported the common-sense view that whereas we do expect others to share our perceptions of the physical world, we do not necessarily expect them to share our social values. In this respect also, then, the Asch experiment may have given an unfortunate impetus to research in this field by directing attention towards that small and atypical area wherein objective consensual judgements are relatively possible. Interestingly enough, and in line with Moscovici's arguments, Perrin and Spencer (1980) have recently reported that in psychology practical classes at Sheffield they are no longer able to obtain the Asch effect. Although other writers in subsequent issues of the British Psychological Society's Bulletin have indicated that they do still obtain the Asch effect, Perrin and Spencer's finding indicates that even in the case of physical judgements the effect is not immutable. Perrin and Spencer speculate that this may be because students are becoming more accustomed than they used to be to the idea that one should make one's own judgements, rather than rely on the influence of others.

Each of the studies so far discussed has used the traditional format of the laboratory-based psychological experiment with subjects who are strangers to one another, manipulation and deception by the experimenter, followed by measurement of change in the dependent variable, which in these studies was the amount of conformity. If one considers field studies of the development of group norms and conformity a rather

different view emerges. Perhaps the best-known study of this kind was undertaken in the so-called Bank Wiring Observation Room, which was part of a factory at Hawthorne, near Chicago, in the 1930s. A particularly cogent re-analysis of the data was undertaken by Homans (1950) in his classic book, 'The Human Group'. The workers in this room - and in the rest of the factory - were engaged in wiring up telephone banks of the type then in use. Basically, what was found was that the workers' productivity was astonishingly consistent over time. Workers at the front of the room completed around 6,600 connections per day, while those at the back achieved 6,000. These figures scarcely varied over the nine months which the study lasted. In contrast to the laboratory experiments, there is no 'objectively correct' norm against which these figures may be compared. Management's work-study men apparently regarded 8,000 connections per day as about right, but interviews with workers repeatedly elicited the comment that the present norm represented 'a fair day's work for a fair day's pay'. Although some subsequent empirical work has reported on work groups who proved not to have such productivity norms, everyday experience underlines the fact that they are widespread, not just in factory work groups, but within all types of organization, including schools and universities. Just as was the case in the original Hawthorne study, such norms usually specify not only how much work is too much, but how much is too little as well.

Homans argues that the best way to understand the creation of these and other norms in the group is by way of a 'systems' theory. In other words, one does not simply note the level of the productivity norm and of consensus to it and then seek to explain it by postulating some causal variable. Instead one treats the productivity norm as both a cause and an effect of the system. Homans differentiates an external system (the structure and history of the firm, the economic situation, the physical layout of the work) and an internal system (the activities, values and sentiments of the group members). Initially the external system 'causes' a particular pattern of development of the internal system. But in turn the evolution of the internal system has powerful effects on the external system. For instance, the existence of the productivity norm affects the company's prospects of profitability, its ability to predict future productivity and so forth.

According to this line of reasoning, the type of norms which arise in a group and the amount of consensus concerning them will be a product both of the context of the group and of the history of relationships within it. This position is more reminiscent of Moscovici than of Asch. Conformity is not seen as something inexorable, but as something whose explanation must be sought within the specific situation of the group. Homans also provides a valuable discussion of the relation between the norms of a group and the roles taken up by each member. Having defined norms as behaviours which are expected of group members, he goes on to discuss the possibility that some group norms might apply to only one or a small number of members of the group. Such norms would ordinarily be considered as role prescriptions. In this manner Homans makes clear that social psychology has no great need to keep separate a conception of role and a conception of norm. A norm is simply a role prescription that applies to all members.

Before one can make a study of the norms and roles in a group some clarification is needed of how best to define these concepts. The definition of norms by Homans which was cited above suffers from an ambiguity which was present in many early definitions. In speaking of behaviour which is 'expected' of the group member, there are two possible meanings to the word. It could mean behaviour which is anticipated of another or behaviour which is required of another. For instance, in a practical class it might be said that since Jane took an active part in the class last week, it is to be expected that she will do so again this week. In this case one is simply extrapolating from past behaviour and predicting or anticipating future behaviour, without any implied evaluation. On the other hand, if the class tutor announces that reports of the previous experiment are expected to be handed in by Friday, he/she is using 'expected' in the

sense of 'required' rather than 'anticipated', and there is a clear implication of disapproval of those who do not do as required.

Most recent researchers would prefer to define norms and roles in terms of required behaviours. A further important point is that the presence of roles and norms in a group should be investigated rather than assumed. Gross, Mason and McEachern (1958) have pointed out how many theorists have assumed that consensus exists in society as to the behaviours required of the incumbent of a particular role. Thus one might discuss the role of students, parents, bus conductors or policemen and incautiously assume that consensus exists in society as to how incumbents in these particular roles are required to behave. At a rather general level, there clearly is a certain amount of widely shared agreement as to what occupants of different roles should do. Nonetheless, where empirical studies have been undertaken of particular roles (e.g. that by Gross et al themselves) a great deal of conflict has been revealed as to how role incumbents ought to behave on specific issues. This line of reasoning is again reminiscent of Moscovici's view. The data collection procedures to be employed must leave open the possibility of conflict rather than consensus, since conflict is just as much a 'normal' property of groups as is consensus.

The study

The mode of investigation to be employed is thus correlational rather than causal. No formal hypothesis is to be tested. Data are to be collected as to how members of the practical class evaluate each of a list of behaviours, considering separately one's own evaluations, and perceptions of the group's evaluations. These data yield a series of indices reflecting the level of normative consensus in the group. Further data are also available concerning the demographic structure of the group, and an exploratory study is made of the relationship between these variables and the level of normative consensus. Both the list of behaviours to be rated and the demographic variable(s) selected can be subject to the control of the practical class, thereby ensuring that the study is concerned with issues which they are interested in, and are willing to make public.

In some ways these research procedures resemble the 'action-research' model employed by consultants to large organizations. In action research the collection of data is collaboratively planned between consultant and client. Once collected it is fed back to the client for the purpose of considering whether or not any change is desirable in current practices within the organization. If the need for such change does emerge, further collaborative planning is undertaken as to how best to create that change. In a similar manner, a survey of practical class norms may (or may not) reveal a situation which class members would like to change. As in the case of all action research, the project should only be undertaken if the consultant (in this case the tutor) is willing to explore with the clients (in this case the students) the manner in which desired changes might be achieved. Some care is also required in conducting this project in a manner which is not personally intrusive to class members.

Methods

TIMING WITHIN THE LABORATORY COURSE. Since this project is concerned with investigating the emergent structures of groups, as much time as possible should be allowed to enable those structures to emerge. This means that the project should be scheduled as late as possible during the term in which it is included. If there is some continuity in the membership of the practical class from term to term, then a later term would also be preferable to an earlier one. It would not, however, be impossible to do the project in a relatively early term. The most likely effect of doing it early rather than late would be that one would find a lesser degree of normative consensus, and that the norms which did obtain would be less distinctive and more characteristic of those found in student groups in general.

GROUPINGS. The precise form of the project to be employed may have to be adapted slightly, depending on the prior history of the practical class group. The guiding principle should be that the study is focussed on that group or groups in which class members spend most of their practical class time together. In other words, if the practical class is relatively small (up to 15, say) and a good deal of time is spent with the total group together, then the total class would provide the 'group' to be studied. If the class is bigger and in consequence is for much of the time broken up into smaller groupings who conduct their studies and discuss their findings separately, then these subgroups may provide a more appropriate focus. If subgroupings are employed, but they vary in composition from week to week, then the total group must be the focus.

PROCEDURE. The project may readily be carried through within a single week's practical class, including most of the required data analysis. A single room is required and the only necessary materials are the questionnaires (to be described shortly). The first stage comprises the selection of a suitable range of behaviours which may provide the basis of the norms of the practical class. Obviously it is not possible to specify in advance which behaviours may become the most salient ones within a particular class. The first half-hour or so of the class should be devoted to introducing the project and selecting suitable behaviours. What is required is a list of the 12 behaviours which are most salient to members of the class. This list of 12 behaviours is to be arrived at through class discussion. Table 1 provides 21 possible candidates for the list, and these should be written on the board in advance or issued as a handout. The final list is to be arrived at by deletion from the list of 21, amendment of items on the list of 21, and additions of new items suggested by members of the class. It is important not to rush this stage in the project, since the validity of the findings rests on the selection of items for the list which do have some relevance to the group's previous history. At this stage one should resist any pressure from the class to take votes or straw polls on which items to include, since this would be likely to

Table 1. List of behaviours which may provide the basis of practical class norms

A. Someone is absent without explanation.

B. Someone consistently argues with the tutor.

C. Someone expresses disillusionment with the study of psychology.

D. Someone shows in discussion that they have done a good deal of reading relevant to the topic.

E. Someone makes frequent jokes.

F. Someone remains silent during discussions.

G. Someone shows keen interest in the topic.

H. Someone 'invents' data rather than collecting it.

I. Someone hands in all the required practical reports on time.

J. Someone expresses difficulty in understanding the statistical tests required.

K. Someone offers to help other students understand something which is puzzling them.

L. Someone criticizes the 'artificiality' of a study the class is undertaking.

M. Someone fails to undertake their share of the task on a group project.

N. Someone criticizes the tutor behind his/her back.

O. Someone prolongs the discussion when others are wanting to leave.

P. Someone tries to manipulate the group to get his/her own way.

Q. Someone proposes that the group shall have greater control over which projects are to be undertaken.

R. Someone behaves in a friendly manner towards others.

S. Someone frequently interrupts others.

T. Someone helps keep the group focussed on what needs to be done.

U. A group member organizes the work of the group.

bias each individual's subsequent questionnaire responses. The criteria for accepting an item on the list should be that it refers to an event (or events) which is felt to be relevant to the group, that its meaning is clear and that the event described is one that people have some feelings about. If the exercise is to be done in subgroups, then each subgroup will need to select its own list of 12 items.

When the process of selecting 12 items is complete, check that the items are on the board in their correct form, or else that class members have amended the list issued to them to match the final version. Whichever of the original 21 items have survived, whether amended or not, should be referred to by their code letters A-U, as in table 1. New items should be assigned code letters from V onwards.

Before the actual data collection commences one further decision is required, namely the selection of an appropriate demographic variable whose relationship to the norm structure is to be studied. In some cases it may be appropriate for the tutor to select this dimension beforehand, in the light of his or her knowledge of the particular class. What is required is a salient dimension of what Homans called the external system of the group: that is, aspects of the structure which are fixed in advance of its meeting. Possible dimensions would be sex, age, race or nationality, or single-subject psychology students versus combined-studies students. The dimension selected should be one which divides the class reasonably equally, rather than spotlighting some small and potentially self-conscious minority. Most often the sex variable, or the age variable in a class that has a reasonable number of mature students, is the most useful. Whichever variable is selected, all that is required is the differentiation of two discrete categories. If age is selected, this can be mature students versus others; if race, then white versus non-white.

DATA COLLECTION. Data collection may be quickly accomplished by questionnaire completion. A suitable version of the questionnaire is given in table 2. It should take about 15 minutes to complete. It may be useful to issue each student with two copies of the questionnaire. When they have completed both copies, one can be used to collect the data anonymously, while the other is retained for subsequent comparison with the class means. The questionnaire asks for three types of evaluations of the

Table 2. Behaviour rating form

Class group .... (e.g. Wednesday morning class) Category .... (e.g. female)

1. You are asked first to indicate how you think <u>this group would react</u> if a member behaved in each of the ways on the list of 12 behaviours which the class has constructed. For each pair of boxes below you should place in the upper box the code letter of one of the behaviours and in the lower box your view of how the group would react to it. In recording your views choose whichever of the following categories is most appropriate.

   1 Everyone would approve of this behaviour
   2 Most people would approve of this behaviour
   3 Some would approve of this, others would be indifferent or would disapprove
   4 Most people would disapprove of this behaviour
   5 Everyone would disapprove of this behaviour

   Now complete your ratings.

Behaviour code												
How you think group would react												

2. Now think again of the list of 12 behaviours. This time you are asked to rank them in order of how <u>you personally would feel about someone other than yourself</u> doing each of these behaviours in this group. Place the behaviours you would most approve of highest. If you find that you cannot differentiate between how much you would approve of some of the behaviours, you can use tied ranks for them. Write the codes of the behaviours in the order you wish to rank them. Make sure you include all 12 behaviours.

   Rank order: 1 ....   7 ....

   2· ....   8 ....

   3 ....   9 ....

   4 ....   10 ....

   5 ....   11 ....

   6 ....   12 ....

3. Finally, think once more of the 12 behaviours. This time rank them in order of how <u>you would feel about behaving in each of these ways yourself</u>. Place the behaviours you would most approve of highest. Make sure you include all 12 behaviours.

   Rank order: 1 ....   7 ....

   2 ....   8 ....

3 .... 9 ....

4 .... 10 ....

5 .... 11 ....

6 .... 12 ....

list of 12 behaviours developed earlier. The first of these is concerned with per-ceived group norms: that is, how each group member perceives the group's usual responses. The second evaluation will be used to derive a measure of the group's actual norms, if norms are considered as the sum of individual members' evaluations. The final question is focussed not on norms per se, but on each person's preferences concerning how they themselves behave.

There is no logical reason why the data deriving from these three questions should not be closely correlated. In practice there is usually considerable divergence, and a richer and more valid picture of the group may be obtained by collecting all three sets of data. The principal reason why perceived group norms are likely to diverge from what are here called actual norms is that the actual norm measure assumes that each group member's evaluation of behaviour carries equal weight in the determination of the group norm. In prac-tice some members' evaluations will be more influential than those of others and this will be reflected in the perceived group norm measure. A divergence may also be anticipated between the personal preference question and the perceived group norms. The breadth of this divergence is likely to show the degree to which the group is cur-rently meeting the needs of its members.

It will have been noted that the first question asks for ratings of how much each behaviour is approved or disapproved, while the remaining two questions ask only for a ranking. The ratings are to be used in a qualitative analysis of the data, to be discussed shortly. For purposes of subse-quent quantitative analysis, these ratings will then be converted into rankings.

When class members are asked to com-plete the questionnaire it should be made clear that they are asked to respond anony-mously, but that the responses will be

shared publicly, in a way which makes it impossible to know which set of data comes from which person. When questionnaire completion is finished class members should be asked to fold their questionnaire once and hand it in to the tutor. When all ques-tionnaires are in they should be visibly shuffled and a start made on quantitative data analysis. This is to be done by tabu-lating responses to Question 1 on the board. This tabulation should not be star-ted before all responses are in, otherwise the anonymity of later respondents will be lost.

Data analysis

QUALITATIVE ANALYSIS. The prime pur-pose of the qualitative data analysis is to determine which of the 12 behaviours on the list attracts sufficiently consensual eva-luation for them to be considered group norms. There is no agreement in the re-search literature as to how strong a group consensus must be before a norm is con-sidered to be present. Bates and Cloyd (1956) made a study of roles and norms in student discussion groups. They judged a norm to be present where at least 75 per cent of group members thought that 75 per cent of members would agree with it. Lieberman, Yalom and Miles (1973) studied the norms of student encounter groups. They accepted as norm-governed all behaviours which were described as 'appropriate' by 67 per cent and all behaviours described as 'inappropriate' by 67 per cent. However, these are relatively arbitrary cut-off points.

This analysis follows the less complex approach of Lieberman et al. The data should be tabulated in the form shown in table 3. For convenience in the later quantitative data analysis, the data for males and females (or whatever other category split is used) should be grouped

Table 3. Example of tabulation of responses to question 1

Behaviour code	B	C	E	F	I	K	M	O	Q	R	S	T
Category of subject												
F (female)	4	3	3	3	3	2	4	4	3	1	4	2
F (female)	3	2	2	2	4	2	3	4	4	2	4	3
etc.	.	.	.	.	.	.	.	.	.	.	.	.
	.	.	.	.	.	.	.	.	.	.	.	.
Sum of ratings	70	50	53	51	72	40	69	80	72	33	82	49
Rank order of summed ratings	8	4	6	5	9.5	2	7	11	9.5	1	12	3

together. When the data are tabulated, it is a straightforward matter to determine the presence or absence of norms. Examine each column in turn and count whether the number of '1' and '2' ratings exceeds 67 per cent. In a similar way, determine also whether the number of '4' and '5' ratings exceeds 67 per cent. In a long-established practical class group it may emerge that half or more of the 12 items do satisfy the definition of norms.

Some time may be now be taken in discussing the results with the class. Issues which could be explored include whether or not the norms shown by this data analysis to be most strongly held do indeed feel like the salient norms of the group; why these particular norms have developed; why the group does not have more (or less) norms; and how far these norms resemble those found in other practical class groups who have done this study. Past groups have, for example, shown norms favouring K, L, Q and T and opposing H, M, O and S.

If it is desired to make most use of the qualitative data generated by this project, then the responses to questions 2 and 3 should now be tabulated in a similar way. In these cases what are available for tabulation are the ranks assigned to each behaviour rather than ratings. This means that it is not possible to use the data from questions 2 and 3 so precisely for determining the presence or absence of norms. However, the data do make it possible to obtain an overall summation of which behaviours are ranked highest. It is the possible divergence between these ranks

and those from the question 1 data, as tabulated at the bottom of table 3, which is of interest. Those behaviours should be identified which show the greater divergence between the data derived from question 1 and that derived from questions 2 and 3. A further period of discussion may now be initiated as to the most likely explanation of these divergences. Assuming that the divergence found is sufficiently large to require some explanation, there are two principal possibilities. The first of these is that the question 1 data have been influenced by some kind of pluralistic ignorance in the group. In other words, each group member assumes that most of the others disapprove of a certain behaviour, let us say appearing too keen and scholarly, while they themselves do not disapprove of it. The perceived group consensus is not a consensus at all, but the group has failed to discover this. This situation is most likely to arise in groups which have kept rather distant from one another, thereby minimizing opportunities for discovering one another's actual feelings and values.

The second possible explanation for divergences in the data is that there is indeed a group consensus about how a certain behaviour is evaluated, but that this consensus does not represent the sum of individual members' preferences. This state of affairs would arise where some members of the group were much more influential than others. Perhaps some members of the class are much more highly verbal than others and their opinions come eventually to be seen as the group norms, while others' views are less heard.

The discussion of these and other possible explanations for whatever divergences are found may be used to provide an opportunity to review with the class, or subgroupings within the class, the way in which their social structure has so far developed. The data should not be treated as a set of definitive 'answers', but as a vehicle for opening up the discussion in whatever directions class members find interesting.

If it is desired to place more stress on quantitative analysis of the data, the procedures outlined in the preceding three paragraphs should be omitted in order to save time and to enable the main hypotheses of the project to be tested.

QUANTITATIVE ANALYSIS. The first step in the quantitative data analysis is to obtain a more precise estimate of the level of normative consensus in the group. This may be accomplished through the use of Kendall's coefficient of concordance (W). This is a statistic for testing the degree of agreement between a set of rankings of the same objects. In order to use the test on the data in table 3, it is necessary to transform each row of ratings into a ranking. This is done by ranking the sum of the ratings in each column. As is the case in the example in table 3, there may sometimes be ties in the rankings. However, this does not invalidate the procedure so long as the appropriate correction for ties is employed. In assigning ranks it is important to remember that tied ratings are assigned the average of their tied ranks. For instance, if two ratings tie for top place, they are assigned a rank of 1.5 each, not 1.0. Full instructions for the calculation of W are given in Siegel (1956).

The value of W obtained reflects not only the presence or absence of norms, as defined in the prior qualitative data analysis, but also the level of agreement or disagreement about the evaluation of each one of the 12 behaviours on the list. This means that the value of W may be substantially affected by which items the group chooses to include on the list. If something is included about which the group is

strongly divided, or if something is excluded about which most groups agree (e.g. approving of being friendly to one another), the value of W will be depressed. The usefulness of the obtained value is therefore achieved not so much in comparing it with values for other samples, but as a baseline for further analysis within the present sample.

The general hypothesis was advanced earlier that the level of normative consensus in the group would be a reflection of its 'external' or demographic structure. A preliminary test of this idea can be made by calculating separate values of W for the data from the males and females in the class (or whatever demographic category was selected). Time may be saved in class by having some members compute the overall W, some the male W and some the female W. Since the values of W are not all derived from a similar number of judges, they must be compared in terms of the significance levels which each achieves. These can be computed as indicated by Siegel (1956), using the procedure for large samples.

A variety of findings is possible. If there is greater consensus within either or both of the single-sex categories than in the total class, this can be taken as indicating that the demographic variable selected is indeed an important one in relation to the level of normative consensus within the class. If there is little difference between consensus in the single-sex groups and the total class, this would indicate that there was a shared perception of how behaviour was evaluated in the total group. This would still leave open the possibility that those evaluations were more acceptable to one sub-category than to the other.

A fuller testing of the general hypothesis is possible through drawing on the responses to questions 2 and 3. What is required is a measure of the degree to which members of each sub-category concur with the perceived group consensus indicated by the data from question 1. To put it another way, what is the match between each individual's views and the views of the group as a whole? There has been a long-standing controversy in social psychology as to how to overcome certain difficulties in the measurement of the 'accuracy' of social perception. This study provides an opportunity to consider these difficulties and to see how they may be overcome. The basic problem has been that when researchers attempt to measure the degree of 'match' between two or more sets of ratings, numerous artifacts may obscure the measurement of the variables in which they are interested. These include such things as the degree to which the rater spreads the ratings along the scale, the average level of the ratings, assumptions or stereotypes the rater may have and so forth. The problems are clearly outlined by Cook (1979). The need to overcome these difficulties had a strong effect on the design of the questionnaire for this project. Cook argues that most of the flaws in 'accuracy' measures may be overcome through the use of ranking techniques rather than ratings. The hypothesis is therefore to be tested through comparison of the various rankings obtained. The fact that responses to question 1 were initially collected in the form of ratings and only later converted to rankings was to allow a more adequate qualitative analysis to be undertaken first.

To return to the data analysis: class members should be asked to refer to their own rankings, of which they should have kept a record. Two rank order correlation coefficients are to be computed. One is between the ranking of perceived group norms obtained from question 1 (to be found on the bottom line of table 3) and their own response to question 2. The other is between the ranking of perceived group norms and their response to question 3. The preferred correlation coefficient is Kendall's tau (Siegel, 1956). If students are already familiar with Spearman's rho, this could be used instead, but it copes less simply with ties. In any event, all members of the class must use the same test. When these correlations have been made, class members should write the two values of tau (or rho) on a slip of paper, making clear which is which, add a statement of their sex (or other relevant characteristic) and hand it to the tutor. Preserving anonymity as before, the tutor should then write the obtained values of tau (or rho) on the board. The significance of the difference between male scores and

female scores on each of the two correlations can now be established. This is best done by t-tests for independent means, using the values of tau (or rho) as scores.

The amount of time required for this project will depend on the length of the discussions of the qualitative data and how familiar students are with Kendall's tau and Kendall's W. If insufficient time remains, the t-tests could be computed afterwards, although this would prevent any final discussion of the findings obtained. It is important that such discussion occurs at some stage because the findings may well show that one or other sex (assuming sex is used to dichotomize the group) does not gain a full hearing for their views and values in the group. If one reveals such a situation, one has some responsibility to explore ways of changing it.

Discussion

The various options outlined within this chapter make it possible to emphasize qualitative approaches or quantitative approaches to investigation, or to sample some of both and to contrast what can and what cannot be accomplished by each approach. The qualitative study is structured in such a way that people are likely to find it interesting and to see connections between what it shows and their experience within the practical class. Rather in the manner of some of the early Lewinian experiments, it uses group participation both as a research method and as a method of motivating people's interest in the findings. It is considerably more structured than the methods employed by contemporary action researchers in the field of organizational consultancy, but it gives a flavour of that approach. Its weakness lies in the lack of cumulativeness of the findings. Systematic recording of the class discussions of the findings might provide illustrations from the history of a particular group supporting one or other theoretical model of conformity processes. For instance, it might be found that, in line with Moscovici's view, the norms had arisen from what was initially a consistently-held minority position. But such findings would be a matter of chance rather than design, and there would be no way of measuring the frequency with which they occurred.

The quantitative study seeks to relate the internal normative system to the external constraints acting upon that system. The form of the data makes it easier to compare different sets of findings, but there is little expectation that the elements of the external system acting on a group will always have the same weightings. In one group age may be a crucial variable, while in another it could be sex. The goal of this type of study is thus not to contribute to a search for generalized laws or explanations concerning conformity, but to provide a more precise estimate than that afforded by the qualitative study of the inter-relatedness of the group's internal and external systems. Neither system is seen as 'causing' the other: they act and react upon one another. The intuitive element in this type of research remains substantial. For instance, the researcher must make an appropriate selection of an external system variable related to the group being investigated if there is to be any hope that the research will be fruitful.

The 'laws' of social psychology mostly concern processes which occur between people without very much conscious attention on the part of the people concerned. Thus one forms impressions of strangers, one attributes traits to individuals, and one comes to expect that a group will or should behave in a certain way. Social psychologists have investigated much less fully what happens when one encourages someone to pay attention to these processes. The evidence that we do have comes from research in such fields as psychotherapy, education, training and consultancy. In each of these areas there is evidence to support the view that enhancing someone's awareness of a social process in which they are engaged will increase the probability that they seek to change that process. Some tentative formulations are available (e.g. Smith, 1980) as to the circumstances under which such change attempts are most likely to be successful. If one accepts this argument, then the usefulness of this practical class lies not simply in the study of practical class norms but also in the creation of possible changes in those norms. The preconditions for successful accomplishment of such changes will include sufficient class discussion time and a willingness to discuss openly current satisfactions and dissatisfactions with the class both on the part of tutor and of the students. Where such changes are effectively accomplished, they provide a vivid demonstration of the manner in which social norms are at the same time both socially patterned in lawful ways, and also subject to change through human agency.

REFERENCES

Allen, V.L. and Levine, J.M. (1968) Social support, dissent and conformity. Sociometry, 31, 138-149.

Asch, S.E. (1956) Studies of independence and conformity: I. A minority of one against a unanimous majority. Psychological Monographs, 70 (9), Whole No. 416.

Bates, A.P. and Cloyd, J.S. (1956) Toward the definition of operations for defining group norms and member roles. Sociometry, 19, 26-39.

Cook, M. (1979) Perceiving Others: The psychology of interpersonal perception. London: Methuen.

Gross, N.E., Mason, W.S. and McEachern, A.W. (1958) Explorations in Role Analysis: Studies of the school superintendency roles. New York: Wiley.

Homans, G.C. (1950) The Human Group. London: Routledge & Kegan Paul.

Lieberman, M.A., Yalom, I.D. and Miles, M.B. (1973) Encounter Groups: First facts. New York: Basic Books.

Moscovici, S. (1976) Social Influence and Social Change. London: Academic Press.

Perrin, S. and Spencer, C.P. (1980) The Asch effect - a child of its time? Bulletin of the British Psychological Society, 33, 405-406.

Siegel, S.E. (1956) Nonparametric Statistics for the Behavioral Sciences. New York: McGraw-Hill.

Smith, P.B. (1980) An attributional analysis of personal learning. In C.P. Alderfer and C.L. Cooper (eds), Advances in Experiential Social Processes, Volume 2. Chichester: Wiley.